SD

250

THE REAL
TINSEL

Rod La Rocque, holding boomerang, with crew of C. B. De Mille's *The Coming of Amos*. Right of La Rocque is Paul Sloane, director; in back of Sloane, Cameraman Art Miller, formerly with George Fitzmaurice; left of La Rocque, William J. Scully, assistant director. 1925.

THE REAL TINSEL

**Bernard Rosenberg
and Harry Silverstein**

THE MACMILLAN COMPANY
Collier-Macmillan Ltd., London

The Macmillan Company
866 Third Avenue, New York, N.Y. 10022
Collier-Macmillan Canada Ltd., Toronto, Ontario

Library of Congress Catalog Card Number: 73-112854

First Printing

Printed in the United States of America

TO
Sarah and Olga

Acknowledgments

When we first embarked on our quest for an era long past, greatly in need of encouragement, guidance, and sound counsel, several generous people came forth to help plot and steer our course. To them all, we offer our most profound appreciation.

Every book begins with an idea. To transform that idea into reality requires a special effort on the part of a few. We therefore give special thanks to them—a small gesture, we know, for such a large rendering. At the start, Raymond Rohauer, formerly film curator of the Gallery of Modern Art in New York, gave his time and energy and enabled us to contact a number of Hollywood personages, many of whom had long since departed from that sometimes mythical place.

And then, Alan Brock, a gentleman who to this writing we have never personally met but who nevertheless responded to our every request, aided us in locating several of this widely scattered group. Without him, we would not have been able to continue our journey.

A most difficult and unsung task is transcribing tapes and typing manuscripts. Five individuals are responsible for that demanding work: Benita Kline, Helen Markarian, Leslie Altshul, Helen Hertz, and Clinton Jones. We thank them.

To our editor at Macmillan, Robert Markel, we owe a special debt. He has been an abundant source of ideas, encouragement, and good cheer throughout—particularly at those moments when the authors believed that insurmountable obstacles stood in their way.

Finally, we can never repay those who spoke so freely of themselves and whose knowledge, perceptions, and experiences are found between the covers of this book. We only hope they gained as much pleasure from our probes as we did their comments. Sadly, since we began this work, six of those whose lives are inscribed on the following pages have now passed on to greener pastures. It is with warm fondness that we remember here Mae Marsh, Albert Lewin, Walter Wanger, Rod La Rocque, William Haddock, and Conrad Nagel.

BERNARD ROSENBERG
HARRY SILVERSTEIN

Contents

THE PLAYER

THE STUNTMAN

THE VOICE ANIMATOR

THE DIRECTOR

THE CAMERAMAN

THE SOUND DIRECTOR

Introduction

When the inventions which "made" movies were developed at the turn of this century, even those who had had a hand in the creation could not have suspected that they had significantly advanced our technological frontiers. Pictures-in-motion were little more than a conversation piece, an amusing and entertaining curiosity; puzzling and occasionally astonishing, sometimes offensive or sacrilegious. Even today motion pictures are regarded in much the same light; save for a bit of sophistication that comes with experience, little in the attitude has changed.

Yet, who among the now revered originators would have dreamed those dreams and conceived of the extraordinary social, economic, and cultural metamorphosis of the motion picture world that has since taken place? For the historically uninitiated, let it be said that Hollywood was not too long ago only a small and insignificant point on the map. The first two decades of American film-making was centered in and around New York City. And then through a variety of partly adventitious circumstances, among which included the need for a good climate with plenty of year-round sunshine, Hollywood was "discovered" as an ideal place to make movies. That signaled the motion picture revolution, a "take off" only occasionally and temporarily grounded during the remainder of its short history. Hollywood was at first the ideal location; it was soon to become the idyllic center of the universe.

Hollywood ceased to be a place as it was transformed into a state of mind like Nirvana with a full panoply of magical, mystical, colossal, grandiose, and phantasmagorical qualities conjured up for an almost insatiable domestic and international audience. In a sense, the entire world was quickly implicated in the motion picture revolution, and this fact suffices to make it perfect grist for the sociological mill, the impetus which provides the starting point for this book.

The sociologist who wishes to approximate the world of human realities frequently begins his journey at the mythical, legendary, and fabled edges of a given situation. Certainly our subject matter is replete with these elements. They come to nothing less than the whole. Hollywood cosmology, its hierarchy of stars, starlets, saints, sinners, heroes, heroines, villains, and monsters. Even the poets were inspired: "She is madonna in an art/As wild and young as her sweet eyes . . ." (from "Mae Marsh, Motion Picture Actress" by Vachel Lindsay in *The Chinese Nightingale and Other Poems*, Macmillan, 1917).

Our special perspective required that we return these shadowy creatures from the netherworld to their relevant humanity (and that is often no small task), thereby gaining a small measure of the human condition in which, for a large share of their lives, each was deeply implicated. Those with whom we spoke were insiders looking in, describing the inner workings of a complex human network. They recite a tale, part history and part biography, but most important, provide us with a chronicle of human events and experiences, perceptions, and attitudes which, when tied together, piece by piece, comprise a totality called the motion picture industry. It is at once a slice of Americana, sometimes rhapsodic, sometimes biting, and always an encircling of an era of days gone by.

On these pages the reader will find a collection of human documents. Whatever measure of authenticity and spontaneity they have derives largely from their social setting, which in each case was an informal three-way conversation. The much too forbidding technical term for what actually took place is "an unfocused tandem depth interview." Which simply means that two of us chatted at length with another person about his life and work. The specific ambience in New York might be our own cramped and stuffy office or the Lambs' Club, the half-demolished Paramount building, a fleabag hotel in mid-Manhattan, a shabby, a genteel, or a fancy Park Avenue apartment; in California, a Beverly Hills motel, a Culver City studio, a dilapidated dwelling, a seaside cottage, and more than one Hollywood mansion. The incorrigible ineptitude of born academics struggling with a tape recorder did not reduce that rapport whose achievement it may even occasionally be said to have facilitated. A constant feature was the sympathetic and empathic triangular relationship that quickly crystallized as three of us sat and talked.

We sought, as faithfully and unobtrusively as possible, to record what a number of men and women with related concerns said to us. Beyond the personal level, their recollections have a fascination to sociologists with a professional interest in the mass media. All these recollections bear on a single—what shall we call it? art form? illusion? industry? Let us settle for "a single phenomenon."

The manifestations of that single phenomenon are even more numerous than the thousands of people directly involved in it for well over half a century. Rare indeed is the individual so insulated as not to have been touched and influenced, if not guided and shaped, by motion pictures. (Is that the right name? Or should one opt for "pictures," as many insiders do? But then, why not "cinema" or "films" or "movies"? Every un-self-conscious or deliberate designation carries a weight of nuances, and habitual use of any one of them provides a significant clue to underlying attitudes.) If only in his role of consumer, modern man is profoundly involved in everything Hollywood has wrought. All the more reason to be curious about what as well as how and by whom it has been wrought. Of painstaking history, the student and the alert citizen can never have too much. Nor has Hollywood lacked meticulous chroniclers of its prehistory, emergence, growth, efflorescence, decline, and resuscitation. We leave the analysis of historians' faults to the disputatious who enjoy quarreling over minutiae which remain perversely buried in an irrecoverable past. Matters of priority (who first invented what) and of historicity (did Mr. X appear on October 1 of 1917 at such and such a place) will probably never be resolved with any finality. This is not to belittle Terry Ramsaye, Kenneth Macgowan, Lewis Jacobs, Paul Rotha, and a handful of lesser but devoted historians. On the contrary, their studies are indispensable. They deserve to be read with care. But our purpose, our cup of tea, is a different one.

As social scientists, we are less interested in history than in the life history, the reminiscence, the brief and unadorned but well-distilled biography. Each life history is wonderfully distinctive. No two people who dwell on the totality of their experience can produce an identical narrative. Moreover, at various points in the life cycle from early consciousness on to decrepitude, the light in which certain singular events are seen will drastically differ. Which is to say, platitudinously enough, that as all men are in a state of flux equal to that of the world around them so is their perception of it. Add the *Rashomon* effect, and one begins to grasp the complexity enshrined in a single Japanese film whose title has come to symbolize this circumstance, that every witness to the same event observes it from his own peculiar angle. Totally contradictory interpretations, not to say wildly or mildly discrepant accounts, may all be equally accurate. That everyone should have a circumscribed and consequently exclusive point of view is an unalterable condition which maddens only the fact-fetishists in our midst.

We do not wish to expunge (rather do we cherish) the eccentricity, the idiosyncrasy, the odd and unusual quality of a producer, a director, an actor, or a stuntman. Such people are all too likely to be treated as featureless abstractions. So, to be sure, is the generality of men who live in an increasingly impersonal and lopsidedly instrumental culture. Depersonalization is all but complete, and nowhere more so than in Hollywood or in its many emanations. Audiences, publicists, image-makers, detractors, and idolators have all contributed to the creation of a "haunted house," a "dream factory," and finally to a ghostly air of unreality that hovers over the whole subject. With cyclic ferocity, the Hollywood figure is exalted and then cut down to size. Viewed as a god or a thing, he is robbed of his humanity. If the dialogue in which we engaged and the statements that followed had an overriding purpose, it was neither to idealize nor to minimize but to humanize people who are so often and so systematically dehumanized.

The final product, the motion picture projected onto a screen, is bloodless, shadowy, celluloidal, ectoplasmic, a powerful and insubstantial species of canned goods. And those who make the product, swallowed up by association with it, are widely regarded as nebulous creatures. Some no doubt suffer from the "ontological itch." Victims of this affliction wonder if they really exist, suspecting that their roles have completely enveloped them in a world made up of others whose behavior is no less inauthentic. Like the rest of us, only more so, they fit the dramaturgic model constructed by George Herbert Mead. That great philosopher understood personality as a mixture of the *Me* and the *I*. The *Me* in Mead's formulation looms so large that it always threatens, but never quite manages, to extinguish the *I*. For the *Me* is that enormous component of personality which does no more than reflect collective social expectations. The *Me* is socialized, broken, domesticated, attentive, obedient—and ever ready to play whatever role it is called upon to perform. The *I*, which represents and expresses individuality, is everywhere and unavoidably weaker than the *Me*. Not so far removed from Freud's id and similar to it in this respect, Mead's *I* stands for that precious part of us which is least responsive to normative requirements, most ungovernable, inner-directed, and autonomous. The *I* suggests an eruptive and destructive force which needs to be contained. But it also means freedom— without which creativity or constructive innovation of any kind would be unthinkable. Our narrators do not seem to us to be atypical bearers of the human personality. They ask the capital questions of our time (Who am I? What am I? Am I for real?) no more frequently than Everyman. If theirs is a world of make-believe superimposed on a gigantic but hardly less artificial stage, the majority still prize their uniqueness. Whether in anguish or insouciance, in loud and brash or hushed and cautious tones, they ring every variation on the theme of independence. To be one's own man, even while being someone else's, is as genuine an aspiration in Hollywood as it is wherever human beings gather together for a common purpose.

The common purpose which allows us to gather these extraordinarily diverse human beings together merely provides a base from which their several perspectives can be brought into focus. Patterns emerge, landmarks appear, recede, and disappear with the crises that precipitate them. Several large-scale processes are seen to be at work as one technical invention follows another, as migration, invasion, and assimilation proceed, as small beginnings lead to developments few among the most foresighted could have anticipated.

Figures of a given age trace for us, each in his own way, how they who were in the midst of it for decades beheld the successive transformations of their activity. A low-level entrepreneur, scrabbling for respectability but shunned by bankers who put their risk capital elsewhere, suddenly finds himself a movie magnate, only to be succeeded by slicker and better-educated bureaucrats. His "one-man operation" is split into innumerable segments. The center of power shifts, its focus now on one Coast, now on the other, is almost always in different hands. The handicraft phase, so vividly portrayed by a number of pioneers, finally passes, and Hollywood makes a belated entry into the universe of high finance, bureaucratic organization, and mass production. Thereupon a bewildering division of labor ensues. With it come countless subdivisions, proliferations, and ramifications.

Film-making has only recently regained some of its old simplicity. Directors who once more improvise, this time with hand-held camera, belong, however, to the so-called underground. As late as 1967 Paul Mayersberg proffered this list of major and minor technicians who work on a Hollywood film:

Director of photography
Camera-operator
Focus-puller
Clapper-boy
Film-loader
First, second, and third assistant directors
Second-unit director
  (under whom there will be a mini-crew)
Production manager

Personal assistants
  (to the director and producer)
Production accountant
Continuity men and women
  (script clerks)
Dialogue coaches
Music composer
Conductor
Musical arranger
Orchestra
Sound editor

Dubbing editor
Sound engineer
  (who has a crew under him)
Film editor
Assistant film editor
Art director
Assistant art director
Special effects man
Scene painters
Prop makers
Propmen
Carpenters
Plasterers
Painters
Plumbers
Gardeners

Electricians
  (gaffer, best boys, operators)
Grips
  (foremen, first and second grips)
Drivers
Mechanics
Stills man
Film publicist
Publicity secretary
Costume designer
Costumers
Hairdressers
Make-up artists
Wardrobe men and women
Choreographers
Special advisers

Since trade unions are a potent force on the contemporary scene, this list is necessarily incomplete. "For example," Mayersberg points out, "under painters you get a foreman, a color mixer, a sign writer, a marbleizer, a furniture finisher, as well as a painter. If you need the help of the studio machine shop to build your sets or props, then you might get involved with a welder, a foundryman, a plater, a buffer, a blacksmith, a sheet-metal worker, and the inevitable foreman" (Paul Mayersberg, *Hollywood: The Haunted House*, Penguin Books, Baltimore, 1969, p. 59). Organized in a finely graded hierarchy of occupations, the technician belongs only to a single stratum within the larger hierarchical structure. He has his opposite number at every other level of production and distribution.

Part of our intention is to adumbrate this intricate mixture or network of new and traditional skills. We could not give every type of worker a voice, for that would have required encyclopedic treatment. Exhaustiveness being unattainable, it was enough, we hoped, to be inclusive. Classification proved troublesome and leaves us uneasy. Where to place the man who moved from reader to cutter to producer to director to writer? Even now, and notwithstanding the inordinate specialization that did set in, a writer may become a producer, a cinematographer, a director, and so on. How much more pronounced this tendency was—how much more fluidity prevailed in the past—our respondences make only too clear. So long as the versatile man was essential, he could reasonably contemplate a leap into the executive suite—from nearly any direction. Nowadays that maneuver is not so simple. Minutely differentiated, highly specialized and unionized work seals off many previously open career lines.

The jack-of-all-trades is at least temporarily out of the picture. (He may come back with further improvement of the portable sight-and-sound camera.) At, or close to the top, the occupational hybrid is still with us, and he cannot be neatly pigeonholed. Transition from the lower echelons, from the shop floor to the office— with its unlimited possibilities—is at this juncture as rare in Hollywood as it is in Pittsburgh or Detroit. "Show biz," including that branch which most interests us, continues to offer unusual opportunities for upward mobility, but in nothing like the abundance of bygone days.

It is precisely this kind of change that can best be discerned when we ponder the significance of our "qualitative data." A subjective, multidimensional reconstruction of the medium that has occupied so central a place in this century yields fruit. For it, we go primarily to the old-timers who have lived within, through, and often, beyond a specific sequence of occurrences that, despite their discreteness, are, nevertheless, prototypic. All America went through what Hollywood rapidly recapitulated for it. Indeed, the astute cultural historian has no richer resource than properly preserved motion pictures. In them he will find, all-embodied and visualized, the passing folkways and mores of an extinct civilization which is yet somehow continuous with our own. We take it that oral life-histories like those transcribed in this book are complementary to, although they cannot complete, that record.

Oldsters were peculiarly well suited to the task we set ourselves. No matter how jaundiced their angle of vision, they alone among the living were witnesses to everything that interested us. After all the tricks of memory were set aside, what residue of impressions remained? Would they help us to piece together a more coherent picture of what transpired over the decades? Nothing else much mattered. We were fully aware of the pitfalls, which consist above all in an inclination to romanticize one's early years and in the intentional or unintentional concealment of truth. As to the first, it is a serious risk. Our cast of characters were, most of them, young when film-making was young. "Nostalgia isn't what it used to be," goes the current graffito. Even so, nostalgia may be expected to produce an immeasurable quantity of distortion. And yet the greater gaiety of youth, the extra energy, the more confident outlook, the comparative innocence—along with the actual misery and the half-forgotten anxiety—can scarcely be gainsaid. To be young in a young enterprise *was* a satisfying and exhilarating adventure of just the sort that could not be matched in subsequent periods.

Concealing the truth is a more complicated matter, especially if it takes the form of self-deception. A man may not be able to live with himself unless he banishes the painful past beyond any possibility of recalling it. On the other hand, psychically induced amnesia has nothing to do with age. More significantly, old people have less reason than those who follow them to suppress material by *consciously* misleading others. For the most part, their careers are behind them. Therefore, they are likely to have achieved some serenity. Time liberates the chronological survivor from opportunism, which no longer avails him anything. Neither does he agonize (if he ever did) over committing indiscretions that might impede his advancement. Old age confers freedom from constraint. Although never guaranteed, its exercise late in life is at least encouraged. This is what William Butler Yeats had in mind when he wrote: "A man may put pretense away / Who leans upon a stick . . ."

The substance of what these graybeards, and a sprinkling of their juniors, tell us is only a little more important than the manner in which they tell it. For that reason, every effort has been made to retain style, tone, idiom, mannerism. (Also, the original taped interviews are en route to historical archives for further, and maybe better, use.) These subtleties will not be lost to the close reader who should discover that they reveal as much about the individual as his handwriting—or his responses to a Rorschach test. The matter and the manner, conjoined in statements drawn from several points of vantage, give us at last a moving picture, with close-ups, flashbacks, and fadeouts. While palpitating and kaleidoscopic, this version of that picture is necessarily linear—for which we offer no apologies to Marshall McLuhan or his devotees. It is one side of a many-sided picture, one aspect of the Big Picture which no one can fully fathom.

Kenneth Macgowan found that "Among the peculiarities of the motion picture is the distressing fact that its history is full of mysteries, confusions and contradictions" (*Behind the Screen*, Dell Publishing Company, New York, 1967, p. 17). We do not find mysteries, confusions, and contradictions distressing. They are the very stuff of life. Still less do any or all of them constitute peculiarities of the motion picture. Dispel one set of mysteries, reduce a few confusions, eliminate some contradictions—which we think the testimony of this book tends to do—and they will be replaced by others. Therein lies a large part of the human predicament. Hollywood, both behind and on the screen, shares that predicament.

"The lunatics have taken over the asylum!" a quipster exclaimed when Charlie Chaplin, Mary Pickford, Douglas Fairbanks, Jr., and D. W. Griffith formed United Artists. It was true. It is always true, and not just for the galaxy represented on these pages. The world *can* be seen as a booby hatch run by one pack of loons or another. None of this precluded sublimity, tragedy, comedy, boredom, or excitement. These are crucial components of the Hollywood syndrome. Hollywood is a microcosm. By happenstance, its mundane message (that a man—however addled—is a man) has been amplified, magnified, and writ large across a million screens. Few of us can escape the medium. None of us can afford to avoid the message.

The Executive

HAL ROACH, SENIOR

I GREW UP as a boy in Elmira, New York. My grandfather, Henry Roach, lived next door to Robert E. Lee in Virginia. He was a very wealthy man with a beautiful Southern mansion. He was also a stone contractor who built bridges and paved the streets of Washington. During the Civil War, he had several hundred draught horses that were used to haul stone. The Northern Army wanted those horses. My grandfather was very friendly with Lee, and he said he'd be damned if a Yankee ever got any of his horses. So both he and my grandmother were made prisoners in their home during the war, and there they both died of tuberculosis. After that, lawyers cut up the family fortune and the family farm. I think my father ended up with about $1500. He had gone to a Catholic school with a boy by the name of Potter, and this man started an insurance business in Elmira. Potter asked my father to go into the business, then he met my mother, and that was the start of our branch of the Roach family. I was born in 1892.

We were a poor family, but mother ran a boardinghouse which meant that we always had plenty to eat and a good place to sleep. Every night after supper, my mother or my grandmother or one of the boarders would read aloud. We all would gather in the sitting room. But I couldn't wait for the nights when grandfather would take his turn. He had been a watchmaker and, because of the strain on his eyes, got cataracts and for seven years was totally blind. He had a gray beard and a long corn-cob pipe that came out two and a half feet so that he wouldn't spill ashes on himself. He allowed me and my brother to invite kids in from the neighborhood and he told them stories too—the most dramatic things you could ever imagine kids hearing. He would make a very peculiar noise in his pipe; this meant fairies were coming to tell him the story. He would build up to a climax. Some of us couldn't keep from asking, "And then what happened?" or something like that. He would bawl us out: "Now you scared the fairies away!" He had to stop and light his pipe and get all set again to tell the conclusion of the story. The reason I'm dwelling on this is that years later I ran into different books having the very stories he told, and I finally realized he was retelling classics in such a way so that children could understand them. I think a little of that storytelling ability was passed on to me because ninety per-cent of the success I have had in pictures has come from my ability to create a dramatic or humorous situation which works in a picture just that way.

When I was seventeen, my father said I should go to Seattle to visit my aunt and see the world, come back to Elmira, get a job on the Lehigh Valley Railroad, become an engineer, and live there happily ever after. So off I went to Seattle. There they were shipping people to Alaska. That intrigued me, so off I went again. It was supposed to be a short trip, but every time I'd start to leave, I got a better job. Finally, I went to work on a pack train. That was terrific, and I stayed all winter. I soon became a pretty homesick kid and went back to Seattle only to get a job driving an ice-cream wagon. I worked for the Seattle Ice-Cream Company which purchased the first motor trucks in that part of the country. I learned to drive, but they forgot that one man now had to do the work of four teams. In order to manage this, I had to drive the truck pretty fast and hard. The company fired me because I was wrecking the truck.

Then a salesman for the White Company which sold trucks on "time" wanted somebody to watch his interests. He wired me to come to Cali-fornia as a foreman in charge of sixteen trucks. It was raining and mis-erable in Seattle, and I thought the nice warm desert in California would be great. But the desert was not ready for the trucks, or perhaps, the trucks were not ready for the desert. I needed about six weeks to tear those trucks apart. That was the end of that job.

I then went to work for a contractor who had long-line mules. Well, we didn't have a twenty-mule team; the biggest we had was eighteen. But through circumstances which would take too long to explain, I be-came a nineteen-year-old superintendent of freighting. Three months be-fore, I had never seen one of those long-line teams, and I couldn't have driven four. Suddenly I was the boss. I did a good job and was moved to another job by the same company. It took five days to make the round trip. They had one or two wagons and a trailer which carried water, food for the mules, and their own camping outfit. The drivers were allowed a day and a half in town. They could get drunk or do anything they wanted to. Then at a specified time the next day, we started out, and no one was allowed to take liquor along. The superintendent of this crew had been called to another camp. He was told to leave the best man in charge as his replacement. I knew about the books. I was a timekeeper, checker, and all, so he left me in charge. I ran the thing for quite a while. For some reason, a replacement was never sent.

One day somebody tipped me off that one of the best skinners we had had taken a bottle of liquor with him when he went out that afternoon. Ordinarily, a team would start about noon, not go too far, and camp out the first day. I had a team of driving mules, hitched them to a little buggy, and went out after him. I found him. He was drunk, good and drunk, and his team was standing there. All these guys carried 30/30s. He had a bottle of liquor, and the first thing I did was to break this bottle over the wheel of the wagon, which made him furious. Then he started for the trailer. I knew that his gun was there so I tackled him as he was running. I got him down and held him, sitting on his stomach. He was spitting at me, and I was trying to make him say he'd be a good boy if I let him up. Then along came Mahoney, the boss, in his automobile. He had a chauffeur with him.

"The rule is you can't drink. He's been drinking." Now by this time, he was sobered up a little bit and quieted down. Mahoney owned the joint.

"All right. Put him in the car and I'll go in and we'll pick up another driver."

"Mr. Mahoney, he's got no more liquor. He'll sober up. I'll stay here the night and take care of his team. I'll put him to bed and he'll be all right in the morning. He's one of the best men you have, and if you fire him, you'll have trouble finding a new one. Just go ahead, I'll take care of it." Mahoney agreed and became pretty fond of me so I was promoted to superintendent of freighting at sixty-five dollars a month and free clothes.

I moved down to Los Angeles and was waiting for a new assignment, when I saw an ad in the paper: "Wanted, men in Western costume. Pay: a dollar, carfare, and lunch. Be in front of the post office." I had nothing to do. I owned a Stetson hat and a bandana handkerchief and cowboy boots. I put them on and stood in front of the post office. I was selected and taken to what was then the 101 Bison Company, which later became Universal. The shot was going to be a crowd scene in a gambling place. There was a big argument among the film people about how to run a roulette table. From my experience in Alaska, I knew how to run one. I breezed up to the director,

"What do you want to know? I know all about roulette."

"We want the leading man to win at the start and then lose all he's got." I told him how to do it. The camera didn't pick up the ball anyway.

"You stand next to the leading man and tell him what to do." At about three-thirty, the assistant came up to me and said, "Be here at eight o'clock in the morning." We had gone out by bus and I didn't even know for sure where I was.

"How much are you going to pay me for that?"

"You get five dollars a day."

You say five dollars today, it means nothing. Bear in mind that when I was a kid, a laborer got ten cents an hour, a dollar a day for ten hours. This was 1913. I quit the mule-train business.

After that, I was willing to play anything that anybody wanted me to play, but I realized that I'd never be a big star. Therefore I was happy to become an assistant director. In those days, the director had only one man with him. That man was his assistant. He hired the people. He paid them off. He told them what to do. He arranged for the costuming. There were no property men, no producers. Today you need sixty people to do what an assistant director did then, and a cameraman even carried his own camera. He also carried a still camera. He made the still pictures while making the moving pictures. And, of course, he turned the camera with a crank. He had to set it up, and the assistant director also worked with him.

At about that time, a local company financed a New York actor to make a picture called *The Hoosier Schoolmaster*. He was to direct it and play the lead. Edwin August was his name, and I got the job as his assistant director. The group of men who financed him retained a very famous Los Angeles attorney who came out every day to watch the picture and see that the money was well spent. He couldn't talk to the director because the director was also the leading man and much too busy. He talked to me. He told me about a young man named Whiting who was eager to get into the picture business. He had an automobile agency in San Francisco, but he wanted to come back to Los Angeles. He also had quite a bit of money. I convinced this attorney that I was one of the best unfound directors in pictures—which is how Whiting and I went into the picture business. We found actors either at their homes or on street corners and went out to make pictures for $350 each. We made eight one-reel comedies and two-reel dramatic pictures. We sent the one-reelers to a company in New York, which turned out to be Warner

Brothers. They, in turn, sold the pictures to Pathé, but kept the money because they didn't have any. They failed to tell Pathé who made the pictures so we didn't get any money. The two-reelers we sold to Universal.

Charlie Chaplin was making a picture for Essanay, a little studio, and I went to work over there as a director. They had five or six English comedians on weekly salary, but only used a few of them in each picture. I took those Essanay didn't use each week to make a one-reel comedy. I had been working there for a matter of months when one of the pictures we had made previously showed up on Main Street with Pathé's name on it. We didn't know *what* had happened to them. I got hold of Pathé, and Pathé said, "We tried every way we could to find out who made these pictures, but United Pictures wouldn't tell us." They wouldn't tell because we hadn't been paid. Now, I was getting seventy-five dollars a week as a director at Essanay. I was not too keen on going back to our own company. (With Whiting, I drew only twenty-five dollars a week.) Finally, Pathé sent a man from New York to offer a contract which was so good that I couldn't refuse it. I started making pictures for Pathé with Harold Lloyd. Two years later, I bought Whiting out.

This is the way we made those one-reelers: Monday morning I would bring the group in and say, "*You* make up as a cop, *you* make up as a garbageman, *you* make up as a pedestrian." We'd go out in the park, and we'd start to do something. By that time, I'd have an idea of what the sets were going to be. By noon, I would tell the set man what I wanted, and he would go back to the studio to get them ready.

I don't think we ever had anything on paper until we started making two-reelers with lights. Nobody but me had *any* idea what the hell we were going to do. We'd try one thing, it wasn't funny; we'd try something else. That was really the fun time so far as making pictures was concerned. Since there were no lights, you had to depend entirely on sunlight. When it was cloudy, you couldn't work. Many times we'd make a one-reeler in a day and a half because that's all the sunshine we got during that week and we had to turn out one every week, fifty-two a year.

In the early days, a show ran an hour for a nickel or a dime. It was composed of a two-reel dramatic, a one-reel comedy, a scenic, and a newsreel. After the second year, we made two-reelers with Lloyd. Instead of making one a week, we made twelve a year which gave me a lot more time. But even then, the cost of people was very small, and you could afford to spend that time. Two-reelers in the early days cost about $12,000 a piece. As the popularity of Lloyd increased, we had to make them better. But I'd say of the two-reelers, we got up to spending somewhere around $40,000. One-reelers cost $1.25 a foot. Then it went up to $1.50.

Anyway, I went to New York to see Pathé. I wanted a considerable increase. They couldn't see it.

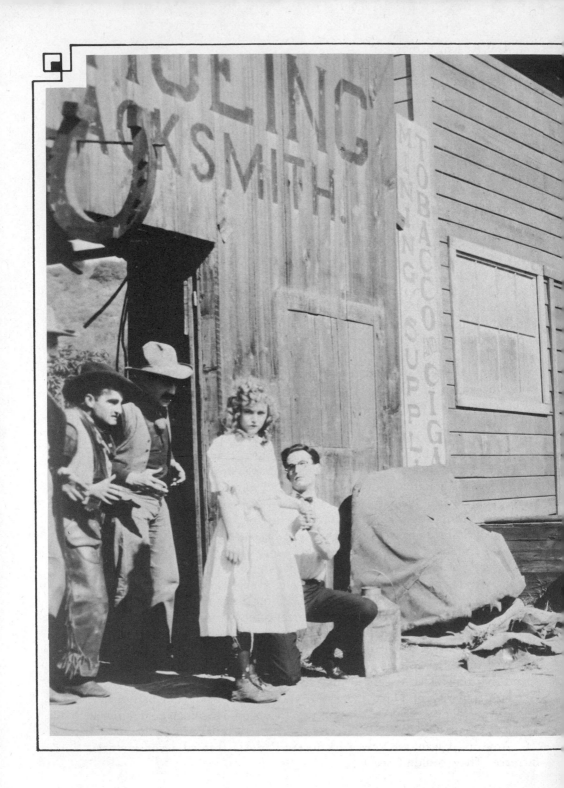

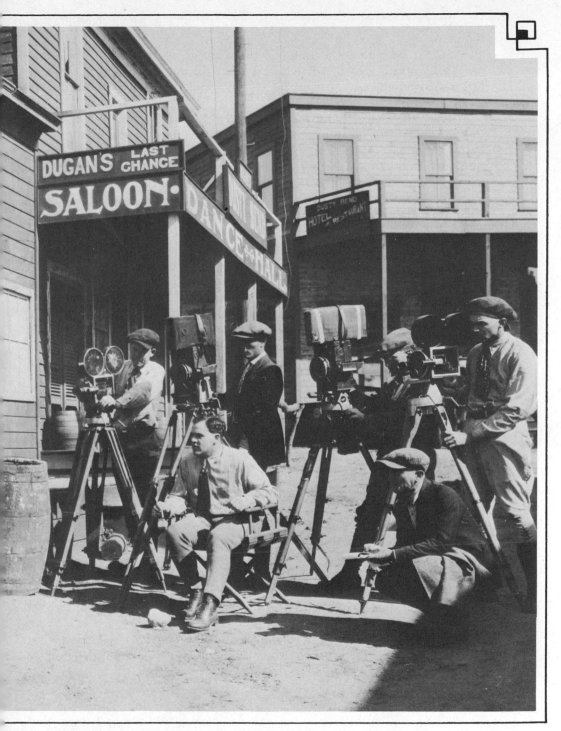

Hal Roach, Sr., president and director-general of Robin Film Company, directing a scene with Harold Lloyd and Mildred Davis. Note use of four cameras.

"What do you think these pictures are going to gross?" They told me. "All right," I said "I'll tell you what I'll do. For the same price as I'm making them now, I want 50 percent beyond what you think they're going to gross."

They were tickled to death. Actually, I wasn't going to get any of that income for a year after the pictures had been on the market. The Pathé Company was displeased with Whiting and approached me to buy him out. We had a meeting at which it was decided that I either buy or sell. I had an option to buy, and if I didn't, I would have to sell out to him. He never thought I would have enough money to use the option. That's another long story, very funny, but soon the treasurer of Pathé was in Los Angeles with my certified check.

On the first year of my 50 percent deal, I received over $200,000. Then Lloyd got big, and we completely changed the contract, paying them 30 percent for distribution. They put up all the money. We moved to Metro–Goldwyn–Mayer and then to United Artists. Those were the only three companies I ever made pictures for.

During the First World War, both Lloyd and I provided for our families and were therefore exempt from the draft. Before we got into the war, *Pathé News* was already the big thing. In fact, everybody called the news, the *Pathé News*. The German–Americans were strenuously objecting to Pathé because they were alleged to be slanting news in favor of the Allies and against the Germans. I was then put in charge of *Pathé News* which gave me a further exemption. In fact, I became a major in the Signal Corps. Soon after, I married one of our leading ladies, Margaret Nichols.

When we started out, we didn't use the name of anybody on the pictures. Then slowly certain people, like John Bunny as a comedian, became known. When I started making comedies, Mack Sennett was well on his way. He was making probably five a week to my one. It took me five or six years before I caught up with Mack, and then a few more years before I passed him. But I didn't pass Mack because of any great genius on my part. Sennett was the guy who decided what was funny, who to hire, and who not to hire. He wouldn't even put Charlie Chaplin under contract. His attitude was: If you don't want to work with Sennett, get out.

"I'm Sennett. I don't need you. I don't need Arbuckle. I don't need Keaton." So Mack let all these people go by. He could have put them under five-year contracts.

I put Lloyd, my first comedian, under a seven-year contract. Everybody who worked for me was under contract, Laurel and Hardy, the *Our Gang* kids, and so on. They were under contract as soon as I knew that they were going to be successful. I soon made a series of one-reelers with Snub Pollard, then I started the *Our Gang,* and after that, I worked with ZaSu Pitts, Thelma Todd, Charlie Chase, and made a series of comedies. I made serials for Pathé with Ruth Roland and afterward with Laurel and Hardy. When we first made those things, we stuck them together with pins. We never even saw a print. Actually we only cut the negative and sent it to New York. The print was made in New York. We never saw a print until it was in the theater. I had to cut it because nobody knew what it was except me. Since I had no script girls, I had to find the pieces that went together.

When some intelligent director started making longer pictures, that thing called the "feature" finally came into being. For a long time, the feature was five reels in length. In a theater, one could see a feature, then a two-reel comedy, a scenic, and a newsreel, all of which ran about two hours. The admission price went up to twenty-five cents, thirty-five cents in the principal theaters. But all during this time, there was a group of vaudeville theaters which fought the motion picture business. They wanted the worst pictures they could buy to convince the public that pictures were no good. Some of the smarter theater owners decided they were not getting any place this way. They wanted to buy better pictures and run them without vaudeville. Now you could go to a theater for a reasonable price and see a good picture plus five or six acts of vaudeville whereas movie houses could run only motion pictures. So they conceived the idea of compensating for vaudeville by running two pictures. Double features became of such importance that the principal comedians—Lloyd, Chaplin, Arbuckle, and Keaton—were practically forced into making feature-length pictures to get the big money. If they had stayed in shorter pictures, the comedies would have been better. A comedy must be built. The laughter must be better as it goes along. The longer it goes, the tougher it is to make a good comedy.

And that, I suppose, is one of the main standards I use when I'm asked to judge who were the great comedians: Could they do sustained comedy? As far as I'm concerned, Chaplin was number one; Harold Lloyd, number two; Arbuckle, number three; then Laurel and Hardy, who may have been a little better than Abbott and Costello, maybe a little better than Keaton.

Some people would include Jerry Lewis on their list. And I guess he deserves to be. But Lewis is the kind of comedian it would be very difficult for me to make funny. He plays the spoiled kid, whereas my kids have always been the sympathetic kind. It's a little hard for me to explain. Jerry Lewis is the brash comedian. I want the audience to pull for him *not* to fall, rather than hope that he does. It's the other way around with Lewis. There was some talk of my doing something with Lewis a short time ago, and I went to see two or three of his pictures. After looking at them, I knew I could do him no good. His brand of humor and mine aren't the same.

Anyway, as the short comedies became a drug on the market, we slowly dropped them. In order to keep the studio going, we had to do feature productions. We were releasing our pictures through Metro, and they were our distributing agents. But they made their own features; they were not interested in Hal Roach making features for them. I moved from Metro to United Artists, where we made *Topper, Merrily We Live, Captain Caution, Captain Fury, Of Mice and Men*. But I was still thinking that short comedies were, in some way, the thing. After making several features for United Artists, I sold them on the idea of "streamlined comedies." The feature had now grown from five to ten reels and from an hour to two hours. If *they* could grow, then the comedy could grow to twice its present size, from twenty minutes to forty or forty-five minutes. I started making comedies with Bill Bendix. I also made a series with kids. This was just before the Second World War. We made seventeen forty-five-minute comedies. They were accepted as features, and we made a million dollars on that first group.

In 1940, I was called back into the Army. I immediately wrote and said, "I don't want to be a colonel; I just want to get out of the Army." They let me out. Then the war started and on the fifteenth of July, I got a notice to report to Fort MacArthur. They told me, "Your commission said that in the event of a national emergency, you could be called six months after your retirement date." I was forty-eight. I was overweight. Everything. But I couldn't even get three days' deferment, and there I stayed for four years. I fought just the Americans.

But there's rather a comedy in the thing. Jim Oviat made movie people's clothes. I called him and asked, "Do you know how to make a uniform?"

"Oh yes."

"Well, make me a uniform." I had uniforms that a Ziegfeld chorus boy wouldn't wear. When I arrived the first time in New York with one on, the colonel took one look at me and said, "Roach, do me a favor. Act like you've never been here and go over to Macy's and get yourself a suit of cotton clothes and come back." It was a funny gag though. Then when I got to Wright Field, a notice came out that if you had any uniforms, you must continue to wear them because things were scarce. So I wore them around to the indignation of everybody who was there. Oh, the pockets were pleated with little scallops on them.

But seriously, I worked on an idea with the Signal Corps. I never could get it accepted, but what I wanted to do was to make film records of everything that went on in the Army: what you ate, where you slept, what was wrong with it, so that there would be a visual report instead of just a written report of what goes wrong. But they were afraid of a report of that kind. Guys in England wanted me for another job, so they transferred me to the Air Force.

Then the studio was taken over by the Army and the Air Force. It was closed for four and a half years. During this time, I had pictures out and was able to accumulate a considerable amount of money. When the war ended, we started making "streamliners" again. They should have cost $150,000 a piece, but they ran from $300,000 to $400,000, and they weren't worth that much money. We lost about a million dollars. But I was now fat and rich, and instead of running my business, I turned it over to my son and other people who were there. And the quality declined. The second batch of streamliners, instead of being a success, was a flop and the result was that we went into television.

About television, Adolph Zukor, a pioneer who goes back further than I do in film-making, was the only one to stick with me when I said that the motion picture business should grab this industry as fast as possible. Well, the motion picture industry reacted to television exactly like the theatrical industry did when motion pictures came in. Theater people would not hire an actor who worked in a movie. They would not let an actor, producer, or a director, or anybody else who had anything to do with legitimate theater in pictures. The theater should have owned the business instead of fighting it. And motion pictures should have owned television, but no, they fought it. It went to radio. Motion pictures were much better equipped to make visual entertainment than the radio companies were. In 1956, the whole thing blew. I cut down my cost of living considerably. Then I went to England to make comedies for MGM which ended disastrously.

Looking back, there are a number of things I've often puzzled over about Hollywood, motion pictures, and comedy. A man once said that there's nothing new! It's all a redo of what somebody else thought of years ago. I believe that's true. I would say that 75 percent of the ideas I got for a comedy, or whatever film I was making, came from looking at other pictures or reading something. I would read a thing that would be very dramatic and think, "Now, if you switched that a little, it would become humorous." If only they had done it this way instead of the way it was done. This is the basis of humor. What people *do* that is funny is my part of the business. The visual comedians are the great actors, and they essentially imitate children. That's the key to almost all visual comedy. People ask why a person slipping on a banana peel makes one laugh? If a person falls down, he's going to get hurt. When a little child walks for the first time, he falls down or off a chair. What's the first thing parents do? They try to laugh the child out of it, to "kid" around. "That didn't hurt," and they start to laugh. And many times a child falls and

Left to right: Stan Laurel, Fred Karno, and Hal Roach, Sr.

Our Gang visiting Mayor Jimmy Walker of New York City. 1929.

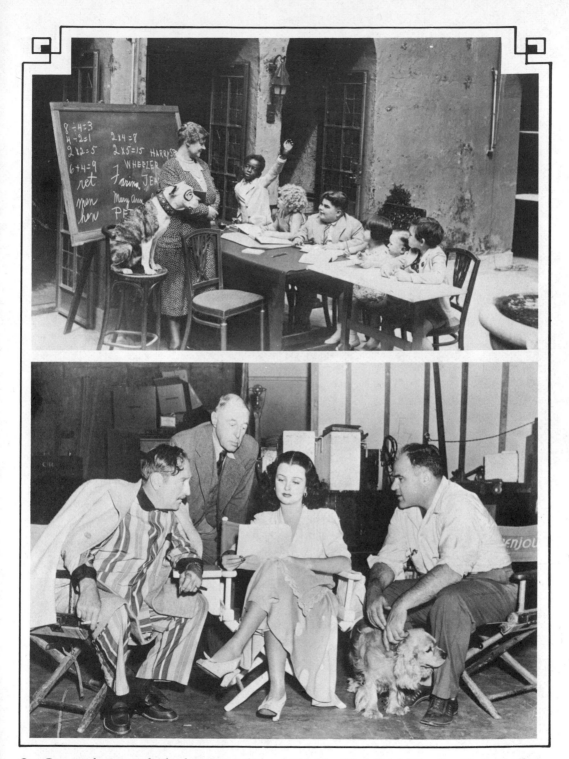

Our Gang in their special school set up on the roof of a New York hotel. Mrs. Fern Carter is their teacher. 1928.

Adolphe Menjou, D. W. Griffith, Joan Bennett, and Hal Roach, Sr. 1939. Picture—*The Housekeeper's Daughter.*

Carole Landis and Victor Mature in Hal Roach, Sr.'s production of *One Million B.C.* 1940.

isn't actually hurt, but it thinks it should have some sympathy so it starts to cry anyway and the parents try to kid the child out of it! Basically, that's the model for construction of visual comedy. So long as children are born, there'll be the same basis of comedy. There's nothing old and there's nothing new so far as children are concerned. When they're born, they're born the same way they were a thousand years ago. Comedy has been the same too.

Another major problem is stardom. It is a very elusive, complex, and sometimes tragic thing. A girl could become a star in one picture because of her good looks. Some who became stars were not great actresses, but all of a sudden, they hit a point where they were tremendously sought after by the public. The girl says, "Gee, I'm a star. Something great should happen. But I still eat the same thing and I like to do what I did before. I'm missing something. What is it?" I remember one girl who had become a star. She had worked for me. She started taking dope and wrecked her life. But she did it thinking there must be some great thing that would happen to her, and didn't. Then there's temperament. Greta Garbo never could understand why she was a star. She was a very quiet girl who happened to photograph terrifically. She could not reconcile herself to the importance she had attained. Her wanting to be alone was a fact. She hated the idea that she was a star, but she didn't know what she could do about it. She just wanted to be Greta Garbo and do what she pleased. Publicity annoyed her. She couldn't go into a store and shop the way other women did. She would rather ride her horse at four or five o'clock in the morning all by herself down by her house at the beach.

A great many male stars were the same way. All of a sudden, they'd find women adoring them and they'd be getting fantastic mail—you know, from women: "Please come and sleep with me," or "What I will give you . . ." and so on. Once I was with a male star on Broadway when he got a package containing the most beautiful watch you've ever seen, with diamonds and rubies around it, from a wealthy gal . . . if only he would come to her apartment. The man had no desire to go; he sent the watch back. For the average person, though, keeping the mind on an even keel under those circumstances is pretty difficult.

But aside from the personal problems of fame, there are those who, once having achieved success, let it slip from their hands. In films, age, perhaps more than anything else, takes the heaviest toll. It was like that with Harold Lloyd. He created a character that I helped him develop, the young man. He couldn't grow old with that character. Every action, every bit of his character was based on his youth. The things that were funny for a boy of twenty were not funny for a boy of thirty-five. Harold Lloyd was a "made" comedian. He worked so hard at developing the character of a certain age that he was unable to let this fellow carry on, to grow up, and still be funny. I once saw him watch a Mary Pickford picture seven or eight times to get one expression that she had. In Harold Lloyd's whole life with me, he never once said, "What do I do?" He said, "What does *he* do?" It was always "that fellow I'm portraying on the screen," never "what I do myself." Acting is exactly what it suggests—portraying someone you are not, not portraying someone you are.

I have been asked a thousand times why I don't have another *Our Gang* comedy. The difficulty would be in finding the kids. It just happened that at the time I started the *Gang*, there were three great kids in Hollywood doing nothing. And I got them. Soon the other kids began to come in. Hundreds played in *Our Gang*. Certain kids could dance; others were great mimics. I've seen Cary Grant sit and watch those kids for half an hour at a time and marvel at their ability to convey an idea. They were natural little actors. Farina could cry great big tears in twenty seconds. You'd think his heart was breaking, and one moment later, he'd be back playing again.

We had a school at the studio which the kids attended. They were there every day. It was a regular public school which we paid for. Because they were a group and they played together, they didn't get as spoiled as individual kids do. They didn't pay much attention to outsiders, but we had all kinds of problems with the parents. The kids didn't care what they were doing, but the parents would protest, "You're getting too much of this other kid and not enough of mine."

I guess the most striking memory for me was when D. W. Griffith came to work at the studio late in his life. When I made *One Million B.C.*, he helped me on it. In fact, he was the one who found Carole Landis. He came to work for me simply because he needed it. Whether his talent had been used up by that time is hard to say. He had done more for directing than anybody else in the business. He had a great sense of the dramatic, unquestionably so, and a great sense, particularly in the silent days, of what was good entertainment. Well, I'll tell you one thing he did for me.

One Million B.C. was a prehistoric picture, a figment of my imagination. D. W. came over to work for me, and I said, "Dave, I'd like you to cast the picture." They brought in girls. I wasn't paying any attention. He looked at them. We had already decided on Victor Mature as the man and Lon Chaney as the father. Every time these girls came in, he took them to the back lot. I didn't know what the hell he was doing out in the open spaces. Then one day he said, "I found your girl." It was Carole Landis. "Come out. I want to show you something." We went out on the back lot where there was street scenery and, on the corner, a telephone post. He looked at the girl and said, "Take your shoes off. Now run to that post as fast as you can. Then run back to me as fast as you can."

She did. I wasn't particularly impressed. That's a hell of a way to pick our leading lady. We know she can run. He said, "I've had fifty girls run to that post and back. She's the only one who knows how to run. You're not going to make a believable girl in a picture of that kind who runs like an average girl. She's got to run like an athlete, a deer." And she could. Her rhythm was really beautiful. In the picture, you never noticed it. But if she ran like most girls, you would damn well have seen the difference.

SOL LESSER

THEY TELL ME I was born in a tent in Spokane, Washington. We moved to San Francisco when I was six weeks old, and I grew up there, staying until 1919 when I went, then twenty-nine years of age, to Los Angeles where I have lived ever since. I had a grammar school education, graduated in 1904, and then worked in the wholesale hardware business until a memorable date, April 18, 1906. That morning at five-fifteen, a terrible earthquake, followed by four days of devastating fire, destroyed practically the entire town. Medical supplies, food, clothing, blankets, and tents were rushed to the city by special trains and were stacked up in the railroad yards. Emergency transportation was needed to distribute these things to refugees who were scattered in parks and playgrounds all over the city.

Of course, there were no automobiles in 1906. Around the corner from my home was a dairy depot and stables. I borrowed a horse and wagon from the owner and began delivering food and supplies throughout the city—until organized relief officials took the horse and wagon away from me. Then fire fighters began dynamiting structures to put out fires because the water supply had run dry. Six blocks from my home stood the famous Blum's Candy Store. We were watching while the dynamiters were getting ready to blow this beautiful candy store to pieces. I asked, "What about the candy?" and was told that everything goes. Our gang was horrified. We were told to help ourselves. And did we! Across the street was a cable-car barn. We pushed the dummy part of a cable car to the front of Blum's, loaded it with gumdrops, jujubes, jelly beans, and marshmallows, pushed the car to the top of the hill, and coasted down the street. Each kid took what he wanted, and we rang bells and passed out candy to surprised takers, whose minds were certainly on more serious matters. Anyway, after the fires were out, everything returned to normal.

It wasn't long after the earthquake that my father learned about the spread of the new motion picture industry. He opened and operated one of the first nickelodeons in San Francisco. I sold ice-cream cones, relieved the cashier, operated the projection machine, and ushered, which was my entrance into the picture business. From time to time, father let me buy a few films. He and I established an embryonic film exchange, purchasing films and renting them to other theaters. During this time, I also produced two pictures in San Francisco and sold them nationally. I was then seventeen.

I may have been the first person to interest a bank in financing motion pictures. I needed $100 to accept delivery of a COD package of film held in the Wells Fargo Express Office. I went to the Bank of America. It was then the Bank of Italy, and A. P. Giannini was president. A great big fellow, he used to stand on the floor, never working behind a desk. I said,

"Mr. Giannini, I would like to borrow one hundred dollars."

"What do you want one hundred dollars for?"

"I would like to pick up a COD from the Wells Fargo Express Company."

"What's in the package?"

"A motion picture film."

"This bank doesn't loan money on motion picture films."

"What's the difference, Mr. Giannini? I'm going to pay it back."

"How old are you, my boy?"

"I'm seventeen."

"I can't loan you any money because you're not of age. We couldn't enforce collection."

"What's the difference, Mr. Giannini? I'm going to pay it back."

"How do I know that?"

"Because I tell you so."

That did it. He looked me over and called to the paying teller, "Give this kid one hundred dollars.'"

"Don't I have to sign a note?"

"You can't sign a note. I'm having this one hundred dollars charged to me."

I took the one hundred dollars and paid it back in time, which launched me with the Bank of Italy. When the bank established a branch in New York, A. P. Giannini's brother, Dr. Giannini, became its top officer I introduced him to Marcus Loew and to L. J. Selznick, the father of

David and Myron Selznick. These were the first of many introductions which helped the Bank of America to become the largest basic bank for the financing of the film industry.

Shortly after that, I made my first documentary, although at the time I didn't know it was one. The famous Barbary Coast, the Tenderloin district in San Francisco, was where "ladies of the evening" were licensed to practice their art, or trade. Since the city government had decided to close this district, the bohemians wanted to stage one last celebration. A great many fun-loving, prominent citizens turned out. Everything that night was free. And when I say everything, I mean everything. My cameraman, Hal Mohr, took a camera down there to photograph the festivities. I called the film *The Last Night of the Barbary Coast* and sold prints all over the United States at twelve cents per foot. In recent years I've searched everywhere for a print for my archives, but I can't find one. It would have been a fine historical item for a museum. Unfortunately, I didn't copyright the subject, and all the prints have gone into oblivion.

In those days, it was difficult to make a business mistake; anything that was produced was bought up immediately. We always began by showing a picture in my father's nickelodeon and then rented it to other nickelodeons. Both my mother and father were dead by 1909. By 1911, the business had grown quite a bit. In addition to the film exchange, I had opened two new theaters in San Francisco, although we lost the lease on the first one. I married Fay Gronauer in 1913, and I'm still married to the same wonderful lady. Today we have two children, six grandchildren, and two great-grandchildren. By 1919, Los Angeles and Hollywood were establishing themselves as production centers and marketplaces for motion pictures, so I decided to move down there. We stayed at the Alexandria Hotel, smack in the center of the film industry, and plunged right into the atmosphere and adventure of Hollywood.

There being no local motion-picture trade papers at that time, agents, buyers, stars, directors, financiers, film-exchange promoters, and speculators would meet at the Alexandria for breakfast, lunch, dinner, and midnight snacks. The central lobby was like a stock exchange floor. The floor was covered with a huge Oriental rug. Most of the film deals were made on that rug. A legend was built about it. Many anecdotes were told about the fantastic terms and conditions of each new proposal, negotiation, and closed transaction. It's no wonder that this rug was dubbed "The Million-Dollar Rug."

It was an exciting experience. The personalities I had known only through celluloid characterizations became real. I had great respect for them. I met Mack Sennett and later worked out a deal with him for a picture called *Yankee Doodle in Berlin*. I arranged for the personal appearance of Sennett's "bathing girls" and toured them with the film. In no time at all, I thus became an impresario, although my ultimate goal was to establish myself in the production field. I had, in partnership with the Gore brothers, two local exhibitors, an opportunity to buy out P. L. Talley, one of the original organizers of the First National Pictures Corporation. This corporation was a combination of motion-picture theater owners, each operating separate chains of theaters in different states. They banded together in protest of the high rental of films to finance their own productions. The Gore brothers and I bought Talley's franchise and his first-run theater in downtown Los Angeles and established the West Coast Theaters. I became the Hollywood representative of First National Pictures in deals with artists which provided an opportunity for many cordial friendships with Hollywood personages, lasting to this day.

I again started making pictures. I signed Jackie Coogan and made six pictures with him including *Oliver Twist* in 1922 in which Lon Chaney played the part of Fagin. This picture did an enormous business. I recall when Adolph Zukor, then president of Paramount, Famous Players–Lasky Corporation, asked me how I expected to come out, since it was rumored that I was spending $175,000 for a picture, and particularly since I was in independent production. He couldn't believe it. Well, that picture did over two million dollars gross and helped finance many new theaters, which the Gore brothers and I accrued over a period of six years. I finally sold out and dedicated myself to the production of motion pictures.

I've often been asked to define the duties and obligations of a producer: In my judgment, a producer is fundamentally a catalyst. There are producer–directors, or producer–writers, and producer–packagers. Obviously no single man can make a picture. He needs technicians, artists, and a director. But a producer puts the elements together and sees the picture through from inception to completion.

There's no rule of thumb on how long it should take to put a picture together. For *Oliver Twist*, the man I thought most capable of doing it was Frank Lloyd, an English director. He was a Dickens scholar and had stage-directed it in England. In addition, he had an outstanding record as a motion picture director in Hollywood. He and I agreed to independently go through the book to see which of the many incidents should be retained for the picture. By lucky coincidence, we selected identical material. Lloyd suggested that he himself write the script, pointing out that it was just a qustion of inserting the scenes in proper continuity and full detail. This he did, and in a matter of four weeks, we were on the floor producing it. We assembled a magnificent cast. It took about six weeks to make the picture. The publicity established it as a road show, and we got excellent percentage terms from first-run theaters throughout the country. The cost was justified. It paid off handsomely in England and throughout the world.

The delightful thing about using a combination of creative arts and techniques like a motion picture does is that each man feels that his job is more important than any of the others. The director feels he is indispensable. He is. So does the art director. He is. The actors and the writers respectively feel that they are the vital element. They are. So it goes.

Obviously, motion pictures have changed over the years. Yet if D. W. Griffith were living today and directing, he would probably be just as socially aware of the realities of modern life as the new producers and directors. The old-timers, like Griffith, sought perfection. Everyone had great respect for their talents. I recall that, prior to my arrival on the Hollywood scene as a producer, I bought the rights to distribute one of Griffith's pictures, *Hearts of the World*. It was a road show with advance admission prices. Since this was before sound pictures had arrived, I provided an orchestra and we had sound effects behind the screen. That was the year of the influenza, 1918, right after the Armistice. At this particular time the public had begun to reject war pictures, but this one was a big success. Griffith made up the basic musical score, which was just perfect for the film. In those "good old days," pictures were musically supported by the local organist. Griffith's music, however, was synchronized and integrated completely to the dramatic structure of the film. I had twenty companies, with orchestras and sound-effects men touring the eleven Western states. When the flu epidemic hit, we had to close down and bring the musicians and effects men home at a terrific cost. All income ceased, and I took a heavy loss.

It has been only in the last five or six years that motion pictures have been elevated to an art form. I never realized the value of the old negatives. Otherwise, I would not have destroyed the negatives from some of my early films. When the business manager came to me and asked, "Are you going to make any more prints of *Oliver Twist?*"

"No," I said.

"Can I destroy the negative? I need the vault space."

I told him, "Sure, go ahead. It's dead."

I had no sense then that it was an art form. The revivals of the old pictures make me just about the most surprised man in the world. Many people have discovered that the motion picture is an art form or, more accurately, that it is a combination of art forms. Of course, it's a communication's medium too, but I think the vicissitudes of life can be unfolded better in a motion picture than in any other form of art. It's three-dimensional, and it has the capacity to tell the truth powerfully. A lot of people still think that the old silent pictures are just merchandise, but more and more of them have come to recognize their artistic value. That's why I am continuing my interest in establishing a Hollywood archives to collect "milestone" subjects.

And herein lies the essential problem of producing films. On the one hand, the artistic aspect, which is a more natural function of the medium, must be taken into consideration. On the other, the business element must also be considered. Sometimes these two collide head-on. Between a painter and his finished product nothing stands but his brush. The product doesn't cost very much except his time. But a motion picture makes such large financial demands that the artist must render a different kind of art than he otherwise would. Let me explain this from the artistic point of view. Recently, I had occasion to obtain a watercolor drawn by James Montgomery Flagg. I wondered if it was considered a work of art. The Hollywood Museum's curator told me:

"Mr. Lesser, this is an example of art of its period. Besides, it is a picture of a great actress, Norma Talmadge. That work was once considered high art. I believe it's a collector's item. We should have that picture in the museum to show what art of another day was like."

If that picture were measured against a Picasso or a modern portrait, it would not be considered an enduring work of art. But as this curator pointed out, it was an art object of that day, just as Mary Pickford's pictures show the art of her day. The art of Buster Keaton and of the Laurel and Hardy masterpieces is still being copied today. Those pictures can be viewed again and again, and in twenty-five or fifty years they will still be seen. Oddly, at first, we thought they were just slapstick comedies!

When sound was invented for the "second" time, I welcomed it as a boon to the motion picture business. Edison's first motion picture for public reception had a sound device. It consisted of a pulley tied to an operating machine which went to the ceiling, across it, and down backstage, where it was hooked up to a talking machine. The operator wound the entire mechanism by hand, thus keeping the projector and sound record-player synchronized. It was the first form of motion picture sound, but so cumbersome and impractical that it failed. So the motion picture industry went forward with silent pictures. Then, in 1926, the sound transition took place. It occurred at just about the same time that I had accumulated my large theater interests and had become so involved with this that I was relatively inactive in production.

It's interesting that each new revolution in the business has produced a new group of so-called tycoons. For instance, those who believed in sound replaced some of the old-timers who thought it was temporary. Actors who had the talent to speak lines began to have greater importance. Embryo producers began to emerge in the new field. The business was turned upside down.

It wasn't until 1931 that I returned to making pictures. How I got back into the business is an interesting story. I knew Louis Brown, an author, who had written *How Odd of God*. Brown was a friend of Upton Sinclair's. He told me that Sinclair had a great quantity of film of an un-

D. W. Griffith observing a scene from his *Hearts of the World*, distributed by Sol Lesser. 1918.

Adolphe Lestina and Lillian Gish in *Hearts of the World*. 12 reels. Photography—G. W. "Billy" Bitzer.

Brenda Joyce, Johnny Sheffield, and Johnny Weissmuller in Sol Lesser's production of *Tarzan and the Amazons*. 1945.

On location with Sergei Eisenstein's *Que Viva Mexico*, later released by Sol Lesser as *Thunder Over Mexico*. Eisenstein is observing cameraman. Circa 1931.

finished picture, photographed and directed by Eisenstein in Mexico. Eisenstein had already achieved great fame as a director in Russia, and Paramount Pictures had engaged him to come to Hollywood to write and direct a picture. Much to everyone's surprise, he chose *An American Tragedy* and was given an unlimited and unconditional contract to write it. He turned in his finished script. The studio management judged it to be a piece of Communist propaganda and promptly threw him out of the studio. He went to Upton Sinclair, who was friendly to the Soviet government, and appealed to him, saying that if he went back to Russia without having accomplished something in America, he would be in very great trouble. He told Sinclair he had a fine idea for a story and asked him to finance it. So Sinclair raised enough money to send Eisenstein off to write and produce a picture in Mexico to be called *Que Viva Mexico*, which later became *Thunder Over Mexico*.

After running out of money twice, Sinclair mortgaged his own home to send more money. The film still wasn't finished. Finally, he had to call a halt. He cabled his friends in Russia to recall Eisenstein, and they did so. As Eisenstein came through Los Angeles, Sinclair seized the uncompleted film. Eisenstein went on to Russia, and that's the last anybody here ever heard of him.

Well, we had a mass of film, several hundred thousand feet, along with duplicate shots. If Eisenstein photographed a cloud, for example, he would photograph it from five or six different angles. The film was mostly scenic with a little bit of a story. It was to be an epic of the trials and tribulations of the peons, really the whole history of Mexico.

I was able to make a film out of it, but the Communists started to attack me for invading the cutting rights of Eisenstein. They said I was desecrating the master's touch. The night we previewed the picture in Los Angeles, they threw stink bombs in the theater. I received all kinds of threatening letters.

In any event, I took the picture on to New York. Everywhere I went, there was publicity about it. And some organizations announced a boycott. At last, one of the theaters down around 14th Street agreed to run only the original uncut version as Eisenstein had delivered it to me, eighty or ninety reels of uncut film. I agreed, but under one condition: the exhibitor would really show it all. I numbered the reels, and the theater advertised the original uncut version. People came and brought their lunches. After a couple of hours, they started to drift out and others came in. Before it was a third over, the house was empty.

No one ever asked for the uncut version again. Writers told the public that the film had to be cut and edited. Eisenstein wasn't available. The boycott stopped. I went to Europe with a salesman, and we were able to sell the rights nearly everywhere. Upton Sinclair got out. I handled the picture for a while until there was no more demand for it. We deposited the film at the Museum of Modern Art; we gave it to them. They were making money on it, and they would occasionally send Mr. Sinclair a little check. They were not obligated to do so, but they felt they should. The film is actually very good.

I have remained friendly with Upton Sinclair all these years. I find he's a very fine man, and no more communist than any of us. Once he ran for governor of the State of California under a program called EPIC, End Poverty in California. He wanted to give old-age pensions. People thought he was worse than a communist, maybe an anarchist. What's happened since makes his predictions look very pallid, indeed.

The picture I produced that gave me the greatest pleasure was *Stage Door Canteen*. I agreed to give the profits to the American Theater Wing for the continuation of their canteen services throughout the world. Half of it was produced in Los Angeles; the other half in New York. We duplicated the sets and matched the photography to accommodate those actors who were in New York in current stage successes. There were over a hundred stars in the picture, each making a dramatic contribution to the story. The script was based on the real Stage Door Canteen, which was a night club type of operation where soldiers, when they were in New York on their way to being shipped overseas, spent their leisure hours. They were entertained by the stars who put on shows and served food. The servicemen danced with the female stars and, of course, the chorus girls, so that their last few days here would be memorable ones. The writer of the script actually went to New York and interviewed many of these illustrious people. The picture did an enormous business. A profit between three-and-a-half to four million dollars was turned over to the American Theater Wing in New York to establish canteens in other cities. I took only 13½ percent for my share to cover overhead for my corporation.

When I subsequently formed The Principal Pictures Corporation, I contracted to release our product through United Artists. I produced two pictures with Edward G. Robinson. One was *Vice Squad*; the other, *The Red House*. Fortunately, both were very successful, so I was able to secure the rights to the *Tarzan* stories from Edgar Rice Burroughs. All told, I made thirteen Tarzan pictures, including five with Johnny Weissmuller, who, up to that time, had been under contract to MGM, playing Tarzan in four pictures produced by them.

My Tarzan experience began when a friend asked if I would like to buy the rights to produce one Tarzan picture. I was told that the rights were granted to an actor by the name of Pierce. One could buy the rights from Pierce by obligating himself to use Pierce in the picture, playing the part of Tarzan. But the date on which Pierce had agreed to pay the author, Edgar Rice Burroughs, had long passed. My lawyer said:

"This is a good contract. It calls for the payment of twenty thousand dollars to Edgar Rice Burroughs, the author and owner of the copyright, and I need that amount to tender to him. If he refuses it, Burroughs must give notice that the contract has been defaulted. We may have to sue, but I'm sure that we can legally establish that the default has been rectified."

So I gave the lawyer $20,000 to cure the default. He went out to Malibu Beach where Mr. Burroughs lived. As he told me the story later, a big fellow answered the doorbell and the lawyer asked:

"Are you Edgar Rice Burroughs?"

"Yes."

"Here, I want to give you twenty thousand dollars," and handed him twenty thousand-dollar bills.

"What's this twenty thousand dollars for?" Mr. Burroughs asked.

"It's in payment for the rights to a Tarzan picture that you gave to John Pierce."

With that, Mr. Burroughs said, "Those rights have expired," threw the $20,000 at him, and slammed the door.

It was a little windy, and my lawyer said it took him forty minutes to recover the money. But he brought suit against Edgar Rice Burroughs on the grounds that any default of the contract required a notice from Burroughs, which he had failed to give. The tender of $20,000 cured the default, and the contract was made good. Then it came out that Metro was making a Tarzan picture and that Burroughs had legally contracted with them that there were no outstanding rights. Metro didn't want any other Tarzan picture in the theaters just then. I agreed to straighten it out by delaying production for a year. That satisfied everybody and Burroughs accepted my $20,000. All this furnished the basis for a fine life-long friendship between Burroughs and myself. This is another illustration of what a producer actually does.

If there's one thing a producer should never do, it's to go on the set when he is not sent for. Only occasionally was I summoned. I remember it happening once when I was doing *Peck's Bad Boy* with Jackie Cooper. At a high point in the story, the scene called for Jackie to cry real tears. I got a call from Eddie Cline who was the director.

"Please come to the stage to help solve a problem." Jackie wouldn't cry. His mother was upbraiding him as I came on the stage.

"You call yourself an actor and all they're asking you to do is cry? They had to bring Mr. Lesser out from his office, and he's a busy man."

"Aw, Ma, I can't cry. I'd cry if I could. I'm not doing it on purpose, honestly I'm not."

One of the crew had a bright idea, so he said, "Jackie, I just heard your dog was run over by a truck."

"Oh baloney, don't try to fool me," Jackie said. We had to get that

Sol Lesser and Jackie Cooper on set during production of *Peck's Bad Boy*. 1934.

Left to right: Director Sam Wood, Fay Bainter, William Holden (seated), and Technical Adviser Ed Goodnow on set rehearsing Sol Lesser's production of Thornton Wilder's *Our Town*. 1940.

scene because the set was coming down. Someone suggested we use glycerine to produce tears, but we all agreed that that would not be effective. Then I had an inspiration. I turned away from Jackie to the director and winked.

"I think it's your fault, Eddie," I said. "This kid is a real trouper and you're picking on him. By God, you're fired."

With that, little Jackie started to cry. "Mr. Lesser, please don't fire Eddie. He's my friend. It isn't his fault." Now the problem was to get him to stop crying.

It happened another time when Sam Wood was directing *Our Town*, one of the better pictures I produced. An issue had developed between Bill Menzies, the art director, and Sam Wood because the scene as arranged cut the head off the actor. Mr. Wood wanted the whole head. The art director maintained that this would ruin the shot. I settled that one by suggesting it be done the way the art director wanted—if necessary, it was a very easy scene to do over again. Wood agreed reluctantly. After he saw it, he was convinced that they were getting a style which was completely Bill Menzies's, and he never set up again without calling for Menzies to approve. That worked out harmoniously. It was a celebrated picture; one which should be remade.

How producer and author may work in harmony can be demonstrated by this story about Thornton Wilder and myself. I went to the Bucks County Theatre in Pennsylvania where he was acting the part of narrator in the stage play of *Our Town*. I talked over with him the problem of transferring the play to the screen. He had never done a treatment before, but was willing to try. We worked for seven or eight days in New York. When he got through, he said he had never worked so hard in his life, but he had enjoyed it. He would take no compensation, but I finally found out from his sister that he wanted an automobile. I bought him one and sent it to him for Christmas. He was very appreciative. I then asked him if he wouldn't work on the script for a consideration. He said no, that screen-writing was a different profession, but that he would be willing to comment on it. The letters we exchanged have been published by *Theatre Arts* as an example of cordiality and understanding between the author and the producer. The point is that a producer doesn't controvert an author's intent. Wilder was pleased with the picture and said so. There's a particular art in writing a screenplay, and it's an advancing art. Some men have the talent for understanding screen movements. Some don't. In this case, we chose well.

Finally in 1958, after fifty-one years in the picture business, I felt the time had come when I ought to end this career. I had reached the age when I realized that one either finishes on top or far below. I decided I would end on top, and I was satisfied.

JOE ROCK

NEW YORK was my birthplace a long time ago, like in 1889. My father was a finisher of hardwood, a cabinetmaker who also built houses and race-track stables. I had a brother and two sisters. I went to DeWitt Clinton High School on 59th Street and 10th Avenue and loved it. Two blocks away was the New York Normal School of Physical Education where I eventually became a physical education director. I played professional basketball in the Hudson River League, for Poughkeepsie, with the Clark House, as well as with the Clark deaf-mutes. I was the only one who wasn't a deaf-mute. I also graduated from the Chattauqua Normal School of Physical Education. I found my first job as playground teacher in Trenton, New Jersey, stayed there awhile, and then received a call from the Pittsburgh Athletic Association. Mellon and Trees and Carnegie and Sloane and Frick—all those millionaires were members. I was physical education director there for two or three years. After that I left for a little town named Crafton, Pennsylvania. John Harris, who later owned the Ice Capades, also lived there and was one of my pupils in the school. I had athletic ability. I won quite a few gold and silver medals in basketball, football, and track and field—and a solid gold medal for the potato race which was popular in those days, in 1905, '06, '07.

When I left Crafton, I came back to New York and did a little dancing in the "subway circuit" with two girls, the Barnes Sisters. I had

Eliza Morris and Joe Rock dancing a ballet. Miss Morris was a graduate of the Louis Chalif Normal School of Dancing. Pittsburgh. 1915.

learned to dance in Normal School. It was ballet then. I've got a photo somewhere of myself in a minuet pose with Eliza Morris, one of the great American dancers from the famous Chalif Ballet School of New York. When Pavlova's show came to Pittsburgh with Mordkin, Miss Morris danced in their show. But I wasn't picked as I wasn't good enough.

I was more interested in football, baseball, and basketball. Being short, I always had to be better than the next fellow. I took nothing from anybody. I gave "schlock" when I got it, and I got it plenty of times. For instance, in one basketball game we played in Jersey, Joe Jeanette was on the other team. He was a well-known heavyweight fighter. Everytime there would be a scramble for the ball, I'd come out with a black eye. Anyway, I could take care of myself.

Finally, somebody from *Theater Magazine* gave me a piece of advice:

"Joe, why don't you go down to the Vitagraph studio and get into pictures?"

"What pictures?"

"Motion pictures."

"Me? I'd never get into motion pictures."

"Why not?"

"I'm not tall. I'm not handsome. I haven't got a mustache."

"But you do stunts."

"What do stunts have to do with film?"

"Well, there are a lot of hazardous things to do."

So I went down to the Vitagraph Company in Brooklyn. Albert Smith and Stuart Blackton and Pop Rock were running it. Pop Rock owned the company. He was the rich man. Smith and Blackton were formerly cameramen, the best in the business. Vitagraph first started in Manhattan in a tall building on Nassau Street, using the roof as a stage. Broadway actors would walk slowly past the entrance, and if nobody was watching, in they'd go. In those days, their names weren't put on the screen. The actors themselves didn't want to be identified because Vitagraph made lots of one- and two-reel films which were used in theaters as "chasers." When they wanted people to get out of a vaudeville house, they'd put a picture on—the picture a real "chaser." So actors were ashamed to have their names on them.

Vitagraph later moved to Brooklyn to an old barn, and they built a fine studio there. I presented myself to Wilfred North, the best director there. He was directing Lillian Walker, then a big star. They also had Anita Stewart, Earle Williams, Maurice Costello, Antonio Moreno, and Norma and Constance Talmadge. I said to Wilfred North: "Mr. So-and-So sent me. He thought possibly you would like to use me."

North looked at me. "Any stage experience?"

"No, no stage experience."

"What can you do?"

"I can do stunts."

"Stunts. Umhmmm."

He took me to a director, I think one of Albert Smith's younger brothers, who was making a picture with Edna Best. They put me in a mob scene, and they told me how I'd be paid. Money didn't make that much difference. I had a little. The pay was $1.50 a day, if you please. I wasn't up to the $5 class yet. The first scene we made was a fight scene. The director lined a bunch of us up on one side. It was a ballroom episode, and a band was supposed to be playing, but since it was a silent film, it was just pretending to play. Another group was on the other side.

"When I blow the whistle," the director explained, "walk toward each other, pick out the man opposite you, and start the fight. When I blow it again, stop fighting."

I looked at my partner, and oh! my God! he was a well-known welterweight prize fighter, a real bruiser. He looked at me, and out of the corner of his mouth, to the fellow next to him, said, "Oh boy," meaning what he was going to do to me was nobody's business.

"Well, Joseph," I said, "you're in for it now and all for one dollar and fifty cents."

The whistle was blown; we walked towards each other, and I watched the bruiser. I quickly moved over to the side, and before he could do anything, I hit him. By that time, there was a scramble. All I did was grab the next guy, and we started to fight. I whispered "If you go easy, I'll go easy." He hit me, and I walloped him one, and he hit me, and I walloped him again. So I told him, "If you don't want to slow down, you don't have to." He slowed down, and we began to pretend to fight all around. But it got so rough and bad that they blew the whistle—they blew four whistles—but the mob wouldn't stop. They used the klieg lights, pulling the switch up and down. That caused all the lights to go on and off and produced a lot of noise, but the fight continued. Most of the fellows were from the fight club nearby, lots of tough guys. The whole orchestra was swept right off the platform. The men fought on the steps. They fought in the big courtyard. The police were summoned. There was a riot going on. Eventually, the fighting stopped. I had a black eye and I was bruised all over. There were more black eyes and broken noses and blood all over the place. From that time on, they were very careful how they started and ended a fight scene. At any rate, I got my $1.50.

Then I was hired to double for girls who had certain action scenes to do, such as catching an automobile on the fly or going off the roof on a rope. I put on a dress and long stockings. From dancing, my calves were just like a girl's. I wore a wig, a hat or coat, and high heels, too. That was pretty tough. I got sick and tired of working for $1.50. I asked for $5. They threw up their hands and said, "Nuts to you."

I didn't work for nine weeks. At last, they asked me to double for an actress because nobody else would do the stunt. They had to give me the five dollars, reluctantly. After that I told them, "No more doubling. If I do the stunt, it will be in a part that I play myself." They claimed there wouldn't be a part for a young fellow like me so I refused to work. Then I met Earl Montgomery who came out to New York from the Coast. He had worked in films as a stuntman with some pretty good people. Montgomery liked me right away. He saw that I could do stunts. We became good friends and worked as a team. We became Montgomery and Rock, stuntmen.

Vitagraph was one of the biggest companies of that time. They had their own releasing organization, composed of Vitagraph, Lubin, Selig, and Essanay. They were sole distributors of a special camera-shutter mechanism. Because of this monopoly, other film companies moved from New York to California to get out of their jurisdiction. That's how Laemmle came to Hollywood. It was Laemmle and William Fox who fought and broke the monopoly. It's strange how we interlock. My sister was Fox's bookkeeper when he was in the "sponging" business. He was a sponger of cloth and quite an important one. When a suit was made, the cloth had to be sponged. Otherwise it would shrink. There was a way of sponging the raw material so it wouldn't hurt the fabric. You'd be walking in the rain and, if the fabric wasn't preshrunk, it would choke you.

My father had seen somebody operating a nickelodeon, a place which contains some benches or seats, mainly the folding-chair type from a funeral parlor, get any kind of films, and run them. So he decided to put some benches in a vacant store, get somebody with a machine from downtown to run films, and charge a nickel. When my mother and sister found out what he was doing, they raised hell.

"Motion pictures? You stop that."

He stopped. But when Fox heard about this idea, it struck a note. He started by renting stores and putting in seats. It wasn't long before he became a very, very powerful man.

Before Montgomery came to Vitagraph, I worked with Larry Semon, who was a cartoonist with the *New York Sun,* and Graham Baker, a cartoonist with the *Brooklyn Eagle.* Graham made one of the first film

cartoons of a mosquito, did all the drawings himself. It ran six or seven
minutes. How wonderfully he made his mosquito! It had a snout that
looked like a drill which bored into anything and everything, especially
people's noses and other parts of their anatomy. He also wrote screenplays, including some of the O. Henry stories, which were wonderful.

Vitagraph made a deal with George McManus for filming the cartoon strip, *Bringing Up Father*. They had Huey Mack as Jiggs and Kate
Price as the wife. Larry Semon came up to direct the series. I worked in
the series, getting my five dollars every day, whether I worked or not.
I received thirty dollars, and then later, fifty dollars a week. I made-up
for the part and played either a young boob or the juvenile. I was agile
and acrobatic. The girl stars were maybe seventeen or eighteen. The two
Talmadge girls, Constance and Norma, were, I guess, fourteen or fifteen
years old. And the Costello girls, Dolores and Helene, were a little bit
younger. Lottie, *not Mary*, Pickford worked there before I arrived.

After we made some films in New York, Vitagraph decided to send
Larry to the Coast. I went along. At that time, Larry was, in popularity,
second only possibly to Arbuckle and Chaplin, but ahead of Lloyd and
Keaton. I must tell you what happened. When Larry directed half a dozen
films or so, he always did a little "bit" himself in each film. He would
work out a piece of business that had nothing to do with the story, put
on clown make-up, his blue overalls with just a shoulder strap, and a
funny little cap. He had a really white clown face. Happy-go-lucky, he'd
come dancing down the park. He'd try to catch a butterfly, anything at all,
just to attract attention. In the foreground was the "business," the actors
acting. As Semon came closer, there would be another shot of him. Finally,
he'd stand in the background and watch to see what was going on, simply
as a bystander. Usually, the actors would act angry, and one would reach
down and throw something, but the intended victims would bend over,
and Semon would get it right in the face, a pie or a bucket of water or
a breakaway vase full of a gooey substance. He would fall and look into
the camera with a dazed expression. That's all he'd do in the film. He
did things like that in three or four films until people began writing in
asking, "Who is that fellow? He's the funniest man we've ever seen on
the screen." Vitagraph came to Semon, "Larry, how would you like to be
featured?" Semon was delighted. Besides directing, he and Graham Baker
were writing comedy scripts. About six of us came out to the Coast with
Semon. I still did stunts. Semon became a big star.

After working for four or five months with Semon, I developed a
grease-paint infection. I would shave in the morning, and then apply
Max Factor make-up which we used before Factor became famous. Max
had a place down on Hill Street. Well, he put too much lead in the
make-up, and we got lead poisoning, all of us, the whole company, right

in the middle of a picture. We were out about a week. Anyway, with this infection I was trying to do various stunts, but missing badly those that should have been easy for me. Larry was giving me a hard time over it, thinking I'd been out the night before. He was a little bit jealous over the leading lady who didn't like him. She liked me, and he wasn't happy about that. He figured that we'd been out. We hadn't, but just the same I got credit for it. He was so mad that finally the assistant director said, "For God's sake, Larry. Lay off him. Look at his face." I had a swollen left cheek and was burning with fever. I had to do a stunt that takes good health to do, one where I'm in an automobile, driving it, going fast up to a haystack. In the haystack were some solid bales of hay so that when the auto hit them, the impact would propel me over the haystack. There was something on the other side for me to fall on. Well, I wasn't timing it properly, and timing is everything in doing stunts. If they aren't timed right, you're going to get killed or hurt. Larry took a look at my face.

"Why didn't somebody tell me?" he said.

"Why the hell didn't you look?"

Here I was, face out like that. I was laid up for fourteen weeks. That was the end of it. We went back to New York, and I refused to work with Larry. That's how I got in with Montgomery. I said to Monty, "Look—you've had experience in films at the American Film Company . . ." I think that's what it was called, up out of Los Angeles somewhere, an old-time, very well-known studio. "You do stunts. I do stunts. Let's not double for anybody else."

We went down to Coney Island and started to write scripts. We would sip beer and write. We finished three scripts. My sister typed them professionally, and they were well done. The gags were well played up. I took the stories to Wilfred North, who felt they were really good. North then took the scripts to Albert E. Smith, and Albert called me in. (I always did the business for both Monty and me.)

"Who wrote these stories, Joe?"

"Montgomery and I."

"You think you can write some more?"

"Oh sure, we can write a lot of them."

"Tell me, do you juggle?"

"No."

"Do you. . . ." I forgot what else he asked me.

"No. I am not even an actor," I said.

"Oh, you are an actor all right. I wish you could juggle. You'd be very good. How long will it take you to make these three films?"

"I don't know."

"Would you take Graham Baker as a director?"

"Oh yes, oh yes, sure."

Left to right: Jack Pearce, manager (famous make-up man), Joe Rock, Ewing Scott (a producer), Murray Rock (Joe Rock's brother), Robert de Grasse (cameraman), last two men unidentified. Circa 1915.

Joe Rock, Earl Montgomery, and Director Elliott "Kitty" Howe on Vitagraph studio lot. Circa 1916.

Rock and Montgomery leap sixteen feet across to a four-story building in New York. This stunt was performed without a net underneath. Circa 1916.

"If you can make these three pictures in three weeks, how would you like to go out to the Coast?"

"Back to California? Of course. We'll do it."

I got hold of Monty right away, "We've got a deal!" It was $150 apiece for the script and $150 apiece for our work. We made the pictures in two weeks, which was easy. The script usually went into a chase right away and finished up by still chasing, but by being chased right into jail. The gags were not very expensive to film. But that was our big trouble. We made the pictures too fast and too cheap. Semon took seven and eight weeks on a film and spent a lot more money. With us, $4,000 or $5,000 was all. Vitagraph had a distribution schedule to meet. When they sold to a theater, it usually was a set number of films for four months, six months, or a year. Every week, they had a new picture and there was a fixed schedule to meet. Larry was screwing up the schedule. He wasn't delivering his quota on time. We knocked ours out quickly. One a week was easy for us.

I sometimes directed and Montgomery sometimes directed. We used to write our stories sitting up in a tree to get away from people, or we'd go up on top of the gantry in the studio, away from everybody. People would shout, "Call for Joe Rock." "Call for Montgomery." Nobody paid any attention. We'd sit there until the story was finished. We started making one-reelers. Then we got into two-reelers. And later, we were not allowed to do our own stunts. We finally were getting $1,500 a week apiece for our work. We always finished our comedies with a shot of us running away from a cop, a schoolteacher, or a principal, and then running smack into them again. If we'd run away from cops, we'd run back into cops. Then we'd break away, climb a roof, and fall through a skylight, look up, see the cops, and smile. We'd turn around and discover that we were behind bars in jail. The kids used to love it. Everything we did was with an eye to them. I played the young boob; Montgomery was the heavy.

When Monty and I started making two-reelers, Vitagraph decided to split us. I'd make mine and Montgomery would make his. They'd have two pictures instead of one. Monty had one director and I had another. We were doing very well individually and were paid in twenty-dollar gold pieces! Everybody got paid that way.

Jimmy Aubrey, a comedian (I made twenty-four pictures with him in the early twenties), was one of the original Fred Karno troupe that came out from England with Chaplin, Laurel, and Billy Reeves in the famous skit called *A Night in an English Music Hall.* In it were twenty to twenty-five all-male roustabout–acrobatic–pantomime–comedians. Jimmy, who hated banks, had a theatrical steamer trunk. He would open it, pull out a drawer, and drop his gold into the damn thing. I said to him,

"Jimmy, you're crazy to keep your money in gold. Put it in a bank." But he didn't trust banks.

Montgomery would take the gold, go down to a bank, and get a thousand-dollar bill. In the films, he wore shoes that were size twenty-two. There was always a hole in the sole of one shoe. He loved to shoot craps and play cards. Monty was born in Alaska, in the gold country. He'd stick a thousand-dollar bill in his shoe with the hole in the sole, then pull out a little piece of it to show that it was a thousand dollars and that it was a real bill. When he was shooting craps, he would sit on the ground and cross his feet so people could see the bill. Someone would usually edge around to get near him, and he would tease him by shoving his foot towards him, look the other way until he reached for the bill, and then slowly withdraw his foot.

Anyway, it wasn't long after that I started producing on my own, featuring myself. Then I stopped acting and made films with Chester Conklin, Slim Sommerville, Lee Moran, Neely Edwards. At that time, New York and Boston did a lot of independent financing. Louis B. Mayer got his money from Boston as did Warner's and various comedy companies. I got my money here from Motley Flint when he was vice president of Security First National. I met Flint through Sam Warner, the youngest Warner brother. Sam actually made the deal with Western Electric for talkies. The other brothers didn't want him to go into that at all. They thought he was doing the wrong thing, but he made the first talkie. The system was Vitaphone, but he never lived to hear it.

After a while, I started producing Stan Laurel comedies. Nobody wanted to use him in a series because he was unreliable. He was a drinker. He also insisted on having his vaudeville partner, Mae, in his films, and she was a pain in the neck. The exhibitors used to write Hal Roach not to use this woman: parents were complaining that she was crude. She always wanted to be pushed over a fence, or through a window, or up a skylight. He would have to put his hand under her dress and push her over. And she'd go "Yeeee," as if she were being goosed. People didn't like it. But she always wanted to get laughs on her own. It was funny, too, and kids laughed, but parents, exhibitors, and censors complained—and Stan wouldn't work without her. She also saw to it that no other young girls worked in his pictures. When I took him on, Laurel was flat broke. He had come to this country in a comedy act in vaudeville called: Stan and Mae Laurel, Knock-about Comedians. Very funny. They reached New York and got onto a big-time circuit which took them all over the country.

I had previously met Stan in New York when he and Mae were doing their act. I believe Hammerstein's was the first to book them on Broadway. When they came out here, Laurel said to me, "Joe, do you think you can get me work if I come out again? I'll fix it so I can stay out here a month."

"Let me know your schedule. Set the days," I said.

I lined up something for him with Larry Semon and Slim Summerville. I called Jack White at Educational Pictures, and I tried others. I knew everybody. I was doing my own Joe Rock Comedies when I left Vitagraph. At Vitagraph, we made a fair reputation, not big-time because they never allowed us to spend a lot of money. But we were consistent. We made films that people liked, and they were played all over the world.

I went to Pathé, which at that time released all of Roach's films. Elmer Pearson was the head.

"I'm going to make a series with Stan Laurel and maybe Jimmy Aubrey." I told him, "Would you be interested?"

"I might be interested in Aubrey, but not Stan."

"Why?"

"You'll have a heck of a time. You might make two or three. We go out and sell twelve, a whole series, not one at a time. Where are we without the full series?"

Then I went to Educational, whose president was Earl Hammons. Same story. He pointed out, "You'd be broke because we'd have to go after you if you guaranteed twelve pictures and only delivered two or three."

I came back and told friends of mine about it. Stan was living with them. One was Gertrude Short, a comedienne in the Telephone series RKO made. She was a funny, cute little fat girl married to the director, Percy Pembroke, who was Stan Laurel's best friend. He made two or three films with Stan in co-operation with Billy Anderson, the "Bronco Billy" Anderson. I told them, "As much as I would like to make a deal with Stan, I just can't do it."

"You've got to, Joe." They pleaded with me. Stan had patches on his pants. He had to pull his coat down as he walked. He had cardboard in his shoes.

"The only way I could do it is if Mae is not in the pictures," I said.

We had a meeting with Stan. He agreed to bring Mae and have a talk. They came up to my office, and I laid it on the line to Mae.

"I presume you want him to make good. I know you want to work, but I can't sell his films with you in them."

"He won't get along without me," she cried.

"Let me worry about that. I'm putting up the money."

I gave him a very good deal. It was his only chance. I also told him that he'd have to stop his drinking and live up to the rules. If he had a call for eight o'clock, nine o'clock, five o'clock, he had to be there and

Stan Laurel. Circa 1928.

remain on call anytime. Also, he had a piece of the deal. I gave him a good salary. He finally accepted.

I provided him with $1,000 to get out of debt, buy a wardrobe, and all that. He and Mae were very happy. We scheduled the first picture, and the sets were built. Tomorrow we work. Up comes Stan, and I look at him,

"What the hell happened to you?"

"We've got a cat at home, and he scratched me."

"Cat? Is her name Mae?"

"What am I going to do? She wants to be in the film."

"What do you mean? She can't be. It's all cast."

"Well, then, I can't be in it either."

"You're kidding. You don't mean that."

"I mean it. If Mae isn't in it, I'm not going to be in it."

"Stan, you've got a contract with me. What are you going to do?"

"You've got the sets built."

"Don't worry about that. I'll do your part, and I've got a number of other comedians I could put in. Stan, if you're not going to do it. . . ."

"Well, I'm sorry."

"I'll tell you what I'll do. I'll tear up the contract." And I tore it in half. I said, "Here." He didn't know what to do. "I'm not going to be blackmailed. I can't make a picture with Mae Laurel in it." He just sat there.

"Stan, she gave you a bad time."

"Yes, she did."

"Do you want me to talk to her?"

"I wish you would." I called her on the phone.

"Mae, this is Joe. Stan tells me you're going to work and he wants to know what clothes you'll wear. Why don't you come over?"

She came bouncing in.

"Mae, I just cancelled Stan's contract."

"You can't do that!"

"Why not?"

"You've got the sets built and everything."

"Oh, I know that. But you're not in the film. I can't sell you. I can sell Stan. He's the comedian. But nobody wants you. I'm sorry. If you love him, you will stay out. I hate to say it, but that's the truth."

She cried and she begged. I said, "Look, I've got money invested in the film."

She was crying, but agreed not to play in the film. "We're going to shoot tomorrow. We'll shoot around Stan because we can't take a chance with his skin."

But we did by putting a little transparent adhesive stuff on the cuts. We made the first and second films. And the third. He was appearing on time and was very co-operative. We would sometimes work all night trying to improve a gag. He would sit in on cutting. He wanted to sit in on the story. Oh, he was good, better than Babe Hardy when the two of them were a team. Babe didn't care. He came in the morning and left at 5:00 P.M. But Stan was interested. He knew cutting, and he'd tell you, "I think if we did this and this . . ." He was fine. And I had good men with me.

Lou Lipton was one of our writers. Tay Garnett, Monty Brice, Al Martin, Jim Davis, and Kitty Horne were others. We had a first-rate staff, and Stan worked along with them. Then came the payoff. Mae was very unhappy. She wanted to go back to Australia, but she didn't have a visa. I asked for her right name which she gave to me, Mrs. So-and-So, an Irish or Scottish name.

"Let me try to fix it up."

"But I don't want to go back broke."

I went down to the Australian consul—an awfully nice man, a Mr. Johnson. I knew him well. I said, "I've got a problem."

"What is it?"

I told him.

"That's no problem. She's an Australian, she is entitled to go back, and we'll fix her up."

My arrangement with Mae was to spend $1,000. Jewelry would be about $300, the one-way passage about $300, $100 would go for clothes, and she could have approximately $300 in cash. The jewelry and the $300 in cash were to be turned over to Mae sometime after the boat sailed from San Francisco. The captain or purser had custody of these items along with $10 to send me a cable when the ship was well out to sea.

My brother was to be with Stan throughout the day of sailing. Stan was somewhat sad and lonely, wondering if it would work, if he had done the right thing, if he would have regrets. It was a cold, rainy day, which did not help matters, as Murray and Stan wandered from bar to bar—with Stan never having felt so low in his whole life. This he admitted later.

The plan was for Murray to take Stan to Lois Nielson's house on the pretext of getting him out of the rain. Lois worked for us at Vitagraph when Montgomery and I made our comedies. She also worked for us at Universal Studios where I made most of my films after leaving Vitagraph. She had been in several Laurel comedies, but Stan did not know her when he was introduced to her that day. Lois was a good cook. I supplied the roast and all the trimmings for a well-rounded feast, augmented by a bottle of wine as well as some hard liquor. Stan was surprised to see me there. I told him that I had brought something over to Lois from Louise (my wife) for Lois to sew up on her machine as Lois was Louise's best friend (which was true) and Lois was good at knitting and sewing. He bought the story, I guess, mainly because he was glad to get in out of the rain. He knew that I was also waiting for the cable. I told him that Louise would phone here when the cable arrived. There was a lovely fire of eucalyptus logs, and the smell of the roast was beginning to fill the air. We all sat close to the fire, and Stan, with a scotch and soda, began to brighten up.

The phone rang. Lois went into the other room and soon came out to say it was from Louise. I went to the phone and returned with the news that the cable had arrived from the purser. Mae had her jewels and money. She felt fine. Stan was overjoyed. He stood up, and being an emotional fellow, he cried and laughed and put his arms around Murray's and my shoulders, danced up and down, and declared that Murray and I were the best friends he ever had, that we were closer to him than his father and brother. We had another drink, and I said I had to go home. Lois pleaded with me to stay, but I claimed Louise was expecting me. Then Murray said he had to go too, and Stan's heart lost a couple of beats. He saw himself out in the rain again. Then Lois, looking at Stan, said, "I cooked a nice dinner and no one wants to eat with me." Murray and I quickly turned to Stan and suggested that he stay. Stan could not utter a word, but Lois made him feel at ease. Of course, all this was the plan. Lois and Louise were in on it too. The cable had arrived hours before, but Louise was not to phone before a certain time.

In six or eight weeks Stan and Lois were married. She was a good wife, made him drop his lush friends who were sponging on him, and got him to cut down on his drinking.

Then along about the sixth picture, Stan became difficult to handle. He kept the company waiting for hours, and the director complained that he was getting behind in the schedule. As I always paid bonuses for bringing the films in on time, and larger bonuses if we finished ahead of time, everyone was affected, especially the director and his staff. No one wanted to antagonize Stan. The director did come to me and made his beef loud and clear. I brought Stan in and said, "What's the matter with you? The call is for nine o'clock and you don't come in until eleven."

"I can't be funny in the morning."

"You so-and-so," I said, "before the wrinkles were ironed out of your stomach, you were funny any time. Don't pull that Ben Turpin gag on me." (Ben Turpin was a cockeyed comedian. His eyes were crossed. When it came to four o'clock, he'd say, "It's four-thirty. The eyes are going to go straight.") Stan's contract specified a five o'clock work stoppage.

"I've been working hard," he said,

"I've got to deliver twelve pictures," I said. "I'll go broke if you don't work."

It kept on like that. We had a heck of a time.

It did not take long for everyone who made comedies to know that Stan had stopped drinking and that Mae was out of the country. I kept hearing rumors that Stan was being approached, not only by the Hal Roach Company, but by most of the major studios. I also heard that Lois was complaining to Stan that he ought to be back at Roach's or with a major studio. In a way this was true. He could have made lots more money with the big companies, and I could not increase his salary because I was contracted for the series. But since I had a contract for four more years and an increase with each series, we would have been sitting on top of the heap, so to speak.

After I got my loan from Motley Flint and we finished three or four months ahead of my scheduled twelve months, Stan said he would not make any more films for me. I knew he was down at Roach's, but did not know what he was doing. I told him that I did not intend to stop him from making a living if he wanted to write, produce, or direct, but I would not allow him to make Stan Laurel comedies, because four or five of my comedies had as yet not been released and it takes nine months to a year or more for a film to recoup its cost. He said he just wanted to go back in the theater. I told him that if he would give me a letter to that effect, I could show it to FBO, and it would let me off the hook on my deal for four more years. He gave me the letter. Soon after this he was at Roach's. I was advised by my attorney to write all the studios that he was still under contract to me. So he sued *me* for a quarter of a million dollars for preventing him from making a living. There was no trial. My attorney and his attorney got together, "Forget the suit. Rock doesn't want anything from Stan. And all Stan wants is his release."

He got his release. We would have cleaned up with four more years in the series. After all, I made him. We were friends and did good work. My wife and Lois had been friends. We all still are. And my daughter and little Lois, the daughter they had, are still the best of friends. After a while, Lois divorced him. He got back in with his old cronies and they were still drinking. Stan married two or three more times. The last, his widow, a Russian girl, was very good to and for him. He married and divorced her and married her again. The one before that, he divorced and married again and divorced.

I made seventy-two pictures for FBO: twenty-four with Jimmy

Aubrey, twelve with Stan Laurel, twenty-four with three fat fellows called
The Three Fat Men series, then *The Blue Ribbon Comedies* featuring
Chester Conklin, Billy Franey, and Alice Ardell. I also made a few with
Slim Summerville, Neely Edwards, Lee Moran of Edwards and Moran,
known as *The Hall Room Boys*.

Long before the Stan Laurel epoch, I started Mickey Rooney in
pictures. He had been in vaudeville with his father, Joe Yule. Mickey
was Joe Yule, Jr. My brother, Murray, as head of entertainment for the
Hollywood American Legion on Highland Avenue, asked me to come
see the Legion show, "There's a little fellow I think you ought to use."

I was making half cartoon, half straight films for Walter Lance's
boss, Jay Bray. They would send me a script, and we'd do our part of
the film with actors. Half live and half cartoon is now familiar to audiences because commercials today do so much of it. Our shooting script
from Mr. Bray was prepared by Walter Lantz and other cartoonists who
did the animation over the scenes we shot. The script provided a full
description of length, which people were in each scene, what actions they
had to portray, reactions by the players (facial as well as physical),
where the hands or feet should be, close-ups, medium or long shots, when
actors should hold still and for how long (timed to so many frames,
possibly to the exact footage), or any other information that had to fit into
what the cartoonist was to draw in, superimposing his pictures over the
live action. Anyone not familiar with this type of screenplay would think
he was reading the work of a lunatic, but actually it was a piece of expert
planning.

The film we made with Joey Yule was full of such cartoon drawings
and actions. Although we had been two days shooting with another
little boy as the lead before Joey came to Universal, we had not wasted
too much time or footage when we decided that Joey was great. We re-
shot the previous scenes, keeping the other children in the film as well.
We took only one day to prepare our work to throw most of the business to Joey. He was a finished little actor with stage experience and
beautiful timing. We did not have to take more than one shot of every
scene he was in after a single rehearsal.

The first scene when we started shooting again took place in a class-
room without desks. The kids were lined up in rows, with Joey in the
last row next to a tall fat boy. The exercise on command *one* from the
teacher was for the children to bend their knees to a sitting position
while both arms were brought straight up sharply to shoulder height,
then quickly, on command *two*, to straighten up and extend the arms
vigorously to the side. Joey did number two when the class was doing
number one, making the fat boy's hands strike him sharply in the nose,
which sent him flying back three to four feet on his fanny with his back

still straight and his legs also flat on the floor. (It was a trick I had taught him before we did the scene.) He bounced back on his bottom several times before coming to a stop. This was funny in itself, with his big wide-open eyes and surprised expression. He put his hand to his nose, then looked at his hand, and not seeing blood, got up, and went back in line to continue the exercise. Again he got a wallop in the nose and did the same kind of fanny-flop and the same hand to nose—and again there was no blood. He got up into line, and once more was walloped in the nose. But this time when he looked at his hand, he saw blood! Looking up at the fat boy, Joey gritted his teeth and with a determined scowl on his face, got back in line. Every time he readied himself to give the boy a sock in the jaw, the number-two exercise was being performed, and Joey's swing missed because the boy was sitting on his haunches. He finally walked toward the front of the class, picked up a stool, climbed up on it, and waited for his chance. He drew back to get more leverage and came around with his right arm, missing completely, which made him turn right around on the stool; but, with his arm still outstretched, he caught the boy flush on the face on the second turnaround. Joey, with a smile of satisfaction, got off the stool and put it aside. When you think that he did this whole long shot without a break, without even a rehearsal, you realize that here indeed was a whiz kid.

At another studio, Larry Darmour was the producer and my old partner, Earl Montgomery, was the director of the newspaper cartoon character Mickey McGuire. They were casting and rehearsing for the start of the series, and all the important characters were practically cast when I phoned Monty. Without enthusiasm, he agreed to see Joey. When he dressed him up in the clothes of the little tramplike cartoon character and put him through some comic business, Monty got Larry Darmour to come on the stage and have a look. Larry placed him under contract at once. Joey Yule's name was soon changed to Mickey McGuire. This took place in 1921 or 1922. MGM changed the name again from Mickey McGuire to Mickey Rooney for the Andy Hardy series. The new character was a far cry from anything he had previously attempted.

Let's skip to a documentary short called *Krakatoa* for which I got the Academy Award in '33. It was something I made in the Far East, when I went there for Howard Hughes's Company, Multicolor. The company made two reels of color tests for me to show, and they paid my expenses. I was sitting one day with the governor of Singapore, Governor Braddle, and, I think, the Sultan of Jahore, Singapore Joe Fisher, and the chief of police. We were all going to the race track, having lunched beforehand at the Raffles Hotel. Joe Fisher looked up, saw somebody (a pilot he knew), and turned to me.

"What do you think of Krakatoa?" he asked.

"What race is he in?" I asked.

They laughed. Joe called the pilot over, a KLM pilot, and asked him, "Have you still got those pictures of Krakatoa?"

"Yes . . ." He pulled out a bunch of pictures. I took a look at the first one showing an explosion in the middle of the ocean.

"That's a good film effect. Who made this?"

"I did."

"Are you in films?"

"No, I'm a pilot. I took these photographs coming from Holland two weeks ago. It's Krakatoa."

"Yes, it's a volcano."

I was told that Krakatoa first erupted in '83, and that every eight or ten years, it erupts again, each time for three or four months. The first eruption blew the island off the earth. That was interesting to me. I went to Batavia from Singapore and got a plane. It could be seen a hundred miles away. I got a cameraman and started to photograph. I made my film, but while I was in the Orient, Joe Fisher, head of Cathay Theater Company in the Far East (representing a large theater chain in the Pacific), received a cable from Joe Schenck saying that Howard Hughes had let Multicolor go into bankruptcy.

"Joe, you are now in the hands of the receiver." He said.

"What are you talking about?"

He showed me the cable, and then I knew why my check or money order was late. There would be no more! I was showing the two reels of color test Multicolor had made for me to producers, distributors, and civic groups, gratis, but now I had to earn some money. So I started to show the films in theaters in the Dutch East Indies, Java, Sumatra, and Bali.

I don't know how long I stayed in Java after getting two or maybe three reels of negative on Krakatoa, but I did get to Shanghai late in January or early in February of 1932. The situation there was tense. The Japanese were giving the Chinese, as well as the other countries comprising the International Settlement, a rough time. The Japanese soldiers were everywhere and cocky as hell. All the Americans, as well as other foreign nationals, were cautioned not to become involved in any incident with the Japanese. Although the British controlled the International Settlement of Shanghai, the Japanese actually broke all the rules and tried to create a justification for declaring war on the Chinese. The Japanese controlled everything, including communications. They even threatened to take over the Customs Department. My Krakatoa film was in customs. The Universal Film man said he would do his best to get my film out with his and ship everything to Hong Kong, which was a free port. The shipment would go by rail to Hong Kong if the roads were open. One morning before dawn, hell broke loose when the Japanese started shelling the Chinese section just outside the Settlement, and the war was on. It raged all around the Settlement. Food got scarce. I stayed for two months until the first American ship was allowed to sail out.

Back in Hollywood, six months later, I had a call from the Customs Department to pick up some reels of negative and pay $150 duty. I argued that I knew of no film that belonged to me, but discovered it was the Krakatoa negatives shipped from Hong Kong through the Universal Film Exchange. A print was soon struck off, and I succeeded in making a deal with Joe Brandt who had sold his interest in Columbia Pictures to go in with Educational Films. We used Graham McNamee as narrator and made a three-reeler which Fox released. It won the Academy Award in 1933. (In 1966, we reedited the film, took out Graham Mc-Namee's narration, and my son Phillip wrote a new text, photographed Joseph Cotten in a prologue and epilogue, and made a 16-mm reduction negative so that the documentary could be released to educational markets.) The original version of Krakatoa opened at the Trans-Lux on Broadway and played for fourteen weeks. Thereafter, it ran in many first-run theaters and was rebooked in the same theaters as many as four times.

Before the Academy Award ceremony, I received an offer to go to London to produce films featuring Carl Brisson. I had never heard of this man. Actually he was a European star on the order of Maurice Chevalier. Paramount later put him under contract when Chevalier left. An American film-cutter in London, connected with a group of British promoters, suggested to them that I might be acceptable to Gaumont Studios as their production man because J. C. Wolff, head of Gaumont's distribution company, knew who I was. They had distributed many of my comedies over a period of years. In an exchange of cables, they sent me an advance of $750 and a first-class passage on the *Europa*. I was to get $500 a week and 20 percent of the profits. When I arrived, John Wolff sent word that he would like to speak to me alone. He intimated that he did not think these promoters had a signed contract with Carl Brisson. They told Mr. Wolff that Brisson had agreed to sign a contract if they could get distribution from Gaumont, but Mr. Wolff said that they would also have to come up with a recognized independent producer. The promoters were supposed to have a suitable first story that Brisson would approve, but it was still being written. In the meantime, John Wolff screened some films with Brisson so that I could judge his talents and personality. The films were delightful. Brisson was a debonair ladies' man, with the right drawing-room manner and a voice to charm all ages of women. He also played the piano and sang. He was primarily a stage star, but had done two or three films.

Winston Churchill reviewing the American Eagle Squadron in England during World War II. Joe Rock is first soldier in the line. 1942.

Joe Rock's production of *5 Ages: From Stone Age to Modern*, featuring himself. 1920.

I knew that Paramount had a representative on the *Europa* who was to interview an international stage star who might be considered to replace Chevalier. I never thought he had Brisson in mind until I saw the films. When the story was completed and Brisson read it, he told the promoters that he was going to wait until I had read it before giving them his opinion. I met Brisson after a stage performance, and he took me back to his suite at a hotel in London where his wife, Cleo, was waiting. We were to have dinner together. While he was mixing a drink, he casually asked me if I had read the story and I said I had. He asked what I thought about it.

"We Americans have a good word for describing certain things," I said. "The word is 'lousy.' "

He let out a whoop, jumped into the air, and clicked his heels like an adagio dancer and yelled for his wife to come into the drawing room, where I had to repeat my opinion to her. Here was a high-class performer worthy of the best in top musicals, but because in college he had been an expert boxer, these promoters presented him with a low-budget fight story! He naturally refused to be signed, and Paramount did indeed sign him right away. I was not about to approve a story with a star like Brisson that I knew would flop, even though it meant being stranded in London. I was put in a first-class apartment/hotel, where meals were a part of the system and served in one's apartment. Men and women dressed in evening clothes for dinner, with a waiter assigned to serve meals. Because the promoters still thought they could lick the story and Brisson had to finish the run of his play, they kept me at this hotel, but did not pay the bills. When the showdown came, Brisson left. The American film-cutter went back to the States because his working permit had expired, and I was stuck with $3,000 in hotel bills.

It was at this time that a film distributor, who had released a lot of my comedies through Gaumont and in Europe, made me a proposal to be his assistant on a film for Gaumont. He advanced me enough money to pay part of my hotel bill and send some to my family in Hollywood. The film was *Forbidden Territory*. I brought Phil Rosen from Hollywood to direct it and Gregory Ratoff for a star part.

When the picture was finished, John Wolff made a deal with me to produce feature comedies starring a British music-hall comedian. After a few films, he became hard to handle, and Gaumont did not care to continue distributing any more. In the meantime, MGM and Columbia had me produce some British Quota pictures, and some were made for an independent group. I did fifteen features. Mickey Powell, well-known for his *Red Shoes, Stairway to Heaven, 49th Parallel,* and other films he directed, made two for me. One was called *The Edge of the World* which made the "Ten Best Pictures List of 1937" as selected by the New York

Board of Review. I built my own studio in England. Joe Kennedy, our ambassador, was a man I had known at RKO, FBO. Before World War II broke out, he urged me to leave.

"I can't. I've got a studio here," I told him.

However, the government took it away for storage, and we got into financial difficulties. Films couldn't be made, but expenses continued. And in England, you pay or play. So we got in bad that way. In 1940, an American there started the American Motorized Eagle Squadron of one hundred Americans. We had fast cars, Tommy guns, and appropriate uniforms. We were attached to the British home defenses. I've got a picture of Churchill reviewing us. I'm standing there, a little yokel in uniform. We were trained by the Scot Guards, the Grenadiers, the Welsh, the Irish, and the Coldstream Guards. We were the Germans in all the exercises, and we never lost. Our CO was Brigadier General Wade Hayes of Pershing's tactical staff in World War I. We made no more films. For two years, I was in the service.

Mr. Kennedy was instrumental in getting my two children on the last boat from England, eight months after the war broke out. My wife and I had to remain. I left late in '42. My wife couldn't leave until '43. She came home on one of the Canadian ships.

I arrived with a thirteen-warship convoy. I had something to do for the American Embassy. I came back with eight bucks. A bunch of PS 188 alumni friends paid my train fare to the Coast. I got to California, where I became a special buyer for the Atomic Energy Commission (The Manhattan Project).

After that, I was an executive producer for Universal when they were planning to get rid of Abbott and keep Costello. I got $500 a week, and all I did was read stories and screenplays. Only the bosses knew what I was doing. While apparently looking for stories, I was getting things ready for the time when the team of Abbott and Costello was dissolved. They hadn't been getting along. Their feuds were costing a hell of a lot of money. There was jealousy between the two families— and even between the two agents. In their last film, they made Costello into another character and Abbott into a heavy. It was a big flop. I was an executive producer. I had sat in on the rushes of this last film, but I didn't choose to criticize because the director was a good friend of mine. I wasn't supposed to say anything. I never did. But I knew the film would flop.

I can tell you I was once rich, with property in Beverly Hills, on Wilshire Boulevard, on the Strip, in Hollywood, and on Melrose Avenue. When sound came along in 1929, I began to lose money. Seventy-two of my silent comedies were still making a profit and providing me with an income. And twenty silent features I had made with Henry Ginsberg and stars of such stature as Maurice Costello, Eva Novak, Shirley Mason, Hedda Hopper, Herbert Rowlinson, and Wanda Hawley paid off. My company was called Sterling Pictures. Our films played in Paramount and MGM houses in New York and that alone earned back the cost of production. But when talkies came in, my revenue dwindled—to the vanishing point. From maybe $20,000 a week, it went down to $1,000 or less to $300—to zero. Finished. And at that point, the market crashed.

I couldn't make it with sound. Only the big fellows were able to do that. They had the studio facilities, the physical assets, and therefore, obtained bank loans. I wasn't able to get hold of a quarter. The real estate, all that property, was shot. I sold good property to keep lousy property. I got into mines and oil wells. Oh, I was a sucker for any good story. I'd finance people, put money in projection machines. None of it was feasible, and I never could make a financial comeback. But, what the hell—I had nothing at all when I started. I'm healthy, and I've had the same wife for forty-eight good years!

ADOLPH ZUKOR

I COME FROM a little town in Hungary. My father died in 1874 when I was a year old, and my mother died when I was nine years old. I was raised by an uncle who sent me through grammar school. Afterwards I took private instruction from a tutor because there was no "gymnasium" in that town. I became an apprentice in a general merchandise store. During the last year of my apprenticeship, I read a good deal about America and felt that I would like to go there. As an orphan, I needed permission to leave the country. Whenever I lacked clothes or money, I had to apply to an overseer who passed on my request to the government, which was in charge of my parent's small estate. The officials asked me to come tell them why I wanted to go to America. They would decide whether to release the money I would need. I was granted the necessary amount, and I left for America in 1888.

I arrived in New York armed only with a few names and addresses of people in the city. I also had a cousin, Dr. Lieberman, who was a doctor of medicine. But I didn't want to go to him because I feared that I might not be well received. I didn't know him at all. I called on other people who were very nice to me. They finally contacted my cousin, told him that I was in New York, and that I would like to see him. He lived on 84th Street and Lexington Avenue, which was way uptown at that time. Of course, they asked me to come and stay with them until I got located and knew what I would do. After I spent a couple weeks there, I realized that there would be no chance for me ever to get any employment out of a doctor's home. I had some friends and distant relatives who lived on Houston Street on the East Side. I moved there and got a job working in an upholstery factory. But that was only short-lasting because of a friend I had from Hungary who was in the fur trade. His brother had been here many years and was a foreman in a fur factory. After I met him, he said, "This work that you're doing is very hard. I'll see if I can get my brother to help you become an apprentice in the fur business." I said, "That would be fine." So, after I was here for four months, I became an apprentice in the fur shop. I remained in the fur business until, I should say, 1903.

However, in 1892, I went to Chicago and was married there. Then the uncle of my wife and I started a fur business in Chicago. But we had to buy and carry too much stock without knowing whether it would be fashionable by the time we produced our neckwear or garments or whatever. Therefore, we decided to move our business to New York. We did so in 1900, and we stayed there with it until 1903.

Then in 1903, I met a man by the name of Mitch Mark who owned a penny arcade in Buffalo and wished to open one in New York. Since he lacked sufficient capital, we invested and opened up a penny arcade on 14th Street. It ran through to 13th. The place was about 40 feet wide and 200 feet deep. A few months after we opened the penny arcade on the main floor, we opened a nickelodeon on the second floor. Subsequently, I went out of the penny-arcade business completely and started motion picture theaters on my own. I built a theater right next to the penny arcade on 14th Street, the Comedy Theater. From there, I branched into the motion picture business. In the beginning, it was a novelty. Many people came in to see the pictures. Admission was only a nickel. A motion picture ran for fifteen minutes.

The years went along and we opened up in Newark and Boston and Pittsburgh and Philadelphia. The seating capacity of the nickelodeons was about three hundred to five hundred seats. About 1908, I began to realize, after watching the audience, that the pictures being made then—a heavy output of chases and comedy—didn't fill the bill. Gradually, our business, instead of being very lucrative, began to go downhill. The novelty wore off, and we hadn't anything to show that would attract a large public. That's when I realized that the only chance motion pictures had of being successful was if stories or plays could be produced which were like those on the stage or in magazines and novels. That way you could give something to the public that would hold their interest.

I talked to many people who had made a number of short subjects at Edison and Biograph and Vitagraph. At that time they released twenty or twenty-five pictures, all one-reelers, every week so that there were enough pictures that they could be changed every day or every other day.

I talked to them about making something even more entertaining, an hour-length film. They weren't interested. They didn't think that anybody would sit through a whole hour watching pictures. From that time to 1912, I finally made up my mind that I was right. At least I felt that way, although none of the other people in the motion picture business, neither the producers nor the exhibitors, had much faith in my idea. There were a lot of reasons why, especially the cost.

In the meantime, while I was trying to get these people to agree, there was a picture being planned by a British producer photographing Sarah Bernhardt in a play she had just closed. It was the spring of 1911. They needed financing and came here to see whether anybody would buy the American rights to their proposed picture. They were advised to contact me. I was the man who might be interested in a picture starring Sarah Bernhardt, to be called *Queen Elizabeth*. They told me what the cost would be, and I agreed to finance the picture in exchange for the American rights, while they retained rights for the rest of the world. After we distributed *Queen Elizabeth* in this country, we leased theaters on the days when they didn't show legitimate plays. For instance, a theater in Chicago, the Booth Theater, had a show with matinees on only Wednesdays and Saturdays. The rest of the week, I used their theater to show our Sarah Bernhardt picture. Throughout the country I did the same thing. Theater owners had to admit that people would sit through a "long" picture.

So that was the very first motion picture such as is seen today. For the first time a movie had been reviewed and written about in the papers. They said Sarah Bernhardt had "starred" in a motion picture. It cost close to $40,000, including a large sum paid to Sarah Bernhardt. It was very long, four whole reels, running a full hour, the longest movie ever seen, just like looking at a three-hour picture today.

Once I was satisfied that the public would patronize a theater showing feature pictures, I organized the Famous Players Film Company. I made *The Prisoner of Zenda* with James K. Hackett. It was the first feature picture made in this country. We sold it "state rights." We advertised in the trade journals, and distributors bought. We sold separately to California and Chicago, down South, and to anybody else who wanted it. Altogether, enough money came in to pay for the negative plus allowing us to make a profit.

After that, we made a number of pictures with stars who appeared on the legitimate stage, like William Farnham, Minnie Maddern Fiske, John Barrymore, Ethel Barrymore. But they did not go over as well in theaters as I had expected. The public attending motion pictures had never heard of or seen these theatrical stars. Matinee idols meant nothing to them at all. Finally we had to build our own stars. So we chose Mary

Pickford, who had worked for D. W. Griffith. Of course, her name at that time was unknown; it had never been printed. The same was true of Blanche Sweet and the Gish Sisters, who had also worked for D. W. Griffith at Biograph in one-reel pictures. Well, we took Mary Pickford, Thomas Meighan, Barrymore, and put them into pictures. It was in 1912 when I organized the company of Famous Players Film Company. The Sarah Bernhardt picture was made in 1911. I was convinced that I was taking no chance by producing pictures because the public wanted to see them. People were eager and anxious. That's how motion pictures developed.

Jesse Lasky started to make pictures in California. Our studio was in New York. Finally we combined and stopped selling the pictures to state's-rights buyers. We organized a distributing company which was given the name of Paramount-Famous-Players-Lasky. Eventually we dropped the other names, and the only name we operated under was Paramount, just as it is today. It soon dawned on us that the better the stories, the better the cast and the direction, the more people we were able to attract. Even though the price had to be raised from five cents to ten cents and then from ten cents to a quarter, people were willing to pay. After a while, the public was willing to pay even fifty cents to see something worthwhile portrayed by personalities developed as motion picture stars. Up to that time, it was catch-as-catch-can.

At first, as I say, Paramount was only a distributing company. Lasky and Famous Players made the pictures along with some other producers. Collectively, they made about fifty-two pictures so that theaters could have one a week. When the Lasky Company and Famous Players and Paramount merged, it became the Paramount Corporation. I had been longest in the business and naturally knew more about it than they did, so I became the head of Paramount, but I never moved out of New York. I spent a lot of time in Hollywood, in the studio, but never lived there.

The star system developed gradually. As the stars got more popular, competition for their services increased, which also raised their price. When Mary Pickford left Paramount, she was receiving $10,000 weekly in lieu of 50 percent of the profits. Whatever the picture netted, she got the $10,000. That risk I had to take. It was big news when I paid her $10,000. I had started out giving her $500 a week, but I finally paid her $10,000. There was no other way to meet the offers she got from other producers. She was very popular because she was great entertainment. Mary Pickford deserved to be named America's Sweetheart.

After she left, we had Margaret Clark, who was also very popular, although less so than Mary. We also developed Pauline Frederick and John Barrymore and Thomas Meighan. I can't begin to name the stars

D. W. Griffith, William Le Baron, and Adolph Zukor on *The Sorrows of Satan* set. 1926.

Adolph Zukor's original nickelodeon on 14th Street in New York City. Circa 1905.

Jesse L. Lasky and Adolph Zukor in the boiler room at the Lasky studio, Hollywood. Circa 1920.

Adolph Zukor, president of Paramount Pictures Inc., visiting set and chatting with Adolphe Menjou, Charlie Ruggles, and Director Elliot Nugent. 1936.

we developed who, in turn, developed the motion picture business. After a few years, people who had small motion picture theaters realized that if they built theaters like the Strand in New York or the Balaban and Katz in Chicago, there would be enough big pictures coming to support them. Each theater had a band, which in itself was an attraction.

In 1926, sound pictures came in. In that revolution lies the whole business. If it hadn't been for an amplifier that the telephone company perfected which made it possible for sound to be heard all over a theater, motion pictures would never have grown to be so important in the amusement world. They had tried to make talkies before by using the phonograph, but without an amplifier, the sound wasn't loud enough.

"Looks" used to count more than ability in the early days. A star still has to have good looks, but more important today, he needs the experience of an actor who can depict characters that make a picture believable to the public. Today, instead of looking first for pretty faces for a picture, you look for talent. Whenever you find talent plus an attractive appearance, you can make a star.

At present, pictures deal with greater and more important subjects. Better producers and directors devote more of their time to making pictures a success. I don't think that process is going to stop. With each year and every day that goes by, more technical handicaps are overcome. Making a perfect motion picture is today a trade. It's something to which a boy coming out of college can devote his time. Writing, producing, or playing in motion pictures has a big future. Not only in the amusement field, but in education and politics, the world is brought closer together through motion pictures. In them, we have an opportunity to see how other peoples live, and they have an opportunity to see how we live.

Famous Players made pictures in association with Belasco, and Famous Players made pictures in association with Frohman. Our Astoria studio is still in existence. The government took it over. When we moved our activities to Hollywood, the location we bought consisted of only twelve acres. It soon became too small. Then we bought the land in Hollywood which the Paramount studio is on and built up a studio with enough stages to produce three or four pictures at the same time. That was in 1915.

Making pictures was my main job. It required courage, and it took somebody who knew much about motion pictures and believed in them. I had one major setback: a studio of mine in New York on 26th Street burned down. Fortunately, we had five negatives of completed pictures, which had not yet been used, stored in a safe. Nothing happened to the safe, and after it cooled off, we were able to find the negatives in good condition. But everything else in the studio was destroyed. We next leased an armory on 26th Street near Seventh Avenue; then we made pictures for a while in a riding academy on 55th Street. At last, we built the studio in Astoria on Long Island. In the interim, we joined hands with De Mille and Lasky and operated on the Coast. With that, Famous Players moved to California. Presently we had to acquire more facilities and did so. Now it's grown to sixty or seventy acres, because we added to it as we went along, but it is essentially the same studio.

Specifically, my responsibility was to provide the finances. I met with the bankers, and I explained to them what we were doing. I also passed on the story and cast of every picture. It was all actually one operation. I kept very busy with that. In addition, I had to establish branches all over the world, in England, Germany, Australia, the Far East. It was necessary to set up a foreign distribution system like the one we already had in America. That was quite an undertaking.

There is no formula for a successful film. You must be like a tea-taster. Above all, you have to know the public, which I have studied from the very first day I opened a nickelodeon. I pondered audience reaction every day. My major concern was to learn what they liked and what they didn't like, what gave them pleasure and what didn't. The experience I gained running theaters was a great help to me later on. Let me put it this way. You have maybe five thousand lawyers in New York, two or three are outstanding, right? They can prepare and defend a case for the judge. They have unique ability. The same principle applies to motion pictures. I had unique qualifications to make and distribute pictures and to show them because I loved the pictures and I had faith in their future. No obstacle was too great for me to overcome in order to reach the goal that I visualized.

A big obstacle would arise when a well-known author wouldn't consent to having his story made into a moving picture. Most of our plays came from England. Some playwrights and producers wouldn't think of letting a play be made into a picture. Or a prominent theatrical producer like Frohman might stand in our way. The growth of motion pictures has always been confronted by different obstacles, either by way of finance or by way of material or by way of individuals. The first four or five years were a hard struggle. Later on, sound solved the problem; it was a lifesaver.

Really intense competition set in as more companies came into existence: Metro–Goldwyn, Warner Brothers, Fox, and many smaller ones, too, like Columbia. I was raided by Warner Brothers. They did everything but murder. I didn't raid anybody because I started the whole business. But I had something others could take. They had nothing, and the only way they could have something was to take it from me. Then the business grew bigger, and there was room for us all. It was only a question of who made the best pictures, and I tried to stay in business on the

quality of what we produced. If you don't make pictures that you antici-
pate the public will patronize, you just exist. But if you use your head to
pick the story and pick the cast and pick the director, that is a God-
given gift. You can't learn it in college. If you have it, you succeed. Those
people who have that quality are still in business. They still do well.
Only illness, retirement, or death can stop them. Louis Mayer had it.
Harry Warner had it. William Fox had it. Those at the head today have
to have the same qualifications. Basically, you either love the thing you
are doing and develop, or you don't.

Pictures of the caliber and quality that we made twenty years ago,
you couldn't give away today. And I am equally sure that twenty years
from now, the pictures we are making today will fare the same way.
You have to keep improving technically and artistically in order to retain
the public's attention and diversify the type of people who go to pictures.
You can get a type now who wouldn't have gone fifteen or twenty years
ago. A college professor, a doctor, a sewer-digger, they all go to see
pictures because each one finds enough amusement in it to spend his
money and his time. Pictures have advanced, and they will have to continue to advance.

My most successful film was *The Ten Commandments* made in 1923.
We made that picture a second time; it was as widely accepted and well
received as the first one. *The Ten Commandments* will be made over again
twenty years from now with new techniques and new knowledge and
new personalities. It will be just as important then as now. If you use
that subject, with its universal appeal, and use present-day methods of
presenting it so that a child of today, not of yesterday, can get as much
out of it as his grandfather got, he'll go and see it. The subject will live
forever. I always believed that anything to do with religion would be
good. There was no precedent for it. But fortunately I found a man who
agreed with me and was willing to spend two or three years writing the
script and putting it on the screen. That was Cecil De Mille. Nobody but
De Mille was mentally big enough to produce *The Ten Commandments*.

I liked New York because all my friends lived here. Now they are
all gone. I'll be ninety-five in January. So you know that of all my old
pals, there's not a single one left. But when you have that association
for forty, fifty, sixty years, it gets into your blood. The atmosphere you
live in gives you what you need. In 1942, I became the chairman of the
board of Paramount. Mr. Balaban was the president. He was much
younger than I, and he carried on the actual work. But I didn't retire.
I am not retired now. What I do now is talk to people. I read about what
they're doing. We discuss the pictures that are planned, mainly subjects,
places, and stories they might do in pictures. But I don't say that *I'm*
doing anything. I just know what's being done. They let me know, and

I tell them what I think if they ask me. I can't tell you I'm retired, nor can I tell you I'm active. I'm just part of the organization. At my age, you can't expect me to run any departments or have any voice in things or to go someplace on business. But I still know what's going on, not only in this company, but in the industry as a whole.

WALTER WANGER

I WAS BORN in San Francisco, July 11, 1894. My father died the year before the great fire; Mother, the other children, and I moved East. I went to school in New York and in Vévey, Switzerland. I attended prep school in America and then went to Dartmouth.

My family has always been interested in innovations. I had three aunts who were brilliant. One was a gifted artist, one was a great linguist, and another was a doctor of philosophy. They were remarkable women who used to travel with my grandmother. They made a *salon* wherever they went. My father came over from Germany after the upheaval there in '48. He was a great reader of Shakespeare and much else. My mother was always terribly interested in the theater. I can see the theatrical scrapbooks she kept just as if it were yesterday. San Francisco was a great opera and theater town. My father went abroad a great deal, and I did too. We lived very well; it was a truly civilized community.

As a student, I took up English, history, and literature. But I left college when Granville Barker came to this country to establish a national theater. He was a protégé of Shaw's. At that time in New York, a group of multimillionaires wanted to build a repertory theater, and they brought Barker over for an experimental season. I was brought down from college to be one of his assistants. He called his headquarters the New Theatre, a gorgeous place that took up the whole block. I think a subscription cost $50,000. It was beautiful, but nobody could hear because the acoustics were so bad. They turned it over to Ziegfeld for big musical

Left to right: Walter Wanger, P. A. Powers, Jesse Lasky, Erich von Stroheim, Milton Hoffman on location for Paramount production of *The Wedding March*. Von Stroheim wrote, starred in, and directed this picture. 1928.

shows. Then the Shuberts got it, and they turned it into a real estate project. But the rich of New York were undaunted, as they are today with Lincoln Center. We finally opened in an old theater on lower Broadway with *Androcles and the Lion* and *The Man Who Married a Dumb Wife.*

I was a nothing sort of apprentice, getting twenty-five dollars a week because I had done a lot of things in college. The day I arrived, Robert Edmund Jones went to work too. Barker was always trying to find new blood. After closing in New York, we did *A Midsummer Night's Dream, The Doctor's Dilemma,* and a number of Greek plays in some college stadiums. I tired of that and went to work for a theatrical agent and promoter, a woman named Elizabeth Nawbry. I made a contract with William Randolph Hearst, who was interested in films, for a serial called *Pro Patria.* I also decided to produce my own plays and did one with Nazimova, which, to the surprise of everyone, was a success.

By this time, the war was breaking out. I had been in London in 1914 during the moratorium getting ready to go to Oxford. I was impressed by all the early British war posters, their campaigning, and recruiting. When I came back here, there was a lot of pro-German sentiment. The Germans were very active and capable propagandists. So I began to organize Allied propaganda on my own. I started getting out war posters; one of the most famous was the Uncle Sam "I Want You" poster. My concept of and experience at influencing the masses came very early. Even my productions at college were international. Well, I went off to war after having had this propaganda seance here in New York. I went into aviation. We didn't even have a plane at that time in this country. We trained without planes to become fliers. We were sent abroad. We expected to go to the French front but instead, in Paris, Fiorello La Guardia, a spirited little fellow, said, "Boys, you're coming down to Italy with me."

After all that training, the American Embassy put me to work on propaganda. The embassy was run by Ambassador Thomas Nelson Page, a Southern writer, married to one of the Marshall Fields. The embassy was pretty old-fashioned and out of touch. President Wilson, realizing he had a problem, sent out Professor Charles E. Merriam of Chicago. Merriam was marvelous, a Lincolnesque fellow, very honest and forthright. Dr. Harold Edgel of Harvard joined us. He worked on propaganda leaflets. The big problem was how to publicize the fact that we were really in the war. I suggested having a film made by George Creel, head of our public information service. They made a two-reeler, showing men marching down Fifth Avenue in civilian clothes on their way to our training camps and coming out a few months later in uniform and getting on enormous transports. We gave this two-reeler to the motion picture theaters all over Italy. That changed the sentiment in Italy, and I was impressed by the force and power of film. That's when I made up my mind that this was going to be my niche.

I eventually returned to this country and started to produce plays again. Jesse Lasky at Famous Players asked me to produce plays for him. I declined, telling him I'd rather work on pictures. That's how it all began. For some time, Adolph Zukor and I occupied offices on the same floor. He would come into my office every morning and stretch himself out on the couch with a big cigar. When things were going well, he'd say, "Mr. Vanger . . . ," and if things were going superbly, he'd say, "Valter. . . ." He would look at the figures because we controlled the theaters and the distribution and exhibition. We would release, say, two pictures a week. Famous Players was simply marvelous to me. I was spoiled. I've never gotten over it. They would encourage me to buy anything. I was Lasky's assistant, and later general production manager all over the world. We had studios in Paris, Berlin, London, Hollywood, and New York.

At that time, films were considered a third-class operation. Bankers weren't interested. Neither were writers. You couldn't hire actors from the theater. They looked down on pictures. It's marvelous to see films accepted as art and high culture now, but what we used to go through in those days to make films. How we changed taste, how we improved sets and clothes, how we finally got great designers interested, that's quite a story! I brought top people from Paris to be interior decorators and now we influence the whole bloody world! I would sign photographers just to do attractive still pictures, clothes' designers to do gloves and hats. I was given great leeway. It would take me hours to tell you the things we did. I found new writers and people from other industries. This experience convinced me at an early age that there's very little difference between statesmanship and showmanship. I think this truth is coming to light right now.

But let me give an illustration of how taste was directly influenced. In those days, De Mille was our top director, Cecil, not William. William was considered a highbrow who didn't "have" the audience, but he was regarded with great awe. Both were from the theater. They had had a lot of experience, and they were very shrewd operators. C. B. was a great friend of mine. He used to have terrible taste in clothes, in sets, and in representing the way parties were given. So I signed Paul Chalfin and his whole staff. They had built the Deering estate, which is probably the greatest estate in Florida. Millions were put into it. Chalfin was a man of superb taste, and he had an excellent staff. I sent him out to the Coast to show De Mille how to lay a table, how a butler should behave. De Mille bridled at all this, but I insisted on it. I was young and brash. It revolutionized that part of film production. And the minute we did it, Metro, Fox, Warner's, and the rest of them did the same thing. In no time there was a terrific lift. You could see the influence everywhere. And the hair . . . why, I took Louise Brooks, a little girl out of the Ziegfeld chorus, who had bobbed hair. The whole world copied that. We were always trying to lift public taste a little bit. Zukor and Lasky were dedicated men who would produce pictures that they thought should be done, even though they weren't going to be profitable.

I did the only article on film that's ever been in *Foreign Affairs*. It's entitled "120,000 Ambassadors," meaning every picture that's around. Not only did we try to make the films popular, we also tried to make them respectable. My purchase of *An American Tragedy* was assumed to be absolutely catastrophic. To use the word "tragedy" when I first went into pictures was ridiculous. Everybody had to be nice; a happy ending was mandatory. And we changed that.

The Ziegfeld Follies used sixty baggage cars to move its production. We moved all that and more in a tin can. I sold General Marshall the idea of using film for training when we had to get an army out very quickly in World War II. I must say he was wonderful about it, and the films were enormously successful.

If you want to put over an idea and you have any intelligence, you can do it very subtly. If The Voice of America makes a film, they're immediately suspect because it is government. But if you pay your money and go to a picture, you relax and you're open-minded. You are much more susceptible to receiving messages. Quite concretely, the Marines asked me to make a picture during the last war about an island in which Colonel Carlson was interested. "Gung ho" was his favorite expression but Carlson was criticized for his confidence in the Chinese. I called the picture *Gung Ho!*, which in itself was tremendous propaganda because the term in Chinese means "working together." Nobody realized that I was making a propaganda film. I shot all sorts of marine training sequences and things like that. Why they asked me to do it, I don't know. It was such a hot subject. While the picture was in production, Carlson came to Hollywood. I had built him up so much that the other generals were concerned about his getting so much publicity.

"We'd like to talk this over," they told me. "Leave the picture for a few weeks."

I had expected that, so I said, "I'm very sorry but I'm lunching at the White House and Mr. Roosevelt will want to see it. So I'm afraid you can't keep it." That's how I got it passed. The picture happened to be a tremendous box-office success. And nobody has ever identified it as a propaganda picture.

I did the same thing in another picture called *Foreign Correspondent* which was tremendously loaded with ideology. And also with Vincent Shehan's *Personal History*. I had twenty-seven writers on that one. Then I made a picture called *Blockade*, which was also "loaded." However, I didn't have faith in it. After we screened it, I said to my press agent, "Johnny, what can we do about this picture? All the way down the line it just misses, although the idea is good." He was a marvel! He immediately sent a wire to Cordell Hull saying it was outrageous that Franco should ban this picture. Poor Franco had never seen the picture or heard of it. It was going into the Music Hall, run by the Rockefellers. We had riots there. The only success the picture had was due to its notoriety. The Communists took it right to heart. They all thought it was a great communist picture.

But getting back to the early days, I first began to make trips out to Hollywood when I was with Paramount. I was representing the establishment in New York. The studio in those days was five days away by train. We used the telephone, but not nearly as much as today. Every night there was a telegram sent from the home office to the studio, and the studio would report to the home office in a very long telegram about everything that went on. That was the only communication. Then I would go out there and raise hell to upset things. I even took Henry Mencken out just to stimulate the studio.

I was assistant to Lasky and sort of a general manager. I laid out the schedule with him. Later on, I became a producer. What does a producer do? Sometimes very little; sometimes a great deal. For instance, John Ford brought me *Stagecoach*, which I made without having a hell of a lot to do with it. On the other hand, I had a lot to do with *I Want to Live!* and *You Only Live Once*—they were completely my idea. In those days, you were pressed to make a lot of pictures to keep your overhead down. I had Henry Fonda and Sylvia Sidney in a picture for which Fritz Lang is given all the credit. He directed *You Only Live Once*.

I had two writers under contract called Towne and Baker. They were great idea men, and they understood films. Towne was an illiterate guy who used to say, "Bring that dame in here and she'll do this . . ." "Then she moves, and then the punk comes in. . . ." He had a collaborator, who was more dignified, to put the stuff down on paper. They would work out all the action: "Oh, this stinks. Nobody will ever stand for that."

They were under contract to me at about $2,500 a week. They would write every sequence on toilet paper and hang it on the wall. When they were ready, I'd go up and comment.

"That seems a little too long. There might be a dead spot there."

"You're right. You're right."

They would tear off two pages of toilet paper. After we got a complete blueprint of the action, the characters, and the scenes, Towne would run around to every restaurant telling every actor he saw "Jesus, Wanger's got a great part for you," He'd build up the mirage. Then when the thing was all finished to the best of their ability, I'd bring in Dorothy Parker, who would rewrite it and insert the dialogue. A great many pictures were made that way.

In any group effort there are always tensions—it's that kind of business. And when the studio got smug after a couple of hits, I'd raise hell—just to upset everything. We had a lot of trouble with Pola Negri and Gloria Swanson, who felt that they were the queens of the studio and that everything revolved around them. Everything in the studio was becoming very difficult. I had an idea about how to counteract that. I took one side of a whole bloody big studio, and we started a little paper about how the pictures were doing all over the country. Beery and Hatten, two comedians of that time, came out on top with by far the biggest hits. Swanson and Negri came out sixth and seventh. That did it.

I don't know whether what we do is an art or a business. Joe Mankiewicz gets angry every time I say "the film industry." He contends that it isn't an industry. It is an art. I don't think semantics has a damn thing to do with it. Films are an influence, a tremendous influence. I remember getting hold of Elinor Glyn. She wrote *Three Weeks*, a sensational book in its day. I called her into the office and offered to give her $50,000 for two letters of the alphabet. She wanted to know what I was talking about. She had referred to a girl and to Valentino as having "It." I said, "Get your friend Mr. Hearst to run a two-part novelette in *Cosmopolitan*, and I will give you fifty thousand dollars. I just want the title." That made Clara Bow the "It" girl. That's not art, but it's showmanship.

In the old days, when we had block-booking, which started Paramount, we controlled the distribution, exhibition, *and* the production. We would sell one hundred and four pictures a year ahead of time, two a week. There would be six "Tommy Meighan's," six "Ethel Clayton's," four "Clara Bow's"—we used to "make" the stars in order to identify the pictures—the stars were our collateral. That's when the star system flourished.

If we saw good-looking girls or boys in the theater, we would give them a screen test and assign a studio press agent. If the tests were satisfactory we would put them under contract. We'd find the right part to introduce them. We'd usually put an unknown girl up against a known male star, or an unknown male up against a well-known woman. There would be a big promotion campaign, and if they clicked, fine. If they didn't, you just wouldn't take up their option. They'd disappear.

A whole aura of myth had to surround the star through fan magazines and fan clubs. We didn't feed the clubs, but we fed the magazines.

In advertising, we had a high-powered publicity organization. When Gloria Swanson came back from Europe after marrying the Marquis de la Falaise, we exploited the wedding to the hilt. We gave her a great ball in the Crystal Room at the Ritz, which was *the* chic place in New York at that time. And we sent her across the country in a private train, not just a private car. When she arrived at Los Angeles, there was a terrific hulla-baloo—as there had been all across the continent. When Rod La Rocque married Vilma Banky, Sam Goldwyn gave a tremendous wedding party. It was more or less a promotional party. When Carole Lombard married Clark Gable, that was a terrific event.

As soon as scandal sheets and gossip columns came along in the thirties, the press agents would plant, "Miss Susie So-and-So was seen last night in such-and-such a restaurant"—whether she was or not, you know, to start a rumor of romance. The power of Louella Parsons was tremendous for a long time. It was not entirely a bad thing. I know she could ruin a guy like she did Orson Welles, or she could try very hard. She tried to ruin poor Herman Mankiewicz after *Citizen Kane* because he wrote it and the picture upset Mr. Hearst. I can tell you a bit about him.

Hearst was one of the big forces on the Coast. I made some pictures for him. My first wife used to share dressing rooms with Marion Davies on Broadway. Every weekend for quite a while, I had to go up to San Simeon. There were special cars on the trains. He'd invite forty or fifty people. Either you were in that Hearst crowd or you weren't. I knew Hearst very well. I asked him one day, "W. R., who would you like to have been in history if you had your choice?"

"Charlemagne," he replied.

He was a fantastic man. We were great friends, but I had a feud with him once because of a picture called *Washington Merry-Go-Round*. In the first scene, Rosalind Russell played a Washington hostess sitting at the head of a table surrounded by national figures. One was a newspaper owner trying to involve us in a war. On account of my great friendship with Hearst, I had purposely picked a little fellow with a black mustache for the role. It was Ralph Morgan, brother of Frank Morgan. At the last minute, my casting director called me and said, "Ralph won't play the part. It's too small." I asked him to hire someone else. So he hired an actor who was a big man and came on the screen just like William Randolph Hearst. I didn't want to do retakes because of a tight budget, and it was one of my first independent pictures. We decided to let it go, but I was terrified. The picture came out and everybody ran to Hearst. "See what your friend Walter Wanger has done."

I was banned from the Hearst papers. They wouldn't even take our advertising.

Walter Wanger and Director William A. Wellman. 1934.

Walter Huston as president of the United States in MGM production of *Gabriel Over the White House*. 1933.

Advertisement for Walter Wanger's production of *Blockade*. 1938.

Marion Davies and Walter Wanger at a party given by Madeleine Carroll. 1937.

"Why don't you apologize?" Louella asked me.

I refused and just let it ride. Six months to a year later, Marion called up.

"Why don't you come to see us anymore?"

"Well, I heard W. R. was angry with me," I answered.

She turned around and inquired, "W. R., Walter says he thought you were angry with him. Isn't that the silliest thing?"

The ban had been lifted. He was like a big child, and yet he was an amazing man in many ways.

Later I made a political picture for his company, my first at Metro. It was entitled *Gabriel Over the White House*. The story was written by Lloyd George's political secretary who had never been to America. It was an amazing picture because it prophesied a lot of things that later happened during Roosevelt's first administration. Roosevelt was running for office at the time I started the picture, and it came out just as he entered the White House. But Louie Mayer had been a big supporter of Hoover and boss of the Republican party in California. Hearst, in 1932, supported Roosevelt and even wrote speeches for him. Mayer got furious with me. I had arguments with him about it. They nearly didn't release the picture. Roosevelt always used to joke with me about it. I went to the White House a great deal in those days.

The picture had many interesting things in it which were way ahead of their time. For instance, the President had a mistress in the White House. This was most daring at the time. We had a scene in which gangsters machine-gunned the White House. Then we had the President addressing the country over the radio at a World Peace Conference. Walter Lippmann saw the picture. I knew Lippmann very well from Paris and the first Peace Conference. He and the *Literary Digest*, which was then the great weekly, proclaimed that this picture was ridiculous. No President of the United States would so undermine the dignity of his office as to get on the microphone and talk to the masses! All this just before Roosevelt began his fireside chats.

You asked me if I had a lot of problems with censorship. Certainly, throughout my career. For example, censorship trouble began with, or you might say was precipitated by, the Arbuckle case. Wally Reid, a tremendous star, used to take dope. And Jack Gilbert didn't behave too well. Stars became so well known that the impact of their private lives was tremendous. Sometimes a cover-up of the goings on was necessary. Every studio had a police department, only partly hired to handle opening nights and traffic problems. If a star was picked up drunk or jumped out of somebody's window, influence could be exerted with politicians to keep his name clean.

The industry itself was unconventional, as were the methods of work

—beautiful girls who had to be made up and ready to work at six o'clock in the morning were playing love scenes on the set by eight o'clock. Then they'd have their meals in the studio and go home at midnight. The reason for these dreadful hours was that management did everything it could to hurry the pictures along. There used to be a big party at the finish of each film. It was a magical world. Young people arrived totally unprepared for this sudden affluence and glory. They would fall into the hands of agents and publicity people and start to believe their press releases. It was very hard, almost impossible, to resist the Hollywood system.

That system and its hierarchy have changed. When I first went out to Hollywood, Mack Sennett was more or less the social leader. He had a great big Mexican house. There were as yet no gossip columnists. He'd give a dinner party, and if you didn't take the young lady on your right upstairs between the soup and the entrée, you were considered a homosexual. And incidentally, at that time out there, they had never heard of a homosexual or a lesbian. It was a very innocent kind of morality, or amorality. Then along came the first organized social system, that of Pickford and Fairbanks.

When they were the social leaders, Pickfair was the pinnacle. To be invited to Pickfair was tops. Fairbanks and Pickford had toured the world. They had friends all over who came out to the estate. They even tell a story that one day, because they hated to miss anybody with a title, they got a message that the Princess Vera Romanoff was in town. They sent a car over to the Biltmore and brought her up there and gave her a wonderful weekend, with parties for her all the time. She was actually a little secretary from San Francisco who went back on Monday morning, having thanked them very much.

After that era, I would say Hearst and Marion Davies took over. They were very jealous of their position. Then, I would say the Selznicks reigned, David and Irene. Somewhere in there, during the war, I was president of the Academy for about six years, and my wife and I more or less held that social position. I was representing Rockefeller and Whitney on the CIAA. I had guests like Wilkie, all the ambassadors, and such people who came through. In the old days, if a man like Maugham or Hergesheimer or Mencken joined us, that was a terrific thing, helping to create a colony out in the desert. But today there are so many important directors, producers, and writers that a lot of the chichi has gone out of it. They're all absorbed in Los Angeles and the new music center. Now all those people have great homes and great paintings and lead much more sophisticated lives.

As president of the Academy, I was motivated to become a sort of social leader. I had great dreams for the Academy. Believing in motion pictures as an international force, I really wanted to see our work become

a respected calling. I thought it was almost as important as the State
Department. Doing things with Whitney and Rockefeller appealed to me
very much, as did running the Academy and building it up. When I took
over, it was in terrible shape. It had no membership. It went into decline
over a labor dispute. I had to go around to the guilds and beg them to
come back in. I think unions have had a big effect on the industry. They
have been very tough in letting in new blood.

To me, that wonderful aspect of internationalism that the motion
picture industry saw years ahead of other industries and incorporated into
its films is responsible for its international success. The British, French,
and German industries were small and ingrown. To go back on that tradition after forty or fifty years of success is very stupid. If the unions
were really so bloody smart, they would make special rates to allow us to
bring in medical and commercial and documentary films, educational films
which are going to be used more widely every year. For the record, there
are no greater plants in the world than in Hollywood, and there are no
greater technicians. So that was my motive in taking charge of the
Academy.

I left the Academy, I went abroad in '49 and I was going to stay
there, when I took Garbo with me. I wanted to make a Garbo picture,
but I couldn't get it financed. I came back and then lost a great deal of
money on *Joan of Arc* and Bergman's escapades, which didn't exactly
help project her image as a saint. When Howard Hughes put out that
damn picture *Stromboli* right ahead of it, I lost over a million dollars. You
see, I had a deal with Metro, and some of the conditions failed to work
out. There was a break in the film market abroad. They wanted to change
things and I refused to, which I regret. I should have stayed with Metro.
Overnight I made a deal with Hughes. He got entranced with Bergman
and when she fell in love with Rossellini, this thing broke. Rossellini made
a picture with her; nobody would finance it but Hughes; and he had my
picture which hadn't been released yet. He brought out *Stromboli* first and
it was a disaster. But with the exploitation of it, he killed the respectability
of my picture. In Europe they didn't give a damn. *Joan of Arc* did very
well there. But I lost too much in the American and English market.

Living in New York you had the privacy of big city life. You didn't
have the Hollywood stupidities because you were in a metropolis. If a star
came to New York from the West, he could have dinner in a restaurant
like everybody else, leave quietly, and get lost in the city. In Hollywood,
wherever I went, it was: "How do you do, Mr. Wanger. So glad to see
you. Want your usual table?" There's a whole dream-world attitude about
everything. For instance, in the morning, no work is done until everyone
has read the gossip columns in *Variety* and *The Reporter*. If anything is

reported that's scandalous about the studio, nobody works. They talk about that item all day long.

Hollywood has always been parochial. There's nothing worldly about the community. They're all anxious for social status. In New York, there is a much more cosmopolitan point of view and a much more civilized attitude.

I've always tried to keep my own point of view and my own objectives alive, and so I've always retreated. When I left Paramount for Columbia, everybody thought I was slumming. Harry Cohn wanted me very badly. Columbia was nothing in those days. I was the first vice-president they had. I couldn't take it because I was used to a much nicer environment. It was pretty tough there and pretty vulgar. Just the same, I was silly not to stay because Cohn gave me an option on a third of the common stock. But I was pretty intolerant and walked out on him overnight. Then I went to Metro and wasn't crazy about that.

There I was an executive producer, with more or less my own unit. I made a Garbo picture, *Queen Christina*. I also did one of the few successful pictures ever made with Marion Davies called *Going Hollywood*, which I had to fight to make. Metro didn't want a Hollywood picture, and I had brought over an actor named Bing Crosby whom they didn't want to co-star with her. She had never been co-starred with anybody. I've always been aggressive and independent. Each time I made a move, they always said I was through. Finally I went back to Paramount and they offered me the whole works, but I went on to United Artists. I had the best contract of my life at United Artists and I left. I should have stayed there, but when the war broke out, I wanted to do an aviation picture called *Eagle Squadron*.

I've always started cycles and trends in pictures. I like to do new things. *Eagle Squadron* starred Diana Barrymore and Bob Stack. My board of directors didn't believe in aviation pictures. I was infuriated and walked out on my contract even though it was brilliant tax-wise and they had just taken up the option for another five years. In my rush, I went over to Universal, which was considered to be the "other side of the tracks." Nevertheless, this picture was the first of about 600 aviation pictures and was very successful. I made another one I had wanted to do for years, *Arabian Nights*, to which everybody had been opposed. That was a fabulous success. These were finished under a contract in which all my income was personal. I became the biggest earner in the country. I was making over a million dollars a year, but the government got 90 percent of it.

Then Metro wanted me to come over and run the whole place. We practically had the contracts drawn. It was a wonderful deal but I was afraid of the politics and at the last minute, I withdrew and remained at

Universal. Within a few months, a new group came in at Universal and made it very tough for me. I had to leave. I went to Eagle Lion because Rank and Robert Young asked me to. That was a mistake. Then I went off on my own, took a studio, and made *Joan of Arc*, which was very unfortunate.

After a trip abroad and some production plans that didn't work out, I went to a little company called Monogram, which later changed its name to Allied Artists. I made a lot of cheap but profitable pictures. Then, the studios came after me again. I went to work under Joe Mankiewicz's contract at United Artists which gave me complete autonomy. I've never seen such a contract. There has never been one like it before or since. That's when I made the *I Want to Live!* picture with Susan Hayward. She won an Academy Award, so I was a big bloody hero again.

To go back a bit: the transition from silent to sound film was very exciting. At Paramount in New York, I had a row about something and was in the doghouse that year. Sound hadn't come in yet. They were trying to squeeze me out of the company at that time. Nobody had any traffic with me. I used to go up to Fox where they were experimenting with sound. I had a great friend up there, Courtland Smith, and he was in charge. They would do recordings of songs by opera singers and bits like a newsreel, just fooling around. I schooled myself in what was going on. At Paramount, there were three fellows, one called ·Kent, head of the sales department, a hero because he brought in the grosses; another called Katz, from Chicago, in charge of exhibition; Kane was the third. We used to call them the KKK. Kane always wanted to be in production, to take my job. They were our Soviet Union, our problem, constantly making it tough. They had all been to Rochester when Western Electric showed them sound. They turned it down and said it was impractical. Of course there was a very good reason to think it was because the success of the motion picture was that you could send it all over the world and just change the titles. Now came a language problem. What to do? And cost! Nobody knew how to solve it. So Paramount turned sound down.

Warner's was in great trouble, going broke, when they heard about sound. At last, they made a couple of pictures with sound, no dialogue, but real sound. They were great successes but everybody said it wouldn't last. They made a couple of features and then came along with the Jolson picture. I was at the opening night of *The Jazz Singer*. I remember going out in the lobby during intermission, calling Lasky on the Coast and saying, "Jesse, this is a revolution!" That did the trick. Zukor, who was the king then, lived at the Savoy-Plaza. He called a meeting at his apartment for about fifty executives. He was a great guy whenever a crisis developed —crying and making emotional speeches. He was wonderful.

"Warner's is making this picture," he said, "and what have we got?

You don't know a goddam thing about sound. A lot of dumbheads. We pay you all money," and so on and on. He turned to Lasky, "You'll go to Europe tomorrow."

Lasky went to Europe and made a deal with Chevalier, not for sound, but for regular pictures. When he came back and put him in sound, Chevalier was sensational. Lasky was lucky that way. Zukor carried on. I got up at the meeting and said, "How would you like to have a sound picture in six or eight weeks?"

"What are you talking about? Jesus Christ, I'd kiss your ass in Macy's window if you could make me a sound picture in six weeks."

"Mr. Zukor, if you will give me the Richard Dix picture that came in today, I guarantee that in six weeks you can have a preview." (It was a baseball picture.) They all looked at me as if I had just come in off a plane from Mars and gave it to me.

I went down to Trenton, New Jersey, to the RCA plant, had the records made, and synchronized them with the picture. When the ball hit the bat—*bang;* when the crowd cheered—*bang.* There was a side show in it, a carnival, and we had all the appropriate noises. I got Walter Donaldson, who was very popular, to write a song that went, "You came to me from out of the sky" . . . or some bloody thing. In six weeks, we had a preview. Zukor came over from his estate at New City in his yacht with all his family. The whole Loew crowd was there. They all wanted to see what our new thing was. The picture went on. I was standing in the lobby. The people came out. They clapped me on the back, "Genius, how did you do it?" They couldn't understand, even after they saw it. So I was reinstated with new decorations and we started building up Long Island for sound.

I think the first picture we made on Long Island was *Applause,* which they recently showed at the festival for Rouben Mamoulian. I brought Mamoulian from the Theatre Guild. Our problem was that we knew nothing about dubbing. We had this terrible problem of how to handle sound. Mamoulian wanted to have the noise of a subway train pulling out of a station while a girl is waving to a sailor on his way to enlist. I tied up the New York subways for a whole day getting one shot. Nobody had ever heard of dubbing. A man named Pomeroy was our sound expert. At that time, Western Electric sent its technicians to us. They wanted to control all the cycles, to have everything perfect. They built a stage about the size of an average room and wouldn't let us use the big stage. We had to work on their size stage, the walls were thick, and there was no air-conditioning. The stars would go in with their make-up, which would be melted by the time the technicians could shoot. Everyone was dying of the heat. You couldn't move the camera. We were bullied like this for months. One day we said, "The hell with them," and threw them out. We just hung monk's cloth around the studio and shot as we normally would shoot. Since then, we've done things in the way of soundproofing, but nothing like what those technicians wanted.

The one problem that worried everybody was what the hell are we to do with the foreign market? When Metro got into it, I remember the idea was that they would make German and Spanish versions, and possibly French versions. Boyer was brought over to make a French version of some picture. Of course, that would have been very expensive. Then when dubbing came in it solved everything. It was a hell of a mess until then. At first we had records, but we got rid of them very quickly. Warner's kept insisting that disks were the only thing, and then one day they changed over too.

You see that the industry has been "brilliant." It has turned down color, then sound, then radio, then television, and now pay-TV. Each one of these has saved the industry.

When moving to sound, we looked for additional attractions. Bill Morris, who was the head of the Morris Agency, asked me, "Why don't you do *The Cocoanuts*? I can give you a whole package." (I don't know if he really said "package." That word was yet to be used.) He said, "It's down at the Casino Theatre. You can have the Marx Brothers and the book and the whole thing for seventy-five thousand dollars."

"All right, I'll check with Mr. Zukor about it," I agreed.

Mr. Zukor was dying for attractions, and I advised him that *Cocoanuts* and the Marx Brothers might be a great attraction for talking pictures at $75,000.

"Seventy-five thousand dollars!" he shouted. "Who said that? Bill Morris? Get him over here. I'll spit in his eye." That used to be one of his favorite expressions. After a while, Zeppo came over with Bill Morris, Jr. Zeppo walked over to Mr. Zukor.

"Mr. Zukor," he said, "this is one of the greatest moments of my life. I've always wanted to meet you. You are the one showman in the world. When I think of what you did for Mary Pickford, of what you've done for pictures, I can't tell you how thrilled I am to meet you."

He went on like that for ten minutes, and the old man started to melt. When he got all through, Zukor wanted to know, "So what's the trouble between Walter and you?"

"Mr. Zukor," Zeppo answered, "all our lives we've worked to perfect this one show. This is our first show on Broadway. It's a big hit. All our jokes are in it, everything we've ever done. We're willing to make a picture for you, give you all our material, all our services, and all those marvelous gags—the whole thing for one hundred thousand dollars." One hundred thousand dollars was never even mentioned. I sat there and gasped. Zukor turned to me.

"Walter, what's wrong with that?"

And that's how the deal was made. The picture spelled a complete revolution in show business. You know how fast the Marx Brothers talk and the gags they use. We opened at the Rialto, and the Marx Brothers hated the picture. They wanted to buy it back, take it off. But it was a sensational success, partly for a funny reason. Exhibitors complained that their customers thought the Marx Brothers talked too fast. People had to come back two or three times to catch what was being said. In this way, it proved to be a fantastic success. That was the first picture we made at Long Island without Western Electric hanging around. I used Joe Santley, a stage director, and a Frenchman named Robert Florey as co-director. We used interesting camera effects never seen before.

Then I made a film with Walter Huston. It was the first of the sophisticated comedies in which a man had a mistress, something never shown before in a picture. What was it called? *The Lady Lies*, I believe. We did some very vanguard things. Somerset Maugham's *The Letter* was a tremendous innovation because of the last line, which was, "I still love the man I killed." Pretty strong for those days.

My problem is that I am very independent and I don't like to be controlled. *Cleopatra* was completely my idea, but I had a hard time getting Fox excited about it. They wanted to do it on a small scale with Joan Collins playing Cleopatra. They had me test some other people. Then they became hysterical and wanted to put Susan Hayward in it, which put me in an awful spot because Susan Hayward is a very good friend of mine and we have had many successful pictures together. I knew she was wrong for the part and, fortunately, she knew it too. I wanted Elizabeth Taylor, and it became a big fight and intrigue. I hired a lawyer, and I approached Elizabeth and offered her a million dollars. The studio went wild. This was the beginning of the million-dollar star. Well, finally I got her. Then the next thing was that I wanted Rex Harrison. Skouras threw up his hands and said he'd resign from the company before he'd have Rex Harrison. Rex Harrison couldn't act. He was no good. The press hated him. Well you see, they had him under contract and had handled him very badly. Skouras said, "Look at this crazy Wanger. Look at what he wants to do. Let me show you what we've lost on this man." He showed me all the books. Then when it came to Antony, I wanted Richard Burton. They had nothing but failures with him. Then Skouras screamed again and went all over the world making statements that he never heard of *Cleopatra*.

Then Skouras insisted on going to London to produce it. I told him he was out of his mind.

"You can't make an outdoor picture in England."

"Yes, you can. The weather is fine there." What he had in mind was that if he dumped a couple of million dollars in Rank's studio, Rank would give him more money for the product, which wasn't very good.

When we finally got the set built, which nobody wanted to build, the horses were skidding on the ice. And this was Alexandria! We just couldn't shoot. We had to rip down the set, and I had nearly every studio in London tied up. We had to tear down all the beautiful sets. We must have dropped at least five million dollars. Then the production was transferred to home.

Ultimately what happened was that they sent over a lawyer, Joe Moskowitz, who had been there many times with Skouras. They had orders to stop production and relieve me. But they never stopped production, and they never officially relieved me. So I stayed on and saw the fight to the end. Zanuck got back in the picture because he was going to be ousted by a minority group headed by the Lehmann Brothers. At the last minute, Zanuck very cleverly got Louis Nizer and Arnold Rand on his side, and they frightened the Lehmann Brothers and everybody else to switch on the vote and back him up. So he got in as president instead of being fired. From that time on, he took over and wouldn't let me near the picture. You remember when it opened in New York? It was bitterly criticized. It was too long, horribly edited, in awful shape. I thought it was a marvelous production, but in awful shape. As a matter of fact, Zanuck recut it three times, and each time it got worse.

Aside from Wall Street, another group that attained tremendous power over the film industry was the talent agency. MCA was the agency that more or less invented the "package" deal. They developed the trend which took responsibility away from the studio, making it easier for the studio bosses, but bad for the whole operation. I can compare it in this way. The studios used to be like Harvard, Yale, and Princeton. There was great rivalry, but great pride too in our responsibility. We had a new writer, a new director, a new actor, producer, starlet. We'd develop them. We'd nurse them. It was our business to find material for them, and we were their haven. If they had problems, anything from dope to divorce to buying a house, there was a paternal attitude shown by the Zukors and the Laskys and by Louie Mayer. But the agencies came along and demanded a percentage: "We want this and this and this."

I've always felt that the motion picture industry was a terrific calling. There were a lot of us who felt that way. Selznick felt that way; Goldwyn, too. And we all resented this intrusion. We had a different outlook on pictures. There was an understanding, a much happier feeling, a much better artistic attitude. There was a lot of jealousy, too, you know. For years I had been developing people who resented my attitude and my behavior. I had been critical, and I had always been dreaming of a different standard for the industry. I've always fought for outstanding material.

When I had my stock company of actors at United Artists, it was the biggest one outside of Metro's. And all were either new people I had brought out from New York, like Henry Fonda, or people who had been dropped by the studios. I took Boyer after all the studios had given up on him. I took my ex-wife Joan Bennett when she was getting $15,000 a picture and ran her up to $100,000. I took Sylvia Sidney, and Madeleine Carroll when she was on her way to Europe. The fact that I had done all these things annoyed many people. They'd love to see me out of the picture. I've never been satisfied to sit on the past. I like to do new things. I am working on something now that is unique, if I get away with it.

When I made *I Want to Live!*, which I thought was a very important picture, I had the Police Department of Los Angeles trying to stop me; I had the motion picture industry trying to stop me; I had the people who had the money trying to stop me. But I was working under Joe Mankiewicz's contract, which gave me complete autonomy. That picture could never have been made had it not been for Joe's contract. I get great pleasure out of doing a thing like that. There was no story purchase at all. It was just an actuality that I built up. I took a lot of legal risks because I was liable for the rights-of-privacy invasion, which is the reason the District Attorney's office fought me all through that picture.

I took over the Academy when it was on its back. It had become involved in the political situation and all the guilds withdrew. At the time it had fifty members. I was president for six years. When I quit, I must say, they gave me all sorts of engraved silver platters, but I don't think they remember me much. For instance, I started a film library up at Dartmouth, the biggest script library in the world. I wrote a letter to a studio president about sending scripts to the college; he hasn't even answered my letter. There is very little gratitude. What I did for the industry I did because I was always devoted to the industry.

In the past, we had a great crowd. In the days of Selznick and King Vidor, there were a lot who were very excited about the industry: Lasky, Zukor, Eddie Mannix. You could do things. It's become a much bigger business today and much tougher.

ALBERT LEWIN

I DIDN'T GROW UP in Brooklyn, although I was born there in 1894. I don't remember it at all. We eventually moved to New York, which I do remember, but most of my boyhood was spent in Newark, New Jersey. After that, I went to New York University and graduated in 1915. Then I spent a year as a University Scholar at Harvard and got my master's in 1916 in English. It was a wonderful place for English in those days! Professors like Irving Babbit. My God, they were great. I was briefly an instructor at the University of Missouri. Then we got into the First World War, and I was drafted. But I never went overseas, and I never returned to teaching.

My father did a variety of things. He helped build the Louisville and Nashville Railroad by being a waterboy on a construction gang. He later worked, as they say, on shirts in New Jersey, and I think that's where he met my mother, who also worked on shirts in a factory. For some time he was the only news dealer in Flatbush. The whole family worked at this business.

I was the youngest, having an older brother and sister. My mother fought very hard to get me into good schools, whether or not they were in our district. I never suffered starvation or anything like that. Kids don't know whether they're poor or rich. I was quite contented as a boy. I always had scholarships. I helped support myself in college by being a kind of correspondent to the *Newark Evening News*, making twenty cents an inch. I used to get the *Columbia Spectator* and several other college papers. I would see what somebody did, and if he came from New Jersey, I wrote him up. They were always glad to get local news.

My mother was illiterate, but an extraordinary, intelligent, and quite marvelous person; very, very capable. The Jews didn't educate their daughters. Her brothers were schooled, but she wasn't. My mother was passionately determined that her children would have the education she didn't have. She really took the reins. Out of a little neighborhood ice-cream store in Newark, she sent three children through college. She did this by Homeric labor. It's a typical immigrant story. My father, with little formal education, was an intellectual. He read Shakespeare and Schiller and Lessing in German. He was also a follower of Ingersoll, the famous atheist. And I was brought up, you might say, uncorrupted by any religious training whatsoever.

My parents were mad about music. They used to go to the opera at the Metropolitan, dragging me up to the family circle, 'way, 'way up there where you needed a spyglass to see the people on stage. But my mother knew all the arias. I still have a tremendous collection of her phonograph records of Caruso and Melba, Tetrazini, everybody from that period. I used to play the mandolin and the violin when I was a kid and that led me to the NYU Glee Club as a mandolin player.

Like many idealistic kids, I thought of myself as a poet. I thought I was Keats and Shelley and Coleridge all wrapped into one. I was a charter member of the Harvard Poetry Society, which was born in 1916. Robert Frost, Conrad Aiken, John Gould Fletcher, and Amy Lowell came to meetings. We wrote bad verses and read them at each other. George L. Kittredge taught the Shakespeare and Beowulf courses at Harvard. He wanted me to take my Ph.D. under him. He told me I had one of the best exam papers he had ever read.

But something intuitive made me feel that the academic world wasn't what I wanted. In spite of that, I ran into the head of the English department at Missouri while he was taking a sabbatical at Harvard. He invited me to come to Missouri, and I accepted pretty much on impulse. At Missouri, we had a marvelous bunch of people. You'd be surprised. Thorstein Veblen was there. He was a very close friend of mine for two years. I saw him every day. And Manley O. Hudson, who became American representative in the International Court was also there.

I had started to do some war work. Also, just by chance—everything was by chance—I had lunch at the Columbia Faculty Club with Manley Hudson and a friend of his named Jacob Billikopf, a famous social worker. Billikopf was head of the American Jewish Relief Committee. After luncheon, I took a stroll with him, and he wanted to know what I was going to do. I hadn't any idea.

"Come and work with me in the Jewish Relief Committee," he said.

"I don't know anything about it," I said. "I'm afraid I'd just be an encumbrance."

"No, you won't. You come."

And I did. I went to work the next day, and within a year, I was Assistant National Director of the American Jewish Relief Committee. I was twenty-three years old. We raised $20 million in one year. I had my experience with social work. I continued for a year or two and knew I wasn't cut out for social work. Meanwhile I finished all the residence requirements in my spare time at Columbia University for the doctorate, except the thesis, which I never did.

A friend of mine was then editing *The Jewish Tribune*. He asked me if I'd like to be the dramatic critic. I did, for no pay, but for the free tickets which I liked. I had just gotten married. We loved the theater, and I became interested in going to the movies at that time. I wrote a column called "Playthings," and it seemed to attract some attention around New York. I received fan letters from some quite famous critics. Bernard Bergman, who was the editor, didn't care what I wrote. I had a free hand. I reviewed films as often as I did plays. I began to get interested in the wonderful films coming from Germany and from Italy. The German Expressionist movement was flourishing, and what really got me going was *The Cabinet of Dr. Caligari*, which I still think was the finest film ever made. It was distributed here by Sam Goldwyn.

I decided I didn't want to be a mediocre poet. I wanted to do something in films. But I was double-crossed by the engineers who invented sound. I loved silent pictures, and my whole interest, technically, stylistically, aesthetically, was in silent films. They were still silent when I went to Hollywood.

I've always been a bit of a purist. It's my feeling that, philosophically at least, an art form exists on account of its limitations, not in spite of them. The fact that a picture doesn't talk or have depth calls on the resources of the artist to overcome these limitations by using his imagination. I'd rather look at an old Buster Keaton, a Mack Sennett, or a Harry Langdon silent comedy than a talking film. I was on the track of solving the problem of the co-ordination of visual and auditory images when I had to stop. I still have ideas about it which I'd be delighted to turn over to some young fellow who had the energy to carry them out. I did do it in a few passages in individual films, and those pleased me the most. But it's a big problem, and I think even great directors, like Ingmar Bergman and Fellini, are still not sure that they have solved the aesthetic problem that lends rhythm—the notation if you like—that a piece of music has to a film. I was aiming at something more precise in the way of cinema rhythm. I didn't achieve it, of course, but somebody will one day.

Von Stroheim was a very close friend of mine. He worked in a film that I co-produced with David Loew when I went into independent production. We brought Erich over here to act in *So Ends Our Night*. It was an anti-Nazi film made before the United States went to war, based on a book by Erich Maria Remarque called *Flotsam* about German refugees without passports. We had a marvelous cast: Freddie March, Maggie Sullavan, Erich von Stroheim, and Glenn Ford playing his first part. He's never forgotten it either. He always tells us we started him. Well, we did; he had a very big part. Frances Dee and a lot of German refugees were in minor parts. It was directed by John Cromwell.

I think von Stroheim had genius as a director of silent films, and I was absolutely mad about his work in *Blind Husbands* and *Foolish Wives*. I admired him intensely long before I knew him. Later on, I used to see him very often because I went to Europe a great deal. He was living in Paris. He worked, however, mostly as an actor. Nobody gave him any more work as a director, which was very unfortunate. At the museums they still run a very much mutilated version of *Greed* based on the Frank Norris novel *McTeague*. I am probably the only person still alive who saw the fifty reels of the original. It took me several days to look at it. I saw the whole picture, and I want to tell you, it was superb, jammed full of symbolism. He liked symbols very much and so do I. I was thrilled.

Years and years later, he begged me to see if I couldn't find the cutouts because MGM had inherited the film. I had Margaret Booth, the head of the department, go into the vaults, and she made a terrific search: nothing. It had all been scrapped. There wasn't a single thing left, but the terribly short version. Von Stroheim tried to do the impossible. He tried desperately to persuade the executives to run it as a feature film serial, to release it as a series of, say, three or four full-length films which, however, were to be continued.

In my own career, I didn't have too much of a struggle. I asked Billikopf to get an exhibitor in Philadelphia to write a letter to Sam Goldwyn. And since he was a very important customer, Goldwyn couldn't ignore it. I didn't see Goldwyn at the time, but a nice man was head of the story department, editor-in-chief for Sam Goldwyn. He gave me a job in New York as a reader. I never gave up any of the other jobs. I continued working for my Ph.D. I used to go at noon and answer mail at the Jewish Relief Committee after I was through with Goldwyn. And I went to the theater as a critic besides.

I was a reader, someone who may be defined as a squirrel in a cage. He reads. He reads books, and he writes synopses of the books because the men who have to decide whether the book would make a movie haven't the time to read them. I started out at fifty bucks a week. Just then, the picture business went into a big slump, and everybody got

Albert Lewin, MGM producer.

Bee Ho Gray, between knife-throwing scenes in *Greed*, roping Director Erich von Stroheim. 1923.

Jean Hersholt and Gibson Gowland in scene from *Greed*.

Gibson Gowland and ZaSu Pitts in Erich von Stroheim's *Greed*. 1924.

a 10 percent cut. I was reduced to forty-five dollars. I called that *reductio ad absurdum*. It took a day or two to read a book. Then you had to knock out a synopsis and write a comment on whether you thought it would make a successful picture or not.

I was a very impatient young man, so after nine months I got Mastbaum, the exhibitor, to write another letter. Goldwyn finally sent for me. He had an office like Mussolini's ballroom; you would be shivering with fear by the time you reached his desk. I walked across the ballroom, sat down, and Sam Goldwyn said to me, "You want to go to the studio?"

"Yes, because I can't learn very much about making films being a reader in New York."

"How long have you been working for me?"

"Nine months and it's time I was delivered." He didn't laugh.

I got out to the old Goldwyn studio in Culver City, still working as a reader, but at least I was on the scene. I used to spend my time on the sets, look on, and snoop around, trying to learn what I could.

I wanted to become a script clerk because I felt that was the most instructive job I could get. I had a terrible time persuading Abe Lehr, who was the general manager of the studio, to let me do this. He used to tell me, "You'll never get anywhere in the picture business, you've got too much education." This was the line he always used to hand me. I wanted him to make me a script clerk, but he wouldn't, claiming I needed stenography.

The script clerk keeps a detailed record of set-ups on continuity sheets. There may be 1500, 2000 set-ups in the picture which are all shot out of continuity. There has to be a record of exactly where each individual shot goes in the mosaic of the motion picture. He has to make sure everything matches. Not only the characters, but the set. He learns to have terrific vigilance. Two or three weeks after shooting one scene, they may shoot the matching scene, and he may have to look up his notes to find out what the character wore, what he looked like, his tempo. You can't trust your memory for that. Things get moved around on the set, too, and they have to be where they're supposed to be. I learned to look at a set in a sort of negative way, asking myself, "Now what's wrong with this?"

I worked as a script clerk, by good fortune, for two absolutely wonderful directors who became my personal friends, although they were important and I was nothing. King Vidor was the first. I worked on a silent picture with him called *Three Wise Fools* which had been a big New York theater success. King did the picture version, which was also very successful. I wasn't much younger than King; he had his success very early. King is still around.

The second one was Victor Seastrom. Seastrom was one of the greatest directors the business ever had. He was also a great actor. He made
classic films that are still shown at the museums. They're rather surrealistic,
anticipating Ingmar Bergman a little. In fact, he worked for Bergman as
an actor in *Wild Strawberries*. He was a noble person. I know no other
word for him. He lived with his family in Hollywood, saw nobody except
me. He liked me, and he came to my house. In Hollywood, when MGM
was formed, he began to work for Irving Thalberg. He made *He Who
Gets Slapped* for him. To this day, it's a superb picture. He used a cast
without stars. They all became stars—Norma Shearer, Jack Gilbert, and
Lon Chaney. He also made a film with Lillian Gish called *The Wind*. Then
came the picture that I worked on, a melodrama by Hall Caine called
Name the Man, with Mae Busch and Conrad Nagel. I was the script clerk
on that one.

I learned so much from King Vidor and Victor Seastrom, it's just in-
calculable. How they directed and how they worked, how they handled
the actors, how they staged the scenes. It was a tremendous education.
Today it's very difficult to become a script clerk because there is a tight
union. They don't want new members, and the initiation fee is very high.
Don't misunderstand me, I am very much in favor of collective bargaining.
But I learned to have a certain hatred of the restrictive union which operates mainly to exclude rather than include.

Camera unions keep talented people as operators all their lives so
that they can't get a chance to be first cameramen. This is an unfortunate aspect of unionism, especially in work where excellence is indispensable. You want certain musicians in your orchestra when you're scoring a film, and the delegate will tell you that you can't have him as your
first violinist; he wants you to have someone else.

"What about the other fellow?" I say.

"He's had lots of work. I have to spread it," he says.

The other fellow's a lousy fiddler; that's why he isn't working. The
difference between something that's good and something that's bad is very
great. But the difference between something that's good and something
that's excellent is a hair. It's that final little push—the better violinist,
the slightly better cameraman, all the tiny things that count. If you compromise, even a little bit, you have a good picture, but you don't have
a wonderful picture.

I've had struggles at times. I wrote and produced a lot of films for
Irving Thalberg before I became a director. The first film I ever directed
was Somerset Maugham's *The Moon and Sixpence*. I had seen and liked
a Javanese troupe. Devi Dja was the head of this troupe. She was an
absolutely superb artist and her whole troupe was adorable. I fell in love
with them. They were Indonesian, not Tahitian. But they knew how to

act, how to walk, how to be South Sea characters, and I couldn't get
Hollywood actors who were able to do the job. But they belonged to the
wrong union and were, therefore, not allowed to perform in my picture
unless I hired Hollywood actors as stand-bys. We were making the picture
on a shoestring. David Loew put up his own dough, and we couldn't
afford to pay people for nothing. I had to do without them.

Devi Dja was a shy, sweet person who wore a Tahitian costume and
walked in bare feet. People who take off their shoes and go about in bare
feet don't walk like the rest of us. That sounds like nothing, but it makes
a big difference. I got her in my office with the union delegate, and I
said, "Devi Dja, I hope you won't be embarrassed, but it's quite important.
Would you be so good as to sit on the floor, get up, walk across this
room, and sit down again for this gentleman?" She did, very sweetly. I
said to him, "You find me any Hollywood actor who can do that and I'll
hire him." He wasn't impressed. I finally used Devi Dja as a teacher for
the girl who played the leading part. And she taught her how to sit down,
how to get up, how to walk. She also acted as kind of a technical expert.
Authenticity is not entirely a matter of having a set that looks correct with
properties and furniture of the appropriate period. It's much more a matter
of how the actors behave.

I wanted to get some experience in the cutting room. I didn't even
ask for that job. The cutters were all my friends. I just went to work and
didn't tell anybody. It was about six months before anyone found out.
I was still on the payroll as a script clerk, but I cut and patched film with
a razor blade the way they used to do it. I learned, and to this day, I'm
a hell of a good cutter. I admit it. I know how to edit films from practical
experience. It's tremendously important. And I think it's important that
you know what to do with a film that's been shot. And when you shoot,
you must know the film that will go together. Now, today I wouldn't be
able to do that under any circumstances because you have to be a member
of the cutter's union.

After my practical apprenticeship, I wanted to write scenarios. This
was still during silent pictures. I couldn't get Abe Lehr at Goldwyn to
give me a chance. I had in my pocket . . . I had had it for months, really
. . . a letter of introduction to a fellow named Joe Engel, who was general
manager of the old Metro studio owned by Loew's Incorporated. Arthur
Loew and Dave Loew were very close friends of mine. We had been
fraternity brothers at college. I ended up as a partner of David's, making
independent pictures. But Arthur, who was the head of the foreign department of Loew's, had given me a letter of introduction to Joe Engel because Loew's owned the Metro studio. Still, I didn't have any confidence
in letters of introduction. But I began to get a bit desperate. I was a
little ashamed about this letter because it was all crumpled and dirty

from being in my pocket for months. But I decided to hell with it. I went over to the old Metro studio and sent this letter in to Joe Engel. I came in to see him and met a charming man. I told him the situation. By this time, I was getting sixty bucks a week at the old Goldwyn studio. He said after fifteen minutes, "You strike me as being sincere, capable, and ambitious. Find out when you can leave there and come over here, and you can write scenarios for me for one hundred bucks a week." Just like that. I was walking on air.

Joe Engel gave me a book to read, but when I read the book, I didn't feel so happy any more. It was by Charles G. Norris, who used to write novels with one-word titles, *Salt, Brass, Bread*. Warner Brothers had made a successful picture of *Brass*. The old Metro, on the strength of that, bought *Bread*, and this was the novel I read. I learned later that they had had a long series of scripts, none any good. And then to hand me, a novice, this script to try to do something with . . . well, that was a little tough. It was a completely undramatic book, a daily life story of a married couple. It had almost nothing you could photograph. I was floored. I had to do something. My whole career seemed to depend on it.

Well, I used to take the Venice Short-Line Car and go out to Santa Monica, a beautiful place and even more beautiful then. It had a kind of palisade with flowers and trees and mountains running down to the sea. Along this almost private beach were the homes of rich, successful people like Douglas Fairbanks. I would walk along, up and down, about two miles on the palisade trying to figure out this story. I looked down at the houses and said to myself, "Those people must be awful rich." I had no envy of them, but, in a matter of ten or fifteen years after that, I built a house on that beach myself and lived there for a dozen years. Funny . . . once I started to hit it, I went fast and really it wasn't too difficult.

I wrote the script of *Bread*, and they were very pleased with it. A fellow named Victor Schertzinger directed it. Schertzinger became very sold on me. My ultimate ambition was to direct. Engel agreed that I could stay on the set with Schertzinger during the production. Mae Busch played the leading part in this picture. When it was in the middle of production, the merger took place between Metro, Goldwyn, and Mayer.

Metro was losing money. So was the Goldwyn studio. But there was a little studio owned by L. B. Mayer way down on Mission Road. It was making money, and a very young chap named Irving Thalberg was doing it for Mayer. They turned out one hit picture after another. The merger grew out of this situation. Irving Thalberg and Louis Mayer were put at the head of Metro–Goldwyn–Mayer. This little successful studio took over the works and moved out to the old Goldwyn studio in Culver City. I didn't immediately go to work for Thalberg, but we had an initial meeting that was interesting.

I got a call on the set to come up to Mr. Engel's office, where I found
a fellow I'd never seen before. He looked like a high school boy, rather
sensitive, quite handsome, slightly built, and attractive. He was Irving
Thalberg, and so young. (He died young, too—at age thirty-seven.) Thalberg was general manager of Universal Pictures at nineteen, and that's
when they made great pictures. He was a genius who had never gone beyond Boys' High School in Brooklyn. I was introduced to Irving, and we
sat in Joe Engel's office. Irving said, "I went East and on the train I read
the book *Bread*."

"Oh," I said.

"I read your script, and I was tremendously relieved." He went on.
"I thought you did an excellent job with that very difficult book."

Well, you know I wasn't displeased with that. I thought, "Here is a
very intelligent fellow."

Then he said, "I have a few minor suggestions, if you don't mind."
And he made two or three brilliant suggestions.

I felt, "Gee, this guy is good. Why didn't I think of that?" Always
he would come up with an idea, and you'd say to yourself, "Why didn't
I think of that?" But then he made a suggestion that I didn't like, and
I argued with him. It was only a way of playing a scene, not too im-
portant, but I didn't agree. I'm a very stubborn character and so was
Irving.

Anyhow, he didn't tell me, "Do it, I'm boss. Do it!" I never, in
twelve or thirteen years, heard talk like that. He always persuaded you
that his way was right. He reasoned. It was never personal. Instead, he
said, "I have to go down to Mission Road. Will you come there tomorrow
and continue this discussion?"

I argued with him for three solid days. I wouldn't give in and neither
would he. I said to myself, "You're a God damn fool, you know, because
this guy is going to be your boss." But I just couldn't give in. I never
could if I didn't believe in something. Finally Irving got tired.

"O.K. It's your picture. I think you're wrong, but do it your way."

Then I was scared and went up to the director, "Vic, look, he told us
we could do it our way, but without saying anything to anybody, let's
do it his way and put it aside. When the picture is finished and he looks
at it and says that it's no good, we will have done it his way."

We did that. It was only a few hours work, and nobody knew. But,
from that time on, instead of being angry with me for arguing endlessly,
Irving always wanted me to work for him.

I didn't work for Thalberg right away because of my arrangement
with Joe Engel. There were reasons why he was never permitted to go into
production. There was a feud between him and Louis Mayer, who wasn't
going to let anybody else make an independent picture to be released by

his company. Engel didn't have a chance, but he insisted I keep working for him. I wrote a couple of scripts that never saw the light of day. I felt so grateful to him that I had to stick along. Finally, I didn't want to take money from him because I thought he needed it. I was making $125 a week, not too good, but plenty for me. I never was interested in money. That's a funny thing to say, but it's true. I made a lot of money. The point is, if you do good work, money takes care of itself.

Thalberg wanted what he thought was just, and he fought for it. Certain frictions grew out of that between him, Mr. Mayer, and Mr. Schenck. I knew very little about that. When the Joe Engel thing didn't work, Irving called me up every once in a while, and finally I did go over to him as a writer. He paid me $300 a week.

I began to work mostly with a producer named Bernie Hyman, a very capable man. Bernie and I had to do a lot of quickies which I agreed to write on one condition—that I got no screen credit. You know, they put my name on one of those stinkers, and I made them remake the main title. I raged at them, "You broke your word. I don't want my name on these lousy pictures." Nothing could make them good. I wrote them as a craftsman. They were terrible stories. I wrote six complete scenarios in five months, terrible stuff. But then I wrote a couple that were pretty good, one for Billy Haines called *Spring Fever* and another one with Billy Haines based on a play by Rachel Crothers. I began to be known in Hollywood. A fellow at First National offered me a job. I didn't have a contract with Irving. He offered me one, but I didn't want it. I reasoned with him.

"Look, Irving, if I have a contract with you and you don't want me anymore, am I going to insist you keep me? If I get tired of you, are you going to force me to work for you?"

"Well, O.K. We won't have a contract, but the terms that were in the contract, that's the least you'll get."

We worked along without a contract for a long time. Then I had an offer of $500 a week from another studio. I went to Irving.

"Irving, I want you to know that I'm not going to work for anybody but you, only somebody's just offered me five hundred dollars a week. You don't have to give me a nickel more. It will be all right. But I want you to know that I've been offered, on the open market, two hundred dollars more a week than you're paying me." He didn't say anything, but gave me $400 in the next check.

After I did those scripts, he made me head of the story department, and I became his personal assistant besides. My God, I worked twenty-eight hours a day. It was terrible. Nights, Sundays, I never stopped. As Irving's personal assistant, I was in his office all day long. I had a very good assistant, Kate Corbaley, a wonderfully capable woman who ran the story department, except for my reading the synopsis and presenting it to the producers. I never had time for myself.

I sat in on all the deals Irving made, on all his story conferences. I ran all the rushes with him. Then one day I opened my envelope and there was an additional check for $600. I didn't ask for it. He never gave me $1,000 a week. He gave me two checks, one $400 and one $600 every week. I had that job for a year, and then I started producing pictures for him. I was one of a half dozen producers working under Irving at the time that MGM became the greatest studio in the world and turned out marvelously successful pictures.

Then we went into talkies. The first talkie Irving made was a tremendous thing for us. We didn't know how to do it. The camera was in a great big plate-glass box. We hadn't heard of pre-recording. We groped. But Irving managed to make the transition. Metro was the last one to go into sound in the whole industry. But we came up with a sensational success, the first *Broadway Melody* musical.

The general public conception of a producer is that of a rather ignorant, coarse, and brutal character who has money and who finances pictures which other people make. One type of producer does set up the business end of it, but most producers don't. The studios and other entrepreneurs do it. Today, most producers are simple employees, just as directors or actors are. Producers used to be called supervisors. Louis Mayer hated the word. He preferred to refer to us as his producers. In a sense, supervisor covers it more accurately.

I was a producer, for example, and an employee at MGM for a great many years with Irving Thalberg. I was responsible, as an associate producer of Irving's, for individual productions, and I was responsible from the beginning to the end. That's what a producer primarily is. He's responsible for the overall job.

Some of the best producers actually are not too literate, for example, Sam Goldwyn. He's a great producer who came out of the glove business, but more power to him. He was able to choose good people like William Wyler. He had the gift of recognizing talent.

Thalberg had a much brighter gift. He was extraordinarily creative. I've seen Thalberg in story conferences with all sorts of famous dramatists and authors, and frequently the best ideas were his. The solution of how best to design a story would often come from him. He always made contributions from a creative point of view, although he couldn't write himself, or thought he couldn't. I believe he really was a good writer, but a little self-conscious about his lack of formal education. Irving had that slight uncertainty which he shouldn't have had because his was a superior mind. He controlled everything in the studio. Later on, he had a unit of his own when the studio broke up a bit. But from the inception of it, he was in charge of production. He had a remarkably extraordinary combination of business sense, good taste, charm, and magnetism. He really created MGM from scratch, and very quickly. To say you worked for MGM was a matter of considerable pride. Under Thalberg, everybody helped everybody else. Thalberg was the team captain and the team was small. Only about half a dozen of us made the entire product. It was particularly good because none of us ever took any screen credit in those days, not even Irving. The fact that it was anonymous made everybody ready and happy to win glory for the team. It wasn't a jealous, political affair, as it became later on.

Irving was also a great editor. He was a perfectionist. If we had an extremely successful preview, as we often did in those days, most people would pat themselves on the back and be awfully satisfied. He would tear the picture apart and improve it. He would push and push to get the very last bit of excellence into a production. After you've seen a picture with an audience, it's amazing what you can do. Sometimes three or four days of retakes will improve a picture enormously, and Irving never hesitated to spend the extra money. His successors were not like that.

When Irving died in 1936, I canceled my contract with Metro. It had about two years to go. Everybody felt distracted at Irving's death. It was kind of an earthquake, not only for Metro, but for the entire industry. He had been universally loved and admired. The whole industry was shaken by his death. When I decided to cancel, all my friends thought I was nuts. It was a very "chancy" thing to do. I didn't think I was particularly well known.

I had no screen credits, or anything like that, and had never sought or got publicity. Well, when I canceled, Mr. Mayer was infuriated with me. Actually, what I thought and never got a chance to explain was that since I had worked so closely with Irving, it was not fair to compel them to keep me for two more years. The honorable thing was to quit and let them make a deal if they wanted me. Instead, Mr. Mayer was affronted, misinterpreted the cancelation, and wouldn't even talk to me for quite a long time. But to my astonishment, within two weeks I had very flattering offers from every single studio in the business. I discovered that Irving had told everybody that I was good. They all knew about me from things he had said. As a result, I had my choice of jobs all over the industry.

I went to Paramount as a producer. I had been with Irving for years without a contract, and before that I had been with David Loew for years without one word on paper. But now I had a very good contract, three years without options and a lot of money. I couldn't be required to make anything I didn't want to make. The deal was made by Adolph Zukor. (He's now in his nineties and still gets around. I admire him very much.) Zukor liked all my ideas. After making the deal with him, I took a vacation in Europe for about three months. When I came back, Mr. Zukor wasn't in anymore. Mr. Freeman was in with a whole new administration, and they didn't like my kind of picture. They may have been right. I wanted to make pictures like those Irving had made as far as I was able to: ambitious and expensive. They had decided that only musicals were really profitable, like the *Road* pictures with Bing Crosby and Bob Hope.

I wanted to make a picture called *Gettysburg*, a big Civil War epic. I also wanted to make a "Knights of the Round Table" picture about the Middle Ages. I had the scripts prepared. Clifford Odets wrote the *Gettysburg* script, but the budgets came to a lot of money. That wouldn't have terrified Irving. I prepared the *Knights of the Round Table* myself, and I was crazy about it. At that time, Stanton Griffis was chairman of the board, quite a bright man. I met him in the hall.

"I just read your screenplay of *Knights of the Round Table*," he said.

"Oh, I didn't think great financiers like you read the scripts."

"I was enthralled," he said.

"Well, Mr. Griffis, I hope you are equally enthralled when you read the budget."

He wasn't. I found myself stopped all along the line. It was an impasse. They were paying me, but I wasn't too keen about taking money and making no films.

I had a contract for three years, but it only lasted a year and a half. I made pictures during that time for Paramount. Two of them were quite successful; one was not. I made a screwy comedy with Carole Lombard called *True Confessions*. It was a very funny picture which Wesley Ruggles directed. This was just before Carole married Clark Gable. I had made two pictures at Metro with Clark, and we were very good friends. Carole was under contract to Paramount. She came in to see me. I didn't know her really.

"Clark says I should latch on to you," she said. "I want to make a picture with you."

"Well, O.K. We'll do that."

I concocted this story, more or less my story, and she liked it. The result was quite an amusing picture. I made another, a big Alaskan melodrama, *Spawn of the North*, and that did all right too. Then I made a flop called *Zaza*. George Cukor directed it. We then decided to settle the contract. It was all amiable enough.

I didn't have too high an estimation of my own work. There were a number of pictures I enjoyed all through my producing time, a few that came out very well like *The Guardsman* with Lunt and Fontanne. I made the original *Smilin' Through*. Sid Franklin directed it, a very successful picture even though the story is a lot of nonsense. But Sidney did a lovely job, and we had a beautiful cast: Norma Shearer, Fredric March, Leslie Howard. The result was very good indeed. And, of course, there was *Mutiny on the Bounty,* the original *Mutiny* with Clark Gable and Charlie Laughton. We were two and a half years on that, but it turned out well. We were three and a half years on *The Good Earth.* Frank Lloyd directed *Mutiny;* Sid Franklin directed *The Good Earth.* They turned out very well, but there were a lot of headaches, heartaches, and crises first.

I was at a loose end, and David Loew was also at a loose end. So we decided to tie ourselves together. We formed an independent company in which we were supposed to co-produce, David handling all the practical affairs and I handling the creative end of the production. That was when we made *So Ends Our Night.* This must have been '39 or '40 because the war had started, but the United States was not in it. David felt strongly about the Nazi problem and wanted to make a contribution if he could, so he decided to make this book, although we were doubtful about its success in the United States. It just about broke even in the long run. It didn't do well in the United States because the public didn't want to feel involved, and this picture rubbed their noses in it a bit. But in England, it was a very big success, which helped.

In a way, that may have led to my starting to direct because we decided that the next picture we'd make very cheaply. I hadn't written a script for fifteen years. David wanted to save the price of a writer, so he turned to me, "You're a writer. For God's sake, write." I wrote the script and let Somerset Maugham read it. I knew him a little bit, and he wrote me that he couldn't imagine a novel being adapted in a better way. The novel was *The Moon and Sixpence.*

We began looking for a director, but a big director in those days cost around $100,000. David said, "Why the hell don't you direct it? Look at all the money we'd save." This was a case of economic determinism.

"Yes, and we might also lose a lot if I make a mess of it." Finally, I agreed. "I'll do it if you take full responsibility. Don't blame me if it doesn't work."

"I'm not worried."

I shot the picture with a totally unknown cast in thirty-two days. It cost us $401,000, fabulous really. I worked hard, and the picture was a very big success. I had worked for a year and a half on that film without compensation, but I owned 50 percent of it. We both made quite a lot of money. And the picture never stopped. United Artists was our distributor. There have been windfalls on television. It's been a meal ticket for twenty years or more. Maugham was crazy about the picture. You know he had a stammer. In spite of that, he made a personal appearance and a speech at our premiere, all without compensation.

The novel had been owned for a long time by Warner Brothers. They

Hurd Hatfield and Donna Reed in Albert Lewin's *The Picture of Dorian Gray*. 1945.

Director Victor Seastrom on location in the Mojave desert where temperature rose to 150° during shooting of MGM's *The Wind*, starring Lillian Gish. 1928.

Doris Dudley and George Sanders in Albert Lewin's *The Moon and Sixpence*. 1942.

couldn't make it, so they sold it to MGM, and MGM couldn't make it. We bought it from MGM for $25,000. The contract came out of the MGM legal department faster than any other contract in my experience, they were so glad to get rid of it. They thought we were screwy. But I had an angle. The reason it couldn't be adapted was that it was told in the first person and because the author at times became a participant in the action. The transposition was very, very hard to do, and the people who had tackled it never solved that problem. For this, I owe a debt of gratitude to Sacha Guitry, who made a wonderful picture called *The Story of a Cheat*, which used a narrative technique for the first time in a theatrical film. He told his story in the first person, the action carried it along, and at intervals when necessary, he talked again. I thought this was a most original and exciting thing, and became the first one to use this narrative technique in American films. I don't claim any originality for that because I got the idea from Guitry, but it struck me that with this technique, *The Moon and Sixpence* was a cinch. I could do the book almost as written, which was what I wanted to do. After that, everybody used narrative technique like mad, even when it wasn't particularly necessary.

Everybody felt we'd make, at most, an artistic flop. David's best friends tried to dissuade him, but he was very steadfast. They said the story of a disagreeable character, a painter whose paintings are burned and who dies of leprosy—this is entertainment? But I always thought that any book which had a continuing sale over more than a score of years, that established a sort of permanent appeal, must have some big vitality in it. The subject matter, Maugham's name, and the title sold that film. There were no stars in it.

I found directing a big challenge. I didn't have a great deal of facility, but I loved doing it. We finally suspended our company, though, because David wanted to go into war work. By this time, Louis Mayer had forgotten his quarrel and asked me to come back as a producer and an executive, which I said I wouldn't do. I wanted to direct, so I went back to Metro. I directed *Dorian Gray* for them, which didn't make anybody rich. It cost $1.8 million. It grossed well over $3 million, got some Academy Award nominations, and won an Oscar or two. Since I had done *The Moon and Sixpence* fast and cheap, Metro had the feeling that when I was spending their money, I did it slow and dear. It looked that way. But *The Moon and Sixpence* had a slashing dramatic design and the detail was less important, wheras *Dorian Gray* was merely a story of an exquisite character, and I got involved with making the picture exquisite. I really went to town on every set-up. When you have two thousand set-ups in a picture, it can take rather long. I was even careful about the table linen and the cutlery and whatever was on the wall. All the upholstery was built for me. I decided that everything was going to be black and white because of the good and evil symbolism. I packed it full of symbols. Now, this picture was made twenty years ago. Recently the embassy in London decided to run a series of distinguished old American films to build the prestige of American cinema in England. So what do they choose to initiate the series? *Dorian Gray.* The picture was handsome because I took all that time and spent all that money. In the long run, it didn't do badly after all.

I left Metro again. I went back with David after the war. We made *The Private Affairs of Bel Ami,* based on the novel of de Maupassant, which was a commercial failure, but was also very much admired by some people. Then David formed a very ambitious company and got a bug to expand, wanting me to have a unit. I wanted to have a modest company, making one picture at a time. So I bowed out and returned to Metro as an executive. I was more or less on the board that ran the studio, and I did a hell of a lot of anonymous doctoring. Louis Mayer—I'd become his fair-haired boy. From being somebody he wouldn't talk to, I had become very popular with Mr. Mayer. He loved *Dorian Gray,* even though it was not a tremendous moneymaker.

I had a lot of notes on an original story I wanted to make called *Pandora and the Flying Dutchman,* and I had the right under my contract to take a year off. I exercised this option. The studio was distressed; they thought I was screwy, giving up my salary. I was always doing quixotic things like that, but mostly they turned out all right even from a monetary point of view. I wrote the script. Then they got excited about it. They were prepared to pay me a hell of a lot of money for the story, the writing, directing, producing—the whole works. I actually had a deal with the studio, but then Mr. Schenck refused to let them go through with it. The budget was $2.5 million, and it was obviously not a commercial picture. Instead they granted me a leave of absence. I could make my picture much cheaper as an independent production without studio overhead and all that. All I wanted by way of settlement was that Ava Gardner should be loaned to me, which they agreed. Then I added James Mason and got a businessman, Joe Kaufman, to promote it. Joe Kaufman was co-producer of the picture. He went to England and persuaded Romulus Films, which was just starting up, to help finance the picture. The American costs were financed here. That meant Joe and James Mason and Ava and I were the American responsibility and all the production costs were British. It was technically a British picture. And I made it. I shot the exteriors in Spain and the interiors in London.

Everyone was impressed when I brought the picture back. I made it in the most extravagant way. And I made it for $1.5 million instead of $2.5 million, in color, without trying to stint. The picture was badly handled in distribution by MGM, but in spite of that, it did quite well. It was a substantially successful picture, and I may ultimately make money on it because I own 50 percent of the Western Hemisphere rights.

You can go out with an unknown cast and an original story and an unknown director and you can shoot a picture for a few hundred thousand dollars, even today. You'd have more trouble getting the few hundred thousand dollars to do that than you'd have getting four million to do a picture with Elizabeth Taylor and Richard Burton, but you'd start off spending a million or more for them alone. Then to buy a hit play or something like that would be half a million more. The production costs are the least. You would have to get a very expensive director with a property like that, and you'd end up spending a quarter of a million dollars for the director and $150,000 for the script because you'd have to have a very successful writer. The whole thing balloons.

I think it's to be regretted that the American companies now have gone in almost entirely for the big spectacular picture. They have left the little interesting picture with originality and taste to the European producers. I rarely go to a Hollywood picture anymore. I go a great deal to the European pictures. They have ideas in them and originality, made by people like Fellini and Bergman. There are several Italians and a couple of very good English and French directors. They have stolen the artistic end of the motion picture completely away from the United States.

I had constant battles with the censors over the most innocuous subjects. *The Moon and Sixpence* had trouble. So did *Dorian Gray* and *Bel Ami*. Even *Pandora* had trouble, and nothing could have been more innocent. In *The Moon and Sixpence*, they just disliked the whole idea of a character who had had an affair with another man's wife who then committed suicide. It didn't have, so far as they could see, any compensatory moral value. Actually, I had to make a few cuts. And not only that. I could tell you a hair-raising story about *The Moon and Sixpence* and censorship. They made me put a terrible title on the front of the picture which read something like this: "We don't want you to have the impression that this character we are telling the story about is an admirable character. He is not." And then we had to repeat that at the end of the film. The phrasing wasn't even in good English. So I came to New York, where a very important Paulist father was a friend of mine. I told him I was very angry with his church for what they were doing to my picture. He was distressed, and he brought me in touch with the head of the Legion of Decency. I appealed to him. My name on the film as writer of the screenplay would cause people to assume that I'd written the title. I didn't want them to think I had, so asked their permission to say, "This subtitle written by the American Legion of Decency." I wanted them to accept credit for the title, but they wouldn't have any part of that.

"All right," I said, "I accept the idea of the title, but it's really not very well expressed. Would you give me five minutes? I will take your idea and put it into good English. You read it and see if you don't find it acceptable. The syntax is no good."

I rewrote the title. There were three or four men and they all read it. They thought about it and read it and reread it and then decided to accept it. I was relieved, but wait till I tell you the payoff. I took the train to California. I got to my office and I found a letter on my desk. They had changed their minds. It went back to the original title. I guess they didn't trust me, even if they couldn't see why. Maugham hated it. Everybody hated it. It finally got lost on most of the prints. The editors cut it off, especially at the end. It didn't seem to make such a difference. People forgot it. They got interested in the picture instead.

Violence has always been popular. Why do the kids love Punch and Judy? Because everybody is always hitting everybody else with a stick. Violence is commercial. In *Mutiny on the Bounty* I added the episode with all Captain Bligh's cruelties, and I really laid on the dreadful things he did to the crew. It made all the difference. People couldn't bear to look, but they loved it. When the admiral at the end refused to shake hands with Bligh, they applauded. That was the difference. It made Bligh even a bigger villain, a villain on a grand scale. Is there anything more violent than Shakespeare's plays? The Greek drama is full of every kind of "cide": fratricide, sororicide, infanticide. So-called classic restraint is a joke. Consider the Parthenon satyrs raping nymphs in the Greek myths or take all of Greek literature, for that matter. Nothing could be more violent. And you look at the great literatures, all violence, and we have to be nice and sweet. Well, life isn't nice and sweet, and if you want to tell the truth, you'd better have a little violence.

I have a book with all the texts of the Punch and Judy shows. They're magnificent adult satires. The people who wrote them were great artists. They wrote the most wonderful stuff about doctors, lawyers, professionals of every kind. Kids really didn't have the faintest notion about that. They couldn't. It was way over their heads. But children love the shows because Punch holds a stick and hits people all the time.

In England, you could have all the cleavage you wanted, but no violence. Over here, you couldn't have any cleavage, but you could have violence. I had tremendous trouble with the British censors about bullfighting. What a struggle that was. This was a problem with the so-called Humane Society. Why don't they call it the Animal Society? They are much more concerned with animals than human beings. They eat their roast beef and let the dogs tear foxes apart alive, but they don't want to see anybody sticking a bull.

Metro built up, under Mayer and Thalberg, a tremendous roster of stars. They went to great lengths to create and sustain a star by giving him good material. I can remember when they made a test of a fellow called Clark Gable, who was a Broadway actor. Well, you know, we used to look at these tests and pick everybody apart. I was there when we looked at Gable's tests. Nobody ever thought he could be a star. They decided, however, that he would make a good heavy, and very often in casting a picture, you would have trouble getting one. He went into a picture with Joan Crawford and slapped her good and hard. The public became mad about him. He became a star with that picture. Nobody remembered that he had big ears. He had a personality that knocked them over, that came right out of the screen at people. You said Clark Gable and you had an audience. Wally Beery was a star. A star didn't have to be a beautiful young thing.

I don't think you can force a star on the public. Hearst found that out with Marion Davies. He spent fortunes on newspaper advertising and full-page ads and all sorts of stuff. He never could make them take Marion Davies. Sometimes great actors don't become stars, like Walter Huston. On the other hand, from the point of view of a director like myself, it was nice to work without stars as often as I did. A good director should get at least an acceptable performance out of anybody, not necessarily a brilliant performance because there has to be some talent for that.

I had a curious experience with Garbo. I was probably the first person to see her in this country. At that time I was Victor Seastrom's script clerk. The cutters were all my friends, and they used to get foreign pictures which the executives wanted to look at. I always saw them ahead of the executives. They had this picture from Sweden, fourteen reels with Swedish subtitles, a very complicated story called *The Saga of Gösta Berling*. The leading part was played by a girl named Jenny Hasselqvist, whom I knew from some of Victor Seastrom's earlier pictures. But there was a supporting role played by a girl I didn't know. There were about seven or eight of us sitting in the room. Nobody could follow the story. It was complicated, the titles were in Swedish, and nobody would have sat through the picture if it hadn't been for this girl. They just waited for her to come on. Every time she came on, all these cutters went, "Aahhh." When it was over, I went to see Seastrom.

"I just saw a Swedish picture with an absolutely marvelous woman in it."

"You mean Jenny Hasselqvist?"

"No, no, I don't mean Jenny Hasselqvist. I knew her very well, but I never saw this girl. I don't know who she is. She plays a secondary part."

"Oh yes, I know who she is. She is a discovery of my friend Mauritz Stiller, and her name is Greta Garbo."

"Well," I said, "I want to tell you, anybody that brings her to this country has a star."

But I was a nothing in those days. I couldn't even suggest it. Well, they brought Stiller over and he brought his girl friend. They wanted Stiller and they accepted Garbo because that was the only way they could get him. However, they liked her and they put her in a picture. They immediately saw that she was something special. The irony was that they ended up firing Stiller and keeping Garbo.

I worked with Garbo when she was tremendously successful, just before her first talking picture, *Anna Christie*. She was absolutely wonderful. Every once and a while I run into her on Madison Avenue. People used to try to get her to come back, but I never thought anybody had a chance. She found making films, I think, very trying. The curious thing is that she was so extraordinary that her fame has grown above what it was at the time she quit. Maybe she did the right thing. Her films are never forgotten.

Occasionally a popular dramatist from Broadway, whose plays weren't worth a hoot but who has had some success with a mediocre play, would talk about art and about how awful Hollywood was and how you had to lose your integrity to be a success. He never had any to start with. Faulkner never complained. He did it for the money, but he was very reticent. Scott Fitzgerald worked for me also at the end of his life, but he was a very sad man by then. It was finished for him, you know. A very charming and lovable man, but he was almost in a trance, it seemed. He was just going along. When I first went to Hollywood, I had met him. Then he was a young man with the whole world ahead of him. And then I knew him at the end of his life. He didn't make too much of a contribution to *Red-Headed Woman*, which is what he worked on. The script was finally written by Anita Loos, but he worked on it.

I always tried to make pictures that would please me and some of my intelligent friends and still please the general public enough to pay off and make some money. On the whole, I got away with it. I flopped a few times, but everybody has some flops. I think the average was satisfactory, although I rarely had a smash hit. But I made enough money for them to let me keep going. I did it as a kind of tight-rope walking. I was a bit of an equilibrist.

I finally retired from making pictures after a heart attack. That's when I decided to begin another career, writing. I find wonderful freedom in writing a novel. It's a looser form. A screenplay has to fit into a two-hour performance. It has to be tightly constructed. It has to follow a progressive narrative line or you lose the audience. When I started writing a novel, I found that I could go off on tangents. I could have my characters discuss questions that had nothing to do with the plot. I began to enjoy myself doing that. I went off in all directions and got a lot of ideas off my chest through the mouths of my characters, which I never would have had the freedom to do in a screenplay. My book is about a woman who is a cat. The title is *The Unaltered Cat*. It is a little allegorical, in the family of *Lady into Fox*. It's in no sense autobiographical, although the characters are synthesized out of people I've known, more or less.

DORE SCHARY

MY LIFE BEGAN in Newark, New Jersey, on August 31, 1905. In the early days, my father did a number of things. He was a real estate broker, a decorator of windows in saloons for special holidays, and a flag decorator. Once he fell off the City Hall building and broke his leg, which finished his labors in that last occupation. My father was a good storyteller. He also had a pleasant singing voice and sang many German and Yiddish songs.

My mother at one time worked in the garment industry. For a while she worked in the Triangle factory, but left there about four months before the famous fire. My mother was a marvelous cook; it was this ability that finally got my parents into the koster catering business. Mother began by making gefilte fish or noodle soup or strudel for some of our neighbors. Gradually, they began to ask her for more. Somebody suggested she cater a wedding. Then my father bought a very old house in Newark and made it into a place which he called Schary Manor. There we began a real catering service.

I owe much to both my parents. Father was a huge man. I'm about his height and I look very much like him. But he was a heavier man than I am. I guess he weighed about 220 pounds. He was a practical joker and a good storyteller. He was creative. He decorated most of Schary Manor himself. And he could embroider. He made wedding canopies with his own hands, out of red velvet, sewn with gold thread. My mother had a calm disposition. She loved being with people. She was a beautiful and extraordinary woman who had a gift for mimicry, steely convictions, patience, and humor.

I learned from both of them attitudes toward living. Mother and Father both endured many illnesses, but they were blessed with great recuperative powers. Each lived to the age of seventy-three. They led very hard lives. It got easier for my mother when I brought her to the Coast in 1938. She and Father had separated after thirty-nine years of marriage. I was also able to help my father, but he lived in the East, and in later years, I did not see him often enough.

As a boy I went to Morton Street Grammar School in Newark, where I was a very good student. I was perceptive and quick. For a child coming out of my environment, I verbalized very well, probably because I read a great deal. By the time I started high school, we had moved to the new kosher catering place, and I worked in the pantry helping prepare grapefruit and salads and also labored in the checkroom. As a result, my hours in school became very irregular. I'd be sleepy at night. In the morning, I wouldn't get up on time. Both Mother and Father were very permissive because they knew I was working hard. High school soon became a series of misadventures for me. I was constantly called to the principal's office. My mother had to go and explain our problems. The disciplined work was hard for me. It required time. However, courses in American history or civics and English, I didn't have to work at. My interest in them came naturally. Finally, I got into an argument, when I was fourteen or fifteen, with a mathematics teacher. I lost my temper and I was expelled from school. Then I went to work full time at the catering place. I also got odd jobs, one with a printing company. I began to do newspaper and magazine selling. I was comfortable. Between the ages of fifteen and eighteen, I'd occasionally go back to school, but these sporadic sessions were not fruitful.

By the time I was nineteen, I had done some sketchy journalism on an Anglo–Jewish newspaper. I knew that my verbal tools were insufficient and that I would have to get some training. By this time my father had a reputation in town as the prime Jewish caterer. Practically everybody had been at Schary Manor for a bar mitzvah or a wedding or an affair of some sort. He got special permission from the board of education for me to go back to school, where I was rather a freak because I had started over again and found myself in classes with thirteen-year-olds. However, the teachers were responsive. They were wonderful and aided and guided me.

A history and an English teacher would often ask me to spend weekends with them. We'd go on hikes and we would talk. The English professor, Benjamin Stolper, encouraged me to begin writing, and his guidance helped me enormously. By the end of a year, I had had enough education to take the regents exams except in mathematics. I did well enough to make me eligible for college, but by then I knew I wanted to work in the theater and newspapers. I had started a mini-paper during the year I was in school and made a living out of that. My teachers had wooed me into areas in which I was reading philosophers and huge chunks of American history. But I finally decided to work rather than go to college, which was a shock to my father, who would have preferred me to become an attorney. The theater, to him, was a sinkhole of sin. But I wanted to work in the theater. By then, I had some amateur work . . . enough to convince me that the theater and show business was for me.

I was a storyteller. During World War I, I knew all the war songs. I went into Army hospitals and sang, wearing puttees and a trench helmet. At weddings and banquets, they would ask me to entertain. I was exposed to all this and liked it. I knew I could engage and win an audience. One becomes aware of that. By the time I was twenty, I began to direct synagogue community groups. I also made the friendship of a playwright, Kenyon Nicholson, who years ago wrote an enormously successful play called *The Barker* with Walter Huston and Claudette Colbert. He suggested that I should write and work in the theater, and got me my first professional job with a stock company in Cincinnati, where I was engaged as a stage manager and a bit actor.

My father was never reconciled. To him, I was doomed to be a bum. You have to remember that a frontier society, such as we were born into, has always frowned on the theater. America had no really significant theater until O'Neill. We did have traveling Shakespearean companies, but theater was mostly minstrel shows and vaudeville, garish, somewhat glamorous, but not very respectable. So, to Father it was a disgrace, a *shonda*, to use a good Jewish word. My mother was reconciled to it, though, as was my older sister.

I continued to work in Cincinnati until I got fired. That job culminated in a fight. It was my first contact with homosexuality. Not being nearly as sophisticated as kids are today, I went into absolute shock and panic when I was "approached," and I hit a guy backstage. Somebody came to his aid, and I took on both of them. I was wiry and fairly strong, so I made kind of a mess of it, and I was fired for "incompatibility" with the company.

I came back home, more or less in disgrace, with a big scratch on my cheek. By then, Father had a hotel in Pleasantdale, New Jersey. He greeted me on the steps by chopping me right across the kisser and knocking me down. He just looked at me and said, "Actor!" That was the last time he hit me because I told him I wouldn't tolerate it anymore. In any event, I then began to write plays and to option them.

My father meanwhile overindulged his ambitions, and the hotel completely failed. He went bankrupt and couldn't stand the disgrace. He was a very proud man; he just ran away. My mother did cooking. Her courage was extraordinary. She had known comfort and even luxury, and she had to give them up. She did—without a tear.

The hotel collapsed in 1928, when I was twenty-three. For a while, Mother worked as a cook and I did anything I could. Then my brother suddenly began to do very well as a stockbroker. He got me a job selling stock in a "boiler-room." I was completely unsuited for it. But I began to make very good money, earning a few hundred dollars a week. It was just before the Crash. One could sell anything. I always felt guilty about it, but that, I suppose, was balanced by avarice, so I was able to survive. Then came the Crash, and things got very bad. Mother and I went back to Newark, where we rented a brownstone. Mother opened a small restaurant, which I helped her run. I was maitre d' and waiter. Then we also secured a concession at the YMHA for the soda fountain and lunchroom which I took over. By now it was '32. Some of the plays I had written over the past several years were optioned. I had met my wife; we had fallen in love and decided to get married. I had no idea how we'd manage. I was earning twenty-five or thirty dollars a week.

By that time talkies were a way of life in the picture business. They began to look for writers. Scouts were in New York, and somebody read a number of my things. He liked them, and I was asked to go to see Harry Cohn of Columbia Pictures. He met me and we got along all right. He was a brash, vulgar, and interesting man.

"How would you like to go to Hollywood?"

"Fine."

"When can you go?"

"Tomorrow."

"O.K."

"Thank you." I got up and started to leave.

"Aren't you going to ask me how much money you're to get?" he asked.

"I know whatever you'll pay me is more than I'm getting now," I said.

"Well, that's very good. You're the first guy who hasn't asked me. You're going to get one hundred dollars a week."

That was nirvana. I had known men like Harry Cohn all my life. I had seen bootleggers and icemen and butchers. I knew his type, an easy-going, rough guy. I wasn't shocked or awed by his toughness. He was the kind of man I always had had to contend with.

I came back, told my wife about it, and we were very excited. But there was a few days' delay during which it looked as though the arrangement wouldn't work. I was prepared to kill myself by then because my faithful friends were giving me a farewell dinner and a briefcase. I was determined to borrow some money, get on a train, go to California, anyway, and look. However, it worked out. Harry Cohn O.K.'d the contract.

We went to California. I borrowed enough money for a couple of suits and my wife's transportation, which wasn't paid for by the studio. I borrowed against my salary. We arrived, hardly knowing a soul. I went to work. My $100 a week was reduced to far less because I had to pay the studio $15 a week for my wife's fare; $10 a week went to my agent; I sent my mother $10 a week; I paid $15 a week rent; and I paid off $10 a week on my cash debts. We were left with $40 a week. But that was enough.

We had come from New York in bitter winter, on Christmas of 1932. I had left the ice and snow, empty stores, apple-sellers, and the sense of deep, deep depression present, even though everybody was hoping that the new administration would bring some relief. The first day in California was damp, but the rain cleared that night. We were met by my dear friend Moss Hart, who had just had a couple of successes and was doing fine. We went to his home on Sunset Strip overlooking a beautiful nightscape of neon signs and bright colors. And then, that night, when he drove us to our hotel, my impression, with the weather so warm and marvelous, was that I'd never leave. I loved it and I thought it was going to be wonderful.

My first contact with the upper echelon came through Norman Krasna, who took a fancy to me, and I liked him. He invited me to a poker game at his house. Norman was doing well, and I went because I felt I had to. I had just bought a Ford on time from someone who was leaving Hollywood for 250 bucks. Somewhere I've got a record of those debts and how I paid them off at $10 a week.

Well, I went to the poker game scared stiff. Although I had gambled before, I didn't know what I was getting into. I remember making sure my shirt was clean. I met some men whose names I had heard, like Joe Mankiewicz and Sam Katz, a big executive at Metro; Sam Marx, head of the writers, and Hunt Stromberg and Larry Weingarten. We ate dinner and the food was good. Then we sat down at the poker table. I didn't dare ask how much the chips were. During the early conversation, as they counted their chips, I found out that each stack was worth a thousand bucks. I broke into a cold sweat. At that time, I guess my cash at hand was about $30 and I owed hundreds more. I began to reason that if I lost $1,000, I could suddenly develop a migraine headache and explain that I'd send a check, then go to Norman, borrow $1,000, and pay him off over a period of time. But calm took over and, knowing something about poker, I decided to watch. I'd go in and I'd ante up if I had to, but I decided to play it very cool, taking no chances. They were bleeding me with antes. Soon I was out about $300. But I began to watch these fellows. They all had nervous tics! One of them was opening his mouth very wide; one of them was popping his eyebrows. If one fellow had a hand, the tic increased. I spotted one guy who was a bluffer and bad at it. So I became a little more adventuresome. Finally I wound up winning $700. That put me into another state of shock. I got into the little Ford, and my foot suddenly began to shake when I realized what had happened to me. Having escaped the possibility of a $1,000 loss, I had $700 in cash! I also resolved never to go back to Norman's house. I showed my wife the money. She was delighted. I bought her a dress the next day, and I got myself a pair of slacks and a sports jacket because that was the writer's uniform. You wore slacks, sports jacket, and a kind of scarf with a sport shirt that had a big Barrymore collar, the mark of a writer.

The first few months at Columbia were interesting. But then there was a 50 percent cut. Three months after we arrived, the banks closed and the studios said that everybody earning $100 or over must take a 50 percent cut. Then the earthquake came along, and I suddenly felt that we had moved into a disaster area.

The early work was absolutely inconsequential. I was handed titles. Those were the days of block-booking when a program of pictures was sold in advance of production. For example, they'd say, "Jack Holt is going to be in this picture. Here's a title." The first one given to me was *Fury and the Jungle* with Victor Jory. That's all I got. I had to look around for a story. I did some reading about the jungle, about piranhas, and so on. Pretty soon I got together a "cockamamie" story. They assigned an experienced screen writer to work with me. We did that screenplay in a few weeks. It was produced instantly. The studio was happy. Then I was given another title. This one was called *Fog*. Fog I knew about. We put it on a ship. Then I was given another title, *The Most Precious Thing in Life*, and then another, called *Man of Steel*, with Jack Holt. The studio only cared about the big Capra pictures or a story by Bob Riskin or by Sidney Kingsley.

At the end of my first tenure at Columbia, I had done four screenplays with Ethel Hill, who was a wonderful lady. She taught me a great deal. The salary cut lasted only for eight weeks. During that quarter, Columbia came out with the biggest profit they've ever shown.

By contract I was supposed to get $125 after three months, $150 after the next three months, $175 after those three months, then $200. Then I was to be on yearly option. But they said that I hadn't proved myself yet, so I had to stay at $100 a week. I saw Sam Briskin, who was in charge.

"I'd like to speak to you, sir, about a raise."

"What do you think you're worth?"

"I think I'm worth what I'm supposed to get now, which is close to two hundred dollars."

So he fired me, saying that one day I'd come back on my hands and knees and beg him for the $100 job. After a couple of weeks, I had the feeling that he was right.

I had no agent out there. I had one in New York, but you needed a Hollywood agent. I went to one who told me, "I'm not interested in you and no agent will be. What's the best we can do for you? Get you one hundred dollars or one hundred and fifty dollars a week and make ten dollars or fifteen dollars a week for ourselves?" He added, "You've got your car. Pack up and go home."

By then we had made a couple of friends in town, among them Al Persoff, who was in charge of writers at RKO. He invited us to a party at his home. Present was Herman Mankiewicz, a real Hollywood figure in those days. He worked at MGM. After a buffet dinner, we began to play parlor games. I've always been very good at so-called mental gymnastics. I used to have a lot of little memory tricks. My memory, thank God, has always been good. And Mankiewicz was impressed with this quick, young, skinny-looking Jew who had just come to Hollywood. He asked what I was doing. I told him I was without work. Through him I reached Sam Marx with whom I had played poker. And Marx put me on as a staff writer at $200 a week. I then sat and waited over a three-month period for something to do.

At last I had an assignment to write a story for Wallace Beery and Marie Dressler. They were to do something in the Ozark Mountains. Metro had brought in an authority on the Ozarks who had a Guggenheim fellowship, a man named Vance Randolph, who was the most unlikely candidate you have ever seen. He was a veteran of World War I, wearing a suit that probably had been bought before the war. It was originally black, but had become shiny green. He went around in army shirts and chewed tobacco. As soon as he entered the office, he put on felt carpet slippers. He got a spittoon from the prop department, and when we began to talk, he'd spit. He was a dear guy though, very funny, very simple, not knowing what the hell he was doing in Hollywood. He had written a number of books, one a definitive work on the language of the Ozarks. We cooked up a story and took it into the producer, Harry Rapf, who was quite a fabulous person in his own right. He told us that he had read the story and he thought it was just fair, but mostly he didn't think it was authentic. Now this was the only time I ever heard Vance Randolph say anything to anybody except me. I remember his chawing on his cud and saying:

"Mr. Rapf, I couldn't tell you anything about whether this is a good story or not. But I want you to know that I have written a few books on the Ozarks, and I am widely considered as a foremost scholar on the Ozarks. So if you tell me this story isn't authentic, you simply don't know what you're talking about, and you can take the script and stick it up your ass."

With that, he spat on Rapf's green carpet. I can just see that carpet and Vance's cascade of tobacco juice. He turned on one heel and walked out. I remember watching that pool which seemed to gurgle and bubble, and I was transfixed. I looked at it. Rapf also looked at it. He pointed his finger at me and said, "Get out." Back at my office, I got a call from Mr. Marx. I had been fired. And Vance was gone. He disappeared. I tracked him down in a room a short distance from the studio. He was already packing. This was the last I saw of him.

So I left MGM, and Mankiewicz got in touch with an agent named Nat Goldstone, who found me a job at Universal for $200 a week. I did an action picture there for Chester Morris. That went well, and then came another one called *Chinatown Squad* for Lyle Talbot. They paid me $250 for that. I developed a small reputation for being able to do an entire script, which was rather unusual in those days. They used to have original story, scenario, screenplay, continuity, and additional dialogue all done by different people. I came to be known as a fellow who could do the whole job and do it quickly.

There followed a period of great activity. I went from one place to another, turning out a screenplay in three or four weeks, free-lancing through the mid-thirties. Each time I made a move, I'd make a bit more money, but those pictures were not exactly noteworthy. In fact, they were highly forgettable.

This didn't frustrate me too much, though, because all this while, I was writing a play based on the San Jose lynching of 1934. That tragedy had moved me, and I began to work on it. By '37, the play was sold and produced. Everyone called it a success. The play got good notices, which helped me in Hollywood, where the trade papers gave it ecstatic reviews, including one that said I was due to get the Pulitzer Prize. People thought I had a big hit on Broadway, and my salary went up some more.

Nevertheless, I ran into trouble with my old friend Mr. Rapf at MGM. For a short time, I was the fair-haired boy there because they saw me as a "doctor." Whenever they had trouble, I was sent for because I could always repair parts or cook up an ending they needed. I didn't mind being run around, even enjoyed it. But then one Friday, Mr. Rapf gave me an assignment, something to read. On Monday I told him I had read it over the weekend and didn't think he should make the picture.

I predicted that it would be a disaster. He got furious and kicked me out of the studio.

I then entered a very fallow dry stretch, the only time I was seriously unemployed in Hollywood. We had one child by then. My wife was pregnant with our second, and things were very bad. I had overextended myself and now I was totally unemployed. We had just moved into a new house, bought some furniture on time, and I had another car. I was ready to sell whatever I could and go back to New York. Then one of those odd circumstances took place.

I had written a script for Spencer Tracy called *Boys Town* which Tracy had refused because he wouldn't play a priest again. He had done one in *San Francisco*. Tracy went into one of his bouts with the bottle at that time. This time he got ill and wound up in a hospital. He told Eddie Mannix, the general manager, "Just let me go back to work at anything." Mannix said, "All we've got for you is *Boys Town*." "I'll do that." *Boys Town* was made during my period of unemployment.

In those days, a picture was finished in six weeks. It was going to be previewed, and my producer, John Considine, called saying that he wanted me to come and see the preview. I went. It was obviously a smash hit, a big picture, because of Mickey Rooney and Tracy. The whole concept of the picture had been mine. They knew it and they were very happy. That night, Mannix came over and put his arm around me and said, "What are you doing? Nobody ever knew where you were." I told him I was out of work, and he invited me to his office. I was immediately put on the Edison picture, and I worked on a big musical, one of the *Broadway Melodies*. I again became that fellow who was asked to do a multitude of jobs.

I read a short story of Paul Gallico's called *Joe Smith, American*. The story fascinated me. It was short, but I figured out some interesting cinematic things about it. I went to my producer and said, "John, I want to make a little picture. I want to direct it. It's a small-budget picture, but it has something to say." About then Roosevelt was planning a "preparedness" program, and this story had something to say about the American spirit.

"Great," he said, "but I can't let you do it. You have to get permission from Mr. Mayer." All during this time, I had never seen Mr. Mayer.

I am now brought in to Mr. Mayer for the first time, quite an experience. He was, indeed, the fabulous figure one had heard about, somewhat awesome, a commanding figure, with very deep brown eyes, a vigorous man. You found yourself in Mr. Mayer's big office, with a huge white desk, all sorts of buttons on it, but that wasn't the impressive thing. The impressive thing was the man who gave you a sense of enormous power.

John told him why I was there and that I wanted to direct. He asked me why, and I told him. He never had much feeling for directors. To him, the producer was crucial. He said, "I don't understand, why do you want to do a little picture?" I explained to him that I thought it made better sense for me to do a little picture than a big picture. That led me inevitably into a discussion of the little pictures they were making. I felt they were God-awful!

"Why does a little picture have to be a bad picture? It should be used as a training ground for young writers, young actors, young directors, young cameramen. You're using it for old people who come up with old stories. It should be experimental." I gave him my whole spiel, which writers had been talking about for a long time.

He listened and he asked, "You don't like our pictures?"

"No sir, they could be so much better and they could make money."

He nodded and dismissed me with, "I'll talk to your tomorrow."

I left with John, who said, "I wish you'd keep your mouth shut." And I rather wished I had. But the next morning I got a call from Mayer, asking me to meet with him. I went to the studio and he put me in his car with his chauffeur and took me out to the Hollywood Track. He had a horse running in a certain race. We talked about horses on the way out. We watched the race. His horse lost, and he took me back to the studio. Not a word. I didn't know what was going on. Then he finally sat me down in the office and questioned me.

"Did you really mean what you said yesterday about the pictures?"

"Yes sir."

"Did you mean every word you said?"

"Yes."

"All right, you're in charge of making all the 'B' pictures."

"I don't know what you mean by that, sir."

"You're in charge. You have carte blanche. You pick the stories, you go ahead. Nobody will interfere. I'm giving you a businessman to watch the money."

"Who's that?"

"Harry Rapf."

I was stunned.

"Mr. Mayer, I have to think about this. I don't know if I can do it. I've never been an executive."

"You'll do it."

I pointed out that I would have to talk it over with my wife.

"That's marvelous. I like men who discuss things with their wives."

Highly sentimental fellow. I went home and discussed with Miriam the prospect of a whole change of life for us. As a writer, after all, I'd work at home most of the time. But, in discussing, we realized that this was what we writers had been talking and dreaming about. The next day I told Mayer I'd like to do it on a trial basis.

"What do you mean by that?"

"I don't want a contract. I may not like it and you may not like what I do. I don't want to find myself in that spot."

"Fine," he said.

I was earning, as I remember, $1,250 a week at the time. Mayer asked me to send him my agent.

"No, sir, I'd rather be a bargain. Then if I'm good, I'll talk to you about money."

They assigned seven producers to my unit and we went to work. There was great enthusiasm, particularly among the writers. When they heard about a writer being put in charge, they were delighted. In a week, I got big-name writers to come in and do scripts. I explained the situation to them, "I can't pay your salaries, fellows." These were two thousand-dollar-a-week writers. They would do a job in a week or two for me. We turned out some very distinguished pictures, like *Lassie, Come Home, Joe Smith, American,* and *Journey for Margaret.* We made stars like Margaret O'Brien and Van Johnson and Peter Lawford. Within eighteen months, we had done twenty-four pictures and had made a fortune for the studio. We were outgrossing the "A" picture unit. Everything was just blooming—and then Mr. Rapf got in the way.

We had started directors like Fred Zinnemann, David Miller, George Sidney, and Jules Dassin. We gave them their first pictures. Rapf began to move in on the rushes and complain. He and I had a terrible fight because I objected to the way he treated people. Then he went along on a weekend with Mr. Mayer, but didn't tell him anything about our quarrel. I went to Eddie Mannix and declared that I wanted to resign.

"Why?"

"I think I've reached the end of the line."

Rapf had told Mannix, but he hadn't told Mayer, so Mannix knew and said, "It's because of Rapf."

"I'd rather not discuss it. Just let me out."

When Mayer came back on Monday, Mannix told him that I had offered to quit and why. Mayer blew his top. There was a ghastly scene with Rapf and Mayer. He wouldn't let me off the hook. He wouldn't let me out of the room. He called Rapf all sorts of obscene things and fired him. I then said to Mayer, "I quit. You've done to Mr. Rapf exactly what he did to Jules Dassin and I can't stand that. I won't return unless you bring him back." He did.

We went along for a few more months until Rapf started up again. Rather than create another climax, I claimed that I wanted to make my

Dore Shary with Dorothy McGuire and Director Edward Dmytryk on the set of *Till the End of Time*, RKO. 1946.

Louis B. Mayer and Dore Shary.

Dore Shary at RKO Studios.

own pictures. Mayer was not angry, ostensibly agreeing that it was time I tried something different. He asked me whether it was Rapf, and I said, "No, no, we've been getting along fine." Of course, Rapf never said anything either.

After the "B"-picture phase, I looked around for properties. I thought of a story of my own, an allegory of events preceding World War II which I saw as a Western dealing with the problem of *Lebensraum*. All the characters were historical. I sketched the story out and spoke to Mr. Mayer. He thought it was an engaging idea.

Then I thought of getting Sinclair Lewis to work with me. I spoke to him on the phone. He came out, very excited about the idea. I enjoyed working with him on the screenplay. Our title was *Storm in the West*. He and I finished the script, but immediately ran into political problems and other difficulties at MGM.

That script had prophetic elements. It was written in '43. Mussolini was Mollison; Hitler was Hygatt, and so on. We had the final assault on a town which these people had taken over. We called it Moon Creek, which was as close as we could get to Munich. In the story, Hitler fights, retreats, and enters a building which bursts into flames. He dies in flames. The character of Mussolini—Mollison—attempts to run away from the debacle, and he is shot down by one of his own men. We describe how, as he falls, his foot gets caught in the stirrup. He is dragged down head first in the mud. Interesting in the light of what actually happened to Mussolini and Hitler.

But there were people at the studio with whom I had previously come into political conflict. They had been opposed to my activities in behalf of FDR and the "one world, free world" concept. They regarded me as someone too far to the left. I was a producer, and I now had to face a hierarchy of executives which was like the college of cardinals. They looked at the script and said it was too political, that Russia was portrayed too sympathetically. My character, the symbol of Russia, was named Steel, who of course was Stalin, and he came from Georgia. He had fought in the Confederate Army and was viewed suspiciously by the Northerners. On the back of his wagon, as he appeared, was a hammer and sickle hanging down as work tools. They thought that was very dangerous. We got into a political discussion, and Mayer sent for me. He said he was sure I was not a Communist despite rumors he had heard. I couldn't help answering, "Mr. Mayer, despite rumors I've heard, I'm sure you're not a Fascist." The discussion proceeded in a fairly amiable spirit. All the same, Mayer didn't want to do *Storm in the West*.

I decided that I had had it. I didn't want to stay there anymore. I went to Mayer and told him. He asked me where I was going, what job I had.

"I don't have a job."

"Do you want more money?"

"No."

"You can only be quitting because you got a better job. We'll meet any offer."

"Mr. Mayer, you're wrong. I'm just not happy."

He thought it over for a week or ten days. Finally, Mannix called to say that Mr. Mayer had given me a release from my contract.

My agent was horrified. Apparently Mayer had intimidated him. He could do nothing for me; the name Schary hadn't been on my pictures. Nobody knew the work I had done in the small unit. This argument was ridiculous. Everybody did know. The exploitation was good and word of mouth from writers had worked. I went to Lou Wasserman, an agent, then comparatively new in California, who agreed to handle me. He contacted David Selznick, a son-in-law of L. B. Mayer's. Selznick hired me despite the fact that Mayer had warned him not to, telling him that I was too difficult, too independent, that I didn't like bosses. Selznick said, "I know how you feel. I don't like bosses either, and I don't want you really to be an employee. I want you to make pictures"—for a new company he was forming called Vanguard Pictures, which was to be a subsidiary of Selznick International.

I had known Selznick very casually, but I had always admired him. I thought he was a brilliant man. We got along well, established a warm relationship, and I took him at his word. He wanted to make small pictures with some content which I had always found interesting. He told me, "As soon as you can, I want you to make a host of them, as many as you want. Do what you did at Metro."

I bought a story called *Double Furlough*, which was later changed to *I'll Be Seeing You* with Joe Cotten and Ginger Rogers. He read the script, hated it, and sent me a twelve-page, blistering memo. He was an expert at memos, especially those that excoriated. I got it, read it. I wasn't well at the time; I had the flu or something. I wrote him an eleven-page memo to the effect that I thought I had done what he wanted me to do. He wasn't to judge my scripts; that was against our whole plan. I offered to buy the script from him so he'd have no loss, and suggested we then forget the whole thing. It wasn't a churlish letter. I just accused him of being abusive and abrasive.

Much to my surprise, I got a call asking me to come and see him. I declined. "I can't. I'm not well and I'm not coming. You hate the script." So he came over to see me. I had made the point in the memo that I didn't want to be a David Selznick. I wanted to be as good a producer, but I wanted to be Dore Schary, no one else. He was very apologetic. He had asked his wife to read his memo and my memo, and her reaction was,

"David, you're wrong." He saw the point: "You can make it, but I won't let you spend more than a million dollars. You will be able to have a star, but you can't have any of my stars." You see, his star, Joseph Cotten, originally was to be in it. I answered, "I'll get two stars." He bet me two hundred dollars on that. Also he promised not to interfere, adding, "It will be a Vanguard Picture. I don't want my name on it anyway." That's what we agreed on. I sent the script to Alan Ladd, who liked it and immediately said he'd sign for it. I gave a report to Selznick. He said, "Why should we pay Alan Ladd two hundred thousand dollars when we've got Joe Cotten?" I was delighted because I loved Joe, and we wrote it for him in the first place.

"Give me one hundred dollars because I got Alan Ladd."

He paid me. Then I sent it to Ginger Rogers. Her agent called me up the next day, "Ginger's crazy about it." I went in to David reporting the news. "Sign her," he shouted. She was big box-office.

"I will after I get one hundred dollars from you."

So he paid off once more. Then he also put Shirley Temple in the picture. He had her under contract. And I was allowed to make the picture.

David was marvelous. I got into a serious argument with the director, Bill Dieterle, who had done a few things to the picture that I didn't like. I was on the set all the time because to me it was a very important picture; it was my first time out with David, and the first time with my own name on as producer, a Dore Schary Production. Dieterle walked out of the set. I called after him, "If you walk out, don't come back. I'll take over the picture." He went to Selznick's office with a report of the brouhaha. Meanwhile, I started to work on the film. Then I was summoned to David's office. Dieterle had given his side of the story; I gave mine. Then David turned to Dieterle,

"This is Dore's picture. His chin is way out. I don't like the picture. I don't like the script, but he's in charge. So you either go back and do as he says, or you can leave."

Dieterle came back, behaved well from then on, and turned out a good picture.

When David saw it put together, he was deeply moved. "It's a hell of a movie. You were right and I was wrong. I'm going to call it a Selznick International Film." He gave it full treatment, and it grossed an enormous amount of money. He made a lot on it, and I made quite a bit because I had a piece of it.

Time magazine gave us an extravagant review and referred to the film as typical of Selznick's taste. David sent me a cute note saying, "It will happen to you later in life when *you* get credit that you don't deserve." We had a marvelous relationship. Every picture I made for him turned out well. Following *I'll Be Seeing You*, I made *The Bachelor and the Bobby-Soxer, The Farmer's Daughter, The Spiral Staircase*, and *Till the End of Time*.

I made some of those pictures on the RKO lot and got to know quite a few people there. The studio head, Charles Koerner, suddenly died of leukemia. Then one day, out of the blue, I was asked to have lunch with Peter Rathvon, president of the company. He announced, "You've been elected a vice-president of RKO in hopes that you will become head of the studio."

"Look, I'm under contract to David, number one. Number two, I don't know if I want to run the studio. And number three, I don't think you should have done any of this without talking with me."

"Well, nothing has really been done that can't be undone. But I want you to know how confident everybody is of your taking this job, and that there will be no bargaining. You name your terms."

I told David about the offer. He wanted to know what my feelings were.

"David, I don't know. It's flattering. It's challenging. I never dreamed of anything like this. But I don't know whether I want to do it."

"Well, I believe you should. If you don't, you might always regret it."

Selznick had been head of RKO many years before, and I listened to him. I went to an attorney, who made up the contract. It included good pay, a percentage of the profits, and complete autonomy. I started the job on January 1, 1947. Our first picture was *Crossfire*, which they had been fooling around with but didn't want to do because it was too controversial. I read it, and I loved what it had to say. *Crossfire* turned out to be a big hit, their alarm notwithstanding. Then we made pictures like *Mr. Blandings Builds His Dream House, The Set-Up, The Window, They Live by Night*, a whole series of pictures that had at least a little distinction about them. People felt that something was going on at RKO.

Then, in the middle of 1947, the Hollywood hearings came along. Two men working for me, Dmytryk and Scott, were named as unfriendly witnesses. They were being branded as Communists. I knew and liked both of them and had encountered neither one in any of the politics I had been involved in. I belonged to some so-called left-wing organizations and had a pretty good idea of who some of the brethren were. I could see the party line, and whenever it shifted, I could tell who went along. But we just never went around branding people we knew or suspected to be Communists. The investigations started. The Un-American Activities Committee came around, asking me questions. I brushed them off with the contempt I felt for them. Finally, I was called as a "friendly" witness, as head of a studio. I spoke with Scott and Dmytryk, "You know I'm going on the stand and I'll say what I think about both of you because you've never done anything that I know of that's been subversive. But I would like to know, just between us as friends, were you, or are you?" They both swore to me that they were not, and I assured them that that was all I wanted to know.

I went to Washington and watched the hearings. I smelled something very wrong because the ten men accused seemed wholly different from the men I thought I knew them to be. I then met with them and their attorney and expressed my dismay. "I don't understand what's going on. You fellows are putting on a very bad show."

They countered with, "What would you do?"

"Well, if I were a Communist fighting for the First Amendment, I'd get up on the stand, say, 'I know I'm placing myself in jeopardy, but I don't believe you have a right to ask me these questions. I will answer any question except a question about my politics.' I'd be very polite, and I'd refuse to answer. Then as soon as I was dismissed, I would call a press conference and I would say, 'I don't think they had a right to ask me, but I'm not ashamed. I'm a Communist. I have a right to be a Communist. There's no law in the country preventing me from being a Communist, but I don't think they have a right to ask me.' Then I think your case would be very clear."

Naturally they disagreed with that. I was called to the stand. I was hammered at by the prosecutor. I simply took the position that I could not and would not refuse employment to anybody on the basis of his political beliefs. I maintained that position though they kept slugging away at it again and again. They kept getting nastier. At last, they let me make a clear-cut statement, and I was dismissed.

This episode made the papers. A big scandal had broken. It was quite obvious to me now that these guys were Communists who really had party cards and everything. But I felt that that was their business. They had done nothing un-American. No motion picture had ever been condemned as being un-American. Afterward, there was a meeting at the Waldorf of all the top motion picture executives. Eric Johnson felt strongly that public opinion had turned against the picture business. It was thought to be riddled with Communists. Samuel Goldwyn, Eddie Mannix, Walter Wanger, and I were the only ones who kept saying, "We have no right to fire these people." Mannix used as his case the law in California preventing a man from being fired because of his political beliefs. I guess Goldwyn and I were a little more emotional about it, as was Walter Wanger, but the general tone went against us.

"How can you fire people who haven't been convicted of anything?" I asked. I was finally able to get a clause saying that no one would be suspended or discharged until the record was clear. I felt that gave me some position with my own board of directors.

By the time I got back to California, Floyd Odlum, who was the real owner and chairman of the board of the company, called a board meeting. He asked me to come and clear up my position. I maintained that mine was an "industry" position, even though it had already been betrayed by Jack Warner and L. B. Mayer and others who got panicky when they arrived in Washington.

"Dore," He responded, "I respect your opinion, but I disagree with it, and we are going to let these two men go."

"If you do, you execute the orders. I will not take any part in it because I think you're wrong. I will vote, for the record, against it."

"Fine, let the record show that."

The guys were fired and then another brouhaha broke out. First I had been under terrible attack by the right-wing papers. You know: "Studio Chief Says He Will Hire Reds," printed in red. I just kept my mouth shut. Then, of course, when this other thing happened, I came under attack from the left-wing boys who said I had fired them. I kept my mouth shut again. I've always found that in public matters, you can get lost in a welter of statements.

At first I thought of quitting, and then when I thought of the actions of these fellows, I said to myself, "I don't really want to be part of their bag." I sensed that a lot more trouble was coming. I felt that I would rather be in a position of some authority to fight it off, which, over a period of time, proved to be a wise decision. I saved a number of people from getting smeared and blown out of work.

But all that passed; the "Hollywood Ten" were convicted. Then in '48, I had ideas for another program of pictures at RKO. The studio was doing nicely. I planned a picture called *Battleground*. About this time, Howard Hughes bought RKO. I had a meeting with Hughes. My contract specified that if the studio was sold, or if somebody else became president, I would have the right to resign. I had a five-year contract. He knew about it and asked me what my intentions were.

"I think I want to quit, Howard, because if I were as rich as you and bought a studio, I'd want to run it. I suppose you want to run it, and I don't wish to be on the spot."

He promised me that was not his intention. Everything went along fine for two weeks until I found out he was asking for scripts and looking at rushes. I didn't say anything about that because I had heard nothing officially. One night he called me at home and said he had read the script of *Battleground* and didn't want to make it. He had seen some rushes of Barbara Bel Geddes. He wanted me to take her out of a picture she was doing.

I put it to him, "Howard, I have only one answer. I quit. You want a messenger boy. Everything I told you has come to pass."

"Let's talk it over."

This took place at twelve midnight.

"When do you want to meet?" I asked.

"Let's meet at three."

"Tomorrow afternoon?"

"No, three tonight," he said.

"Oh, no, I've been working all day and I'm tired. I'll meet you anytime tomorrow morning from seven o'clock on, but not at three o'clock."

We finally settled on a noon date. I went to see him. He was very quiet, couldn't understand why I wouldn't take his orders, why I wanted to make *Battleground*, why I wanted Barbara Bel Geddes.

"Howard, this makes no sense whatsoever. Please let me out before we get into a big fight. It will become dirty and involved. I'd rather not get into that with you. Just let me go."

"What do you want?"

"Nothing except the right to buy *Battleground* because I'm going to make it into a good movie."

He yielded. Hughes is a very interesting man. We left very amiably, agreeing that I could depart two weeks after I showed somebody what was going on at the studio.

But I still insisted, "I'll execute no orders for you, Howard. I'm not going to take anybody out of anything, and I'm not going to cancel anything."

Then Mr. Mayer called me. MGM had had much success during the war years, but right after, their pictures slipped. The number they were making declined, and they had not been good. I didn't know at the time that Mayer was having difficulties with Joe Schenck. Schenck was asking him to get somebody to head production, a vacancy since the days of Thalberg. Schenck evidently had been watching RKOs pictures, which consistently got good reviews and did good business. So Mayer offered me the opportunity to run production. My attorney and I had a meeting with Schenck and Mayer. Schenck told me what he wanted, but I had to have certain guarantees about my prerogatives as head of production.

"We've never given them since the days of Thalberg," he reminded me.

"Well then, don't count me in. I will not get caught up in that maw at Metro. I've been there. If you want a head of production, O.K. but it has to be on these terms." I got that contract.

I started at Metro in August, 1948. They all agreed that what they wanted was active production. They had been making only eighteen pictures a year for which they had one hundred writers, one hundred stars, forty producers, and forty directors—an incredible mass of talent. I went away for about six weeks with a trunkful of material they owned and other stuff that had been submitted. By the time I came back, I had a whole slate ready. The first year we made thirty-five films and everybody was happy. That year I turned a $9 million loss into breaking even. The next year we made $6 million and so on. Everything went fine.

Now, inevitably, Mr. Mayer began to chafe because with the studio's reactivation, there came up derogatory stories about him. I was doing my job, but I detected that Mayer was becoming very uncomfortable. One day, in the spring of '51, I think it was, I went into his office to ask him some questions. I'd usually see him every few days. I would prepare a list of questions and go in and discuss them with him. I had no right, for instance, to buy properties that cost more than $75,000, but I could buy anything I wanted at a price below that figure.

On this occasion, Mayer seemed very indifferent to my questions. I knew something was troubling him. I couldn't help asking, "L. B., what's the matter?"

"Nothing, nothing." The phone rang. It was the treasurer of the company, the second in authority, calling from New York. I heard only Mayer's end of the conversation: "Yes, I think it's true. Yes, yes. Well, I'm sorry too, Bob. You tell Nick for me that he can take Dore Schary and both of them can choke on the studio," and he hung up. Then he looked at me with that penetrating gaze of his as if to say, "And now what?"

"L. B., would you brief me? What's going on?" I said.

"I'll brief you, you son-of-a-bitch." As he said that, I got up.

"L. B., you don't talk to me that way. I don't know what's going on, but I will not endure this," and I started out.

"You come back and sit down when I order you."

"No," and I walked out.

I didn't know what the hell to do. I called my attorney, David Tannenbaum, who observed that something must have happened between Schenck and Mayer. I was not going back in that office. No one told me anything. I didn't want to get into a power fight. I could find another job doing any number of things. He called Schenck and Schenck called me right away. He placated me. "I can't tell you what's going on now, but I want you to go back into Mayer's office and just ask him how he'd like things to work from now on."

"I'd rather you just accepted my resignation."

"I will not accept your resignation, and I will not tell you what's going on except to say that Mr. Mayer is leaving. You'll find out in time. Do me a favor and go back." So I swallowed my pride, or whatever it was, and went back.

I buzzed Mayer and asked to see him. He said yes and snapped off. I went in. "L. B., I don't know what's going on. There are a lot of questions I have to ask you that we never got to."

John Hodiak, Van Johnson, and George Murphy during filming of *Battleground*.

Dore Shary talking to Director Vincent "Vinnie" Donehue during shooting of *Sunrise at Campobello*.

Part of running a studio: Dore Shary playing host to Queen Juliana of the Netherlands.

Dore Shary, Adlai Stevenson, and Marlon Brando during filming of *Teahouse of the August Moon.*

He used a rather obscene expression about what I could do with the list and continued to abuse me. "Now, while you're here, you bastard . . ."

"L. B., I've been through this before and you're too old a man for me to fight with. I'm leaving." I walked out again, and called Mr. Schenck. "Nick, this is hopeless. I'm going home. I want no part of it."

"Well, if you want to go home . . ."

"I certainly do." I started out when Mannix came in with another man who was in charge of contracts. They had both been with Metro for many, many years. They said Mayer had told them a big blowup was going on and that I should apologize.

"Apologize for what?"

"Well, you know, when he gets mad, he calls people all kinds of names. You just go in and tell him you're sorry for getting him angry."

"That's as absurd an idea as I've ever heard. I don't like anybody to talk to me that way, and I will not go in and apologize for something I never did. I don't want him to apologize to me. I'm going home." They pleaded with me, but I left.

That night, Nick called to inform me that there would be a meeting of the executives in Chicago two days later. We all went. Schenck told us that Mayer was leaving, that he had quit. Nick wanted to set up a triumvirate of some kind to run the studio. I told him, "Nick, I don't want to go through this all over again. I'm sorry Mayer is leaving, but if he is and you want me to stay, you have to leave me with the authority I had. I won't answer to Eddie Mannix. I think Mr. Mayer knew a good deal about how to run the studio and these men are all right, but they're not as capable as Mr. Mayer."

Then Schenck asked them all to leave the room. He showed me a letter Mayer had written him in which Mayer laid it on the line that he was tired of Dore Schary usurping authority and getting credit for his work, and that Schenck had to make up his mind: it was either Mayer or Schary. Then he showed me his response, which was that he had gone over the records, and if Mayer was forcing a flat choice, he just had to opt for Schary. That had blown the roof off. I just murmured, "I wish you had told me this before. Maybe I could have met with Mayer and worked out a *modus operandi*, and he would have stayed on in an emeritus capacity or something."

"No, that was impossible because he doesn't like you."

He asked me whether I would stay, and I said only if I could run the studio. My contract did state that in the event Mr. Mayer left or retired, nobody could be placed in charge over me without my approval. All I was asking for were the terms of my contract. They all agreed to that. Mayer left.

It was so foolish of him. Mayer could have stayed there for the rest of his life. He could have been an ambassador of good will and kept a position which would have made him comfortable. I felt no hatred or bitterness for him. By now I was a lot more sophisticated about these matters. I told Schenck that I assumed there would be many resignations from people Mayer had started. With a half-smile I'll always remember, he said, "Of course." I wondered what that meant. I thought perhaps he was just being agreeable. Actually, not a soul offered to quit. I realized then that when my time came, I could depend on nobody saying, "We're for him." I knew that when you lost an important job in Hollywood, you fell like a stone in a pond, only without any ripples. You were just gone.

From '51 to '56 everything went pretty smoothly. To be sure, we had arguments over certain pictures. Some I wanted to make which Schenck didn't want me to turned out marvelously. And some I wanted to make that he didn't want me to make turned out God-awful. I did *Battleground* my first year there; it was the biggest money maker of the year, got Academy Awards, and so on. That was an enormous success and solidified my place. Later I found out that Mayer had said to Schenck, "It's a war picture, but let him make it. It will teach him a lesson and we will be able to control him." That judgment hadn't done him much good.

There were a number of crises. In '51, another series of hearings came along, this time involving the American Legion. I had been rather vocal about that, and it got me into some trouble with Schenck. But the American Legion ultimately agreed with my position. Then there was the crisis of 3-D to which I had been very much opposed. Fortunately, it turned out right for me after a lot of money had been wasted buying those ridiculous glasses which were blinding people all over America. I continued to be active in community affairs, as chairman of drives, and the like. I was interested in the '52 campaign for Stevenson; also the '56 campaign.

Mayer had begun a proxy fight to gain control of MGM. He and Schenck had a lot on each other. They both had indulged in shenanigans, and each was afraid of too much publicity. Part of Schenck's bargaining position to hold onto his chairmanship was to agree to Mayer's proposal to bounce me out. My contract was due to be up in November, 1957. Schenck had already stepped down from president to chairman of the board, my first clue that something was up. I had advised Arthur Loew that at the end of my contract, I no longer wanted to be head of production because it was becoming more administrative than creative. I would have preferred to make my own pictures as an independent producer.

The whole thing blew up when Arthur Loew quit as president. Loew was an incorruptible man who would want no part of any duplicity. The new president, Joe Vogel, was one of Schenck's men. New stories began to appear indicating that a certain studio head was in difficulties. I read these items and figured *I* was the studio head in question. I called Joe Vogel, "You know, Joe, there are a lot of stories appearing and they're directed at me. I'd like to issue a statement that I have a contract and. . . ." He shouted, "Don't you issue any statements." His voice was very harsh.

"Joe, I detect in your harshness reason enough for me to come to New York right away."

I got there and met with him. He told me I was going to be fired. According to him, politics was the reason. He claimed, "We get hundreds of letters from stockholders demanding to know what the studio head is doing in politics?"

"Can I see some of those hundreds of letters?"

"I don't have to show you anything."

"I know you don't have to, but I would just love to see."

"Well, I've got a letter here I'll show you."

He dug out a letter that was typed in blue ink which said I was in politics. Also that I was playing gin rummy with actors at the studio, and if they lost to me, I gave them parts. I never played gin rummy with actors. I was also alleged to be guilty of shacking up with several girls at the studio, which didn't happen to be true. In fact, I got rid of a number of little chippies at the studio who had been kept there for the board of directors. I think *that* irritated some of them. But my private life was always my private life. I happened to have been very devoted to my family.

This letter was anonymous and obviously written by somebody with an axe to grind. So I said, "Joe, you'll have no trouble with me. All I want is out." They sent for the head of the press department, Howard Dietz, who announced, "We'll get out a statement that you've resigned."

"No, I'll be party to none of that mealy-mouthed mush. You get out a statement saying that I've been fired. I haven't resigned. Who are we kidding?"

He then asked Arthur Loew to come in. Loew was still at the studio as head of foreign sales. Vogel had told me, in addition to other things, that new bookkeeping techniques had been instituted and some of the pictures which appeared to have been successful had turned into losses. Loew came in. He was very cordial to me, but very diffident to Joe. Arthur is an independent man. Joe told him, "I wanted you to know Dore is leaving. You're aware of the reasons, the losses that we have found." Arthur looked at him. "I'm not sure of anything like that. You shouldn't have sent for me, Joe." He turned to me, "Dore, your record is better than you know it to be. I'm very sorry that this is being done to you." He walked out of the room.

I said to Joe, "There's no point in our talking anymore. I'll send my representative in tomorrow and we'll clean it all up." The next day I came in and introduced them officially. I was still at work on one picture, *Designing Woman*. I asked them if I could make the final cut in New York. They didn't mind.

One day I was up at the New York office, looking at some things with the cutter, when Mr. Schenck walked in on his way to lunch. He greeted me very cordially, "Dore, come in and have lunch with me." I went into his lunch room.

"You know why this happened, don't you?"

"No, the reasons I've been given are all lies."

"Well, I'll tell you your trouble. You don't listen to anybody. You didn't listen to me. I got into trouble because of you and I'm responsible for getting you out of this studio. It was my decision."

"I don't know why you sent for me now, Nick, unless it's to get me to take a knife and cut my wrists, if that will make you feel any happier."

"No, I want you to stay and have lunch."

"I have no appetite to lunch with you, Nick." I got up and left.

Miriam and I went away for a few weeks to California to the desert. I wanted to think things out. There were some job offers. We'd never been abroad. Our older daughter was married. Our other daughter was engaged. Our son was just finishing high school. I asked my wife, "Why don't we all get on a boat and go to Europe for a while? For the first time we've got enough money. I think I'll write a play." In the desert, I was thinking of things to do. I read a lot of new books, including one about FDR. Quite suddenly, I got the idea to do *Sunrise at Campobello*.

The story came into quick focus. Maybe a psychiatrist could analyze why it occurred to me: the story of an apparent defeat visited upon a guy who then got back up on his feet. That stirred me. I knew I wanted to do it. What may have propelled me most was writing a political play after receiving all these political attacks, you see. I did a draft of a story outline, contacted the Roosevelts and got their approval. I met with Mrs. Roosevelt, came to New York, and laid out my trip to Europe. I spent some weeks in New York working with Mrs. R. at the library.

We boarded the *United States*, went to Europe, and spent four months over there. I worked on the script. I guess it's one of the most chichi scripts ever written in longhand. Some of it is dated on the S. S. *United States*, part in Portofino, some in Deauville, some in Paris and London, some in Rome, Haifa, and Tel Aviv. I came back with the first draft of the play.

After a little more work, we cast it, opening on FDR's birthday, as planned. I was very lucky. It clicked, and I saw my path. I didn't want to go back to Hollywood where I knew I would always be "the former head of MGM." So I stayed on. We sold our house in California and got an apartment in New York. My other daughter married before we came on. Our son moved to New York with us.

I directed *A Majority of One,* co-produced it with the Theatre Guild as I had done with *Campobello,* and that was a big success. Then I did *The Highest Tree,* which was a dismal failure. Then *The Unsinkable Molly Brown* came along and that was good. I determined to stay and work in the theater. I have been doing it ever since, the last few years with no startling success at all. I made *Campobello* into a movie. Warner's came to me to do *Act One.* I loved Moss Hart. Moss had died. Out of my feeling for Moss, I decided to try, and it didn't work. That was the last movie I made. *Lonelyhearts* I did right after *Campobello* as a play. The reaction to it was mixed. Some people liked it very much, but others, particularly Nat West people, thought I had betrayed the ending. In retrospect, I wish I had put his very bitter ending on it.

The Publicity Director

ARTHUR MAYER

I'M PROBABLY almost the oldest man around who's still active in motion
picture production. I arrived in 1886. It will surprise you, but my birthplace was Demopolus, Alabama, a town founded by refugees from one of
Napoleon's marshals. My father settled in Demopolus, and when he died
prematurely, my mother brought us back to live where she was born,
New York City. She devoted the rest of her life to the rearing of her
children. I was the youngest of two boys. Mother had read somewhere
that Harvard University provided the best education in America. She resolved to save enough money to send her two sons to Harvard University
—and proceeded to do it. My brother is a very distinguished surgeon, so
at least in one case her idea proved successful. He is two years older than
I am, still very active, operates twice a week. The other one disgraced his
family by going into the motion picture business.

As a student I was particularly interested in literature and art. Upon
graduating, I didn't know what to do. After Harvard I went over to
Europe, intending to be a writer. In fact, I fooled around with a large
number of things before I decided that the "picture" business was what
I wanted. I went to see a friend of the family's who was a banker, and
he asked me what *industry* I'd like to go into. My answer was, "I think
I'd like to go into pictures." I meant etchings, engravings, maybe someday,
oil paintings. He took my breath away by saying, "Pictures? Wonderful.
I think it's a marvelous idea. I'm all for it. There's going to be a lot of
money made in pictures. It's a comparatively new thing, of course you

realize, Arthur, but the developments are phenomenal. Everybody is going to make money in that business." He added, "By good luck the bank just loaned some money to a fellow named Sam Goldfish who is in the picture business. He's making movies, hand over hand. They're going to be an enormous success."

Unfortunately, or maybe fortunately, the phrase "picture business" misled my friend, the banker. He couldn't conceive of any bright, vigorous young man becoming a painter, so naturally I must have been talking about motion pictures. That was the beginning of my career. Goldfish had been a glove salesman, in business at that time with a man named Archie Selwyn. They didn't get along very well, and when they separated, Selwyn said, "Not only did he steal a large part of my money, he also stole half of my name." He had become Goldwyn instead of Goldfish. Now the industry joke, not very funny but constantly repeated, is that he stole the wrong half. He should have called himself "Selfish."

The banker gave me a letter of introduction and over I went to see Mr. Goldfish who was very nice. The year was 1918. But he seemed anxious to get rid of me, and why not? He was *in camera* with a charming young woman. I met Mr. Goldfish. I also met Mabel Normand who was in the office at the time. It occurred to me suddenly that possibly this might be a business I would enjoy, that it was well adapted to my particular talents. So I went to work for Mr. Goldfish. He asked me what I wanted to do. I gave him the normal answer, the one I get from my students every day, "I would like to direct, to make pictures, of course."

"Well, you can't just do that to start in with, Arthur. You have to find out more about the kind of pictures people want and how the business is conducted. I'm going to send you out to my office in Chicago." "Office" was the wrong word, actually they were "exchanges." Originally, motion pictures were bought by theaters that exchanged them with other theaters. Back in those early days, they weren't covered by copyright. You were able to buy and exchange them with other people, and then you returned the picture to the company exchange for the one you got.

So Mr. Goldfish sent me to his exchange in Chicago. I was shocked to discover very quickly that they were stealing money from him right and left. I was so ill-advised as to inform Mr. Goldfish/Goldwyn to that effect. If I had had any sense, I'd have known better. Chicago was a rough, tough place. The gangsters were running things. Mr. Goldwyn was upset by the report, but delighted that he had someone dumb and inexperienced enough to tell him about it. So what happened to me was that instead of getting trained for Hollywood, for making pictures, I was routed around to other exchanges to see if any hanky-panky was happening there.

I'd probably still be traveling around in exchanges if Mr. Goldwyn hadn't been fired from Goldwyn and replaced by a new man as head of the company. That happened largely because Goldwyn imported a picture called *The Cabinet of Dr. Caligari. Dr. Caligari*, a very unusual film, was, shall we say, a flop. I got involved because after he showed the picture in his projection room, Goldwyn wanted to know from his staff, "How was it?" Not a word. Yes-men usually say how marvelous the boss's selection is, what a wonderful picture it was, regardless of what they think. But not a soul said a word after watching that film. It was a very natural and understanding reaction, more or less the way people feel today when they see *Last Year at Marienbad:* what the hell is it all about? That was their reaction to *The Cabinet of Dr. Caligari*. My own position at that time was equivalent to assistant office boy. I said, "I like it."

"Ha!" he said. "We have one bright young man in here. I'm going to let you help me out on the campaign."

The campaign was a catastrophe. Theaters sued us. We ruined their business for weeks. People wouldn't come back after we played *The Cabinet of Dr. Caligari*. However, it was and still is a very great picture. It's the daddy of all our horror films, when you come down to it. But America wasn't ready for anything of that nature. It was surrealistic.

Caligari cost very little. Ufa, the German film company, was way overbudgeted at the time. To satisfy its directors, they decided to make a few cheap pictures, *Caligari* among them. They didn't select the story because of its artistic potentiality; they just wanted to make a cheap picture. My recollection is that it ran about nine and a half reels, a fairly long film for those days. Anything much over an hour was considered quite long. However, there were exceptions even then. Not like now, of course: the three-hour picture is, on the whole, a real menace. But we might have been better off then if they had run somewhat longer, which would perhaps have precluded the rise of double features.

With *Caligari* to sell, I temporarily stopped reporting on exchanges, going out instead to various places trying to persuade distributors to take the picture. You didn't actually show the picture if you could help it. You knew if the exhibitor saw it, he'd never play it. You went out with stills and a press book instead. At that time press books were very misleading. They still are. They give an erroneous impression of the picture. We tried to conduct a campaign about the horror, the hair-raising nature of *Caligari*, deflecting attention from its artistic qualities.

As I say, they showed a picture that did no business whatsoever. Goldwyn was fired; *I* wasn't. My salary was so small that nobody paid any attention to me. It was my only salvation. I only earned twenty-five dollars a week. So they got rid of Goldwyn. The man who succeeded him was a remarkable character named Godsol. Godsol brought me back to New York and again we had the performance, "What would you like to do, Mr. Mayer?"

"I'd like to make pictures."

"You can't make pictures until you know more. I'm going to send you out to some theaters in the Middle West."

Remember that it was during the early twenties when major companies were acquiring theaters. Goldwyn Company wanted to be in there with Paramount, Loew, and Warner. And vaudeville was still holding its own at this stage of the game; it hadn't been affected yet by pictures. Moreover, we were in the early stages of the star system. It had just started rolling. Up to that time, actor anonymity had been the rule. Names of the first actors would mean nothing to anybody today. Those in control of the industry feared that actors would ask big salaries, as much as $150 or $200 a week, something outrageous like that, if you publicized their names, so they were much opposed to identifying them at all. But Carl Laemmle changed all that. Before Laemmle had Universal, he ran a company which was the first to publicize the early stars. He was even ahead of Roach. Mary Pickford was maybe not the first star, but she was the first really great star. She always looked down on Chaplin as a kind of a newcomer. When Chaplin got a salary as big as hers, she'd raise almighty hell about it, and she had to get a bigger salary. As far as she was concerned, they weren't going to give a Johnny-come-lately like Chaplin as much money as she got.

From a financial standpoint there is no doubt that the success of the early American motion picture business was predicated on the development of stars and the incredible following they managed to establish. People went to pictures in a way they won't today. I don't care how popular Liz Taylor and Julie Andrews are. They won't do an incredible business with a bad picture. But you put Fairbanks, Chaplin, Pickford, or Lloyd in *any* picture then, and that did it. All you needed with Chaplin, for instance, was to put a sign in front of the theater announcing, "*He's* here this week." If you had an advertising display of Chaplin in front of your theater, you did business. People go out now to see *a* picture, not a star.

On the negative side, let's compare Hollywood to Europe, which is possibly the best contrast. Europe placed its major emphasis on directors rather than on stars. Great picture-makers were all-important. Consequently, we've had a regular succession of great French directors, such as René Clair and Renoir. There was Eisenstein in Russia. The Germans, too. This tendency gave the Europeans a genuine aesthetic advantage over us. But at the American box office, it was star value that counted. Not many directors' names were or are widely known by the American public.

The stars we did deglamorize a bit, somewhere in the late forties. But originally the star-centered–era companies would distribute one star picture, and to get it—to get Fairbanks or Pickford—a theater had to buy all the rest of their product. Films were sold in big blocks. As long as you could use the star as a leader, he was invaluable to you in selling all your bad pictures. The star pictures were frequently just as bad also.

Then, one day the Supreme Court ruled that block-booking, was illegal. In addition, the companies owning theaters had to dispose of them. That changed their production policy. No longer was there any interest in making a large number of pictures. They wanted to make a limited number, which in turn caused them to break up their "stables." Every company had had huge stables of stars under contract who were now let go.

Another thing happened during the same period: a tide of rising income taxes. Stars discovered that working for the major companies meant they couldn't hold on to most of their earnings. Each star thereupon sought to establish his own company. For example, if you own a company, you can arrange your taxes quite differently. In the 90 percent bracket, you can sell your stock for which you're taxed only 25 percent. So the stars all went out for themselves. Hardly any of them remained under contract, and the companies learned to be less interested in the star system. And they stopped developing new stars.

In my youth, the major companies always had scouts around, much like football or baseball scouts from major American industries seeking executive material. In those days, they scouted the countryside, schools, colleges, any and every place for young talent. No one does that today. Independent production began to flourish as a consequence of judicial decisions; the independent producer isn't interested in developing stars for the future. Even with all the faults of the old-time heads of the major companies—each was so singularly arrogant, self-assured, greedy, and bad-mannered—they still thought ahead. What would happen five or ten years later was of central concern to them. L. B. Mayer ransacked the world for fresh, young talent. Today, the independent producer is interested only in the picture he's making at the moment or the picture he's going to make next month, not in the long-range future at all.

In this eclipse of the stars, something new had occurred: the American director had begun to acquire some power. For a long time, he was just another hired hand. "Here's your next picture, go ahead and shoot it." He wasn't even consulted about the writing. He wasn't even consulted about the cast or the amount of money to be spent. The director only had a chore to do. As soon as he completed one picture, he was given another. With the rise of independent production, though, important directors became producers as well. The director–producer is now so exalted that he frequently claims 50 percent or more of the profits on a film entirely financed by others.

Von Stroheim fell victim to the older system. Griffith, on the other hand, was more the victim of his own errors. He had been an independent producer, not originally, but as soon as he became strong enough. And *The Birth of a Nation* made a tremendous amount of money for him. He lost it all on his second big picture, *Intolerance,* and was in financial trouble from then on. Griffith got a job with Paramount after he lost all his money, but his sort of picture was no longer popular. Von Stroheim was different. He worked for one major company after another and invariably got into trouble because he spent monumental sums of money. Budgets meant no more to him than they mean today to the average director–producer. Consequently, he was shuffled around. His films just weren't profitable.

Possibly Orson Welles has been the one director sacrificed by our system. Welles has had a tragic career. He was able to make very good, not necessarily unprofitable, and not overly extravagant pictures, but it has been impossible for him to get along under the American system. This is true of Von Sternberg to a lesser degree. John Huston's case is also tragic. If Huston had died ten years ago, you'd have had to say that he was the fair-haired boy of American pictures. But not the Huston of recent years. I have much admiration and affection for him; he is a man who is very hard not to like enormously. It hurts me when he turns out a poor picture. I try to explain the failures away by saying that the front office must have interfered with him, or something like that.

To be a successful director, you used to need the capacity to turn pictures out rapidly, to adjust yourself to whatever the front office gave you. The director had no time and no encouragement to place any emphasis on art. Now this may have all been for the best. I'm always a little bit afraid of ART in big capital letters. All in all, the best work in Hollywood has been that of people who didn't regard themselves as artists in any sense of the word. They were craftsmen who had a job to do. And in retrospect, many pictures they turned out ever so casually in the twenties and the thirties and the forties look very good compared with the so-called artistic pictures some of them tried to make.

Of course, before the time of the big studios, an independent like Sennett would shoot off the cuff. If he heard there was going to be a fair or a flood somewhere, he sent his company out with orders to shoot a picture. And it got shot as they went along. He would cut films himself. They would come back with the stuff, and Sennett would go to work. You can just see him sitting in his bathtub, editing a film. He also had a rocking chair, and you could tell if you listened to the squeak of that chair whether he liked the picture or not. If the chair squeaked a great deal, that meant he was rolling backward and forward and he wasn't too happy. But if he was really intent on the picture, you heard no squeaks. Sennett laughed when he read in later years about "the art of Mack Sennett." He was no artist. He was just a maker of pictures, trying to get as much fun, as many belly laughs, into them as he possibly could. His pictures were good if people rolled in the aisles. That was his test of their quality. He discovered by experience that certain things are regarded as funny. A well-dressed man with a high hat falling down the stairs is funny: dignity overthrown. Incongruity is a very good word for his type of funnies. You have to deflate the pompous, which is what Sennett did all the time. That's why he was such a successful comic film-maker. Whether he would have as much appeal today, I don't know. *It's a Mad, Mad, Mad, Mad World* redeployed some of Sennett's techniques on a gigantic scale, and it clicked. Apparently people still like the belly-laugh comedy.

Anyway, after a while I was supposed to know something about theaters, so I got sent out to the Middle West. I had the misfortune to go in the summer. Ordinarily, in those days, the summer was the worst season for movies. These days, it is the best. Air-conditioning brings people into the movie theaters as soon as it really gets hot. But that summer was a wet one. It rained day after day—and business was tremendous. No one in New York watched the weather in Chicago; all they knew was that the receipts had doubled. So they came to the completely false conclusion that this fellow Mayer was a very good theater operator, only I didn't know the front of the theater from the back. They looked at the receipts and the receipts were good, so just as Mr. Goldwyn had made me check the film exchanges, the new Goldwyn Company, revised under Mr. Godsol, decided I was the ideal theater operator and they kept me in theater operation for a good many years. I really knew nothing about theaters. There's no modesty in this whatsoever. I mean, business was good, maybe not due to rain alone. The pictures could have been better or perhaps they got all the receipts that had formerly been withheld. But it certainly wasn't my genius at work.

I did inaugurate a bonus system which was practically unheard of in the motion picture business. We'd give the manager a little extra money if he had a very good week. By benefiting in that fashion, he'd have somewhat less reason to steal the receipts.

I made my headquarters in Chicago for four years or so, covering the Middle West territory. That lasted until the collapse of vaudeville, with which it had been tied in. Then the head of Paramount Public Circuit, under Mr. Zukor's leadership, decided that the best way to control the industry was through the ownership of theaters. They built up a circuit of well over twelve hundred theaters. Twelve hundred theaters might not sound like so much, but they were located at the most strategic points in key cities, exactly the places we avoid today. One of my jobs was clocking traffic. The place you clocked the most traffic was where you located your theater thirty years ago. Today it's the last place you locate your theater because you have a parking problem which didn't exist at that time. But then, that's what you most wanted, and Paramount theaters were situated in heavy traffic areas. They formed a company known as Paramount Public. The head was a man named Sam Katz who had been the head of Balaban and Katz in Chicago. Katz wrote me a letter asking what we could do to fight vaudeville. Vaudeville was beginning to climb. How could we take over that business for motion picture theaters? I wrote what he thought was an intelligent letter. He asked me to come East, and I became one of the directors of the Paramount Public Enterprises.

I must have been operating 500 to 600 theaters. That was in 1929. All our large theaters had what we called presentations, live shows that accompanied the picture. You didn't have double features in those big Paramount Public Palaces. You might have them only in the secondary houses; in these large, so-called palaces, you saw stage shows. We would build a big stage show in New York and then route it around the country. These shows, though we took great pride in them then, were pretty awful. Only two or three movie companies could afford to do this. Paramount was the leader, with the most theaters and the deepest involvement in presentations. They called this whole theory of theater operations deluxe, a nice fancy-schmancy word. Katz had done this before in Chicago for the Balaban and Katz Theaters.

Ten years before, people looked at his places and said they were monuments of bad taste. Then, people were beginning to say that, though hopelessly rococo, there was something special about them. Going out to one of these theaters was an event. Today the most popular theaters have 700 or 800 seats. They're not palaces; going to them is an unimportant event. You go because there's a picture you want to see. But going to a Balaban and Katz Theater in the old days was really something. First of all, you couldn't get in for quite a time, but the crowd was not ignored. Lobbies were big enough to hold more men and women than could be seated in the theater, and we entertained a few thousand people during the waiting period. A band would play outside; food was served. They had ushers trained by West Point cadets. Just going into a rest room was an eye-opener. The idea of these palaces was to provide a paradise which folk in moderate circumstances could look forward to. Admission wasn't so steep in those days: fifty or sixty cents was a high price.

Paramount gave me a comparatively small area, and I ran theaters through Iowa, Nebraska, and Minnesota. As things went well and they began to have more and more faith in my capacity to do the job, they gave me a larger and larger territory. Eventually I was running theaters from as far East as Ohio, all the way out to Kansas. I must have been making $150 a week, big money. I had one of those sliding-scale contracts which they gave everybody. You made $100 for the first two years, and the next two you made $150, and then you went up to $200. If you lived to my present age, the chances are you'd be getting $1,500 a week.

My Mother was not overly pleased with my career. My brother became a doctor, and according to the natural course of events in a Jewish family, I should have become a lawyer. The motion picture business . . . well, it wasn't as bad as running a house of ill-fame, but it was in that category. Also, I unwisely decided to show my mother *Caligari*. She concluded that I must be working for madmen. Eventually, mother was reconciled to it.

I was now a film distributor for all intents and purposes. I finally prevailed upon the higher-ups to let me go out to Hollywood. I still wanted to be a director. But this is the problem that faces all of us in the motion picture industry. The boy who comes in tomorrow to see me is going to say, "Mr. Mayer, my father would like me to go into his business, but I really want to make motion pictures. I'd have my father's permission if I could go home and tell him I had found a job. How do I get started in this motion picture business?" And I'm going to say to him, "Brother, I don't know how you can get started in motion pictures . . . I can get you work as a salesman or as an advertising man. But that doesn't mean that you're ever going to make a picture. If you're a writer, yes. If you're a director, I don't know." Once you get started writing for movies, you may get a chance to drift into picture direction. Once upon a time if you wanted to become a director, to do it was first to become a cameraman or a film editor. But today these craftsmen are organized in closed unions. That makes it very, very difficult for a young man to get started.

When I got out to Hollywood they put me into the advertising department. What to do with a young man who could write a little bit . . . ? I was never particularly successful as a writer. Hence I got to be head of advertising at Paramount. It happened in the early thirties when Paramount had such rising stars as Marlene Dietrich and Mae West.

In '29, '30, and '31 when the country was in real depression, the motion picture industry was in very good shape. Its troubles came a little later, in '32, '33. During the early phase when a man was out of a job, he couldn't sit home with his wife all day. He'd go to a motion picture for twenty-five cents and sit there all day. The theaters were doing well. Deep depression really hit the industry at the time I went to Hollywood. But Paramount was fortunate in having had some very remarkable stars. Mae West was an enormous success. The early Marlene Dietrich pictures were very profitable. Cary Grant was starting his career; he had his first important part in a Mae West picture. Paramount sustained a good level— and then got into trouble over the large number of theaters it had acquired. Paramount had bargained about price, about what to pay for them.

Adolph Zukor and Arthur Mayer. In the rear: right, Howard Peterson, assistant secretary of war; left, Sam Dembow, executive vice president of Paramount Publix. Circa 1943.

A meeting of the War Activities Committee of the Motion Picture Industry. 1st Row: Brenda Marshall; Ned Depinet, president of RKO; President Harry S Truman; Myrna Loy. Behind President Truman: Cecil B. De Mille. Left of CBD: William Holden. Right of CBD: Harry Brandt, president of the Independent Theater Owners Association. Behind CBD: Arthur Mayer. Right of Mayer: Abel Green, editor of Variety.

The old Rialto Theatre in New York City in its most sadistic days. Theater owner—Arthur Mayer.

A large number of these deals were made on the basis that Paramount stock would be given for the theaters and that it would be guaranteed to reach a certain price within ten years. Far from reaching that price, Paramount stock went down. As time ran out, the company found it was in no position to pay for them. And Paramount went into what they called "77" deals, a polite form of bankruptcy. You didn't call it that. Instead, the company was reorganized. They brought Mr. Balaban East to head what was actually the new company.

As advertising director, I had quite a time. One of my favorite stories is about the first campaign for Mae West. We didn't have an industry code at that time, but it was evident that handling her would present problems. She was tremendously popular. She had gone to jail for a previous legitimate production she had made in New York. There was no doubt that her pictures were going to be very sexy. I simply prepared one big still for my advertising campaign. It was just a bust. I built up the beauties with which nature had already so bountifully endowed her, and I wrote one line of what I thought was safe, chaste motion picture copy. The line was "Hitting the high spots of lusty entertainment." Nothing happened. We sent out all the advertising, and it was too late to change a thing. Mr. Zukor liked it. Then, one day, he called me in! "Mr. Mayer, I'm shocked and surprised. I thought you were such a gentleman and you use a dirty word."

"What do you mean, a dirty word?"

" 'Lusty.' What a word to use."

" 'Lusty,' Mr. Zukor, you know, comes from the German word *lustig*, for life, energy, vigor. There's nothing dirty about the use of that word."

"Look, Mr. Mayer, I don't need your Harvard education. When I look at that dame's tits, I know what lusty means."

Well, that was more or less typical of the problems I faced with motion picture advertising. But it was too late to be squelched. Mr. Zukor always moved very discreetly. He would go on record as having disapproved and protested against the advertising, that he had given Mr. Mayer and the advertising department a severe talking to, but he'd also wait until it was too late for changes to be made.

Depending on how I stood in his estimation, my name varied all the way from "Arthur" to "Meyers." It hinged on whether he was angry at me or not, and let me assure you, I was "Meyers" most of the time. But I do have a high regard for him. Among my most priceless possessions is a telegram from Mr. Zukor written only a few years after that Mae West episode. It reads: "You're herewith discharged. Best regards. Remember me to Mrs. Mayer." He couldn't fire me. I had a contract. Nevertheless, his wire was the first blow in a battle and eventually we worked out another deal—to my disadvantage. I got the Rialto Theatre and he cancelled my contract. The logic was as follows:

If a motion picture does well, it's because the picture is a fine, good, remarkable box-office attraction. If a motion picture does badly, it is because the advertising was poor. And although the advertising man almost invariably is the butt for any unsuccessful venture, he rarely gets much credit for any success. This, at least, is an advertising man's picture of the situation.

Previously, as a theater man, I had quite a bit of experience in advertising. I had a press book with ads laid out by the company. I looked at them and felt I could do a lot better than that.

A press book tells you all about the picture. It's company propaganda. In addition, the book has ads which the theater can use and send for. These ads are filled out in accordance with billing requirements, a major problem of advertising. You fulfill all the billing requirements and you find you have nothing but the names of the picture-makers all over the ad, with very little room for any copy saying what the picture means or why you should go to see it. Everybody connected with the picture insists on having his name in the ad, and not only his name, but it must appear in a certain size. You spend a large part of your time trying to persuade people that their names, in proportion to the other names, are exactly according to contract. That you happened to put in a name in light instead of heavy print has nothing to do with it. I've had girls who hired men to climb to the top of tall buildings to measure the precise size of their names in proportion to the title of the picture.

This is an example of one of those amusing incidents. I handled the campaign on *War and Peace*. Mr. De Laurentiis and I walked up from the Paramount office to the Capitol Theater where it's going to play. De Laurentiis has an interpreter with him. He can't speak English, quote unquote. He talks in Italian, and the interpreter says to me, "Mr. De Laurentiis, he wants you to know how much he appreciates all you do for him. Mr. De Laurentiis, he love you like a brother. Mr. De Laurentiis, he learn English so next time he has a picture maybe you can talk together and maybe he can understand what you have to say better than he's understood in the past. . . ." All this palaver until we reach the Capitol Theater. Mr. De Laurentiis takes one look at the marquee and he then says to me, in perfect English and in a perfect rage, "Good God, Mayer! You know that my name was to be as large or larger than that of anyone else in connection with this picture, *certainly larger than Tolstoy's.*" This is how you spend most of your time when you're an advertising man.

Advertising is designed to give you an opening for the picture. After you've opened, you want to get the people in. You have one name in the picture, at least only one name of any great consequence. So you have to advertise it on a very, very big scale, which may get you that opening. It may even get you a week's good business. If you receive good reviews, you talk about the critics. But the only important thing is an intangible; it's much harder to ascertain immediately. That's what we call "word of mouth." What are people saying about the picture as they leave? All the advertising in the world won't help you if they're going out and saying, "It's a dog. Did I get fooled on that one." The job is to get them in to see the picture in hopes that they'll go out and say they liked it. Today they're starting to advertise pictures the day they begin to make them. That's to build up the advance to promote a broad desire to see that picture. It's all to get that first week or two. And a picture looks a lot better in a house that's crowded with people than a house that's half empty.

That reminds me of the case of *The Outlaw*, for which, for two years, the billboards showed two big breasts and nothing else. Actually, the picture was an anticlimax, at least by the time it reached New York. In a sense, by then the breasts were sagging, and so was the exhibitor's confidence in the film. It ultimately made money, though. At least I suspect so. But this brings us to figures and statistics and who knows whether it made money or not. That's always the advertising man's dilemma.

Through all this I was never a Hollywood man in the sense that I established my home there. My wife and three children stayed in the East. I'm married now fifty-two years. This is quite a record. If you ask me what I have done that is of an unusual nature in the motion picture business, I would answer with the fact I've been married to the same woman for over fifty years.

The Player

〰〰〰〰〰〰〰〰〰〰

CONRAD NAGEL

Most people think it is a vaudeville gag, but I was born in Keokuk, Iowa. Keokuk was named after Chief Keokuk of the Sac and Foxes, one of the few tribes friendly to the white man. Under the aegis of Chief Keokuk, many of the railroads, the Burlington, the C and B, and so forth, were put through that part of the country. My father was a musician who had a school of music in Keokuk. In 1900 he went up to Des Moines to take a college job. I grew up there. I naturally went to the school where my father was dean of a small college of music, Highland Park College. Highland Park was a college which I think all colleges should be like. Dr. Longwell founded it with the idea that most boys coming off farms in that part of Iowa didn't have four years to spend getting an education, so he boiled it down to two years. It only took me two years to get a four-year degree. I went to school forty-eight weeks a year, six days a week. Classes started at seven every morning and ran all day.

At the age of fifteen, I played the part of Ebenezer Scrooge in Dicken's *A Christmas Carol*. This experience settled my fate. I was going to be an actor. Since my mother was a singer and my father a pianist and composer, they encouraged me in every way they could in any artistic bent I went off on. I took every course college had in dramatic arts. I got into every amateur play within a radius of fifty miles of Des Moines and received my degree at age eighteen. I got it done and out of the way. It's interesting because today, my own son is attending the University of Kansas. Out of 365 days each year, he's actually in class only about 160 days.

It's a waste of time. At eighteen, I was on my way, and by the time most of these kids graduate, I was established and doing well on Broadway.

It was easy to get a job in show business in those days because there was a stock company in every city in the country, including Des Moines. They had professional actors in all the important parts, but there were always bit parts. They just couldn't afford to bring actors from New York, and this is where the local talent came in. I had no trouble finding work. The only difference between then and now consists in what the unions have done. Then you played ten shows a week, seven nights and three matinees. And you opened a new show every Sunday matinee. That meant you were in the theater from ten o'clock every morning until after the show at night, seven days a week, and for that, my pay was five dollars a week. You couldn't live on that.

At the end of one season, I had appeared in forty-five hit plays, "hits" because only the hit plays got to stock companies. I also attended all the rehearsals studying how the leading man got his effects, how the comedian got his laughs. The character man taught me how to put on beards and whiskers. So after spending a year in one of those stock companies, if you had anything on the ball, you came to New York, and bang, you had a job.

I had letters of introduction from people in the stock company and I got a job within forty-eight hours of my arrival in the big city. There were never enough actors to go around then. I went through two or three plays around the subway circuit. Finally I landed the star part in one of the great hit shows of the time and toured with it for two years. The play was called *Experience*, a modern version of *Everyman*, the old morality play. I had the part of Youth, and Youth was the center of *ten* great scenes. It was the dream part for any young actor. And at nineteen, I was earning $150 a week. It was 1916. That's the equivalent of $700 or $800 a week today. I was a rich boy, while father was still dean of a college at $75 a week.

Then I had my chance on Broadway, in *Forever After*, starring Alice Brady. We opened in 1918 at a beautiful theater, the Central Theater at 47th Street and Broadway. The play was a big hit and so I was a successful young actor on Broadway at the age of twenty. By this time I was getting two hundred dollars a week. Unfortunately, at about this time, Highland Park College had gone under. My father came to New York and went into teaching. He became associated with the Opera School, and the entire family moved into an apartment up on Riverside Drive.

In 1918, they made almost as many motion pictures in New York as they did in Hollywood. I don't need to itemize: there were studios all over New York City. I worked at one on 48th Street. Adolph Zukor had his Famous Players Studio on 56th Street where the City Center is now. Biograph was way uptown around 175th Street. Vitaphone was out in Flatbush where NBC now stands. I also worked in that studio. The Famous Players in New York and Lasky in Hollywood affiliated and became Famous Players–Lasky. In a very short time, they became Paramount and built their studio out in Astoria, Long Island, which is now the Army Pictorial Center. I worked there in 1923. We stage, or legitimate, actors considered ourselves the real actors. These movie actors, you know. Anybody who worked on Broadway always had offers to make motion pictures around town, particularly since half the pictures in those days were being made in New York.

I hardly had gotten started in my hit play when picture offers came in and I decided to take them. I was young and healthy and could take the punishment. It was punishment, you know. You didn't get home from the theater until eleven or twelve at night and you had to be out in Flatbush, at Vitagraph, at nine o'clock the next morning. I had to get up about six o'clock to make it out there on the subway. It was a little easier working on 56th Street. They had to let you go at twelve o'clock on Wednesday and Saturday so you could play the matinees.

I did my early pictures in New York. The first one was *Little Women*. I had a theatrical contract with the famous producer, William A. Brady. He was also the head of World Film, a big production unit on 48th Street. They had decided to make a motion picture version of *Little Women*, and they cast me as Laurie. Henry Hull was the professor, and the girls were all well-known picture actresses. Brady thought it would be a fantastic idea to go to Concord and make *Little Women* right in the Alcott home. We went up there, found the home still intact, and filmed it on location.

Practically all pictures in those days were six reels. They lasted an hour and a half. In addition to the feature, the movie house would show a two-reel comedy and usually a travelogue or a newsreel. It was also around that time that The Strand Theater, run by Roxy, originated the idea of featuring a symphony orchestra and a singer. You got a terrific show for seventy-five cents. And they had their choice of the best pictures. It was Roxy and the Strand that set the pattern for movie houses all over the country. The Capitol Theater and Loew's State also came along with this type of program. Not just a picture, but a stage show, too. The whole Loew's circuit was like that.

Much later, I came into the "live" part, so to speak, through a back door. Around 1930, there was a slump in Hollywood. If we were under contract, they had to pay us our salaries. They decided to send us on a tour of the Loew's theaters. I was the only one who did pretty well simply because they provided me with a very good act. Edgar Allen Wolfe, a famous vaudeville writer, wrote a one-act play for me. I didn't just go out and say, "Here I am making a personal appearance, you lucky people. Aren't you fortunate to see me alive?" No, I had a good legitimate act which also was entertaining.

Anyway, I was well prepared to be a movie actor. I had not only worked my head off all those years in college and on tour, but I'd sit around at night with fine old actors who just loved to talk theater to young actors. That's how you soaked up the art of acting: just as a good painter would acquire a complete knowledge of his art, I learned about acting. To act before the motion picture camera, therefore, came very easily.

Many of us benefited from that complete theatrical background. Even Mary Pickford had had stage experience, and her competence was proven, for in her first talkie, *Coquette*, she won an Academy Award. People made a great mistake thinking that *all* of those silent picture actors were dumb puppets who did just what the director told them to do. Theirs was definitely an art. If not, why did some become great stars while others fell by the wayside? There were dozens and dozens of "baby stars" every year, all very attractive. They photographed beautifully. They'd have little careers of two or three years—and then disappear without a trace. Without credits, people like J. Warren Kerrigan; Bunny, the Funny Man; Flora Finch were certainly well known. So why did Mary Pickford become a big star while twenty other beautiful blonde-haired little girls become nothing? Nobody can explain it. But if you're right, they just sprinkle that stardust on you and you're, say, a Gertrude Lawrence or a Mary Pickford. I never worked with Mary, and yet I knew her very well. Mary was one of the few great stars of that era who had a social conscience. She was always lending her talent to causes. For example, she was a founder of the Motion Picture Relief Fund, whose board I later joined. In 1930, I became president. But Mary helped found the Fund when she was at her peak in 1918, or the early 1920s.

But let's get me out to Hollywood. Well, along comes the actor's strike in 1919. I have just finished my run in *Forever After*. I have made not only *Little Women* but several other pictures in New York, and just then—the strike. Actors' Equity Association was founded in 1912, but it had no power and no authority until 1919 when we demanded recognition from the producers, and they said, "Oh now, you actors . . . you're nice charming people, but you can't be taken seriously and we're not going to have a union in the theater." They refused to recognize us, and we went on strike. Nobody believed the actors would go out, but we did. It was a tough fight. An awful lot of the stars didn't believe in a union. The art of the theater and so forth. So a group of them formed another organization called the Actors' Fidelity League which we quickly named the Fidos. They tried to defeat us, but fortunately we won the strike. We had parades up and down Broadway with the Barrymores, Eddie Cantor, Ed Wynn, and other famed actors. One by one we were closing the theaters. If there was a theater open, entertainers like Cantor or Wynn would go around in front and out in the street around eight o'clock and put on an impromptu show just to keep people from entering the theater. Ultimately, we closed all the movie theaters. Then we joined the AFL, and with their help, we won the strike.

In August, I was supposed to go on tour with *Forever After*. It was a successful show. We expected to do great business. But I got an offer right after the strike to go out to Hollywood and make a picture for the director I had worked with at Famous Players, Charlie Maigne. He offered me more money than I had ever dreamed of getting in the theater. And California—Hollywood—that sounded pretty good.

So I went out to make this picture for Famous Players–Lasky. I got there in December of 1919. It ran over into 1920. I was among all those big movie stars, but they thought I was terrific because I was a stage actor. They would point to me and say, "Look, he's an actor." Big movie stars didn't usually consider themselves actors, but they were. At any rate, they were much impressed with my performance in this particular film. When it was finished, they offered me a contract. It was an adaptation of a best-selling novel, *The Fighting Chance*, by Robert M. Chambers, a very popular author of the day. I was the leading man and Anna Q. Nilsson was the leading lady. Anna Q. was quite well known, but we were not big stars like Gloria Swanson and Tommy Meighan. We were what you would call "featured" players.

In those days it took a long time to travel to Hollywood. It took five days by train besides that long ridiculous layover in Chicago. And when I got there, I hated it. Oh gosh, did I hate Hollywood. You see, we came out of the bitter cold of New York into the terrific warmth of California, and it was all I could do to stay awake. I'd get on the set, and if I could stand still for two minutes, I'd doze off. So after four or five days, I went to the railroad office and got a pullman reservation back to New York to make sure I'd leave the minute the picture was finished. Then Mr. Lasky called me in and offered me a five-year contract with options at the end of every year. And the salary—it was money never heard of in the legitimate theater. And fifty-two straight weeks. I couldn't do a thing except sign it. I went out to make one picture and stayed twenty years!

My preconception of Hollywood was well attuned to the completely false picture everybody had. Hollywood was good copy, and it sold newspapers. Not at that particular time, but a bit later, there were 75,000 people there making their livings in the motion picture industry, and out of those, at any given time, you couldn't find six people involved in any kind of scandal. Like most people, most of us were and are, privately at least, rather uninteresting. You don't hear about these people. They go along in their calm sensible way saying, "I hit it big, but this may not last." For example, take Anna Q. Nilsson or Rod La Rocque and Vilma Banky, three of my oldest and closest friends. There were dozens and dozens of these as against the few who were built up into good spicy reading matter. Of course, tragedies occurred, but when don't they? Like that of Jean Harlow and Paul Bern. I knew Jean very well, and I delivered the eulogy at Paul Bern's funeral. But they were caught in a genuine tragedy, not a scandal.

But let's go way back. I can tell you about the "notorious" Wallace Reid. I made his last picture with him. Wallace was the number-one box-office star, the King. And he was one of the most charming, most lovable, wonderful guys I've ever known. There wasn't the slightest bit of conceit in him. He never took himself seriously. No ego there at all. But perhaps he was overwhelmed. Even though he was married, there would be five or six women at his doorstep every morning. He'd have to fight his way out. It was the same thing with Clark Gable, besieged by neurotic women. Now just what happened to Wally, I don't know. It was supposed that he took dope. First he would drink and carouse around until late at night, and then, in order to stimulate himself for his work, he probably took dope. Anyway, when he died, the explanation given was a combination of drink and dope. This got into all the papers. There was nothing secret about this.

I didn't have Wally's problem because I never got that big. Technically, I never did become a star. I was earning large amounts of money, but I was also very happily married. Lupe Velez, Clara Bow, Marilyn Monroe? I don't think that any of these people went sour as human beings. There was something wrong with them psychologically. Perhaps a good psychiatrist could have straightened some of them out. But most of those I knew took the Hollywood life in stride.

The influence of silent pictures on the general public was far greater than that of talking pictures. The silent picture didn't require translation into foreign languages, so American films enjoyed far greater success all over the world than they do today. All you had to do was change the subtitles. The impact of the motion picture on the customs, thinking, and habits of people everywhere was enormous. In fact, there was a saying in the twenties that the trade followed the film. It comes to mind all of a sudden now. A perfect example of this was Wally Reid and the soft white shirt. In 1922, all men wore starched detachable collars, and the "Errol Collar Man" was the famous model. Their ads were sensational, featuring handsome Greek gods wearing Errol collars, some of them three inches high. Then Wally Reid came out in a picture wearing a soft white shirt. What happened? All over the country millions of men wanted to buy soft white shirts. The Errol people came running frantically to the

Motion Pictures Producers' Association, "Can't you do something about this? The collar manufacturers are being put out of business. Can't you get Wally Reid to wear a starched collar?" Well, they got the logical answer, "Why don't you start to manufacture soft white shirts?" And they did!

Another example comes to mind. About the same time I made a picture with Gloria Swanson. It was one of the first pictures Sam Wood directed. One day he wanted a prop for Gloria, a bottle of perfume. He told the propman to go to the drugstore for a bottle of perfume and to be certain it was in a distinctive-looking bottle. It had to be a distinctive prop so that in another scene which took place five months later, the audience would remember it. So the prop man bought a little black bottle, very oddly shaped, of perfume called "Christmas Night." Nobody had ever heard of this very expensive perfume. After the picture came out, they sold a million bottles. A million bottles of that perfume; "Christmas Night" was *the* thing.

Then there was a picture called *Over the Hill to the Poorhouse.* In it, a dear old lady was shown working on her sewing machine constantly. She would put a piece of cloth into this machine and somehow it would come out a finished dress or a shirt. Of course, everyone in the audience wanted one of these machines. The Singer people even got an order for one from Thailand.

When the prohibition era and the "wild and reckless youth" era came in, parents and reform organizations all over the country became much concerned with the influence of pictures on teenagers and the younger generation. After Joan Crawford played in two or three "wild youth" pictures, the idea of censorship began to germinate. There were even arguments from some reform organizations that the picture business was a public utility and should be put under suitable regulation. Then came the biggest scandals of them all. First, the Wally Reid thing, then Charlie Chaplin's involvement with a teen-age girl, and finally the Arbuckle scandal which split the country wide open. Reform groups started referring to Hollywood as Sodom and Gomorrah. Roscoe Arbuckle was tried in court three times and completely exonerated three times. But a San Francisco district attorney, wanting to make a reputation for himself, seized the opportunity, and Arbuckle was ruined. And the reform organizations began to demand censorship. They had twenty-five state legislatures considering twenty-five censorship bills. Passage of these bills would have ruined Hollywood. What would have been allowed in Florida would not have been allowed up in Oregon. By the time you got through, your picture would have been cut to pieces.

Some time later, I made a tour speaking to various censorship organizations. Things were in complete chaos. In Massachusetts alone, I found censorship laws for the Commonwealth of Massachusetts, others for the City of Boston, and a third set for Boston only on Sunday. Just in that one small area, a film would be sliced three different ways. It was utterly impossible. Hollywood panicked. What did they do? They looked at baseball with its "czar," Judge Landis, who had cleaned up the game, and thought, "We'll get a czar to clean up Hollywood." They went to Washington and got the Postmaster General, Will Hays, the greatest politician of that era, and they organized the Hays Office. Hays went to work, brought the censorship organizations together, and said, "Tell us what you object to, and we will try to cut it out at the source." That was the code's primary function. The producers signed up. Hays was their czar. What his office said went. Every script was submitted to him. Hays didn't censor it; he merely said, "Look, if you shoot this, they're going to cut it out in Ohio. If you shoot that, they're going to cut it out in Massachusetts." Of course, writers and directors hated the Hays office, but as a matter of fact, Hays saved the motion picture industry. In no time at all, he got most of the censorship bills dropped. I think only five or six states ultimately wound up with censorship legislation. But all of this had been brought to a head by the Roscoe Arbuckle case.

Writers, directors, producers, even actors, felt rather squelched by the censorship. At one time or another, we all complained about it. We'd get what we thought was a very good scene, and then somebody would come out of the front office saying he'd talked to the Hays Office and they were sorry. Sometimes it was so ridiculous as to be childish. I remember a scene I did with Jane Wyman in a picture made about eight or nine years ago, *All That Heaven Allows*. I played a friend of the family's, a fussy old guy with aches and pains. Jane Wyman played a very attractive woman whose husband had died. She had kids who were grown-up, in college, and so forth. She was lonely and looking for companionship. Everybody thinks she should marry me, but I'm a pain in the neck. I've always got aches and pains. I'm a fussy old guy who, however, belongs to the clan and the kids want her to marry me. Then we have a scene where we are decorating the Christmas tree, and I say to her, "Oh, I got this wonderful new doctor. . . ."—kind of an intimate little scene. Well, so help me they cut it out because they claimed the censors would interpret it as our having an affair. Now she could barely tolerate me. I'm dull. To claim there was anything remotely suggestive there was absurd. They cried, "Wait a minute, in Maryland and in Ohio, they're going to interpret that as you and Jane having an affair so we have to eliminate the scene." Actually, the real romance, quite pure, was between Jane and Rock Hudson, who played a horticulturist much younger than she.

After I had become accustomed to the Hollywood climate, my good heavens, I loved it. I was successful. I was active. I was working all the time. It's true that my first love was the theater. I kept thinking each year I'd go back to my true love. But I just went on from year to year, I put more and more money in the bank, yet I was doing things I enjoyed.

I loved working with Cecil B. De Mille and with William deMille. It was a special pleasure, in those years, for me to work with them. William deMille's approach was entirely psychological. That was very good for a good actor. He picked everything to pieces so that you knew exactly why you were doing what you did. Cecil De Mille was more of a showman, one of those truly great figures of show business. A lot of people claim that he was a phony, a show-off. He was not that; he was just a superb showman. At the time of his death, somebody totaled up the millions of people that had seen Cecil De Mille pictures. And everyone he ever made showed a colossal profit. He never had a flop.

I was terribly fond of the silent film, but when talkies came along, they were also much to my taste. Because of my theatrical experience, I was among the first to get a break. Since I was already established, I had been trying all along to organize the motion picture actors by bringing them into Actors' Equity. In 1927, when the wage dispute came up in Hollywood, the only organization around was my little group of Actors' Equity. I got up on a soapbox. We had a great many meetings. The crisis was touched off by a big general salary cut, but under pressure, the producers called off the cut.

At the time, I was under contract to MGM. So Louie Mayer was mad at me. The worst punishment he could think of was to lend me to Warner Brothers for a picture. At that time, if you were under contract to one studio, never were you loaned to another one. It was one of those things that MGM wanted you shown at the Capitol or the Loew's State, not in the Warner Theaters which were only for Warner stars. Well, they loaned me over there and the result of it was that I made a picture with Dolores Costello at the same time *The Jazz Singer* was being released with Al Jolson. *The Jazz Singer* was not a talkie; it was a "sound" picture, a silent picture in which the only sound was Jolson doing his numbers. But when it was released here in New York, *The Jazz Singer* created a sensation. Meanwhile we were working on our picture when Jack Warner came running onto the set with Darryl Zanuck, who was then in charge of production. Warner said to us, "Darryl's got a great idea. You've heard about *The Jazz Singer*. Darryl wanted to put some talking scenes in this picture." As a result, we finished the picture and then put some talking scenes into it. Remember, there were only two or three theaters where you could run a picture with sound. In the Vitaphone, the sound was on a record, not on the film. Ours was the first feature-length picture that had any talk in it,

Conrad Nagel, Charles Bickford, and Kay Johnson in *Dynamite*. 1929.

Conrad Nagel and Joan Crawford in *The Hollywood Revue of 1929*.

Conrad Nagel and Dolores Costello in *Glorious Betsy*. 1928.

real dialogue, not Jolie singing. The picture was called *Glorious Betsy*. The night that it opened, my God, all of Hollywood was there to see it. It was a fantastic event.

Then I did the introduction for the first picture that was all talkie, *The Lights of New York*, with Helene Costello, Dolores's sister. Bryan "Brownie" Foy, a director at Warner Brothers, made it. They worked six days making a feature picture out of it, but spent a little bit over the budget, all of $25,000, and Jack Warner was so sore that he fired Brownie. And here was the first 100 percent talkie which everyone wanted to see to be able to tell his grandchildren about. That picture made over a million dollars.

Just imagine what a catastrophe hit the industry at that time. You must stop and think. The motion picture was about to be revolutionized, its whole basis reversed. In silent pictures, you wanted as little talk and as much action as you could get. All of a sudden, now you wanted as much talk as you could get and as little action as possible—if only because you couldn't move the microphone. It was a couple of years before that could be done. So in every talking scene, there was a huge mike placed in the eternal bowl of flowers, and you had to sit there and talk right into it. The Vitaphone that was all on records had been difficult to synchronize, but even when they started putting the sound on film, there still were the colossal mikes. The first time we ever tried to move the mike, the scene was two of us moving over to a window, and two or three propmen had to carry this huge, heavy mike over to the window with us.

The transition was very difficult. I made Cecil De Mille's first talking picture with him. It was called *Dynamite*, a super-colossal production. That was 1930. Even then, there was no dubbing. The climactic scene in *Dynamite* was a huge explosion in a mine in which Charlie Bickford, Kay Johnson, and I are trapped. There's only one way to get out. I'm the rich, young socialite, she is a very social dame with millions of dollars, and Charlie Bickford, the rough miner. There's a bulkhead blocking our way, a concrete bulkhead. We find some dynamite, and we've got air for just so many hours. We've got to get out by a certain time or we'll all die. Again, there's only one way to get out. The dynamite has no caps to set it off; we have a big sledge hammer instead. Now which one of us is going to swing the sledge? It winds up that I do the deed. But there were a lot of technical problems. How to simulate the proper sound effects of the explosion rumbling and roaring. Cecil De Mille, from his old stage days, remembered that when you wanted a roar of great thunder, you had a big trough built backstage and you rolled cannon balls down it. So they built one, and it was perfect. We got the roar of the mine exploding

In another picture, I had to fry two eggs. They experimented with all sorts of ways to get the right sound. They rattled cellophane. Finally, I made a suggestion, "Why don't we just light the fire? I'll fry the eggs and see what happens." That was it!

The sound revolution wreaked havoc, some of it needless. Take the fate of my very dear friend, John Gilbert. (Our dressing rooms were next to each other.) He should have survived; he was a fine actor. He had a distinct and forceful way of talking. Whenever he spoke to you, he was extremely powerful about it, but unfortunately, with that microphone, his voice came out funny. Now if they had just been wise to this, they would have slowed him a little bit and had him talk lower. A year later, with dials, they could have taken care of anything. But he was finished. One picture and they laughed him off the screen at the Capitol Theater. Still, he continued to try. He did many pictures with Garbo and then they broke up. When Garbo did *Queen Christina*, she insisted that they give Jack a part. He played it, and he played it damn well. But no go—even though he had been the top male box-office attraction in silent films.

Corinne Griffith, the great American beauty, was another example. Apparently there was nothing they could do to fix the sound of her voice. Vilma Banky, who didn't care much, had a deep Hungarian accent that just wouldn't work. On the other hand, Garbo's accent accentuated her appeal. My old pal, Rod La Rocque, one of the greatest romantic stars of that time, had a nasal thing. He worked and he studied, but it just somehow didn't work. Yet many made the transition with no trouble. Garbo became even greater. So did Joan Crawford. And Norma Shearer, with whom I did many pictures, like Mary Pickford, won an Academy Award with her first talkie, *The Divorcee*. Mary Astor was another. In fact, the great majority were like that. But there were a few casualties, not all of which should have been.

Radio was an important part of the sound phenomenon. I went on radio before it got really commercial. We would troop down to the station and go on for free. I'd tell my friends, "You know what I am going to do? I'm going to be on the radio. Be sure to listen." You know, on the old crystal sets. "You listen and I'll say something to you." We'd have little secret codes. Radio developed very quickly. It came to full fruition with the Jack Benny and Amos and Andy weekly broadcasts.

I had a weekly radio show for years at the same time Cecil De Mille had his famous radio show. He narrated for the Lux Radio Theater, and I had the same type of show, the Silver Theater. C. B. and I competed for stars, material, plays, and everything else. As often as they could, Lux would do a radio version of some picture that was not yet released. Louella Parsons also got into the act, by doing the same thing. Competition was quite fierce among us.

It took a lot more time to make a talkie, and it was a lot more expensive than to make a silent film. The studios began to overwork their actors. You'd work until midnight and be back on the set at nine o'clock the next morning. You'd work all night Saturday because you could sleep on your own time on Sunday. Very often you'd work on Sunday, particularly if you were on location. Then when the Screen Actors' Guild finally got organized, they set out to define a working day. They established the working day and judged everything on the basis of the freelance player, not by the contract player. The contract player was getting paid week after week whether he worked or not. The Screen Actors' Guild helped to eliminate many abuses. For instance, if a director didn't know what he wanted, he would experiment, try a thing fifty different ways, all on the actor's time, and run until seven or eight o'clock at night. But when he knew he could only have an actor eight hours that day, he'd do his homework and make things a lot easier for the actor. Then, of course, the five-day week finally came in. That was a bit of a struggle because once a picture is started, the overhead continues twenty-four hours a day, whether you're shooting or not.

What eventually happened to me was that I made too many talking pictures too fast. I had made the first two or three talkies so they knew I was O.K. Whenever they were casting a picture, when they came to the leading man, the reflexive reaction was, "Get Nagel. He can talk." That was the gag in Hollywood. Louie Mayer found that he could make a lot of money loaning me out. He loaned me out for far more than I was receiving from MGM. So long as you were useful to him, nothing in the world was too good for you. But if he could use you, why, he would wring you dry. And I guess he did that with me. In the first two years of talking pictures, I was either featured or starred in thirty-one talking pictures. I mean that would kill anybody. You couldn't avoid me.

Altogether, I made a couple hundred pictures. I don't enjoy seeing myself on the late late shows because I get mad that I'm not being paid for them now. The actor only gets residuals on pictures he makes specifically for television; it is the producer who makes money when "his" picture is released to television. But to tell the truth, I never took much pleasure in seeing myself on screen. It was just a business. That thing up on the screen was the commodity I sold. It was a product, nothing personal.

By '31, '32, I was making fewer and fewer pictures. And then my contract with MGM ran out in '33. They did not renew it. So I hopped back to New York. It was my chance to return for a stage play which I wanted to do and did. I, thereafter, would go back to Hollywood every once in a while to do an occasional picture, but nothing very important.

Then in 1949, I was in a hit play on Broadway, just at the time television was beginning to be important. They were having trouble with a panel show called *Celebrity Time*. I was asked to be the emcee. Since the play ran only six nights a week, Sunday night I could work on TV. I took a crack at it and liked it. John Daly was originally on the panel, but later went to *What's My Line? Celebrity Time* was a good steady job.

As television became popular, Hollywood again went into a panic, just as it did when the talkies came along. But this time two things hit film-makers at once: television and the damnable decision of the Department of Justice forcing producers of motion pictures to divorce themselves from their theaters. What reasoning was used there, God only knows. But it signaled the end of an era. The producers' biggest interest, strangely enough, was not the pictures they made, but their real estate investment in huge theaters. They made movies simply to keep the Capitol, the Music Hall, and the others open. Ten times more money was invested in theaters than in the studios. This is what accounted for the large amount of employment in Hollywood.

Hollywood was always a strange place. Whether you worked or not depended mostly on chance. For example, once they were going to do a picture with British dialogue. "Nobody can write this except P. G. Wodehouse, or a literary man of his caliber. That's it, get P. G. Wodehouse." So they started calling, looking all over for him. They couldn't find him. It turned out that he was right there in the studio. He had an office there for six months and was drawing a salary right along. This is a true story.

And there were many other stories like it, always revolving on one or another luminary. Actors were constantly brought out like that, but then the pictures they were supposed to make got postponed or canceled. And they would sit there. If you're an artist, you want to work. You don't want to be pensioned off at the height of your career. For instance, young Carl Laemmle, Jr.'s, father had said, "If Irving Thalberg could run a studio when he was twenty-one years old, my boy can do the same thing," and Carl Jr. was put in charge of Universal. They got ready to shoot *Bad Sister*, a picture with three people in it nobody had ever heard of, brought out from New York under seven-year contracts with very small salaries. "Get Nagel. See if you can borrow Nagel from MGM." So they borrowed Nagel, and Nagel came over to make a picture. Well, the little girl that had the leading part—Carl just thought was going to set the world on fire. The three other people, he called in one at a time and told them they had nothing to offer. They were colorless. No fault of theirs. They just didn't photograph. He suggested they all go back to New York. The people were Bette Davis, Humphrey Bogart, and Rosalind Russell.

At the same time, Irving Thalberg let Margaret Sullavan go from MGM. Carl Laemmle, Jr., signed her up at Universal, and she became one of the brightest stars at Universal. Around the same time Fred Astaire made a test at MGM and . . . I mean, this is famous. Somebody got a copy of the test results: "Lean, thin hair, can't be photographed very well, not much personality, and so forth." The last item: "Also dances." They let him go.

I knew Thalberg very well, first at Universal and then when he came over to MGM. I had gone from Paramount to the Goldwyn Studio in one of those crazy switches. Richard Dix was unhappy at Goldwyn; I was unhappy at Paramount. So Paramount wrangled Dick away from Goldwyn. To get even with Jesse Lasky at Paramount, Abe Lehr, who was in charge of Goldwyn then, started negotiating with me and I signed up with Goldwyn, not because he particularly wanted me, but because Jesse had taken Richard Dix. I was with Goldwyn at the time the merger took place between Metro-Goldwyn, and Louis Mayer, who had been an independent producer. Two-thirds of the pictures I did after that were under the aegis of Irving Thalberg. Each of these pictures was assigned a producer like Harry Rapf. Even Dave Selznick was a producer at MGM.

Thalberg was never satisfied with a picture. He put MGM at the top of the heap, made it the Tiffany of Hollywood. How? By originating the retake. Up until Thalberg, you had a schedule, you finished the picture, and that was the end of it. Good, bad, or indifferent, it was released. People were in the habit of going to movies. Whatever their quality, they made money. Don't misunderstand. No one made bad pictures on purpose, but obviously, with fifty-two pictures a year, all of them couldn't be great works of art. Thalberg conceived the idea that a picture could be redone. It occurred to him after he had seen a film and said, "You know that little sequence there. If we could just change that, it would alter the whole picture." This was unheard of.

"You mean call these people back?"

"Yes, call them back."

They called them all back, spent a few thousand dollars more, and the picture turned out to be terrific instead of just ordinary. The retake became policy. They would finish the picture. They would take it out and preview it. Then they'd come back and fix it up. On one picture I made with them, they shot three-fourths of it over again. Irving also had an uncanny ability to see exactly what was wrong with something and to be able to doctor it up. You know, it's easy to find fault, but then what are you supposed to do? In von Stroheim's picture *The Merry Widow*, there were scenes which, at that time, were insuperably offensive to censors. So Thalberg cut it himself. He was extraordinarily clever. But he killed himself working. Every night when I'd go home and walk out that front gate, Thalberg's office was right up there. No matter what time I went home, his light was still on. That was the boss. He could do everything.

To me, the writer is always number one. There's nothing wrong with the theater, with television, with the motion picture, that writers can't cure. Writing is where the money should go, not to these million-dollar stars. They should get million-dollar writers. Now I'm talking against my own craft. Television would be great today if one writer could be paid enough to work on the next episode of, say *Bonanza* or *Gunsmoke*. If they could pay him enough that he could spend three months on an episode instead of having to knock one out every two weeks, everyone of them would be good. A good writer should have to do only a couple scripts a year. Pay $50,000 a script. What's the point of making any more money? This is the heart and soul of any phase of show business. Take radio, theater, and television—if you have a good script, you don't need anything else. With a bad script, you can get the best actors, the best directors, the best everything else, and you're still lost.

If I had it to do over again, I'd avoid overexposure. The fault was really my own. I could have gone on strike. I was young, I was healthy, and I loved to work. I just didn't think. If I had thought, I would have gone to Mayer with, "Look, L. B., this is too much." When I got to where I was only working on two pictures at once, it was practically a vacation. Very often I was actually working on three or four different pictures at the same time. How can you do that? Well, they've got ways of shooting around you.

I remember doing a picture with William deMille and another one at the same time with Cecil De Mille. I'd work with William in the morning and Cecil in the afternoon. I'd have to ask myself, 'Gee, what part am I playing now? Then I would work with Fred Niblo in the evening. And the next morning I would go out with Harry Rapf. We were doing a big musical, *The Hollywood Revue of 1929*. It was the first musical with no story, really a review. Jack Benny and I played the two masters of ceremonies. Everybody said Harry Rapf was crazy for making it. It wouldn't make a dime. But it was a sensational box-office hit because every star at MGM was used. The audience thought they were getting a million dollars' worth of entertainment for a buck. And they were. Now that thing is shown on television again and again and again. All they've done is change the title to *The Hollywood Revue*.

When I was young and healthy, I loved working so much. I bragged, "I worked eighteen hours yesterday and I feel great." I had one stretch in which I went thirty-six hours without a break. They had to stop twice to let me shave: all day and all night, twenty-four hours and twelve hours the next day.

I was never a big star, so I never had a role like Moses or D'Artagnan. But being assigned thirty-one pictures in twenty-four months, I had an opportunity to play every type of part. The variety, though, didn't keep me from becoming a drug on the market. My wife would say, "Well, let's go out and see a movie tonight." We'd get in the car and discover that I'm playing at the Paramount Theater. And I'm playing at the Universal

Theater. And the MGM Theater. We couldn't find a theater where I wasn't playing. So we'd go back home. I was an epidemic.

I'd love to work in Hollywood again. All they have to do is ask me. Hollywood is such a nebulous term. It covers so much territory now. It's the most dreadful place in the world to be if you're not working. It's worse than being in a cemetery. And it's a great place to be if you are working. In New York, nobody knows whether you're working because there are so many different things that you can do here, and they care less. Out there, it's pictures or television and that's it. In New York, there's even a surprising amount of radio, and there's always the possibility of a play. But so far as Hollywood is concerned, as I said, all they have to do is ask me.

BLANCHE SWEET

M Y FATHER happened to be in California when I was born in Chicago. The year was 1896; Mother was seventeen and a half. Father was much older, a handsome, charming, and attractive man. He was a champagne salesman. He just went around, led a very gay social life, and drank nothing but wine. A fabulous person, he did rather well. Mother died when I was a year and a half old. She was still terribly young and very beautiful, a professional dancer. My mother's mother brought me up. I suppose that's why when Grandmother was left with me, she gravitated me toward the theater. She had never been connected with it herself, except through my mother. We were poor, darn poor, but nobody had ever had kinder upbringing than I. Our troubles were not serious. I had no difficulty adjusting to any condition that arose—and I'm sure it was my grandmother's care that gave me that feeling. After all, when you are an only child and you have one grandmother who makes up your entire family, she has to make up for all the missing members. I wasn't even aware of my father's absence. It just seemed to me to be a normal thing. I knew that other children had fathers. I didn't, and that was that. When psychologists speak of broken families and broken homes, I wonder if they don't attribute too much to the fact that both parents aren't around.

I grew up all over the country, maybe because of money and my grandmother's relatives—first, second, third cousins, something like that. Since she came from Cincinnati, we soon moved there, and it was there that I made my debut. As a baby I was carried on stage in *Blue Jeans*, a

Blanche Sweet and Conrad Nagel in *Tess of the D'Urbervilles*, Metro Goldwyn. 1924.

popular melodrama of the day. It was a Pollard Stock Company production. Stock companies then were quite the fashion. Every city had one it was proud of.

We didn't stay in Cincinnati for long. I never stayed very long in any one place. Even during the good many years I spent in California making pictures, I jumped back and forth from the East Coast to the West Coast, constantly changing. By age four, I was in vaudeville. I don't remember my sketch too well, but I can tell you one thing I did in it. I ran away from home with a little boy about the same age. When we returned, we were given bread and jam which I looked forward to at every performance. It was fun.

Richard Mansfield had a play which included parts for children. Instead of carrying them around, to cut expenses he recruited them wherever he appeared. He could get them easily because the children didn't have too much to do. When he came to Cincinnati, my grandmother applied with me in hand, and I was selected from among the other children. Then Mr. Mansfield came along, and I guess he liked my blonde hair. But I didn't like him. I wouldn't do a thing. I balked like a mule. I can remember my grandmother taking me aside and begging me to accept. I said I didn't like his face. It was my excuse for refusing to play with him. They even offered me the Christmas tree that was used in the play, all the toys that went with it—anything if I would just cooperate. I finally gave in. After that, as a veteran of seven, I went with Chauncey Olcott. The steady work meant security for my grandmother and myself. We stayed with Olcott for three years, three seasons of traveling around the country. Throughout this period my grandmother gave me schooling. She tutored me in reading, writing, arithmetic. I read incessantly. I didn't go to school until I was nine years old.

Then quite suddenly my father appeared when we were playing Denver, Colorado. He chanced to go to the theater and saw me. At that time my grandmother used *her* name for me, Blanche Alexander. He recognized the name and came around. It was the first he'd seen me since my infancy. He wanted us to join him in San Francisco. We did. I went to school there for a short time—until the earthquake and fire came along. That put an end to school, and almost to us. We were right in the midst of everything. I thought it was great, a wonderful show. We went to the Presidio and lived in a tent. What more could a nine-year-old child ask? Of course, my poor grandmother must have been terrified. Our hotel was dynamited, and we lost all our possessions. I ended up in a private school in Berkeley for a few years. Over vacations I made a couple of stock appearances in Oakland and San Francisco. When I started going to school, I used my full name, Sarah Blanche Sweet. I always wanted people to call me Sarah. It would have been a lovely name—Sarah Sweet. Nobody would have believed that that was a real name. In fact, nobody believes it now because so many actors take on rather syrupy stage names.

My grandmother actually taught me to be an actress. She particularly helped me to memorize my parts. I was rather good at that. A short time after we would open in a play, I knew everybody's lines. I could have stepped in for any of them. Apparently I had great self-assurance. I lost some of it later on.

After we moved to Berkeley, my father remarried. He lived in San Francisco, and when he didn't come over to see me, my grandmother would take me over to visit him. Grandmother finally decided that it would be better for us to go back East into the theater, but instead I took up dancing, which I loved. I auditioned for Gertrude Hoffman, who was a very well-known vaudeville performer. She gave imitations of various people and an especially good one of Isadora Duncan in *The Blue Danube*. Once we did one of her dances, dressed in little chiffon wisps, skipping around the stage barefoot. To this day, when I hear the opening bars of "The Blue Danube," I feel like kicking off my shoes and skipping around. I loved that.

Then I made a picture with the Edison Company in 1908. I did two pictures for them, as an extra in the first and with a small part in the second. Someone suggested we go down to the Biograph Company. I made out a form, left it, and didn't hear a word. We were completely ignored. I did a few things in between, a couple of plays, and then somebody suggested that I go down again and ask for Mr. Griffith. He was the man in charge there, the director, producer, everything. We saw him and he put me to work that day. Just a bit part, a walk-on thing, in a picture called *A Corner in Wheat*. All I remember was that I played the New Year. An elderly character in the company, Mr. Miller, played the Old Year. He went out and I came in—with another wisp of chiffon wrapped around me.

The transition from the stage to film presented no problem. I never had any difficulty going from one medium to another. I enjoy working in them all: radio, television, silent pictures, talking films. It just seems that whenever there was a change, I changed along with it. The stage experience I had as a child gave me confidence in myself. After I made quite a few pictures, Mr. Griffith decided it would be best to take his company to California, but just for the winter. In the meantime, I had an offer from Gertrude Hoffman to go dancing with her again. Mr. Griffith wanted me to stay with him. I had to say, "I'm awfully sorry, but I'm going to go dancing." He was to have been paid me $125 a week. Hoffman offered me $40. Imagine what my grandmother thought. She had lots of influence with me, but every once in a while, I got independent notions in my blonde head. I wanted or didn't want to do something. Maybe I really wasn't as bad as I sound, but I was stubborn, you know. So I went dancing. Hoffman had her own act in a musical revue. I came on between the first act, comprised of one group, and Hoffman, who had another act with her own company. It was a separate unit. When that ended, an entire season had passed.

I did a play called *Charlotte Temple*. And I was fired. It was the first time that that happened to me. You may be sure it hurt. But the reason was a good one. I played a young girl who elopes from a convent with a reverend. Because she doesn't know that he is one, she has terrible experiences straight through to an unhappy death. My lover and the villain have a duel while I'm shrieking and screaming and falling down steps. I didn't have enough maturity to understand the role. I was then between thirteen and fourteen. The girl had to be young, and yet, I was too young to play it.

That led me back to making pictures. Grandmother suggested that we write to the Griffith Company and see if the opening was still there. They invited me to come on out. We went. That was the real beginning. I stayed in pictures with Mr. Griffith until I left for the Lasky Company which Cecil De Mille and Lasky had just started. Now I was box-office, with a name that made money, and they needed somebody. I went to Mr. Griffith hoping that he would tell me not to leave. But he didn't. "No, I think it's good for you. You know enough to get out on your own now and it'll be best for you." He said the same thing to Lillian Gish and Mae Marsh, too.

I doubt if any of us wanted to leave because we were all devoted to him. There wasn't a member of that company, male or female, who didn't love that man. It's difficult to explain this devotion. We had great respect for his ability and understanding as a director. He opened up vista after vista. He was a marvelous actor himself, although he didn't make good as an actor. One minute he was discouraging to you, and the next minute he was inspiring you. I say "discouraging to you" because if you weren't getting the scene as he felt you should, he would show you how it should be done. He'd show you so beautifully that you felt, "Oh, I'd never be able to do it that way," and you'd sulk and mope and *then* you'd get to work and do the best you could. Did you know that he was also interested in singing? Mr. Griffith had a beautiful, deep, resonant voice with coloring to it. All in all, there was something magnetic about him that everybody felt. If *he* told you something was good, that made your day. You wanted so to please Mr. Griffith, you considered him and his judgment more than that of the public. It was always the director who mattered. *Mister* Griffith: everyone called him Mister. Once or twice I heard him called Larry, but not by anybody in the company. It must have been a visitor, maybe somebody who knew him before he went into pictures.

When I got into the company, it was well established and was doing all right financially. I don't know what their pictures sold for. They were only one-reelers. Mary Pickford had been there, but Mary left for an independent company before I came down to the studio. It was after the first or second season in California that Mae Marsh appeared. I was also there when Dorothy and Lillian Gish appeared. We're all around the same age. So many people have asked (and I can't answer) how it happened that we all arrived practically at the same time. Forgive me if I include myself in this group: we *were* all talented and almost all had had stage experience. It wasn't that Mr. Griffith was looking for fourteen-year-old girls because Florence Lawrence and Marion Leonard, both blondes, had also been with him. They were the older, more established, leading women. Florence Lawrence left to go to the independents, and Marion Leonard was there in my time. The group I have in mind was composed of Mary Pickford, Mae Marsh, Lillian and Dorothy Gish, and myself. Mae had had no stage experience whatsoever. She was a gifted girl with a lovely, expressive face. Her work was, naturally, helped by Griffith's direction, but she had native talent. All the rest came with stage experience and that, too, was enhanced by Griffith's direction.

I made the first, so-called big picture, his *Judith of Bethulia*, and that was a breakthrough, a step forward, because it was to be four reels. We'd only gotten to the production of two reels, but even that was thought to be, you know, amazing. Those were released separately. One week one reel would come out, and the next week, the other reel. But Griffith conceived the idea with *Judith* of making a longer, larger picture. It was to cost $50,000! Everybody in the front office fainted. The businessmen in the East cried, "No. It can't be done. It will lose money. The public won't accept it." But Griffith fought, and they reluctantly consented. We started the picture in California and finished that year in the new studio. It was a real high point and a great success.

By that time we had formed an alliance with the Klaw and Erlanger Company, which wanted to enter the picture field. They had many plays but no titles to them. The arrangement wasn't the kind with which Griffith could be pleased. He was a one-man show. He had to do everything himself: develop the original idea, carry it through, do it his own way, spend what he wanted on it. He was never good at working with anybody else—except Billy Bitzer. They were like fingers on a hand, and they got along beautifully. But that was different because Billy wasn't in a position of control. He would have ideas and then bat them back and forth with Mr. Griffith—you couldn't really know whose idea it was. Often they didn't know themselves. From a control standpoint, from a management standpoint, the new arrangement was difficult for Griffith. The Biograph Company had great confidence in him and let him proceed as he wished, but when they merged with the Erlanger Company, he wasn't very happy.

He was supposed to supervise pictures. We had two floors of studio space: the top floor for daylight and the other which had to be artificially lighted. We were shooting two pictures simultaneously, which wasn't what he wanted to do. They were plays. Not that he objected to doing plays; he did them repeatedly after that. Anyway he left.

On the eve of his departure, he invited several people to go with him, but he didn't say a word to me and I was heartbroken. I didn't want to be left behind with the thought that he didn't want me. I was the last person he asked. I don't know what got into that man, whether he did it deliberately or just couldn't make up his mind. I suspect he just wanted to teach me a lesson. I was the rebel of the company with rather strong ideas. We used to battle a little, occasionally, and maybe that wasn't altogether tolerable to him. So he made all his preparations and then finally asked me to come along. Most likely he had intended to from the beginning because everything was all set for me.

We did Paul Armstrong's *Escape,* a well-known play. Mr. Griffith moved us into a tiny studio. Before, we had had the big one on 169th Street, built especially for our company, which was the apple of his eye. We'd started out in a two-by-four down at 11 East 14th Street and then built the big one from which he walked out. Back we went to a little studio, not the same one, but on 23rd Street and Broadway, actually a small loft. We started making *Escape.* This represented a radical advance for Mr. Griffith: he had formed his own company, the Griffith Company with everything the way he wanted it and he'd staked his all on this first picture —and I got scarlet fever. That was simply appalling. It tied everything up when we were at least halfway through. We were impatiently awaiting the release, all our money was invested, everything depended on the outcome. I had to go to the hospital. I stayed there for three or four weeks. Eventually I straggled out and we finished *Escape.* I don't think I was ever forgiven. I felt so terrible, you've no idea. Things turned out all right, but the experience panicked everyone. You have to remember the horrible financial situation. Players didn't ordinarily have any money invested, so when I say "we," I mean that from an interested standpoint. Everything was "us," "we," "our company." We were very clannish. And we were very snooty, too. The news had reached us that we were good—that we had the best director and producer and, without a doubt, made the best pictures. I'm afraid we felt pretty important.

Although the girls of the company are so often mentioned, we also had wonderful male actors. Henry Walthall was one of the best in both films and stage. The men were never given enough credit: Arthur Johnson, James Kirkwood, Lionel Barrymore. They all came from the theater. Robert Harron was a young fellow in our age group who had been a prop boy, doing general errands. You did everything in those days; there weren't a

lot of specialists around. You were just as likely to carry on a piece of
scenery as to put on your make-up. At any rate, I don't know how Bobby
got his start, whether Mr. Griffith had the idea that Bobby could act or
whether Bobby asked for a part. But he used to hang around all the time
and watch. He was interested all right and somehow started playing. Bobby
was like Mae. He had that natural gift, the inborn talent. He absorbed a
great deal just watching. Bobby became one of the finest, most sensitive
actors of all. He played in *Intolerance* as Mae's husband. How lovely he
was in that. What a beautiful young actor. But Bobby died young. It was
a tragic end and a real loss.

Anita Loos began to write for Mr. Griffith when he was still with Biograph. I remember that she was present one day and found out afterwards
who she was. She was a fourteen-year-old script writer. It's odd that so
many of us were young, but we were in a young business, not yet part of
an art form. Griffith turned it into an art which hadn't existed before him.
And we who worked for him didn't realize how great he was, at least not
in the beginning. I myself had no clear impression of him for the first two
or three months. I wasn't overcome at all. Not until I went back and
really started working with him did I begin to realize the magnitude of his
contribution.

I didn't see too much of him after I left the studio. I visited with all
my fellow actors and eventually saw him again. But I never heard from
him. He never said I'd done a good picture or a bad picture. He made no
comment after the time I left, and I've never been able to figure that out.
Perhaps he was hurt, which is something he would not have admitted.
How could somebody have wanted to go off and leave the company?

Mary Pickford was the first to do it. She came back and then went
off again, the year before she joined Zukor's Famous Players. A few
months later I left, going over to the Varsity Company. It's true that we
weren't making much money with him. He didn't pay well. We worked
for the love of the man and for the company. Even Mr. Griffith didn't
make much money. I don't think he was ever very far ahead on account
of his constant ambition to do something bigger, better, and finer.

I left before *The Birth of a Nation*. I was to have been in it, but they
hadn't even started rehearsing when I received another offer. When I
came back to visit, he had *Intolerance* with the Babylon scenery set up
and made much to-do about it. He never said a word to me like, "How
are you doing?" or "How do you like it?" Instead, he took me across the
street to see the set. He was trying to impress me, and I admit that I was
most impressed. That was a tremendous thing, the likes of which we had
never seen in pictures before. I thought, "I'm sorry I'm not going to be a
part of it." The set was beautiful and so was the picture.

I recently saw *Intolerance* again. I had some charm bracelets on, three

D. W. Griffith, Blanche Sweet, unidentified gentleman, and Bessie Love. 1930.

Blanche Sweet and Ronald Colman in the MGM production of *The Sporting Venus*. 1925.

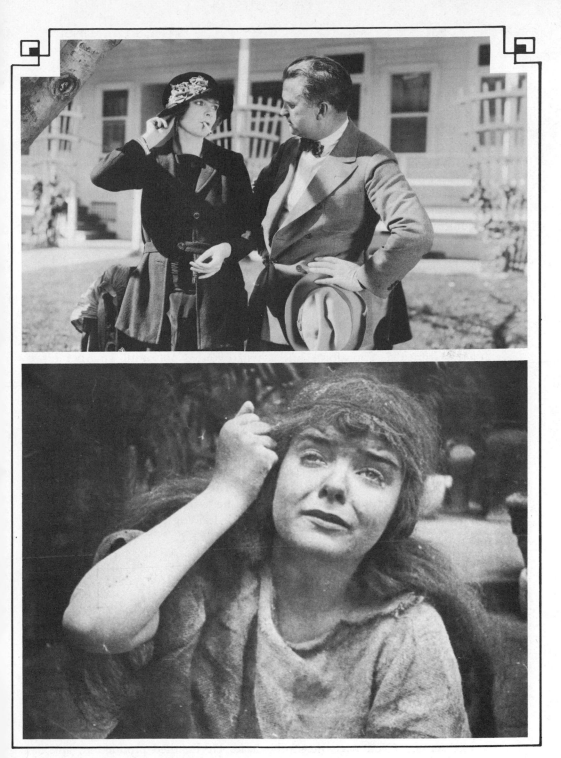

Blanche Sweet and Thomas H. Ince, producer of Eugene O'Neill's *Anna Christie*. At the Ince Studio, Culver City. 1923.

Blanche Sweet in D. W. Griffith's *Judith of Bethulia*. 1914.

of them, which made a little tinkling sound. Everytime I moved my arm and this little tinkle came, the woman sitting in front of me turned around and glared. Since it wasn't a sound film, my tinkling bracelet didn't interfere with her hearing. She just wanted complete silence. I got so I was afraid to move my arm. Once the picture unfolded, the woman became so intent that I could have shot off a cannon in back of her and she would not have heard it. The second lovely thing occurred during a melodramatic sequence. Bobby Harron is to be executed, and Mae Marsh, his wife, and two others are in a car racing against time to get a pardon to save him. A woman down front who wasn't an exhibitionist, as I could tell from the quality and tone of her voice, exclaimed right from her heart, "Hurry!" Isn't that extraordinary? You can still get wrapped up in a picture like that after all these years.

It was 1914 when I left the company. The Lasky Company made me a handsome offer. I believe it was $500 a week. I can't recall what I was getting at the Griffith Company, but I know it wasn't anywhere near that. When I went to Lasky, I was frightened. I knew that a great deal was expected of me. I didn't know whether I had enough or how much was Mr. Griffith's. You don't know what you've got until you get off by yourself. I was scared. The funny thing is that Cecil De Mille, several years later, said he was scared of me. But I was scared of him and of the company. I was scared of the world. I didn't know how I was going to behave. I planned to try very hard. He directed my first picture, *Warrens of Virginia*, and he directed my second picture, *The Captive*. He later confided, "You used to look at me so intensely, I thought you were saying, 'What a fool he is' to yourself." Cecil hadn't any reputation for pictures at that time. He was just starting, he was learning, and I, looking at him, was trying very hard to understand what he wanted, how he felt about the part and the play. There we were, both looking peculiarly at each other, each scared to death. But we got along.

After the two pictures with Cecil De Mille, we never worked together again. There were various reasons. In a company like that, a director wasn't confined to one star. You changed about. I also got star billing, whereas with Mr. Griffith, nothing about the players was credited. But the public learned our names anyway. At one time they tried awfully hard to keep our names from being known so that we wouldn't become box-office and other people would outbid the company for us.

As I say, I worked with several directors. William deMille was a very bright man. Cecil, his brother, outshown him, but I think William was more intelligent. Cecil was not stupid, but he was, above all, a showman. He made pictures that would appeal to the public, which indeed they did. I think that Billy deMille could make finer pictures. That happens in Hollywood. Cecil was the studio head. He handled production, and Sam

Goldwyn was there too. They came to a parting of the ways. I never knew Lasky or Goldwyn too well because they were exclusively in finance. We'd see them now and then at parties.

I worked more than anything else. If you're making a picture, you don't have any social life, or you're not supposed to, and usually you don't feel like it. Only Saturday night was reserved for play, and that, not always. It was the one night you could go to a party, stay out late, and sleep till all hours the next day. Otherwise, you worked, went home, had your dinner, and got to bed as quickly as possible. You were tired, you'd worked a long stretch, and you had to be up at the crack of dawn. Then you didn't make a piddling one or two pictures a year. You made a lot of them. And it was great fun. You tried not to do a picture you didn't like. I always made that attempt, but I didn't always succeed. For instance, I was considered a dramatic actress, but I got tired of playing dramatic roles. I wanted to vary my field. "I can't go on playing dope fiends and kleptomaniacs. Give me comedy to do." But they claimed, "People don't expect that of you." It's the same old problem that's plagued most actors and actresses. ZaSu Pitts tried it the other way as a tragedian in Frank Norris's *McTeague*. The film version was Erich von Stroheim's *Greed*. But the public didn't accept her in that role. In time they did give me a comedy. I loved it, hugely enjoying myself, but I went back to dramatic roles.

I stayed at the Lasky Company for two years. Then in 1916, I organized my own company, Blanche Sweet Productions, and we made a war movie called *Unpardonable Sins*. We made another one which didn't work out too well. The motion picture business was in an incredibly fluid state. Different people were constantly coming, and conflict arose between directors and producers. As a result, directors started forming their own companies. So conflicts arose between directors and exhibitors. Everybody wanted the last word and the most money. The First National organization was formed. While controlling production, it also exhibited films. After my company dissolved, I made any number of pictures for them which eventually led to *Anna Christie*.

O'Neill loved our *Anna Christie*. It's the only film of a play of his he did like. Pauline Moore was in the original stage play. Then Thomas Ince bought *Anna* for me. It was the first O'Neill play that had ever been done as a movie. For the longest time, we hadn't dared to do unhappy endings. Ince deserves great credit for challenging tradition. He was a good director and producer, but one who always used what he thought was going to be popular. He bravely departed from his own policy, and produced *Anna*. Of course, I was delighted. Those of us influenced by Griffith wanted to improve pictures. We knew we weren't doing great things and wanted to do at least better things. Doing them and making money didn't always go together. I was very happy to have the opportunity Ince gave me. *Anna Christie* didn't have a happy ending, but it was successful, the public liked it, and O'Neill liked it. I was frightened that he wouldn't and elated that he did. O'Neill was biased against actresses. If he praised an actress, it was more than a real compliment, it was a tribute.

Similarly, *Tess of the D'Urbervilles* had an unhappy ending. We wanted to do a great story by a fine writer, and we believed it would be good for pictures. By that time, my husband and I were under contract to Metro-Goldwyn. We were making our own pictures with them; that is, I did them in association with, then, my husband, Marshall Neilan, who was a director and a producer. (Later I was married to Raymond Hackett. You probably know of him as a very fine stage and film actor and director.) We worked on a percentage basis: they shared half the profits, and we held complete control of production. But then the exhibiting end of the company got worried. They were afraid that the public wouldn't accept a sad ending. It was a fierce fight all over again. Neilan proposed that we make an alternative ending—on the condition that we run both and see how they went. We wound up with the unhappy ending, a happy ending for us.

In the twenties, things were very different from the previous decade, different in so many ways that you can't just say this or that way. At the tail end, as a climax, talking pictures came in, and we went bobbing around in every direction. Censorship also took hold in the twenties after one or two uncalled-for scandals concerning actors prompting the morality clause. That clause was put into every contract. What a perfectly foolish thing! It confined you to "the usual activities of people" and stipulated that you were not to cause any trouble by scandalous behavior. They began by censoring off-screen behavior which grew into the censoring of films as well. De Mille and others put suggestive material into their epics. I felt even then that such stuff was more funny than dangerous, unintentionally funny, of course.

The role of writers changed drastically. At first we had no scripts, no stories, and that changed and changed again. Anita Loos was an early one. Frances Marion was a highly paid writer. You'd talk to whoever wrote your script before it was finished. Quite often you consulted with them about how it was going, and the writer would come to you for ideas. Writers say that this relationship doesn't exist anymore. One told me recently, "Writers are nobodies. They are well paid, but they have nothing to say about pictures."

I always tried to be selective in choosing my material. Once I was annoyed with myself because I didn't stick to what I had decided. Once when we were in England, we saw Gladys Cooper playing the wife in *Diplomacy*. Florence Reed had played the other role, Countess Zita, in stock in Los Angeles. The countess was a villainous, bad woman. I had always wanted to play a part like that, and I was enchanted with the play. I said, "That's it. I want to play *Diplomacy*. Only, I don't want to play the wife. I want to play Zita. I'll wear a black wig, and I'll be bad." I cabled back for the rights to *Diplomacy* and got them.

Then when it came time to produce the picture, I heard a chorus of protest, "You mustn't play Zita. Your public isn't looking for that." I had played *Anna Christie* and my public wasn't offended. I don't know why they would have objected to Zita, but I let them talk me out of it. They made an awful uproar about it, saying, "You do it if you want to go against everybody's best judgment." They ganged up on me. It was silly of me not to have stood up for my rights: I would have been much better as Zita than I was as the wife.

I also did too much just for money. I was ashamed of myself, but I couldn't resist. Ten thousand dollars a week is awfully hard to resist. Why else would I have done *A Lady from Hell?* That title alone should have stopped me. But, you know, I went to John McCormick, who was general manager at First National. I discussed the offer with him and asked First National to let me do it. He replied,

"You could, but I wouldn't if I were you."

"John, how can I turn down all that money?"

"I see your point. Oh, I guess this once wouldn't hurt too much. But don't make a practice of it."

I've forgotten, but I don't remember seeing that picture. I'm sure I saw the rushes, and let's say I wasn't very proud. But there were other wonderful high points that made these situations less damaging and unfortunate than they might have been.

I ought to tell you about Mr. Griffith and silent pictures. Mr. Griffith didn't insist on our learning too many lines. They weren't necessary. We said a few things because movement of the mouth had to take place. People playing a scene together have to say something to each other, but we said as little as possible. Still, what we said had to be proper. A certain number of lip readers were in the audience. We kept talk down to a minimum because, after all, a mouth that's moving constantly and says nothing audible doesn't truly convey the scene.

And then came sound. In a way, I mourned the passing of silent films. For my personal fortunes, the change couldn't have come at a worse time. I was in England making a picture for Herbert Wilcox. It was called *The Woman in White*, written by one of their standard writers. We had practically completed it when news came to us that *The Jazz Singer* would open. That shot our silent picture to pieces. Either we had to remake the whole thing in sound which involved lots of money, or just wash it up and absorb a terrific loss. There was some indecision. They rushed around

trying to determine whether sound had come to stay. It came to them that
the best idea would be to release the picture immediately in England before
The Jazz Singer got over there. They'd extract what money they could by
racing against sound.

The sound wasn't any too good either at that point. When I came
back to the U.S., I stopped in Chicago between trains and dashed to the
theater to see another sound film, *The Lion and the Mouse*. It was a
standard old play starring Lionel Barrymore, with one scene in which he
swept a plastic bust off its pedestal. It fell, and you heard the crash half
a minute later! That kind of thing lasted quite a while until they settled
down and started to synchronize with greater efficiency.

My first talking picture was *Night Hostess*. The mike was set, and
you couldn't move it. Some of us wondered about that, "Why do we just
have to stand in a knot, hardly able to lift a finger, glued to that mike?"
We started experimenting, taking little chances, moving around. Things
eventually worked out.

I left Hollywood in 1931, came back to New York, and did a play
with Raymond Hackett, whom I'd met *once* out in California. Only once.
Then we did the play together and that was it. We were married a year
later. He was a wonderful, wonderful man. We had great happiness together. We enjoyed working together. He was a fine actor, did some
directing also, and made quite a success in pictures, like *The Trial of Mary
Dugan*, which he had played on the stage, and *Madame X* with Ruth
Chamberlain. We did a number of plays that year together. I've never
made another picture.

Oddly enough, when I was doing *The Petrified Forest* with Leslie
Howard and I had a run-of-the-play contract with Arthur Hopkins and
Gilbert Miller, Metro-Goldwyn-Mayer invited me to do a picture. If I had
gone to Walter Hopkins and asked him, he would no doubt have released
me. He was a decent fellow, a fine director, a great man of the theater.
But I didn't ask. I felt honorably involved. I said I wanted to do theater,
that I had a big, successful play on my hands, and that I wasn't going to
walk out on it. So later they did the film. I wasn't in it. I think Metro-
Goldwyn-Mayer was angry because I wouldn't do the picture. But by then,
after all, I had had a full career.

MAE MARSH

I WAS BORN in 1895 in Madrid, New Mexico. My father was a traveling auditor for the Santa Fe Railroad. Whenever they opened a new station, he would set up the accounting system and then move on. He was working at one of the new stations from Albuquerque to Santa Fe when I was born. There were five other children besides myself, and because of my father's traveling, each of us was born in a different state.

My mother was from Asheville, North Carolina. Her mother was married to Edward Tenbrock Warne from St. Louis. He and his friend Caldwell invented barbed wire. My cousin John Warne Gates, nicknamed "Bet-a-million" Gates, who was just starting out as a salesman, sold barbed wire all over the West. Eventually he did so well that he bought out Grandpa and Caldwell and took over the business himself. He began producing it in a factory and brought it to Texas, where the people all thought it was wonderful to have such a thing. Ultimately, this invention changed the entire character of the West.

My grandfather on my father's side was Walter Marsh, a professor of English at the University of Kansas in Lawrence. William Allen White speaks of him in one of his books.

My father died quite young, mother remarried, and we moved to San Francisco. I was in the San Francisco earthquake, and my stepfather was killed in it. My mother was then brought down to Los Angeles by her great-aunt, and we youngsters were placed in school there. My oldest sister, Marguerite, was studying to be a nurse at the French hospital and stayed in San Francisco after my great-aunt took us to Los Angeles. She married and later became an actress in New York. She was with the Raymond Hitchcock Company as a chorus girl. When she came back to Los Angeles with her daughter to join the family, she went into pictures, beginning at the old Burbank Theater with Charlie Ruggles.

I always wanted to be an actress, too. In fact, when I was in school, I remember having to write an essay on what you wanted to be when you grew up. I was about eleven years old then. My answer was unequivocal —I wanted to and would be an actress.

So when I was seventeen and my sister Marguerite was doing pictures with D. W. Griffith and Mack Sennett, I got her to take me out to the studios. She told Griffith that her kid sister would like to work in movies and asked for a job for me. At the time Griffith was rehearsing and suggested we speak to Sennett. Marguerite was working for Mack Sennett that day, and he said, "Oh, yes, she can be one of the girls sitting on the porch." We went down to Redondo Beach, to the old Redondo Hotel. It was a beautiful hotel with a veranda across it and the lovely rocking chairs they used to have in the old days. I sat there on the porch, watched Mabel Normand swim, got a free lunch, and $3.50. I was a millionaire. I never wanted to go to school again.

School to me was just a bore. I asked mother's permission to work in pictures, and she said, "If you continue to work and earn money, it's all right with me." I asked Mr. Sennett if I could come back and he said, "No, I won't be needing you tomorrow. We'll see if Mr. Griffith can use you." Mr. Griffith was still rehearsing, but he said, "Yes, I can use her. I'm doing *Ramona* with Mary Pickford and Dorothy Bernard. She can come out and work with me at the studio at seven o'clock in the morning." I was there on time, and we drove to location at San Gabriel. There I was, standing around not knowing what to do, when Mr. Griffith said, "Well, don't you know what to do? Get your clothes."

"What clothes?"

"Well, all right," and he called Bobby Harron. "Have this child put on a señorita costume and have her hair done." He said, "Do you know how to make up?"

I said no, so he called Mary Pickford and asked Mary if she would make me up. So Mary Pickford made me up and Dorothy Barnard fixed my hair for me. I worked there three days, and from then on, I did extras about three times a week. Mr. Griffith insisted, though, that I finish my schooling, so mother arranged for a teacher to come to the house, Mrs. Stokes, who put me through the rigors of high school and college.

When Mr. Griffith began rehearsing a picture called *Man's Genesis*, I got my first chance for a lead role. In the film a girl had to wear a grass skirt which would show all her limbs. Mary Pickford didn't want to do

Mae Marsh in *Polly of the Circus*. 1917.

that. "Give the part to the little girl. She doesn't mind showing her limbs." In those days, they wore skirts down to the ankles. You couldn't show the calf of your leg. And I said, "Oh, yes, I would like to do it." It was immaterial to me whether I showed my limbs or not.

I received five dollars a day when I worked on *Man's Genesis*. Mr. Griffith would tell me exactly what to do. On the first day, he explained, "I want you to sit on that rock wall over there. This boy you're sitting next to, you're very, very much in love with him. But don't do anything but look at him like you're in love with him. Have you ever been in love?" And I said oh yes, which I hadn't. He said, "Just think that you're terribly in love and look up at him shy-like." So I did, and then he said, "Look up at him again and then put your head down," which I did. Then he said, "Now get up and run away." So I got up and ran away. That was my first acting part. I loved it. I said to Mr. Griffith, "When am I going to do it again?" He said, "You've done it once. You can't do it again. That was fine. Maybe you can do something else tomorrow."

Mr. Griffith put on one two-reel picture a year, which was his prize picture of that year. Naturally, Mary thought she would get the part because she was the star. But when rehearsals were called, he didn't call her. He said, "Mary, as long as you refused to do that shot, I'm going to refuse to give you the part in this picture." He called me. I think Mary was a little angry with me for a while, but not for long. And over the years we've been great friends. However, she soon stopped working with Mr. Griffith and went to New York to play in *The Good Little Devil* with David Belasco. I believe it created some friction between Mr. Griffith and Mary for quite a while.

Later, when he was shooting at Biograph in New York, I got a telegram from him which said that Mary Pickford refused to work with him after a certain date and I could come there. So I went and did one picture with Mary called *The New York Hat*, by Anita Loos. Naturally she played the lead in that and I did a small part. After that, she left.

It was at the Biograph Company studio on 14th Street that Griffith changed my name. I was born Mary Marsh. He said, "We can't have two Marys in the company, so I'll call you Mae."

I signed with Griffith when he terminated his contract with Biograph to do features with Mutual, whose studio was uptown on 118th Street in New York. All the Biograph players went up there with him.

In my first beautiful picture, which was the one that Mary thought she would have, I was anonymous. In the Biograph days, only exhibitors knew the names of people who appeared in the picture. There weren't any fan magazines then. The picture business wasn't big enough yet to advertise, and they didn't spend any money on it. They would sell only to the exhibitors.

However, some people knew us. For example, Vachel Lindsay wrote a poem about me in his book *The Chinese Nightingale*, called "Mae Marsh, Motion Picture Actress," written after *The Wild Girl of the Sierras*, the title of a picture I made in the first part of 1916, just after *The Birth of a Nation*. I met him in New York several times. In fact, he proposed marriage to me, but I didn't care for him. He was red-haired and funny-looking, and so much older. And the poem didn't even phase me, partly because I had had other poems written about me and partly because I never knew he was so famous to begin with.

So even though we weren't billed, people were able to find out who we were. Especially in the Mutual days. The public began to know who was in the picture about the time that I appeared as a waitress in a comedy part in *The Avenging Conscience* with Blanche Sweet and Henry Walthall. Somebody down South had written a little verse about me. We had a fan magazine in 1914, '15. But there was no such thing as the "star" system. There was "D. W. Griffith Productions," though. Then our credits appeared on *The Birth of a Nation* in the first part of 1915. That was the first time I can remember my name being on a film. The credits read: "D. W. Griffith Presents," and then it listed the people who were in it, like Henry Walthall, Lillian Gish, Mae Marsh, all the way down.

I was with Mr. Griffith from 1912 to 1917. Mr. Griffith was a great teacher. He taught us spacing and timing. After he gave me my first part in *The Lesser Evil* (1912), he pointed out, "They always say you don't have any lines to remember. But you do have lines to remember in your head. You don't speak them, but they are in your mind. Think of your lines first and have them register the same way as they do when you're speaking." Sometimes we talked in pictures, but our lips never moved very much because it looked funny to have your mouth going all the time. Instead, we moved them very lightly and slightly. We learned pantomime, expression, and timing. There was a great emphasis on timing. Though Mr. Griffith was an exacting pedagogue, at the same time he was a most generous, understanding, and sympathetic man. If you didn't do a scene right, he'd say that you weren't thinking, that instead you were trying to act it. "We don't want actresses," he'd say. "We want people to think what they're doing. If you think what you're doing, the expression on your face will be right."

The only name we ever called him was Mr. Griffith, and a few of his close friends called him D. W. He was sort of an exalted figure, our teacher and advisor. I think he had a fatherly feeling toward all the people who worked for him. His great genius was his understanding of human nature. Of course, he was a great reader and was always on top of world affairs of the day. He would tell us about such things. Once Lillian was reading some book that didn't amount to much, and he said, "Well, why don't you read something worthwhile? Why read that trash? Read some of the old authors. Read some beautiful poetry." He would tell us what books to read, and talk to our teachers to see if we were getting the right studies. He would say, "You can't get very far in this world unless you have an education." Actually he didn't have a formal education, so he educated himself. He had great vision and he was very bold. He visualized *The Birth of a Nation* as a great document that everybody would understand. When he did *Intolerance*, he said, "Let's hope that this will be the end of all wars because war is so cruel." That was his reason for starting *Intolerance*, to portray the cruelty of war. Later on, during World War I, he took a number of prints of the film to the English government.

He later made two pictures in England. He wanted me to go over with him, but I was under contract with Goldwyn and couldn't. Even then, Griffith continued to work on some of these rather important ideas of human affairs and showed them in his films, hoping to alleviate these conditions. But many people misinterpreted him. Recently at a discussion at UCLA, I was saying that Mr. Griffith was against war, and a fellow got up and said, "How can you say that when his pictures were all about wars?" I told him, "He did it for the terror. He did all those death scenes to show how horrible it was." Ultimately, I think Mr. Griffith was frightfully disappointed that he was unable to get backing for his pictures. Yes, they acknowledged he was the master, but banks only gave money to the big studios.

I think *Intolerance* was the greatest picture Griffith ever did, although I understand it lost a great deal of money. But I remember one year, some years later, when I was in London, they showed it, and the crowds were enormous. I think his decline came a bit later than that. Afterwards he had his own company and made some big pictures with Lillian Gish, such as *Way Down East* and *Orphans of the Storm*. I remember that he had difficulty getting money for those.

When we put on *The Birth of a Nation*, I was still making thirty-five dollars a week. It was a big salary and I was very grateful. I wasn't supporting myself, so I was having a grand time. I was living at home and I had thirty-five dollars a week to spend on candy and other things I wanted. But when I made *Intolerance*, my salary went up to eighty-five dollars because of my success in *The Birth of a Nation*. Griffith said, "Don't you know that you have become a star?"

"I have?"

"Do you remember seeing one day on the Brooklyn Bridge a big sign of the name of some oil company?" He said this to Lillian Gish and me both. "Someday your names are going to be that big."

"Oh, wouldn't that be lovely. That would be heavenly," we said. Then Sam Goldwyn phoned me from New York and said he wanted me to be his first star for the picture company he was forming. He would give me $2500 a week. Of course, that floored me. I told my brother and mother about that.

"I hope you're going to take it, aren't you?" my brother said.

"Oh, no, I wouldn't leave Mr. Griffith. I don't care for the money," I answered. "You'd better take it. That's the most money anybody is getting in pictures today," he said.

So I went to Mr. Griffith and he said, "What is he going to pay you?"

"He's going to pay me twenty-five hundred dollars a week."

"My God, that's as much as Mary Pickford is getting. Take it. You take it and make a lot of money. What is the rest of the contract?"

"Well, it's twenty-five hundred dollars a week for the first year, and thirty-five hundred dollars for the next year. It's a two-year guarantee with an option of four thousand dollars a week the third year."

"Take it and when you're finished, come back to me and we'll make a picture. Of course, all the pictures at the Goldfish company are going to be lousy. But you come back and then we'll make a good picture."

I signed with Goldwyn in 1917. He was Mr. Goldfish then, and still is as far as I'm concerned because I can't remember his name as Goldwyn. It was Sam Goldfish and Edgar Selwyn who formed the Goldwyn company. I stayed only two years because I had married in the meantime and the "Act of God" was on the way. After that, I went back to Mr. Griffith.

I made only two good pictures for Mr. Goldfish, *Polly of the Circus*, directed by Charles Thomas Horan and Edwin L. Hollywood and *The Cinderella Man* directed by George Tucker. They were the only two pictures that were worthwhile. The others were very poor. Mr. Griffith was right. I'd have a two- or three-week vacation after each picture, but I wasn't having any fun because I was making bad pictures. I didn't like it there at all. I was not having nearly the fun I had with the Griffith Company making good pictures. Still it made me very rich. But I don't think it turned my head at all. It made me very sad to know I was wasting so much time putting on bad movies. I didn't care about the money. I wanted to be a good actress. I know this was Griffith's influence. He always used to say, "Be a good actress."

I recall that when we rehearsed *The Birth of a Nation*, he was very happy that I was playing the little girl. Although it was taken from Dixon's novel, he had written a great deal of the script himself. He understood the South, having been born and raised there. And he said, "You remind me so very much of my little sister. You are a little sister." He was very happy and he liked what I did. I'm sure he never dreamed it would be the success that it was and create the controversy that it did. I definitely remember that. I never heard any anti-Negro conversation when we shot the picture. In fact, we had many Negroes working on the

Top left: Mae Marsh in the Fox Film production of *Over the Hill*. 1931.

Top right: Mae Marsh on location in Fort Lauderdale, Florida, for the making of *The White Rose*. 1923.

Bottom: Tom Moore, Mae Marsh, and George Fawcett in Samuel Goldwyn's production of *The Cinderella Man*. 1917.

Mae Marsh in Samuel Goldwyn's production of *Polly of the Circus*. 1917.

Mae Marsh and Robert Harron in D. W. Griffith's *Intolerance*. 1916. Released separately as *Mother and the Law*. 1919.

set, and they loved the picture. There was one whose name was "Madam," a skinny, tiny little woman and a wonderful actress. Mr. Griffith liked her very much. Although it was a glorification of the Ku Klux Klan, it didn't trouble him because he knew he was doing the right thing. Of course, when it opened in Boston and in the South, there was a terrible uproar, which took everybody by surprise.

Mr. Griffith personally cut every bit of the film. One evening while he was cutting with Jimmy Smith, he said to me, "I'd like you to bring your niece and all her neighborhood friends in to see this picture because I think children have a wonderful, honest value of what's good. If the children like it, I think it will be a success." So I asked my mother to gather all the children to see the picture that evening. And the kids just loved it: oh, they clapped and clapped at the end. They said, "When can we see it again?" Mr. Griffith said, "I think I have a success."

Mr. Griffith worked on every aspect of his pictures. He would tell Billy Bitzer, his famous cameraman, "Let's not do it that way. Let's try something else."

"I don't think it will photograph that way," Bitzer would say.

"Try it, try it. You never know until you try it."

I remember once he was doing a scene, I think it was with Blanche Sweet, in which he wanted her to look misty. He said, "Put some gauze over that camera. Quite often when you look through a gauze you see something, but it's fuzzy and soft. I want this scene to be soft, but we still need the lights on it to photograph it."

He was also the one who introduced the close-up. And in *Intolerance*, *he* built an elevator outside of the set and put the camera on the elevator. He also shot from a moving automobile. I think the first time I remember seeing him use the camera in an automobile was in an Indian chase in *The Battle at Elderbush Gulch* with Lillian Gish, Lionel Barrymore, and myself. My niece was also in that. It's a wonderful two-reel picture shot on location in the summer of 1913 in the San Fernando Valley.

We used to see the first rushes on all the pictures because it was part of our schooling with Griffith. Of course, it got so that we wanted to do it. In fact, I also saw my rushes when I worked for the Goldwyn Company. Many years later I did an independent picture at Columbia, and I asked the director if I could see the rushes. I told him I hadn't worked in a long time, and I wanted to see how I was doing. He said, "Go ahead. They are running them in the projection room." So I went to the projection room and opened the door.

"I've come to see the rushes," I said.

"Who are you?" someone answered.

"I'm Mae Marsh."

"Who said you could come?"

"The director said that I could come and see them."

They finished about two minutes of the rushes and he pushed a button to stop and said, "That's all." He didn't want me in. The attitude had changed.

Anyway, immediately after Goldwyn I did a couple of films, one of them, *Flames of Passion*, with Sir Aubrey and Eva Moore in London. Then I came back to America to do *The White Rose* for Griffith. But he wasn't ready, so I went back on the same boat to London and did *Paddy the Next Best Thing*, which was a big comedy success on the West End. I didn't like England because it was terribly cold and miserable, but I loved the people and I loved the countryside. Then I came back to America, turned around again, and went to Germany to do a picture called *Arabella*. It was freezing when I arrived in Germany, even thought it was in May. Then I went to Paris. Mama wanted to see Paris, and we went there for a short time. The next year I went to London and did *The Rat*, adapted from a play by Ivor Novello, who was also in the picture.

When my second child, Brewster, was born, I retired. I went back to work about six years later (1931) and did *Over the Hill*. From then on I was in and out of pictures because I got tired of making them. I did about one picture a year.

Many years later, Mr. Griffith passed away. I recall the funeral with real sadness. There were hundreds of people there. They hired a big hall on Hollywood Boulevard. I never saw so many flowers. I was working at Twentieth Century–Fox when he died. It was in the newspaper that he had taken sick. I immediately phoned the hospital, told them who I was, and asked how Mr. Griffith was. They said that he had passed on at eight o'clock that morning. That was heartbreaking because he had been taken to the hospital only the night before. I got in touch with Herb Stern, a mutual friend of ours, a publicity agent in Hollywood, and asked him to make the funeral arrangements. I told him, "Herb, you've got to tend to this. He was a real person. He was a genius. He was the greatest motion picture producer and director that the business ever had. He put pictures where they are today and everybody understands that." But fortunately, the Academy heard about his death, and we had the funeral. Donald Crisp, one of Griffith's actors, was one of the speakers. I was thankful to hear him speak because he had been in *The Birth of a Nation* and had played for Mr. Griffith for many, many years.

Griffith's death was tragic. In his last days he had done very little work. When I went to see Griffith when he was working at the Hal Roach Studios, he told me, "I'm nothing but a figurehead here. They're not taking any of my advice. I don't know why they have me. I'm just taking the money and that's all, but I'm not going to stand for it much longer. I just can't."

I had gone to see him because he wanted me to play the mother in *One Million B.C.* He said, "They refused that. They refused to have other people I wanted in it. They're not taking any advice of mine. First I was asked to direct it; then I was asked to give advice. They're not letting me do either, and I think I will not be able to stand it." He quit. We had lunch, and he said he was very sad. That was the last time he was in any studio that I know of.

But getting back to my own career. When sound came in, it was hard for me to learn lines. I would memorize them by using Griffith's old technique of thinking *what* you're saying, not *how* you're saying it. Thinking was the key, and timing and spacing were all thinking. Acting is acting, no matter whether it's pantomime or voice.

In talking pictures I worked a good deal for John Ford. We had known each other for a very long time, all the way back to the early Griffith days, when he was a little extra boy during *The Birth of a Nation*, riding as a Klansman in the Ku Klux Klan. In all the other pictures we made, I'd be a blue-eyed Indian and he'd be a cowboy. When he became a director, I was in many of his pictures, such as *Two Rode Together* with Jimmy Stewart and Richard Widmark. I would play what they call cameo roles, because I didn't care to get up every morning at five o'clock to be at the studio by seven. I did this at Twentieth Century–Fox for thirteen years.

Looking back, there's surely been a change in the film business over the decades. First it was a little family, then it became an industry, and then it became a match factory. It was still a match factory when I was last there. Of course it depends on who you work for. Andy Stone does his own work. That's different. John Ford also does his own work and is his own boss. But with the other directors, if it isn't in the script, you don't say it. Ford says, "Throw away the script. I don't want you to have the script. You know the story." Andy Stone is the same way. That's why they're the only two or three directors I've worked for that I really like.

It's odd, but after all these years in Hollywood, I have never been a part of the social life. When we were young, we weren't allowed to go to those night clubs where Mabel Normand went. I guess that carried over, for my husband and I haven't been to a night club in forty-nine years. Even there, a little bit of Mr. Griffith remains.

EDWARD EVERETT HORTON

NOBODY'S OLDER than I am. Oh, a few people are, but they are not in circulation. They're generally in asylums or old men's homes. The fact is I was born in Brooklyn on the eighteenth day of March, twenty minutes after St. Patrick's Day in 1886. My father was a printer. He had been on the *Baltimore Sun*, *The New York Times*, and the *New York Herald*. About 1900, he was put in full charge of a contingent sent with linotype machines and printing equipment to form the *Paris Exposition* edition of *The New York Times*. My mother was born in Scotland, as was her mother. I still own an antique clock that came on their sailing ship from Scotland to this country, which was all filled with feather pillows to protect it. We have some of the feather pillows to this day. That must have been a hundred years ago.

I have two brothers and one sister. I'm the oldest. I went to kindergarten in Brooklyn. Then I went to School Number 11 in Brooklyn and from there to Boys' High School. We then moved to Baltimore for about three years, and I went to the Baltimore City College. I didn't finish because we returned to Brooklyn. Eventually, I went to Oberlin College. I was out there for three years until my family discovered evidences of my interest in the theater. That annoyed them no end. If I was getting theater in a strict school like Oberlin, my word, something had to be done. If you were going to be an actor, why go to college?

My father was a great enthusiast, though, of the theater. He just loved it. Near Baltimore, out in the country, my grandfather lived near

Julius Brutus Booth, who was the father of Edwin Booth. I understand that in his delirium tremens, you could hear him yelling and shouting all over the valley. My father used to tell me that they were never allowed to go anywhere near there. But I think that when my father was on the *Baltimore Sun*, he must have been sort of an interviewer because he seemed to have talked to Mr. Booth and he knew Joseph Jefferson. And as a young fellow—I couldn't have been more than five or six years old— he would take me to every show that he could. My mother was horrified. She thought he was just ruining "that boy."

My father was the youngest of six brothers. They were all named after famous Americans. My oldest uncle was George Washington Horton. He was the chief of the fire department in Baltimore during the great fire of 1912. Then there was Millard Horton, Henry Peter Clay Horton, and Herbert Berkeley Horton. My immediate uncle was Winter Davis Horton. I remember him very well as a young man because I never knew where that name came from. It wasn't until my niece majored in American history at Swarthmore that I found out Winter Davis was the senator from Maryland who, no matter what Lincoln said or did, was against it. My father was named Edward Everett after the famous orator of the same name. I'm Junior. Originally, I went under the name of Edward Horton. My father said, "I think you're making a mistake, Edward. Anybody could be Edward Horton, but nobody else could be Edward Everett Horton." I said, "I think I like that." Nobody seems to have objected at all.

At Oberlin, I majored in German. I lived with a German family for three years and spoke nothing but German. But I began trying to organize little one-act plays, getting the kids together. We were going to have a big junior prom, and I thought it would be nice if we put on a play. So in the women's gym, we arranged a stage that had little footlights in front with candles behind them. We didn't think it was necessary to ask for permission. Just about the time we were about to start, the dean of women came in and said, "Mr. Horton, what is this? What is this? Oh no, no, no." So we weren't allowed to do it.

My folks heard about such things, and they thought maybe I'd better stay home and go to the Polytechnic Institute in Brooklyn. I was there a whole year, majoring in German, English, and history. Suddenly they decided to do away with the arts courses and make it a purely technical school, which it is to this day. So I affiliated with Columbia and stayed there until I got fouled up with the *Varsity Show of 1909*.

This was the first time I had really ever been on the stage. I was running around with a bunch of fellows there, and they said, "Why don't you try out for the Columbia show? You can tell stories and everything." I tried out and was given a part right away. The rehearsals started, the music started, the dialogue came along as did the dancing, and finally we opened the show. Ran it for two weeks at the old Waldorf-Astoria, when it was down on 34th Street. By the time Saturday night came, I was almost as good as I thought I was. After that, to put it gently, Columbia and I came to an amicable parting of the ways. They were just as glad to see me go as I was to get out. I ended up in the chorus of a little opera company on Staten Island. That lasted for three or four weeks, and then I got into another chorus.

You didn't need voice-training in those days. I found out, too, that if I sang with all the rest, no one could tell what I was singing and I couldn't help being on key. I was in the baritone section. In this second chorus, I had a very unusual experience. It was in a musical comedy that had been quite successful in New York, called *The Newlyweds and Their Baby*. They were going out all over the United States. They needed one chorus boy who had to be a certain height because the chorus line started with a big bruiser and came down to a little fellow at the end. They needed someone to be the second guy. I had met somebody on the street who had been in the little opera company, and he said, "What are you doing, Edward?"

"Well, I don't know if I'm doing anything." I said.

"Listen, you get down to the Irish AC near the Hudson River on 52d Street and . . . Is that the best suit you have?" he said.

"Yes."

"Oh," he said. "Go anyway and see what happens."

I went down there and I didn't need to try out. I was just right, you see. Now, as a chorus boy, you were supposed to know certain steps because there was no choreographer in those days. You went forward and back, and you did this, that, and the other thing. All these boys knew the steps, so I had to learn them quickly. Now the fellow ahead of me, was a very big bruiser with the biggest hands and the biggest feet I had ever seen. I tried to keep out of his way while doing these steps, watching over here and watching over there, because I knew if he ever stepped on me, my career would be ruined. But he didn't, and we finally got along all right. You know, that chap was Wallace Beery. Years later, I played with his daughter Carol out in Ephrata, Ohio. She knew all the stories about her father except that one. She never knew that he had been a chorus boy.

Finally, I returned to New York and found out you couldn't get anywhere without an agent. You had to have somebody working for you. So I decided on an agent named Chamberlain Brown. I used to get up to that office in the morning when the office was opened. Somebody would come out, glance at me and be not very encouraging. Finally, other actors and actresses would come in, all beautifully dressed with their hair combed, tight shoes, and, oh gee! I'd sit there, and then it would be lunchtime, and I had about thirty cents to spend. I'd go out, have lunch, and come back.

I did this for three days. I stayed until they were locking up. Nobody paid any attention. At last, one day the head man, Chamberlain Brown, said, "What do you want?"

"I'm looking for a job."

"Are you an actor?"

"I'd like to be."

"What have you done?"

"I haven't done anything special."

"If you haven't done anything, we can't do anything for you here."

"Well," I said, "I had a part in the *Varsity Show* at Columbia University."

"Oh," he said, "what's your name?"

"Edward Horton."

"Here, you take this card and tomorrow morning you get over to the stage entrance of the Lyric Theater. Go right in on the stage. Go there about nine or nine-thirty. There you'll meet a very fine, well-known actor, a great star, who is looking for a young man to be in his play."

I couldn't wait for the next day. I went to Brooklyn and could hardly sleep all night. Here's my big chance. I got over there in the morning and I went on the stage. This man looked like a tragedian! He had on a fur hat, a fur coat, and a great big tie. In front of him were six or seven fellows, all with white cards the same as mine. I had thought I was going to be the only one there. I went to the back of the line. He was taking these cards and listening to what the fellows said. As I got nearer, I'd hear them saying, "*Bought and Paid For*," "*Paid in Full*," "*Butterfly on the Wheel*." I thought, "Golly, there's no use my staying here. I can't say anything." I wanted to go away. Then I thought, "No! I'm already here. I must see what's going to happen." It got to be my turn and I handed him the card.

"All right, all right, let's have it," he said.

"There's nothing, sir."

"What?"

"Nothing."

"What do you mean, nothing?"

"I have nothing to say."

"You haven't done anything in the theater?"

"No sir."

"You want to be an actor?"

"I am very anxious to be."

"Well, well, well, perhaps we could teach you. Thank you, gentlemen."

And I was engaged as a stage manager, twenty dollars a week. That man was Louis Mann. In those days, Louie Mann and Clara Lippman were a great team. We started the next day on a new play, *The Cheater*. I had only been getting twelve dollars, and oh boy, I was there with a script and watching everything. Finally, he let me write some letters for him. I had some very fine notepaper. At the end of the second week, he said, "Horton, how much did I say I was going to pay you?"

"Twenty dollars," I said.

"Well, make it forty dollars."

My word! Forty dollars! I couldn't believe it. I haven't had that much money since. Well, I was with him for three seasons until I heard that the manager of the famous resident company in Philadelphia, the Orpheum Players, was up in New York looking for a juvenile. Now, as much as I enjoyed being with Mr. Mann because we traveled all over the country and I was now getting sixty dollars a week, I went over to see this chap.

Most of my money went home. I was helping my brothers and sister with their education because my father, as a printer, wasn't too affluent. He was making fifty dollars a week. I was getting sixty dollars. The Philadelphia manager was very pleased with me. He talked to me about salary and said he could only pay twenty dollars a week, but here was the chance to be the juvenile in a famous company. I accepted and we opened on my birthday in 1912 at the old Chestnut Street Theater in a play called *The Man from Home*. I played a silly-ass Englishman. I was there for three seasons.

While I was a stage manager with Louie Mann, he let me play parts every now and then. Sometimes when an actor went away on vacation, I would play his part. I watched Louis Mann. He was a great artist, oh, a great artist. He was fabulous. He was a dialect comedian, you know. It was just as if I'd gone to school to be with him. Eventually he wouldn't come to rehearsals at all. He'd say, "Horton, you know the play." And I could imitate him, and I'd do all the other parts. It was a great experience. Whatever I know about the theater, I learned from him during the time I was with him.

Another theater soon opened called the Chestnut Street Opera House. In that theater I played my first leading part in a play called *The Typhoon*. The original leading man, Thurston Hall, came to me after rehearsal one day and said, "Edward, I can no more play a Japanese prince than I could play Sarah Bernhardt. Why don't you play the Japanese prince and I'll play the German doctor?" Well, I did. I tackled the part of the Japanese prince. At that time, at the University of Pennsylvania, there was a fabulous Japanese student named Sato who was surrounded by very interesting Japanese friends. He had the whole top of a dormitory, and everybody said he was a prince. I contacted him about the play. He read it over and gave me, phonetically, what he felt this Japanese prince would say, and on opening night, who was in the audience with all his Japanese friends but

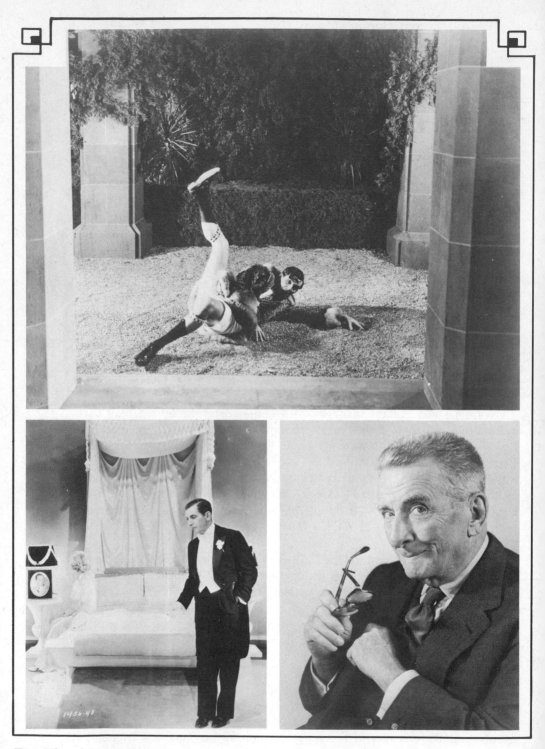

Top: Edward Everett Horton.

Bottom left: Miriam Hopkins and Edward Everett Horton in Paramount production of *Design For Living*. 1933.

Bottom right: Edward Everett Horton.

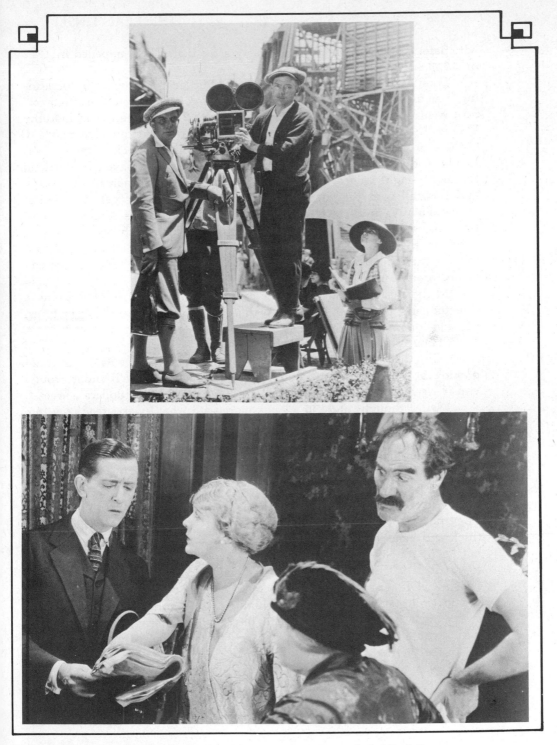

Director James Cruze and Cameraman Karl Brown filming *Ruggles of Red Gap*. 1923.

A scene from *Ruggles of Red Gap*, starring, from left to right: Edward Everett Horton, Louise Dresser, Lillian Leighton, Ernest Torrence. Paramount Pictures. 1923.

Mr. Sato. They gave me a little party after that. This happened in 1912 or 1913.

Soon after, I got an offer to go up to Portland, Maine, to be the leading man at $125 a week. "Oh, Horton, is he good? He gets three figures." So I went up to Portland and played the Keith Theater there with Dorothy Dalton, the leading woman. She eventually married Arthur Hammerstein, Oscar's brother. She and I played together for thirty weeks. Oh, she was lovely. I think she lives up on the Hudson today. I played in Portland for eighty-eight weeks. From there, I went as leading man to Pittsburgh and then all over the country in different plays, always getting a better salary. Finally, in 1919, I was invited to come out to Los Angeles to continue my work at the Wilkes-Majestic Theater on Ninth and Broadway. I was in that theater for six years, starting at $200. Then they put in a Sunday matinee after about the third week and gave me $250. At the end of six years, I was getting $1250.

In the meantime, I did six or seven silent pictures. Jesse Robbins a director came to see me. He said, "I think you'd do wonderfully in pictures, Mr. Horton. Would you like to make a picture?"

"How can I when I'm in the theater?"

"Oh, that's all right. We'll make it in the daytime when you're not playing or not rehearsing. You just come down and we'll shoot around you if we have to. We'll give you one hundred and fifty dollars a week."

Well, I thought of $150 a week more with what I was already getting. Let's see, there's Rockefeller, Ford, and Horton, right there. So I decided to do it.

We worked at Vitagraph studio. It was an original called *Too Much Business*. I was very nervous. They thought they'd give me something to do the first day so that no matter what lay in the future, it could never be worse. I was called upon to report down to the L. A. Athletic Club. They put make-up on me. In those days, in silent pictures, it was sort of thick and yellow all over. I had never appeared on the street in make-up before in my life. It was something I wouldn't do. Nevertheless, I had to do it, and then I had to walk down to the corner of Seventh and Broadway. It was teeming with people, walking by on the street and riding in trolley cars. I was to wait until I saw a dolly coming along with a box on it that looked as if it might contain an upright piano. But in it was a camera. I am to get in back of that box, keep about twenty or thirty feet behind it, and walk slowly to the front of it. If people stopped me, I was to make as though I was talking to them. Nervous? I was shivering. The next day I saw the rushes, and they were terrible. That was my first picture.

By and by, they wanted me to play something on the order of Douglas Fairbanks. I was pretty active, jumping around and all that. I used to play handball a lot. I still play tennis every day.

I did four pictures, and then I was asked to do one with Jimmy Cruze and the Famous Players–Lasky. I thought, "This is it. I can get rid of the theater now." But they wouldn't allow me to leave the theater. Equity claimed that I had no right to go. I said, "I have a two-week clause, and I want to make a picture." But Mr. Cruze said, "All right, we'll pay them to let you go for two weeks." And in two weeks, I made a picture called *Ruggles of Red Gap*. Red Gap was the little town of Eureka up in Northern California. It was shot in a great big house all made of scrolled wood, very viciously Victorian, but rather handsome. I was Ruggles. That was very, very interesting indeed.

They liked my movie efforts. I was a young fellow, not bad looking, I had nice clothes, and I got to play all light-comedy parts in pictures. I was doing straight dramatic leads in the theater with only a few comedies. I played in *Bought and Paid For, Paid in Full*, and *The Ideal Husband*. I did a comedy every now and then, such as *Never Say Die*. The cast didn't like a comedy to come along because you had to work in a comedy. If you weren't getting laughs and you knew it was a funny show, you had to get together and say, "What's the matter? What can we do? How can we be funny?" In a dramatic play, if you didn't remember a line, you just stood perfectly still, not moving a muscle, and people would say, "Oh, what an actor! For five minutes he didn't say a word. You could hear a pin drop. Marvelous!" You couldn't do that in a comedy. You had to keep going. Well, I don't know how the comedies came along.

Then came the talkies in 1927, and I was invited to be in the second talking picture, a six-reel, 100 percent-Warner Brothers, Vitaphone talking picture. It was called *The Terror* with May McAvoy, Edward Everett Horton, Alec Francis, Louise Fazenda, and a number of other people. The first one was called *The Lights of New York*, and it also had May McAvoy as the star.

There had been one or two little two-reelers before them, and I was in one of those with Lois Wilson. The producers didn't seem to know what they had since *The Jazz Singer*, which was really the third feature-length talkie, hadn't come out yet. In those days, there was no boom that followed you all around. The microphones hung down, all wrapped around with material to make them look like part of the backdrop. We had three or four cameras. In a great big ensemble scene these cameras were sort of coffins covered with tarpaulins so that you couldn't hear the buzz of the camera. They were on turnstiles or something like that. We were instructed not to talk until we felt ourselves in the center of the camera. So the scene would go around: "You see this man?" . . . Camera turns . . . "Yes" . . . Camera turns . . . "You know what happened?" . . . Camera . . . "No" . . . Camera . . . "Killed." . . . Camera . . . "What!" . . . Camera . . . "Who did it?" . . . Camera. Of course, then they took it all and cut it up and put it together again. We didn't think anything could be better than that. It was the last word in progress. No boom to follow you around. You waited until you were in the center of the camera and then spoke your lines.

Making pictures was quite exciting in those days because it was a brand-new field. It was not like the theater, but it was exciting because everybody was excited. Along came *The Jazz Singer,* and that was the beginning of history. The other two, somehow, were thought to be tricks. But Jolson started it. I've been at this business ever since. By 1927, I had bought this property where we are now, and I had started to build my house. My mother came on, as did one of my brothers. And my brother George still lives next door. He graduated from Yale, majored in bacteriology, and was with Dupont for a while. He isolated some sort of germ afflicting chickens. He came out here and started teaching at the old Lincoln High. Eventually he retired.

I was in that Majestic Theater morning, noon, and night, rehearsing a new show all the time, making a picture, then coming back. In pictures, I wasn't under contract. I was just "invited" to come and make them. I was very pleased to get to know somebody like May McAvoy or Louise Fazenda. I'd have parties and invite them out. In fact, when I made a picture with Lily Pons, *Hitting a New High,* I had a very big party in my banquet hall. Rod La Rocque was with Vilma Banky; this was some time ago. I never married. However, I have not given up hope. This is Leap Year, you know. I have a nice disposition, a lot of antique furniture, and I still have two acres of ground.

The theater was delightful. It is the only thing I ever wanted. I used to have the key to the stage door of the Majestic Theater. I'd get down there at seven in the morning. In my dressing room, I had couches and things to drink. It became known as Majestic Alpha, and everybody in the world was always welcome. I remember a young fellow coming in there one day. Oh, a nice-looking chap, well dressed and everything, but on fire! He had a play for me to read and he wanted to know if I would listen to the first act. Well, I did and it was pretty good, but I didn't know how to encourage him because I had nothing to do with the selection of plays. He wanted to know if he could come again when he finished the second act. Well, he did. Two or three weeks later, he came down again. I told him all I could do was to suggest it. I never knew what happened because that was the last time I saw him, but I have never forgotten his forceful personality and how ambitious he was. I found out that he later went into pictures and got to be the head of Twentieth Century–Fox. His name is Darryl Zanuck.

I was going to do a play called *Her Cardboard Lover* in my own theater now, acting and directing. I'd taken over the Majestic and instead of working for somebody else, I was working for myself. I was wishing for a certain type of leading woman, someone very patrician and elegant. A charming woman did come down to see me. She had been playing the lead in Denver. She and her husband had just arrived. She said, "Mr. Horton, I've never played comedy. I've played *Six Characters in Search of an Author* in New York." I said, "I think you'll be delightful in this part." Her name was Florence Eldridge. She was great in the part, oh great. Her husband was Freddie March, who eventually got a chance to do *The Royal Family* at another theater, playing the Barrymore part and playing it so much better than Barrymore. He was immediately put under contract and went right on up and up and up.

I was making $1250 a week in that theater. The movie people would offer me $500 or maybe $750 and ask if I would sign a seven-year contract, you know. I would think, "Wait. Suppose I'm no good in the motion picture business and they rent me out to another studio where they give me parts I can't play? Anything to get rid of me. Here I am my own boss." So far I have always been a free-lance player. Never under contract to any studio. In films I got to feel that I was sort of a scavenger. Some contract player at Paramount or Universal would say, "I won't play it." So they'd say, "Don't worry, we'll get Horton." And they'd get me. A director would say, "Now, Eddie, we know how good you are. Just ad-lib. The part isn't really written yet, and we would like you to see how you feel about it. You know, you can't go *too* far, because you have to keep the plot. After all, you're not under contract to the studio." I would say, "Well, it's five thousand dollars a week, seven weeks guaranteed. You don't even have to use my name. I don't give a rap. I'll just play the part and take the money." So that's what happened, picture after picture. I didn't give a rap about the billing. I had no ambition at all. All I wanted to do was. . . . Well, seven weeks' work, what do you know? I can build another room. I can go to England. I can do a lot.

I couldn't take movies seriously. I like to be the show-off. I like the electric "something" that comes with playing a part in the theater "alive," don't you know. The audience is with you and they're laughing at you. At the end of the show, there's enough applause for you to come on and make a little speech. "Something accomplished, something done." That's never happened in the movies. In the theater, even if they don't ask for it, I'm out there making a speech anyway. I say, "The older I grow in this wonderful profession of which I have the honor to be a member, the more convinced I become that you can listen to waves on the shore of a brook in the forest, the wind in the trees, or the rain on the roof, but there is no more thrilling, no more exhilarating sound in all of nature than applause, and I never get enough of it." Mr. Gleason on TV has shortened it to "How sweet it is." You never heard that in a movie. All the director would do would be to signal "O.K." I was known as "One-take" Horton. I did it right the first time. How lovely. I didn't have to do it again.

At the same time it was grinding work. I had to get up at six o'clock in the morning. I had dogs to feed and chores to do around the house, then get in my automobile, and drive to MGM, which was forty-five minutes away. You get into the make-up; go on the scene. The director would come up and say, "Do you know your lines, Mr. Horton?" Well, I would have about three lines. I would say, "Yes."

"He knows his lines. He knows his lines—great!"

Well, since I had been learning one hundred and twenty-five pages for every play for years, one page was no effort.

Lots of times, you'd do a scene, a long scene, and you'd do it over and over again. Film meant nothing in those days. And you often wondered why? Why do we do this thing so many itmes? No comment of any kind. Actually, the director hoped that one of the actors would do something that might change the scene and make it a little better. He wouldn't know what he wanted, but maybe the actor would do or say something accidentally. Finally, he would say, "Well, all right, we'll keep the last one."

There were some extraordinary directors, of course. I did five pictures with Mr. Lubitsch, who was a frustrated actor to begin with, over there in Germany at Ufa where he was a director. He always had the actor in his mind. In no part of any Lubitsch picture did he have an actor who was not just right. You rehearsed a whole week on the picture without shooting anything at all. We rehearsed in the sets. No matter what you thought or what you wanted to do, Mr. Lubitsch had gone over it in his mind and had come to a conclusion. Just as soon as you could put yourself *en rapport* with him, you were very happy. He knew these actors very well, and he wanted something from them that even they didn't know they had. He was a genius, you see. Just a genius. The "Lubitsch touch" meant bits of business that he supplied. For example, there was one scene in *Trouble in Paradise*, I think, in which another actor and I are photographed behind a big glass door that looks into the bar of a fabulous hotel. I'm saying to another actor, "Do you want to go in?" and that sort of thing, but you couldn't hear a word. All pantomime. Only Lubitsch could think of a scene like that.

The Merry Widow stands out above all in my memory. It was filmed on a gorgeous set at MGM. Never was there a set like it, with a palace and all that sort of thing. Chevalier and Jeanette MacDonald were the leads. I played the Baron Popoff. In the Lubitsch version, there was a king, and I played the prime minister. Anything I did that the king approved of prompted him to pin a little medal on me. If something happened that he didn't approve of, he'd take the medal off. No great reaction of any kind. But very amusing. Well, when we finished the scene, we'd all retire. Chevalier and MacDonald would go off with the French actors Chevalier had brought over with him, the French director, and the French dialogue director. MacDonald wasn't allowed to say a word that wasn't passed. It had to be excellent French. Then we'd watch them doing the scene that we did. They had a king and a prime minister, and whenever Popoff did anything that the king liked, the king would kiss him on both cheeks. Then, when he did something wrong, there was a terrible scene and you'd think a revolution had started. Lubitsch used to look at me and say, "Why? Why all that?"

One day Lubitsch came to me and said, "Edward, there's trouble and it's going to be three or four weeks before things are straightened out. I understand they want you at Warner Brothers. Why don't you go over to Warner Brothers and play and you'll still be on salary here. Go over and make the picture. Let me know when you're finished." So I was getting two salaries at once. I remember that very well. Why wouldn't I? Then I did another picture with Gary Cooper that was a lot of fun. *Design for Living*, that was it.

It wasn't very long before I had an invitation to make a picture in London for United Artists. I did that for Gainsborough. It was called *Soldiers of the King*. I went over and made the picture in 1930. It took thirteen weeks. From 1930 to 1939 I was over and back often. The last British picture I made was with Jack Buchanan and Googie Withers. It was called *The Gang's All Here*. That ended in March, 1939, although we started it in October, 1938.

I never minded being asked to do a film. I didn't want to be under contract, that's all. I'd make them, and I still will. I've just recently done two, by the way, that are out now. One is called *The Perils of Pauline* (1967). The other is called *2000 Years Later*, which was released in 1969.

Only once did I feel I was really playing myself. That is, really acting. It was in *Summer Storm* with Linda Darnell and George Sanders, taken from Chekhov's *The Shooting Party*. I played a Russian nobleman in it. Oh, so very stuffed shirt. Delightful. Has billions of dollars, and then the revolution comes and he's picking up cigarette butts. It was like a stage play. I was really playing a new type. That's what I like to do. I thought it would be the beginning of a whole new career in films. It was a part that Lionel Barrymore could have played, though not as well as I did of course. It was that kind of part, sort of a pathetic comedy part.

I liked doing *Lost Horizon* with Frank Capra. I had read the Hilton book. Suddenly I got a call from Mr. Capra. He wanted me to come down and be in the picture. "Oh," I said, "Mr. Capra, what could I play in it? I don't see anything." He said, "What I want you to do is not in the book. I am going to write it in just for you." Well, you couldn't say anything to that. I was a paleontologist. Did you ever see *Lost Horizon*? Well, I'm the fellow who carries the vertebrae of a prehistoric animal around in a little box. We are all in the airplane, and I discover that we are going in the wrong direction. I say, "Something must be done about this." Then we get to Shangri-La, and I like it there.

Capra was entirely different from Lubitsch. Everybody who worked for Capra had had stage experience. We were all stage actors. He hand-picked them. He said to me one day, in a fabricated room up there in the Himalaya Mountains, a great big place with wonderful Chinese embroideries, all built on that set, "Edward, in this scene I want to get over a feeling, not of fear, but sort of an eerie feeling. What goes on here? A mysterious something. What do you think?"

"Well, Mr. Capra, I don't know."

"What do you mean you don't know? You've been on the stage for fifteen, twenty, thirty-five years. What do you mean you don't know?"

I knew I had made a mistake and covered up quickly. "Well, I don't know quite what you mean by eerie. If I were in a room like this and I happened to see that long curtain moving back and forth, I'd be a little. . . ."

"That's it. That's it. You're behind the curtain."

"I am?"

"Yes, you're behind the curtain."

So I went over and stood behind the curtain.

"Now sell me the fact that you're behind the curtain. I can't feel it unless I see some sort of a form of your body. Get up closer to it."

"What am I doing?"

"Give him a sword, one of those samurai swords. Now let's see the sword come out back and forth in front of the curtain."

"What am I doing?"

"You're sharpening a pencil or something like that."

"Ed, I'm stuck." He then said, "How do I know it's you?"

"I have no idea, Mr. Capra, unless I thought I heard something and I looked around the curtain to see what. . . ."

"That's it, that's just right. Now it's nobody, so you go over to the desk." I went over and just as I sat down I jumped up.

"What's the matter?"

"I forgot the sword."

"Oh well, go and get it." Now at the desk he said, "Go ahead, what do you want to do?"

What do I want to do? I mean, what can you do behind a desk? I'm trying to see if there's any dust on it. Then I saw a Chinese lacquer box. I opened the thing and looked in it. And as I looked up, I saw that it had a mirror in it, and there's my face! I screamed and shut the thing.

"Perfect, that's just right," he said.

Well, it was fun working with Capra because you were thinking all the time and you tried to please him. He knew what he was after, but he wanted to see how you'd get around to it. Both Capra and Lubitsch were extraordinary directors.

On the other hand, you find the kind of director who is under the absolute thumb of the producer. The play has been gone over. It has a wonderful writer. It's all been timed. The movement is here. The close-up is here. You come to the close-up. It's all in the book and this is the way it's got to be shot, and it's done in a certain amount of time. There's very little leeway for anything the actor might do that is very funny. So the run-of-the-mill comment is, "No, keep it this way." "You said 'and' instead of 'if,' Edward."

"Oh did I? So sorry."

"Take it again please."

So "if I go," not "and if I go." Everything like that is watched. I'd improvise anyway. They'd take it that way and then they'd take it the way it should have been. Sometimes my way was better.

I think I hold up a mirror to domestic nature in my portrayals. A man and wife will come backstage to see me and say, "Mr. Horton, it's just wonderful. You're just like my husband. He can never pass a mirror without fixing his tie or stopping. Sometimes he picks up pins and puts them under his. . . ." And the husband will listen to her and say, "Mr. Horton, nothing of the kind. You're just like her brother." And then the battle starts. Certain things could happen in that family, if not with that husband, then with some other husband and wife, which will make them just boil over with rage at each other. They may even divorce. But they see me playing a situation exactly like what they battle over, and instead of being mad, they sit there and yell, "Isn't that marvelous?" They're laughing at what they were going to scream about at home. I'm not trying to be funny. I'm just trying to be the man next door or the man up the street, something like that. So I think that any audience-interest I have is that I represent, to the average male or female, somebody they know. "This is that nut who used to live down the street, who used to put on a Roman toga and come out in the yard with a sword. Wasn't he a pest? We all said he'd come to no good and now look at him up here on the stage. Dreadful." That's the only theory I have about what makes me click.

Slapstick is different. Take some of the English comediennes who came over here. They were fabulous. I remember them when they arrived. They had comedy songs that had us rolling in the aisles, they were so funny. They were all founded on a very sad, and kind of a pathetic, little incident. For instance, "There was I, waiting at the church, waiting at the church, waiting at the church. When I found that he had left me in the lurch, Lord did it upset me. All at once, he sent around a little note. Here's the very note. This is what he wrote. Can't get away to marry you today. My wife won't let me." Oh, they laughed. That's kind of a sad thing. Almost tragic. Then there was another one: "John took me around to see his mother, his mother, his mother. When he'd introduced us to each other, she sized up everything I had on. She put me through a cross-examination till I fairly boiled with aggravation. Then she shook her head, looked at me, and said, 'Poor John, poor John.' " Well, that's sad, too, but it was very funny. That was also Chaplin's secret. He came out of the same English music-hall tradition at about the same time. So did Stan Laurel. Wasn't he marvelous?

Do you know the difference between farce and comedy? I will tell you. A comedy is a play written for the stage that could be played either as tragedy or comedy. It depends on the tempo. It's written around a situation that could happen, and it is treated either for laughter or for tears. A farce is something that couldn't possibly have happened, but it is played so that it seems to be happening while you're looking at it. Like *Up in Mabel's Room.* Something of that sort.

I made one Western, a two-reeler for Harold Lloyd. He asked me to come under contract with him. They were enthusiastic about my work, so I signed the contract. They were going to start off with some two-reelers. I was supposed to get into six-reelers and get to do all the wonderful comedy. Marvelous. One of the two-reelers was a Western, my idea. I didn't write it, but I gave them the idea. I would be a grown-up Little Ford Fauntleroy, very nervous, who lives with my two very well-to-do aunts. But I'm Ferdie, who is very nervous. I mustn't play with rough people and mustn't make noises on the street. I'm leading a very cloistered, very sheltered life, very snooty, very snobby, wearing glorious clothes. Finally, my aunts find out that I have been visiting a soda fountain where I have been known to sit and talk to a blonde. So something has to be done. They're going to send Ferdie out to their brother's in the far West. Their brother has a hotel, so they think, out in Death Valley or Devil's Gulch, way out in Colorado, and they think it would make a man out of me to go there. Well, I get out there and I discover that this hotel is a night club, the likes of which has never before been seen. All these women with no clothes on. I'm a little bit shocked, but I assume that as soon as they know I'm annoyed, they'll stop all that piano-playing. I want to see the proprietor. Now the proprietor is the bad man of the comedy. I go into his office in the back of a shack and find this fellow wearing a frock coat and combing his wavy hair. I take one look at him and I say, "I'm sorry, sir, but you can never wear a tie like that with that kind of coat." So I rip off his tie, take off my bow tie and put it around his neck, and get behind him to tie a bow. Well, all this fellow's life, he'd been trying to tie a bow tie and he's never been able to. So he and I are buddies right then. Finally, I get the cowboys to take some baths, and I get them smoking tailor-made cigarettes. And soon I'm out on a horse and enjoying the cowboy life too.

My mother lived with me in California. She passed away six years ago. If she had lived two more months, she would have been 102. She was always saying, "Edward, I wish you'd give up this line of work you're in and settle down and amount to something in the community." Well, I would say, "Isabella. . . ." Isabella was her name. "Isabella, this is the community. Twenty-two acres I've got here. All I need is a post office. I'm the boss." She went with me to England three times. I'd see something antique and she'd say, "Oh Edward, where are you going to put it?" I'd say, "Don't ask me where I am going to put it. I don't know. I just want it, that's all." So we'd store a whole room full of furniture and finally build other rooms.

Well, I have some ideas for the future. I want to build a great big tower out here, about sixty-five feet high with a deck around the top. Then I want to put on the top of it a very ornate water tank that will work electrically. Then when I press a button, all over the grounds, a marvelous fountain system, fed by this thingumajig way up on top of the tower, will flow. Like Versailles. About $175,000 and I can do it. Life begins at eighty-two.

I had a very nice luncheon one time when I was doing a picture with Douglas Fairbanks called *Reaching for the Moon*. Mr. Fairbanks had asked me if I would like to join him at lunch with Sam Goldwyn, Mr. Schenck, and another tycoon—I don't know who it was. I sat there and listened. It was there I heard Mr. Goldwyn say, "Douglas, it's not how much they like you in this town; it's 'are they going to like you in the next one.'" That's been on my mind ever since—every time I play a play and I hear the applause. I know it's Friday and Sunday night is the last performance and then I'm going to play in Ohio. I wonder if they are going to like me there. They did here, but will they like me there? I think Robert Browning put it this way: "A man's reach must exceed his grasp, or what's a heaven for?" Well, Mr. Goldwyn said it a little differently. It isn't how much they like you in this town; it's "are they going to like you in the next one?"

ROD LA ROCQUE

M Y MOTHER was Irish, my father French. He and all his brothers were in the hotel business. I derive from a family of chefs. La Rocque really is my name. I enjoy *haute cuisine*, the wines and the sauces. Mrs. La Rocque, who is a native European girl, brought a lot of Hungarian recipes to this country. We have wonderful goulashes, stuffed cabbage and peppers. With all that, I'm the string-bean type.

I had only intermittent schooling. As a boy in Chicago, I thought it was more interesting to hang around the stage doors of stock companies than to have a paper route or run errands. I broke in with Willard Mack and Maud Leone. They were married then and had a stock company. At age nine I went to Willard Mack to inquire about boy parts. He told me they were going to do *Salomy Jane* using a boy in the second act. Pay for a performance was one dollar. If he had offered me twenty-five cents, I'd have been perfectly satisfied. It turned out that my uncle, Bill La Rocque, was a friend of Willard's. He advised me against telling my father about this transaction. I agreed to keep it a secret. We did the play two weeks later, and afterwards another one called *Samson Valley*. Because there was a bugle boy in that, I had another part. Mr. Mack's advice helped me so much. I was an amateur. He took it upon himself to direct me gently, kindly, firmly. I thought you had to give it everything. Once he called me over, told everyone else "at ease," and turned to me "You want to be a trouper, don't you?" A trouper in those days was the real thing. You could ad-lib, you could do anything. I thought, "Oh gosh, isn't this marvelous? He's taking an interest in me."

"Yes, I want to be a trouper."

"Then forget everything you've done up to now, but remember this: try as hard as you know how to make the other fellow believe what you are telling him."

That didn't fully register with me until years later, but it is awfully good advice. First of all, *you* have to be convinced. Then you have to make the other actors believe what you are telling them. Finally, pick up their cues. It's almost that simple. Of course, there are additional techniques you acquire by experience: the fencing thing, the boxing bit, the dancing routine.

When summer vacation was over, I went back to school. But the Forbes Stock Company came to Chicago the next summer. I surmised correctly that Mr. Forbes might be acquainted with Willard Mack. Mack was a well-known stock performer, and later a great personality on Broadway. He married Marjorie Rambeau first and Pauline Frederick next, became involved in films, and starred for Mr. Belasco. With Gus Forbes, I did *The Middleman, When Knighthood Was in Flower,* and *The Professor's Romance,* all common stock pieces. Like everyone else, I'd be doing one play this week, forgetting last week's while memorizing next week's bill. That was a fabulous and wonderful discipline.

Uncle Bill got tickets for Mother and Dad when I did the boy in *Salomy Jane.* Dad didn't know whether to be furious or elated. But he gave in. It was harmless enough. The company had dedicated people. Salaries were nothing like they are today, but they loved the theater and lived within their means. That was a great lesson. I started out as an impressionable kid. It would have been so easy for me to go wrong, not by chasing the bluebird of ecstasy, but just by not learning to be contented. Loving people should be our greatest pastime, and I was schooled in that direction by the people I met who were friendly and showed me how to be the same way. I might have been taught underhanded things, not "Make the fellow believe what you're telling him," but "Fake it, Rod. This is all just make-believe."

Let's see now. I was born in '98, so in 1914 I was sixteen years old. The stock companies for some reason stopped coming to the North Side of Chicago. There was something over on the South Side, but long trips didn't interest me. I thought about motion pictures because of the Essanay Company on Argyle Street in Chicago. And I liked films such as *The Million Dollar Mysteries,* the serials, with Pearl White and Kathleen Williams, actresses I later came to know whom I didn't dream of knowing then. I played in vaudeville with Jim Carroll around Chicago where there were maybe a hundred movie theaters. Usually on weekends, actors tried to hop up to the picture studios. I asked our laundryman, "Do you know where the Essanay Studio is?" One of his colleagues had that route. He got me the address. I went over on a Saturday. Carroll and some of the others were horrified. "You're not going to do that, Rod. Dear old boy, you've played in the theater!"

It so happened that E. H. Calvert was making *The Snowman* with Dick Travers. It had a saloon scene requiring lumberjacks. He asked me what I knew about make-up. Fortunately make-up had interested me. Willard Mack and Gus Forbes were character actors. They had taught me how to use crepe hair and that sort of thing. If there was no boy part, they'd let me be in a mob scene. I'd put on a beard, a wig, or an old hat. So I exaggerated a little bit, "Oh, yes, I can do it. What do you want? A man with a beard?"

"No, just stubble."

I remembered a trick which Willard Mack had taught me. You put spirit gum on your face and instead of using burnt cork or painting it or trying to cut hair so fine that it looks like stubble, you take a sack of Bull Durham tobacco and flake it across the spirit gum on your face. It was the texture of tobacco, but you could get away with it. That was that. When I left, Travers and Calvert asked me to be back on Monday.

"Sure."

I left with a check for $3.25. It was what they paid extras. The 25¢ was for carfare. Nothing for lunch, but we would go to Sternberg's at the corner of Argyle Street and Broadway for a glass of beer and a meatball for five cents. I was always in make-up, so no one knew my age. I would get my glass of beer and a meatball. The older actors made up for our paltry expenditures. They'd buy booze in the evening, highballs and liquor.

I came back on Monday. Calvert said he wanted to do close-ups the next day. He picked two or three of us to stand near Travers. I returned on Tuesday—and that was finished. I asked Mr. Calvert if I could come back every day to see what was doing. He thought that would be a good idea. Gloria Swanson was there, but she was just another girl working at the studio. Gloria and I started at the same time. She also came from Chicago. Bryant Washburn played the juvenile, Ruth Stonehouse was a leading lady, along with Nell Craig and Lillian Drew, and Francis X. Bushman, who was the big male star.

The name Essanay derives from Spoor and Anderson. Spoor was a real-estate tycoon in Chicago. Anderson was Bronco Billy. He represented the West Coast division of Essanay. We didn't see Bronco Billy in Chicago, but when Chaplin broke with Keystone, they got him. He made some pictures out there, and I had a chance to see him. When Chaplin left Essanay, Spoor made an attempt to replace him with Max Linder, bringing

Linder to America for that purpose. However, Linder was no Chaplin.

In those years, 1914, '15, '16, '17, I hung on, finally getting up to five bucks a day because I had a wardrobe. I could put on tails or a dinner jacket. That was an elevation or a promotion of sorts. Then I got better and better parts. I was fascinated. I had always been interested in photography, camera angles, lighting. The people were very interesting. While I was there, D. W. Griffith released *The Birth of a Nation*. That was a must for all of us to see. Nothing like it had ever been done before. I was greatly impressed. The medium seemed to possess tremendous possibilities. After that, Mr. Spoor made a deal to get Henry Walthall, a star of *The Birth of a Nation*, to come to Chicago to join the Essanay Company. It was very exciting. We worked inside with artificial light. Doors and windows were painted on the scenery. We were making Black Cat pictures which were two-reel features. Black Cat was a brand name for our melodrama and comedies. I played both. I did General Grant in a two-reel picture and generally developed toward character roles. I was the heavy many times.

But Essanay finally gave up the ghost in Chicago. Bushman left. Washburn got an offer to go to the Coast. Ruth Stonehouse had other interests. It was slow disintegration, or gradual metamorphosis. I asked Mr. Calvert what he planned to do, and his answer was New York. I told Mother and Dad that New York was a possibility. They had no objections. My parents were very sensible. I also had very loving sisters. We were a happy family, with none of this "did you hate your mother, was your dad a villain" business. Mother did admonish me to keep in touch. Off I went to New York, with sixteen dollars in my pocket. I arrived at Grand Central Station. My train was late because of the snow. I had a suitcase with some things in it. I asked a policeman, "Would you please tell me how I could get to the YMCA?" He directed me, "You get on the so-and-so streetcar and get off at 57th Street. Then walk west." I thought New York was going to be a production you couldn't possibly understand, at least for the first week or so.

I got to the "Y" and to my friend, Ralph Graves. We lived in a dormitory, eight of us in one room. The first night I'll never forget. When we woke up in the morning, I said, "I've got to see Mr. Calvert. I wonder what kind of weather it is?" It was an inside room, naturally, so we had to stick our heads out of the window and look up at the "patch of blue," as prisoners call the sky, if you can believe the line from Oscar Wilde. I looked fairly decent, so I tried to find Mr. Calvert. I went to his hotel, but they knew nothing. I thought, "Gee whiz, what does a fellow do now?" So I asked Ralph. He directed me to Eddie Small, the agent who eventually became quite a big producer. I presented myself to Mr. Small and filled out a little card for him. No one had yet thought of saying, "Don't call us, we'll call you." You just kept going to see if there was something at Vitagraph, or at Paramount up on 57th Street, or at the New Jersey studios in Fort Lee.

There was a little place on Seventh Avenue where they had chocolate cake for five cents, rice pudding for five cents, and two cups of coffee for five cents. We would go over, have good cake, rice pudding, and coffee. It was a feast. We were getting along. Then I went one day to Eddie Small, who asked me if I could ride a horse. I had ridden, in some Essanay pictures, on horses rented for our Westerns. Oh yes, I could ride.

"But can you ride a horse with armor?"

"What do you mean?"

"Wear a suit of armor and ride a horse."

I thought that this was no time for timidity. "Sure, I've worn armor."

"In that case, go up to Paramount Studio."

I went up and found a man named Ford, the casting director. In time we became very good friends. He explained, "This is a dream sequence. It's a Billie Burke picture, and, of course, the knight on a horse rides in, that sort of thing." We were to do it on Long Island at a castlelike building. There was ice on the ground. The armor was cold. It clinked and clanked. I felt awkward. The director, however, was very kind. He saw that the armor didn't fit very well and that it annoyed the horse, which didn't like all that ice. Finally, he gave up, and I thought, "Gosh darn it, this is a devil of a way to begin a career in New York." But he asked me to come again in the morning for interiors. They hadn't given me a script, and I didn't have the temerity to ask if my part was long. Any salary would have been satisfactory. That didn't matter. I went the next day, got into the clinking thing, and we shot some interiors. Then, another break: The director told us more exteriors would be made in Florida. That meant they were keeping me on salary and would pay my fare to Florida. We were all going to the same hotel. Florida!

It turned out to be an agreeable initiation into Paramount Pictures, but I still wanted to keep a foot in the theater. I wondered whom to see and where to go. I had read a lot about William Brady and his daughter. He owned the World Film Corporation, and Alice was his star. Robert Warrick was another, Carlyle Blackwell yet another. Mr. Brady we remember as a diamond-in-the-rough kind of man who wore a little pinched hat, always chewed on a cigar, and acted gruff. He was supposed to be a tough Irishman. Everyone warned me that I'd tremble in his presence. I doubted that it made sense to tremble in anybody's presence. His secretary, major-domo, and girl Friday was a Miss Healy. We got along from the very beginning. I went in on the hoof, off the street, and announced that I'd like to see Mr. Brady.

"Have you an appointment?" she asked.

The door opened and Mr. Brady stood there. "Did you say you wanted to see me?"

"Yes, sir."

"Come in."

Well, I must say that I did tremble a little at that. What do I do now? Where do I go from here?

"What experience have you had?"

"Oh, I worked with Willard Mack and Gus Forbes and J. Quigley and Maud Leone."

"You're pretty young."

"I started young."

"I'm going to do a thing here, *Up the Ladder*, with Alice and there's a part in it if you can read. Will you read for me?"

"Oh, certainly. Have you got the script here?"

"Yes."

"May I take it home? I'd like to study it just a little bit."

Actually I wanted to catch my breath. I went home to one of those third-floor walk-ups in a theatrical boarding house on 45th Street. It was ideally situated for walking everyplace to see agents and producers. I studied very hard that night, but easily, unfrightened, you know. I was concerned, but a funny type of confidence seemed to envelop me. I remembered Willard Mack's slogan, "Try to make the other fellow believe you." Just by being honest and sincere, I might get away with it. In fact, I did. Mr. Brady wanted to know what my salary was. I'm not sure what I said, but it endeared me to him. I said, "Mr. Brady, I haven't got a salary."

"What?"

"I haven't got a salary. I'm looking for work," I repeated.

"How are we going to get together?"

"Mr. Brady, a man of your reputation and ability knows what this part is worth. I imagine you're willing to pay what the part is worth and the actor who plays it probably isn't worth any more than that. However, if the actor isn't equal to your demands, you wouldn't want him, I'm sure, even if he'd do it for nothing. I mean, you know what my salary is, I don't."

"Are you kidding?"

He signed me for the part at $125 a week. Honestly, it would have frightened me to ask for that amount. I knew that in movies we were getting $100 and $110 for juvenile parts. But you weren't supposed to make that kind of money in the theater. We tried the play out, but it wasn't for Broadway. We played Atlantic City and a couple of the other places. Alice felt shaky about it too. So we folded. But I had established one more contact.

Then I went back to the movies. We made *Paying the Piper* directed by George Fitzmaurice. And at Paramount I worked with Reginald Denny. Throughout that period, I free-lanced, simultaneously at work on a movie and a play, or moving back and forth. Most of the time I was moonlighting.

I had been corresponding with my family all the time. Every once in a while mother would do a wonderful chicken in aspic and send it express. I'd have a feast in my room. With two salaries coming in, I thought it was time to get a little apartment. I looked up some places at Cathedral Parkway, 110th Street, rather a nice neighborhood at that time. I found one and sent for my mother and sister. Just then Goldwyn needed a leading man for Mabel Normand, who was under contract to him in Fort Lee. I took the test and, by Jove, got the part. Goldwyn kept me. I played with Mabel Normand, Madge Kennedy, and Mae Marsh—comedy with Mabel Normand, tragedy with Mae Marsh. The Madge Kennedy picture was fluff about "young lovers with problems." Willard Mack came out to Fort Lee when Pauline Frederick left Paramount to star for Goldwyn, and he brought Mary Garden over for *Thaïs*.

Mr. Goldwyn decided to give up Fort Lee in order to establish the Goldwyn studio in California. He took over the old Triangle Studios. On his invitation, I went to see him about going out West with the others. He always held it against me that I turned him down, though I did so politely.

"Mr. Goldwyn, I can't leave New York. I'm hung up with the theater. You've been very generous. We've had a happy association."

"It's all right. If you don't recognize an opportunity when it comes, that's okay," he said.

I felt that I had unintentionally hurt him a little bit. That would have been about '19 because about two years later, we were making *The Ten Commandments* for De Mille.

I returned to the theater with Mr. Brady. Bob Leonard and Mae Murray came to the theater one night. Bob introduced me to Miss Murray, who was his wife of that period. They asked me to go out with them after the show. They enthralled me. She was charming; he was a lovely fellow.

"I want you to come to the Coast with us. I've got two pictures. One is *Jazzmania*, and there's a gigolo in that I'd like you to do." (He had seen me as the heavy in a play.) "The other is *French Doll*—and you'd have the lead in that."

"It's very interesting, but I will have to take it up with Mr. Brady. I am under contract to him. The play is closing and I don't know what he has in mind. He has first call," I hedged. Bob volunteered to talk to him. "Well, look, this is a personal thing with Mr. Brady. He's been like a father to me, and I don't want anyone to intercede. I'll present it to him."

In the egotism of youth I was sure Mr. Brady would insist, "You stay with me, boy." I guess I was considering myself indispensable and nobody ever is. I went to Mr. Brady and told him that Bob Leonard wanted me to go to the Coast. Mr. Brady was a San Francisco boy who had never stopped loving California. He said, "Rod, jump at it. You take it. Go." I was hurt for a moment! "You want to get rid of me?"

"Don't be silly. It's the opportunity of a lifetime."

"You know I was out there for you in *Thy Name Is Woman* with Mary Nash," I reminded him.

"Didn't you like it?"

"Well, we were only in San Francisco a week and then in Los Angeles a week."

"It will grow on you."

"But I'm coming back to you."

"Listen, they're going to pay you more than I could afford, and I wouldn't stand in your way for anything. I'm very fond of you, Rod. Grab whatever you can get. Go on out there and feel free. Please."

I did go and made both pictures at the Metro-Goldwyn-Mayer studios. Mr. Goldwyn had pulled out of his company. Mr. Mayer was having trouble running his studio in Glendale. Metro, with Bert Lytell, Grace Allison, Harold Lockwood, and Alice Lake, went down the drain. By an act of absolute magic, Mr. Mayer organized a company out of these three failures: the Goldwyn, the Metro, and the Mayer enterprises. With Mr. Thalberg, he pulled these three strands together and created the great Metro-Goldwyn-Mayer that it became. That was our studio when we made *The French Doll* and *Jazzmania*.

Thalberg was about my age. We always used to call ourselves brothers. He was a boy genius. Thalberg had an innate understanding of tempo, timing, character, philosophy, psychology. Why? That's like asking why does Heifetz play the violin so expertly. Many people studied with the same masters, maybe worked as hard as Heifetz, but they're not Heifetz. Irving started out as personal secretary and major-domo to Uncle Carl Laemmle at Universal. Somehow or other, he absorbed everything. Thalberg and that very different man, Mr. Mayer, made a team. They complemented each other, each displaying an uncanny acumen for his craft. Thalberg's feeling for story was terrific. On two occasions I know, they had collected a bunch of junk which, at best, mystified everybody. Irving would be called in. He'd ask Mr. Mayer for another $150,000. And money counted then. They weren't making million-dollar pictures every day. We would come in mostly for two or three hundred thousand. *The Ten Commandments*, *The Covered Wagon*, *The Big Parade*, *What Price Glory* didn't cost millions of dollars. Anyway, Irving would take the money and make the necessary cuts and retakes, put the thing together, get another score for it, etc. It would open to hurrahs. He had that kind of genius; a fabulous story sense, just fabulous.

After the pictures with Leonard, while planning to go back East, I sent for my mother and sister. I got a bungalow for them, thinking they would like to see the Coast and might not get another chance. They could come out, look at the place, see Santa Barbara, and have some fun, maybe drive up to Arrowhead, give it a gander, and we'd all return together. One afternoon I came home to the bungalow. It was over on Orchid Avenue in Hollywood.

"Mr. De Mille wants you to get in touch with him," Mother said.

"Oh yeah, I'm sure he does."

"Rod, there's a message on the desk."

We were always kidding one another. When I'd leave in the morning, I'd casually remark, "Oh, by the way, Mother, if De Mille should call, tell him I'm busy," some inane comment like that. I went over to the desk and there was a message to call Lou Goodstadt at Paramount Studio. Going along with the gag, I called at about six o'clock. A secretary answered.

"He's waiting to hear from you."

I thought, "Nobody is waiting to hear from me at this hour. Everyone's gone home. But anyway, I'll call and then I can say I've rung him," but . . . there was Lou Goodstadt.

"Can you come over to the studio . . . ?"

"Do you mean now?"

"Yes, De Mille is in his office."

I later learned that De Mille never quit. He worked until seven-thirty or eight o'clock and loved it, late dinner and all. I freshened up and went over. Mr. De Mille was kind and sincere from the very beginning. Why had he called? Because "We're going to make *The Ten Commandments* and there's a part in it you might like."

"What makes you think so, Mr. De Mille? How did you find out about me?"

"Paul Iribe."

Paul Iribe was his art director, a Frenchman who had worked with George Fitzmaurice when we did *Paying the Piper*. I had played a ne'er-do-well, an absolute wastrel, just a son-of-a-gun who left a wake of sorrow and regret wherever he went. Paul Iribe remembered, "There's a guy out here by the name of La Rocque who does this thing and seems to get away with it." Mr. De Mille got a copy of *Paying the Piper*. The great De Mille addressing me:

"I think you'd like this part. It's a heavy. I understand you just played a lead for Mr. Leonard. I hope you don't mind playing a heavy."

"I prefer it. I'll take a heavy any day."

Richard Dix was to be the lead.

"We're going to do it in two parts. In the first part, we have Pharaoh and the opening of the Red Sea and so forth. Theodore Roberts will be Moses. Then in the second part, we do a modern version. Regretfully, we will have to show that everything would be the same today: that these truths are still violated, things Moses and Jesus tried to tell us continue to be ignored or disregarded. You'll like the script."

He assembled us: Nita Naldi, Leatrice Joy, Richard Dix, Theodore Roberts, Charles De Roche, people who had played with De Mille for years and years. I was probably the only newcomer except for Nita Naldi. It became a family affair. The "modern" cast went up to the desert as assistants and extras in biblical mob scenes. When we did the modern segments, players who had been in the biblical part joined in our scenes. It was integrated, undivided, one story—which, at that time, was a remarkable thing.

There were spectacular events—like the opening and closing of the Red Sea. We had a technician, a miniature specialist, Roy Pomeroy, who was really fantastic. You wouldn't believe how he did the Red Sea scene. Two blocks of Jello, carved with waves, were set on a huge table which was split in the center. These two blocks were held together with water rushing over them. On cue, things on winches turned the blocks and separated them as water came over the edge. With the screen Jello shimmering and going away, they ran the thing forward, and it closed. When it was reversed, it opened. We had double exposures which were so realistic that we were hounded by the Society for the Prevention of Cruelty to Animals, who wanted to know why we had treated the horses so cruelly. Chariots, horses, and riders had tumbled into the Jello. Mr. De Mille asked these people, "Aren't you worried about the human beings at all?" They were only concerned about the horses. When we proved that it was double exposure and a trick, all was forgiven.

The picture was a sensational success. There were subtle things in it; for instance, a title that was completely overlooked. I remember the son, Danny, whom I played. The mother was overly religious, very arbitrary, and dictatorial. I was the bad son, the contractor. I had built a church and cheated on the sand and mix. The church caves in and kills my mother while she is in there praying. Naturally, I "pay the piper" in the end. But the son, when the mother is remonstrating, says, "Mom, darling, you think you're carrying a cross, but it's a whip." Most people miss that.

Later, we used a couple of similar subtle touches when we made *Feet of Clay*. (Vera Reynolds was in that with us.) We're despondent and make an attempt at suicide. We turn on the gas in our cramped two-bit apartment. There's all this mist and all of us lost souls are going beyond to the other world, one guy with the noose still on his neck. He had been hanged. We're walking, mystified, hand in hand. Victor Varconi is the judge, maybe St. Peter, who knows? One person must go this way, another that way, depending upon the judgment that Varconi makes. When one of us starts asking for mercy from him, the hangman says, "I only turn the pages. The writing is your own." He turns a piece of cellophane. It's crystal clear.

De Mille and Jeanie Macpherson kept writing together, concocting these lines, really collaborating. De Mille would ask a player, "Is there something wrong with that? How do you want to say it?" Dialogue was modified all the time. It's one of the traits that kept De Mille going so long. He had more serious intentions than you might suppose. It's true that he always managed to inject sex into even the most sacred subjects, but to him it was the only reason that any of us were here. You might have to hunt for it, but his underlying themes showed deep hostility to discrimination and prejudice. His emphasis on sex, apart from its entertainment value, signifies that we're all born the same way.

The Ten Commandments made me a star, whatever "star" means. I had been starred before, but not with such impact. The reception in London was wonderful. Allan Dwan and I then went to Paris to see about another picture. But the female star became seriously ill, with appendicitis I believe, and the picture we had in mind was called off. It would have been *The Golden Coast*. Then I got a cablegram one morning in the Savoy Hotel. It was from Mr. De Mille. He had decided to resign from Paramount. The cable read, "Your contract is with me, not with Paramount. We're organizing the Producers' Distribution Corporation, PDC, taking over the old Ince studio in Culver City," which later became the Selznick Studios, but were now to be the De Mille Studios. I sent a very simple cable, "Am with you—hook, line, and sinker. Good luck. Carry on. Love. Rod." And so when I finally did leave London after another two weeks or so, I went to Culver City, PDC.

De Mille made individual stars of us all. I did *The Coming of Amos*, followed by *Hold 'Em, Yale*, and what was it? With Lupe Velez, poor darling Lupe, not *To Have and to Hold*. Anyway, we had Noah Beery under contract with us, and Bill Boyd, and Alan Hale. I made *Strong Heart* and ten or twelve other pictures. After that, Mr. De Mille left and went to Metro-Goldwyn-Mayer. He wanted to take me with him. But I didn't feel like it: "Let me rest for five or six months. I've been doing so much of this. I want to go to New York and Europe. I'm in some kind of a rut."

I had met my wife-to-be, Vilma Banky, the first night she spent in Hollywood. That was in 1925. We were married in 1927. She hadn't yet made *The Dark Angel*, her first picture with Ronald Colman. We met at the De Milles'. I loved Mrs. De Mille. She was a charming hostess and a lovely woman. I was pleased to be present at one of her gourmet dinners. De Mille had reminded me, "It's black tie. Mr. Goldwyn will be with a young lady he's brought from Europe and we'd like you to fill a spot." That's how I met Vilma. There was a language barrier, but I had had high school German. You know that she's Hungarian. I had made some pictures with Victor Varconi, who was also Hungarian, and he taught me a few words. We struggled a bit trying to communicate but it added gaiety to the encounter. She was beautiful, wholly feminine, charming, and marvelously European. Since she had seen *The Ten Commandments* in Berlin, she didn't feel completely strange with me. The evening was splendid. Afterwards Mr. De Mille, who had a projection room, ran a picture for his guests. Vilma and I ran into each other from then on. We were both involved in the same studio just a little later. We bumped into each other, got along, loved being together.

Then one day I got hold of Victor Varconi and told him: "I'd like to be able to say 'I love you' in Hungarian. I want to say that to Vilma." He worked with me on this until I could imitate every sound. We got there. On a particularly pleasant evening, I was dreaming of what I would tell her. I had ordered dinner at our favorite restaurant. The music was playing. I thought, "Well, now how am I going to say this?" I leaned over and whispered it very fervently. She screamed, she laughed, and pulled back and said, "Oh Rod, you've been going with that Varconi man again." In my most loving tones, I replied, "Go to hell." But we survived that. I was in love with her and wanted to spend the rest of my life with her. I proposed and she accepted. That's how it's been—and that's how it goes.

I didn't fall for my own publicity. I couldn't carry all that corned beef and cabbage. I was lucky. Naturally the studio made a big thing of our real romance. Vilma and I wanted to go to Santa Barbara to be married in the mission. Vilma's father was a Lutheran; her mother, a Catholic. She went to either one church or the other. But my mother was a Catholic and my father was a 32d-degree Mason. I'd been an altar boy. We wanted it to stick. Well, Mr. and Mrs. Lehr had a dinner at their home. Ronnie Colman was there again. I forget who came with him. Also present were Ben Lyon and Bebe Daniels, George Fitzmaurice, Florence Vidor, and Vilma and myself. I had purchased the engagement ring. When I called for Vilma that evening, I put it on her finger and kissed her. We went to the Lehrs'. The girls in the cloakroom told Mrs. Lehr, who told Abe. After dinner, Abe stood up and announced, "I have a toast. Cupid is in our midst." Vilma had been Ronnie's leading lady in four or five pictures. Florence Vidor and Fitzy were very interested in each other, and so were Bebe and Ben. It was a tossup, musical chairs, roulette, bingo. Abe said, "To Vilma and Rod." Bebe excused herself from the table. We didn't know it at that time, but she called Louella Parsons. So the next morning there it was in *The Examiner*. Boom!

The *Times* resented it because of the scoop and Sam was really furious. He told Vilma, "I brought you to this country. I acted like a father. I protected you. What are you, ashamed? You want to go someplace and hide, disappear?" To pacify him, the wedding was arranged at the Church of the Good Shepherd in Beverly Hills. Oh, it was big. Vilma's bridesmaids were Constance Talmadge, Bebe Daniels, and my sister, Mildred

Rod La Rocque and Nita Naldi in C. B. De Mille's *The Ten Commandments*. 1923.

Rod La Rocque and Richard Dix in *The Ten Commandments*.

Left to right: Vilma Banky, Samuel Goldwyn, and Lois Moran. Goldwyn discovered these two European beauties in 1925. Their American debuts: Banky in *The Dark Angel*, Moran in *Stella Dallas*.

Rod La Rocque, Jetta Goudal, and Noah Beery in *The Coming of Amos*. 1925.

Rod La Rocque and Vilma Banky returning from European trip.

Davis. The best man was Papa De Mille. The ushers were Donald Crisp, Harold Lloyd, Ronnie Colman, and Victor Varconi. They had cameras going and we were shot from every direction.

Our own preference was to avoid all the hullabaloo by going quietly to Santa Barbara and sneaking off on a little honeymoon. But that's not how it was destined to be. Tom Mix drove up in a coach-and-four. Everybody was there. After it was over, we had a reception at the Beverly Hills Hotel. There was a huge buffet with turkey and salads and lobster and shrimp, an abundance of everything. But because of the lights, they made space for two papier-mâché turkeys. As soon as the food was consumed, it was replaced on a conveyor line at the front table. Turkey after turkey after turkey. And salad upon salad upon salad. But someone wrote that it was a motion picture banquet with papier-mâché turkeys. They never forgot that and kept referring to it. Sam would have been terribly offended if we had not complied with his wishes. He was truly fond of Vilma. When we were in the reception line, greeting all our friends with all *their* friends, 1500 or 2000 guests, De Mille wished Vilma happiness and told me I was a lucky guy. Sam almost had a tear in his eye. He looked at me, "Rod, you're going to take good care of her, aren't you?" We went to Canada, to Banff. We fished and hunted. Vilma likes to do both.

By the time we got back, Mr. De Mille had withdrawn from PDC. I told him I was mixed up. My very good friend, Archie Selwyn, had come out to Hollywood and lost his son, run over, I think, by Mary Pickford's chauffeur. I had loved Archie for a long time. He was so smitten. Vilma and I'd sit and talk and have a drink and try to soothe him. One day out of the clear sky, he asked us to do a play for him. I started to equivocate, "That would depend on the play. And I don't know whether Vilma would like that or not." In Europe she had been on the stage, but never in this country. I knew all about the critics here because I had had theater experience in New York, and hell's bells, nothing could hurt me. I'd been torn to ribbons in some beautiful flops. But I didn't want to hurt her. I hew to that line of Samuel Johnson's, "A good wife is like the ivy that beautifies the building to which it clings, winding its tendrils more lovingly as time converts the ancient edifice into a ruin." And marriage can be fragile.

Well, Archie was reasonable, "Look, why don't you leave it up to Vilma?" I didn't think for a minute that it would interest her, but I was wrong. She thought it would be fun. Then again I didn't think he would find a play, but if he did, why not? So long as Vilma agreed. He found a play that Anita Loos had written with her husband, John Emerson. It was an adaptation of a Hungarian farce called *Cherries Are Ripe*. We read the play together and Vilma was all for trying it. They sent us the script. We took the train to New York, and while Archie was getting a company together, Vilma went to Paris for a gown. She came back, we rehearsed and opened in Wilmington, Delaware. It was a riot. They were standing up all over the place. Vilma Banky and Rod La Rocque in person. I guess we were the first film couple to do a legitimate play. We had a run-of-the-play contract and a guarantee against the percentage. With the curiosity that it excited, we were able to make an incredible amount of money. It compared favorably with our movie income. We played one night in an arena wired for sound to 47,000 people. I think it was in Tulsa at the Cotton Palace. Echoes came in all over the pace. It was murder. But the audience loved it.

But there was a lot wrong with it. Anita and John always promised to rewrite, but they never did. It was, "Next week. Next week" or "John is ill" or "We can't get to Anita." Of course Archie was satisfied because it made so much dough. We stayed with it the full season, including eleven weeks at the Erlanger in Chicago. We had some long runs, but I avoided either Coast. Archie expected us to continue through the next season, swearing up and down that the play would be rewritten. "If not, call it off." The production was amusing, but it just wasn't sophisticated enough for New York or L.A. And since they didn't rewrite the thing, I signed a release. They got Basil Sidney and Mary Ellis to play it and opened in the Globe Theater in New York. It closed in four days.

We had another amazing experience. Our headquarters were in Berlin in '31, '32, and '33 when that clown, Adolf Hitler, walked in. I was working for Universal. Uncle Carl Laemmle had made *All Quiet on the Western Front*, a milestone in the new talking picture era. We were to do bilingual pictures. With our visits to Europe, I had caught up on my languages. Our starter was to have been *S.O.S. Iceberg*, with Leni Reifenstahl and Tay Garnett directing. We'd do the English version, "Hello, how are you?" And so forth and so on. Then we would switch to, "*Guten tag*," etc. But somehow or other, the idiom didn't work. You can't just give tit for tat. Also we were surrounded with those Nazis. It was quite an experience. To see schoolboys walking around with armbands and pistols was incredibly shocking to me. By chance, then, we knew quite early that Hitler and his gang were mad.

Vilma made *The Rebel* over there. She did talkies: the first, *They Knew What They Wanted* with Eddie Robinson at Metro-Goldwyn-Mayer, *Child's Fifth Avenue* for Sam, then another, and that was the end. She didn't want to renew her contract. Vilma thought that when we married it canceled her contract. Being a European girl, she was trained for wifehood as an all-time thing. They thought I put the idea in her head. I went all over the place saying, "I know a contract is a contract. But it is the way the kids were schooled over there. When they marry, it becomes a career."

I went on with some pictures. I made a couple that Walter Smith wrote. He was interested in a Mexican bandit, Lastro, a fantastic character. We made *The Delightful Rogue* and *The Gay Bandit* for RKO and *The Swan* with Marie Dressler and Lillian Gish, which George Fitzmaurice directed as a sound picture for United Artists in '28 or '29, using cameras in booths called iceboxes. We made *The Sign on the Door* for Fitzmaurice and United Artists. Then I did an English picture. Gee, I don't even remember the name of it or the time. Let's see, when was I last in England? In '38? Then we felt the great upheaval on its way from Germany.

We were back in the United States, still right on top. But things were getting confused. Our ranch didn't seem to be going well, the Japanese were being rounded up, and you couldn't trust itinerants. We decided to protect that investment in our property and in our way of life. Neither of us was ever completely stage-struck. We loved what we were doing. We're still interested in watching others try, but we've kept our own distance. It was good to be in—and it's great to be out.

DAGMAR GODOWSKY

L IKE MOST women, I never remember the dates and times when things happened, nor do I care to. Let it suffice to say I was born. When is unimportant. My father was a Russian and Mother was American, a New Yorker. But when I was six weeks old, I was taken to Europe by my parents and was brought up there, so that when I was young, I didn't speak English. I spoke French and German.

When father was living in Chicago, he was the head of a music school. He was a concert pianist, but had run the school for some time. Then he had a big, big concert success in Berlin, where we had moved. It was on account of that that the Emperor of Austria sent his emissary to ask my father to take over the music of Austria-Hungary. The whole family moved to Vienna. We became Austrian citizens and lived there quite a few years. Thank God, I have a bad memory. Dates escape me. But one thing I have always remembered very, very well were the wonderful years in Vienna. I loved and adored it.

My mother's family was in the tobacco business. They loved music and the arts, but they were in business. They were well-to-do. Father was brought to their home on Riverside Drive in Manhattan by his uncle. He had just returned from Paris and was asked to play piano in the house of my grandmother. He at once fell in love with my mother.

Father was sort of a shy and bashful type. Each time he visited my mother's home, he left without his belongings. First he forgot his umbrella, the next time he forgot his galoshes, and after that, he sort of forgot everything. Grandma said, "Leopold, you don't have to come here to get your forgotten things. Just come anyway." He became a full-fledged member of the household. Grandmother was so impressed with the young virtuoso that she finally left her family and went with him to France—taking care of him while he studied with Camille Saint-Saëns. It's an amazing thing for her to have left the whole family for this young boy, but he was extraordinarily talented.

I had the happiest and most wonderful childhood. If ever I dream of anything, I'd want it that way all over again. My parents were just too wonderful for words. When my father would introduce me with, "My daughter," it was always spoken with great pride. I don't know why he should have been so proud of me, but he was, and Mother always said, "Am I not lucky to have such a good daughter?"

I remember that on my fifth birthday, I wanted a piano. All I cared about was music. When people now ask me, "Did your father play very much?" it occurs to me that I was never conscious of his playing. I was only conscious of his not playing. As a little girl, I would sit under the grand piano and listen to him. It may sound a bit whimsical, but one could say that I practically grew up under the piano. It was quite natural, then, that I gravitated toward piano lessons. I studied and practiced quite hard because I loved it so much.

We had a German governess who used to practice with me, and I remember that one day—which I'll never forget because it changed my whole life—I was playing something and she said, "You don't think you'll ever be as great a pianist as your father, do you?" She was very harsh about it, and I remember putting my head on the piano and crying. I think I wept for hours, and I never, never forgot that experience. It was so cruel. And it changed everything. It shouldn't have made a difference because Father told me many times that I had more talent than almost everyone he knew. Even recently, I ran into a pianist, quite a well-known teacher who said to me, "You know, you play beautifully." So now I play when I feel like it, but it doesn't matter, for one does not have to be a professional to enjoy music.

I continued to play piano, but never with the same verve. That's when I decided to go into the theater. I wanted to be an actress, I guess, because I've always been an extrovert. When we came back to the United States (some time later), I studied for the stage at the American Academy in New York.

Father didn't like my going into the theater business at all. Still, he knew everybody there was to know, which made things a little easier because every door was open to me. I didn't have to struggle to see someone, as many budding actors and actresses often do. But then again, I had to walk in, and that wasn't always so easy.

Anyway, he introduced me to David Belasco's manager, and I became Belasco's *protégée*. Eventually, I was given the part of Nora in Ibsen's *The Doll's House* at the Lyceum Theater on Broadway, and the play was a great success.

I worked hard in the theater for a while. We were living in New York and enjoying it. A little later my father agreed to teach a master's class in music in Los Angeles. Mother had been quite ill for some time and had to stay home. My father couldn't wait, for his classes were starting, and I convinced him to take me along. And, you see, I knew that he had a friend by the name of Charlie Chaplin whom I was dying to meet.

We arrived in California, and soon after, I met Chaplin. He was very kind and took us to the studio where he was making pictures and then to the Universal studios. The casting director saw me, and in an hour I was in a picture. I know it sounds ridiculous, but they put me into pictures as the leading lady opposite Art Accord, and off I went on location with a lot of men and guns. Father sent a chaperon along. He was terribly old-fashioned about those things. I almost think I married so that I could use powder and lipstick.

In that first film, I had to be on a horse a great deal. I knew nothing about horseback riding. I also remember I wore a Spanish dress, a mantilla, and a rose in my hair. The noise of the guns and horses was terrific, and I was so confused. I honestly didn't know what was going on. I was so unprepared, and it was nothing at all like the stage. But now I was a film star. It was just not to be believed. Instant stardom.

Truthfully speaking, I don't think I ever was a great actress. I was very, very proud that I achieved stardom and fame, but I don't know how good I was. Once the *Manchester Guardian* said that I was one of the great actresses and that Chaplin and I were the only great ones. Well, you can imagine how I felt. It was a little difficult to keep my equilibrium.

I always laughed at myself because when my father and I would come out of a theater, people mobbed me. They'd just seen a picture I was in and would try to get a flower or piece of clothing, and there was my great father somewhere in the crowd. And I thought this was really the funniest thing that could have happened. I was the great success, and he was the great man. The lesson I learned was that mediocrity is really more appreciated than greatness. Some lesson.

You must know that silent pictures were much superior to the talkies. First of all, I am enamored of pantomime. It's a mysterious form of acting which allows a performer to dream all sorts of things into the characters he plays. It is truly an impressive art form, and it was the foundation of silent films. And it is an international language. It also gives the director an opportunity to develop the dramatic action through the gestural expressions of his actors. There were some great directors in those days.

Among the ones I worked with, I most admired John Ford. I made a film with him called *Hitchin' Posts*. Ford is truly great. He has an extraordinary imagination and a special way of seeing things. Of course, we shouldn't fail to mention Griffith with whom Ford originally worked and who I knew quite well, though I never worked with him.

After Ford, I made many, many pictures with the man I married, Frank Mayo. He was well known in the film industry then. This was my first marriage. It occurred in the midst of the gay life of Hollywood. All of us there were terribly young, full of happiness and life. It was exciting and it was a new thing, and it was just wonderful. We were making a great deal of money and were being admired for no good reason.

It never bothered me to be a star. I thought it was divine. On and off stage we were playing to an audience; yet in Hollywood, you didn't feel it. Nobody paid any attention since we were all stars. It didn't matter. We were all great friends, went to hundreds of exciting social gatherings, and when the public wasn't around to offer adulation, we played to each other.

My greatest success, however, came as the leading lady opposite Valentino. I first met him at a night club in New York. In fact, it was the first time I had ever gone to one. I went with Father and Mother, another couple, and Enrico Caruso. I remember sitting there when Caruso introduced him as Mr. Rodolfo Guglielmi, whose real name was Rodolfo Alfonzo Raffaelo Pierre Filibert Guglielmi de Valentina d'Antonguella, and *that* was Valentino.

I didn't see him again until I went out to Hollywood. I had a contract then with Universal Film Company. We were at a dinner party that Maxwell Karger, the director, had given. There were many stars and starlets invited. I didn't know too many people. Then I saw someone I seemed to know and thought, "That's the man I met through Caruso." He came over to greet me. When I introduced him to the others at the party, Nazimova just looked furious. Everybody there followed her example, because he had been in some sort of a scandal in New York. His great friend Bianca de Soeul had killed her husband for love of Rudy.

Nazimova could hardly be contained. When Rudy went away, she said, "How dare you introduce him to us," and then she said a word which I don't want to repeat. She was quite angry. Naturally, all the others followed her example since she was then the queen of Hollywood. It was an innocent breach of etiquette, if that.

I went home and I was troubled. What in the world is all this? Why would she be so annoyed? And she was really annoyed. Ironically, two or three days later, Jean Acker, who was also at the party, married Valentino. Rudolph had called and asked me to be their witness, but I wasn't home. I don't think it was later than eight o'clock the next morning that

Dagmar Godowsky and husband, Frank Mayo, pose in front of portrait of her famous pianist father, Leopold Godowsky.

Dagmar Godowsky and Rudolph Valentino in a scene from *The Sainted Devil*. 1924.

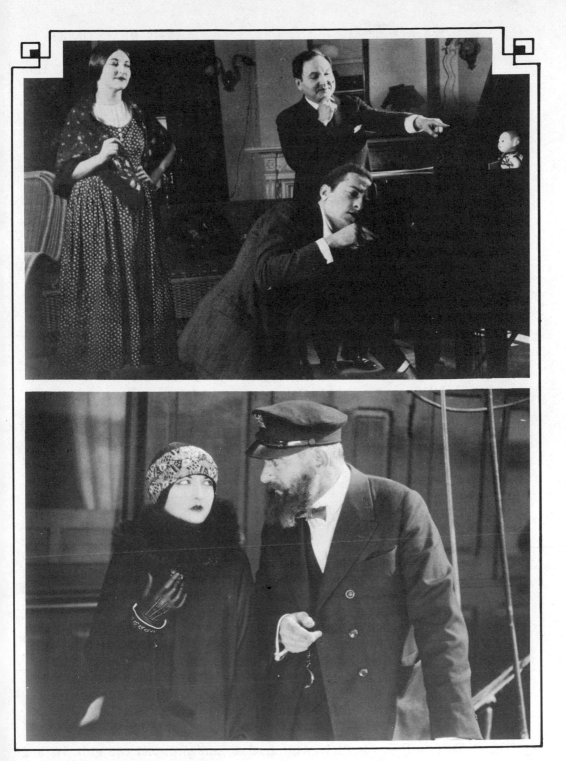

Dagmar Godowsky and Jascha Heifetz in Ray Foster's *Celebritypes*. 1930.

Dagmar Godowsky and Tyrone Power (Sr.) in *The Story Without a Name*. 1924.

I received a phone call from Rudy, "What in the world did I do? How could it happen? Will you help me? It was a terrible mistake."

I talked to him for hours and tried to calm him down. Anyway, soon after, he and Jean were divorced.

It was much later that I made my first film with him in New York at the Long Island Studios. I was very fond of Rudy, but really fond of him. He was sort of shy and I found him very naïve. You know, it's funny that when I first met Rudy, I just saw a very nice-looking Latin. When I came to meet him again, I still saw a very nice-looking Latin. Well, he looked to me like an attractive maitre d', or the way one should look. I found him attractive, but I wasn't overly impressed. Then one day I was on the Paramount lot with Jascha Heifetz, his two sisters, and a friend, and I was showing them around. They had all just arrived on a ship from Australia, where he had done a concert tour. I was talking to them when suddenly Rudy appeared. (By then, he had changed his name and had been Valentino for quite a while.) He just sort of waved to me and said, "Hello, Dagmar."

"Hello, Rudy," I said.

He was walking away from us down a spiral staircase when the two Heifetz girls started to swoon. They said, "It can't be! Who is he? Who is he? We must meet him."

"Who? Rudy?" I said.

I couldn't understand. But I rushed to the steps and said, "Rudy, will you please come up right away," and I introduced him. I thought, "My goodness, I didn't realize how devastating he must be." That's when I really became conscious of how attractive he was. I liked him very much. But I didn't think he had much sex appeal.

He met both his wives through me. Now isn't that a strange coincidence? First, he met Jean Acker that horrible evening when everyone refused to speak to him. That was a whirlwind affair. And then, one night years later, when I was making a picture, I had a party in my home. I was living with my parents at the time. Nazimova, Natasha Rambova, and Rudy were invited. But I couldn't be there. I had to work late at night. My parents took over and hosted the party, and I came home later. That's when Rudy met Natasha.

They eventually married, but it didn't turn out particularly well. It was so sad. It lasted quite a few years, though they were separated. When the papers came out about how very ill he was, she kept saying, "Publicity! Publicity!" She didn't believe a word of it. She was in Europe and stayed there. Oddly enough, I saw him the last evening of his life before he was taken to the hospital. I was having dinner at the Colony. I can see us now. I was at the table on the right with Ullman, his manager. At another table facing us sat Rudy with another gentleman and two girls. He and

Ullman must have had some sort of a misunderstanding. What happened, I don't know. But I couldn't even say hello to Rudy because Ullman and he weren't on speaking terms. The next day, he was taken to the hospital and shortly afterwards died. I was very unhappy because I was terribly fond of him.

And then there was our family relationship with Charlie Chaplin. He loved my father, and I think he loved me at that time. Chaplin, you know, is music-mad. He plays the violin left-handed. He played quite well and, as most people know, composed quite a lot. Sometimes he'd ask me to see his pictures with him, but I never watched the picture. I watched him watching himself. I adored it and would laugh. He would nudge me and say "Shhh!" And then he'd laugh his head off. He enjoyed himself terrifically.

But Chaplin is angry with me. He won't talk to me anymore. You would think that he had a sense of humor. I had written in my book, and it was the truth, that when I started in Hollywood, I was so young that Charlie Chaplin fell in love with me. And he didn't like that, not a bit.

Soon after I had arrived in Hollywood, I went to a party given by Dorothy Wallace. There was a huge garden surrounding the house. On a bench, I saw Chaplin stretched out. On another bench, I saw Mary Pickford. You must remember I was quite young and impressionable. I thought, "Now I understand why Hollywood has such a bad reputation. These people are drunk all the time." To my surprise, when I went in, I saw that the very people who were stretched out on benches were dancing. What they had done was to make life-sized dolls of themselves and let them lie all over the garden. It was perfectly mad.

Every week somebody would give a party. They were all gala events. If you say it was wicked, no, I think it was very naïve, and rather childish and sweet. We were happy. We were exuberant. We were rich. Of course, my own family was different, but these people weren't used to having so much and thus engaged in a bit of extravagance.

I never liked personal property and didn't build a great home. It's a simple case of claustrophobia. That would have forced me to stay put, and I loved to travel. So I was perfectly satisfied with a small home.

I knew everyone. I never thought acting a great art, and I never will think so. For me, it simply provided a wonderful life. I just can't have great respect for acting. I think it's nice, it's wonderful, but as an art, it's nothing much. Writing, yes; acting, no! And that's why I could never take myself very seriously as an actress, I'm sorry to say. It was very hard work, but I liked that, even adored it.

The trouble is that everyone believes his publicity. That is the great danger. When that happens to performers, it's impossible for them to live with either themselves or anyone else. Fortunately, I didn't believe a word of it. I maintained a sense of reality. But remember, I was born into a family where my father was great. Whatever I could do would just have been a shadow of his achievement. And that helped me keep my sense of proportion. Some of the publicity was "made." For instance, my hands would peel. So what did they put in the papers? That I was a snakewoman. Dagmar Godowsky, the snakewoman. Unbelievable things like that. On occasion, they would concoct imaginary romances, but in my case, they didn't have to work too hard. I truly had them. I had quite a few suitors.

Eventually, I married and tried to settle down. But there is a problem in being married and being in the limelight at the same time. It definitely tears people apart. Still, I don't think the divorce problem is exclusive to Hollywood. The whole world is like that now. Nor do I think it is peculiar to the acting profession. Back in those days, perhaps more so. Not now.

My first marriage ended in divorce. As I said, my husband was a film star, Frank Mayo. I married a second time, and I left him too. If I hadn't left him, I would be too embarrassed to mention the whole episode. It was the shortest marriage that ever was in the whole world. As I said, I have claustrophobia, and when he put his arm around me right after the ceremony and asked, "Who do you belong to now?" that was that. I couldn't stand it. I had him take me for dinner and after that I said goodbye.

One of my problems in the movie business was that I was always type-cast as a vamp. Once you're type-cast, it's very difficult to break away. As a matter of fact, when I made a picture with Nita Naldi, also a "vamp," everyone thought that we would hate each other. Not at all.

We were all friends, and we never let any aspect of the business come between us. And then we had those parties. Every week somewhere else. Once my husband and I gave a costume party. It was supposed to be a baby party. Everybody in Hollywood showed up. Nazimova arrived as a Hawaiian baby. She wore a bikini sort of thing with a few grapes. And my husband wore a nurse's uniform which killed me because all the stars were saying, "Nurse, nurse, would you take me to the little girls' room?" All the little girls, Viola Dana, Shirley Mason, Mae Murray, etc., were there in different costumes. I was a Chinese baby, of course, because I looked Chinese. So I thought. It was one of those wild, fun nights. In the morning, I found Edward Everett Horton, still in his costume, sleeping in my bathtub.

After a while I left films and went to Europe—my mother wasn't well. Then I made a short return to film-making, doing one picture in London. I was engaged to make a film in Berlin for Ufa, but Mr. Hitler changed my mind, so I never got to do a sound film. Anyway, it really didn't matter because I so enjoyed my career in silent films. There were any number of marvelous experiences I like to tell about.

I recall a film with Nazimova, *Stronger Than Death,* in which I did Oriental dancing. Bobby Leonard was the director. Every morning, Nazimova and I would get up very early and take Oriental dancing lessons. As a matter of fact, I did a great deal of dancing in films. In one, I did the famous tango with Valentino. I was quite a good dancer, if I have to say so myself. It's very much against my feeling to talk so well of myself. There's one thing about me which I must repeat, I don't take myself seriously. Really, I don't.

Valentino and I did many love scenes, but I really was only attracted to blond men and bald men. I *liked* Rudy, and I liked working with him, but it wasn't easy. Especially when we did two takes—one for Europe and one for America. For America, the takes were very circumspect. You couldn't kiss but just a second, and then nothing. But for Europe—ohhh— were they hot, those love scenes, so hot that outsiders weren't permitted on the set. It was very hard work, even with Rudy.

Yes, we worked hard night and day, there were no taxes, and we made quite a bit of money. But I don't care for money. I only care about *not* having money. I'll tell you a story. I was having lunch with a little starlet one day. We probably had no takes scheduled, and we were lunching somewhere near the studio when along came Lefty Flynn, a very famous stunt flyer. Well anyway, Lefty Flynn came up and said, "You ought to buy property. Some day this real estate around here will be very valuable." I thought to myself, "Well, that's not a bad idea." I was living at home, had no expenses, and I was making nice money. Fine. So my friend, Lefty Flynn, and I left the restaurant, and I bought four lots on Hollywood Boulevard, four lots on Sunset Boulevard, some lots in Culver City, and so on. Every time I made money, I bought and I bought and I bought. My God! To be so intelligent and not know it. This was terrific. Then I got my divorce and went home because all I wanted was to be with my family. That's really why I didn't want to get married. I was so happy at home, why get married? I figured that as long as I was living with the family, I'd give them the property.

"Here, Pa, this is what I bought all these years. You take it."

A few years later my mother came to me and said, "Do you know what your father did?"

I knew she was angry when she said "your father." I said no.

"He sold that property of yours."

"Oh, he did?"

And as I never worried, I didn't think of it again. The subject, however, popped up many years later. I was leaving for Europe, and my brother, sister-in-law, and I went to a big dinner party. A man came up.

"Miss Godowsky, you might not remember me. I was with the law firm for some contracts you made many years ago."

He mentioned the office of the man who was my father's lawyer, who had advised father to sell that property. He thought it a ridiculous investment. So father sold. He got very little for it. But the lawyer died a multi-multi-millionaire.

"Tell me, how much is my property worth now?" I asked this man.

"Fifty million," he said, and not a second did it take him.

And you know, it's a sad story, but still in a way, if I had had all that money, I wouldn't know who were my friends.

WINI SHAW

WE WERE a theatrical family. My father was half Hawaiian and half Irish; my mother, half Hawaiian and half English. During the reign of King Konatoua, my father was his favorite tenor. They called him The Royal Hawaiian. Born in 1910 in San Francisco, I'm the youngest of thirteen children, seven boys and six girls. We put together a family act, known as Joanie's Hawaiians, and came to the states in 1915, where we played at the World's Fair in San Francisco. We went on the road and finally wound up coming into New York City in 1917 or '18. I worked at Rise and Weber's here with Sophie Tucker. I performed continuously in our family act from the age of eleven.

School consisted of a private tutor who traveled on the road with the family. Every one of us had that. I was as tall as I am now when I was eleven, 5 feet 7½ inches in my stocking feet. I wore high heels. And, quite different from that of most children born and raised in the business, my life was beautiful. It seems we never stopped traveling. We went on the Interstate, the Keith-Orpheum. We would go sightseeing. I can remember when I was thirteen swimming the Salt Lake, going to Yosemite Valley and the Grand Canyon. I saw every part of the forty-eight states and Canada at that time. We even took the act to Newfoundland.

The family always performed as a unit. I sang and danced. When I was fourteen, we worked the Audubon Theater in New York City. I was friendly with a girl named Lillian Shea, who was rehearsing in one of the music-publishing houses. She was kidding around, doing a Helen Kane type of thing, the boo-be-doop style. While she was resting, the piano player played "The Man I Love," and I started to sing. There was a knock at the door. It was Phil Baker, but I didn't know who he was then. He asked me if I could start to work with him the next night at The Little Club on 44th Street. I expressed my regrets and explained I was tied up working with my family. He asked permission to discuss it with my mother—who gave her approval. And with that, I started out on my own.

I was young and unsophisticated. I can remember Phil Baker pleading with Mama, "Will you please have her put some lip rouge on?" We girls never used it. I had brothers who, once the show was over and we started to leave with make-up still on, would take us into a corner drugstore and wash our faces for us. The family was very close and affectionate. I used to drive everybody crazy because all night I'd say, "Good night, Mama dear; good night, Mama dear; good night, Mama dear. . . ." Finally my brother would say, "For the love of heaven, will you go to sleep already." It was a beautiful family. They all stayed in show business.

After a while, the family act split up. My brother Charlie went into the Ziegfeld Follies of 1926 and 1927. My other brother worked the speak-easies and night clubs. My sister Esther played the Lexington Hotel along with my other sisters. Once after working with Phil Baker, I was in the town of Tonawanda when Helen Kane found me, and I went into *Simple Simon*. That's where I sang "Ten Cents a Dance." At fifteen, I ran away and married a musician. By the time I was eighteen, we had three children. It runs in the family. My husband joined the act. He passed away eight days after my third child was born.

I went into the Ziegfeld Follies. Then I made a test for Fox Studios, which is how I got to the West Coast in 1934. I stayed on and on at Fox Studios and finally got into one picture with Claire Trevor. I had a tiny bit, a walk-on, and that was it. What a letdown. I had been just sitting around for six months, collecting my checks. I had gone to Hollywood with an excellent contract, especially for those days, $750 a week. In 1934, that was equivalent to $2,000 or $2,500 today. But it did something horrible to my ego to have to sit—and without a thing to do. Before that I had been one of the stars. I had replaced Ruth Etting in *Simple Simon*; then I replaced both Ruth Etting and Helen Morgan in the last Follies that Ziegfeld produced before he died. After that, to go out to the Coast with a great contract, and all of a sudden to have nothing happen. You just sit there, and I did. They kept bringing other people in from the East Coast to do things you knew you could do, but didn't get a chance to do.

When I look back at that waiting period, I realize I had been a little too cocky. Until then everything had come too easy. Because of my family, I had had an entrée. Bookers knew the family, knew me, and everything came a little easier than to an outsider. Hollywood gave me the one knock I needed. Out there, I had no one to fall back on.

After that setback, I got involved in a musical show called *The Shim-Sham Revue*. I invested a bit of money in it and also had a part. A boy by the name of Jack Osterman, who was a fabulous comedian, performer, and singer, starred in it. Diane Lewis, William Powell's wife, was also in the show. While I was doing that, a scout from Warner's came in and soon I had a contract with Warner Brothers. Then everything went well again.

In California, I was the lonesomest thing in the world. I lived at the Beverly-Wilshire Hotel. When you meet people out there, they say, "Wini, you must give me a call." And then they go off, and you learn that they're not in the directory and you can't find them. Before I had been with just my family. All of us were together. We didn't need other people. If we were going to a dance, there were always our brothers to take us. Overnight, the protection and warmth were gone, and I'm out there by myself. I would sit in my hotel room and wait for the maid to come in so I'd have somebody to talk to.

But one day I was walking down Wilshire Boulevard. Right across from the Beverly-Wilshire Hotel was the Brown Derby. And I started to cry. It was time to eat, so I went into the Brown Derby and ordered liver and bacon. I couldn't eat it. When the food arrived at the table, I could no longer hold back my tears. I was so lonesome. Shortly, the captain came over, "I beg your pardon, but what's your name?" I told him, figuring he had taken me for someone else. He thanked me and went away. A note came over reading: "Dear Miss Shaw: You look so lonesome sitting over there. I wonder if we may join you?" It was signed, "Mary Pickford." I'll never forget that act of kindness till my dying day. Here I am, a punk kid, and she's the queen. So far as I'm concerned, she always will be. After that, I was invited to Pickfair for many informal dinners and for her very, very formal dinners where there were "hundreds" of butlers. Each guest had one right behind him, dressed in pantaloons. It was beautiful.

In the beginning, I felt I'd take Hollywood by storm. The family, naturally, always said, "Baby sister, there's nobody like her." Instead, I sat and sat. It's a very strange set-up. You can't ask for explanations because you don't get to see people. Everyone is very, very busy. It was a "Don't call us; we'll call you" type of thing. But it was just at that time that the Fox Studios came out with a big build-up for Alice Faye. They were so involved with Alice Faye and Shirley Temple that everyone else suffered because of it. I couldn't understand the whole thing when it was happening.

I knew quite a few others who didn't get work and were very discouraged. Some never made it, and I feel sorry for them because it's

Seated left to right: Wini Shaw, Mervyn LeRoy (director), and Donald Woods. Standing: Hugh Herbert, Ned Sparks, and Joseph Cawthorn. On set for Warner Bros. and First National production of *Sweet Adeline*. 1934.

On stage in filming of *Ready, Willing and Able*. Wini Shaw and Ross Alexander rehearsing the song "Too Marvelous for Words." 1937.

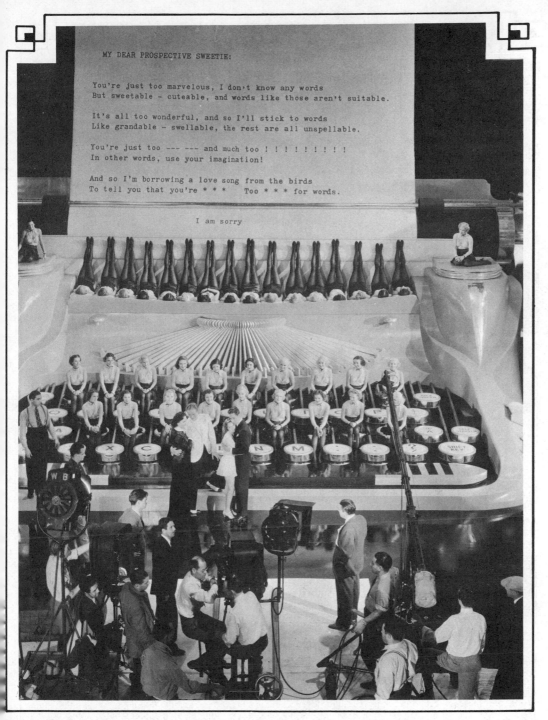

Wini Shaw, Lee Dixon, Ruby Keeler, and Ross Alexander on the set of *Ready, Willing and Able*. Busby Berkeley, dance direction and choreography. 1937.

Entertaining New Zealand troops just outside Cairo during World War II. Left to right: Anna Lee, Jack Benny, Wini Shaw, and New Zealand officers.

Ross Alexander, unidentified woman, Wini Shaw, and Ruby Keeler chatting during filming of *Ready, Willing and Able.* 1937.

heartbreaking. But I had come from the theater and I had had the background. I had gone out there, and I was going to make a picture by hook or crook. I simply had to, that was all. I couldn't let the family down. I would never have quit.

That's why I invested money in the *Shim-Sham Revue*, which I hoped to make into a showcase. And it worked. I wound up doing most of the Warner Brothers' musicals. The first thing I did there was *What No Man*, a short with Phil Reagan. Buzz Berkeley happened to see it and decided that he wanted me to sing "Lullaby of Broadway" in *Gold Diggers of 1935*. I also introduced "Lady in Red" and "Too Marvelous for Words." Then James Morton and I did *September in the Rain*. In fact, I made thirty-two pictures, all told. In those days you could do two or three pictures at the same time. The studios could flip you from one to another. And I never refused a part.

I'm a very good girl. I believe in direction. I think other people can see you much better than you can see yourself. When I picked songs for myself, my accompanist used to say, "Wini, that's not right for you." And nine-tenths of the time, he was right. Sometimes I'd fall in love with a certain piece of music, but it wasn't for me. It was for an opera singer or a concert type, but I'd love the lyric. I'm strictly a girl who goes for lyrics.

Berkeley was a wonderful director. He got his effects by working at them. There wasn't any aspect he didn't know about making motion pictures. He knew camera angles; he knew lighting. He knew what he wanted, and he'd explain it to you. Some directors, even though you feel more comfortable picking up a glass with your left hand, insist that you pick it up with your right. He wasn't that type. Once he explained it to you, he let you do it on your own. If it was wrong, he'd tell you. He would point out what was wrong and yet he wasn't a finicky director. His direction was so clear that often you'd only do a single take.

For instance, "Lullaby of Broadway" I did exactly once. That was the first time anything had been done "live." I mean it was shot and filmed with sound, everything all together, on one of the big sets. The set was on a dolly way in the back. The orchestra was there. We got it on the first shot and just left it that way. Before that, you would record your numbers, synch them with the sound, and then play them out. Berkeley also originated overhead shots of the dancers. What Jackie Gleason does today was perfected by Buzz in the thirties.

Some people, I think, found him a little difficult to work with, but I can only go by myself, and I'm prejudiced in his favor. I'm the type of gal that if I like somebody, I like them all the way and they can do no wrong. And Berkeley had pretty much the run of everything he did. If you're a winner, as he was, nobody fights you. The "powers" were in the business for the money, and all they cared about was that he brought it in. Berkeley got what he wanted.

Most of my friends were actors and performers. When I was out on the lot, they were Glenda Farrell and Joan Blondell, Kay Francis, Ann Sheridan, Anita Louise, Gail Sondergaard. Yet I was very unhappy in Hollywood. All my family was in New York. I missed them. My children were with my mother in St. Albans, where they went to school. Then we bought a farm up in New Hampshire. My daughter and sons graduated from high school in New Hampshire. It would have been very difficult bringing them to Hollywood. Mama was head of the house after my dad died. I mean she was "it." Since everyone else was in New York, I thought it best for the children to be with her. In fact, she told me point-blank that they were going to stay with her. She wouldn't have them out in California with some maid taking care of them. As I said, I did thirty-two pictures. You went to the lot at five-thirty in the morning, and in those days you didn't get home until maybe seven, seven-thirty at night. So she raised them.

Once I had a contract with Warner, I started to save my money. I've always been a little frugal, and I had three kids. Phil Baker used to sing a song which I'll never forget. The lyric was "Put it in the bank, girls; put it in the bank, girls, 'cause that'll be your sex appeal twenty years from now." I remembered it. So I saved my money. Other actors and actresses bought everything in sight, but don't forget my background. I was always able to have what I wanted within reason. Therefore, when I was making good money, I wasn't overwhelmed by it as so many other kids were who had been deprived for so long. Those are the ones who go on sprees. My only indulgence was a mink coat and a Ford. Then I graduated to an Oldsmobile which I stayed with until I came to New York and bought myself a Cadillac. But that's as far as I went because who needs more?

I think one of the cutest things that happened in my career concerned Phil Reagan and myself. We had done so many pictures together that Warner's decided they were going to build up a romance between us. We were sent on the road for a personal appearance tour. Josephine, his wife, went along as my companion, and with my three and Phil's six kids, we had a baseball team going for us. They did things like that to get your name in print. Some didn't care what was written so long as they got publicity. If they hadn't wanted it, they could have stopped it very easily. If you were a matinée idol, the rule was you shouldn't be married. If unfortunately married, you weren't supposed to have children.

When we came for the opening of *In Caliente*, for instance, in which I did "The Lady in Red," the press knew I had children, but the studio tried to keep it hush-hush. So I said to the children, "Now, as we walk through the lobby, be sure you say, 'Mama, mama' all the way up." They did, and that was the end of that. No, you didn't deny that you had them, but in those days, it wasn't popular. In fact, I've got ten grandchildren now. Anyway I had children, and I was darn proud of it. I wasn't going to keep them in the background and all of a sudden, later on in life, wind up with a twenty- or thirty-year-old girl. That's happened to many actresses, and it's rather embarrassing to them.

In a seven-year period I made all those films. The grind was very difficult. Cameras don't lie, so you've got to get sleep. You've got to get rest, but you're working maybe two or three pictures at the same time, doing the shorts, and holding interviews and personal appearances in between. Although most of my films were musicals, I also did *Front Page Woman* and *Satan Met A Lady* with Bette Davis which were strictly dramatic. She's a great artist. And she's wonderful to work with. *Front Page Woman* was the first really dramatic thing I did out there, and I was nervous. For one whole scene, Bette turned around and said, "I planned this. No close-ups of me. Keep the camera on Wini, and I'll turn my back." She had nothing to fear because she had so much going for her.

In 1941, during the war, I stopped making pictures and went overseas for twenty-two months. I was over there with Jack Benny and Larry Adler for the War Department. We went into Italy eight days after the invasion. Then they grounded me because I contracted malaria. After that I continued in show business, first working in the road company of *Call Me Madam* and then back into night clubs. One thing I had missed terribly in Hollywood was "live" audiences.

In 1955, I married Bill O'Malley. I actually first met him in 1943 when he was enamored of a prima donna who was in a show with me. Then I bumped into him in '47 and again in 1955. That was it. I left show business, and we have been happily married ever since.

The Stuntman

GIL PERKINS

M Y ROOTS are in northern Australia, where I was born a little over
sixty years ago. I always wanted to get into the theatrical business, mainly films, but Father didn't like that at all. He gave me no encouragement. We don't use the word "bum" in Australia, but he implied
there'd be no tramps or deadbeats in our family. Mother was more in-
dulgent. Her children could do what they wanted to so long as it wasn't
criminal.

During the First World War, we did little school plays for charity.
And then I got into the pantomimes at Christmas time. Folks in the United
States don't know much about them. Pantomimes were musicals based on
English folk tales, strictly for kids, with some good music in them. The
principal boy was always played by a girl, and the principal girl was
always played by a girl. But there were always other kids' parts, and that's
where I came in.

I went through grade school and on to the Malverne Technical School.
That background gave me a second interest, but I really didn't care to
become an engineer. Then I tooted around the Pacific for four months in
my eighteenth year, having virtually run away from home to ship on a
Norwegian freighter as deck hand. Two years later I came over here with
a buddy of mine. He set up a garage and car business. I sometimes helped
him out, but by 1928, I was on my way in pictures. I appeared that year
in a film called *The Divine Lady*, directed by Frank Lloyd.

When I arrived in Hollywood, they were making pictures, part talkie and part silent. None were completely talkie. I remember Conrad Nagel in *Glorious Betsy* with Dolores Costello. It was part talkie. Hollywood was just about getting to the full sound film. At that time many English pictures were being made over here, and people thought my accent was English. I was hired to play young Englishmen. I was twenty and well set-up. I'd been a champion athlete in Australia and a trackman. I was also a very determined young man. I would go around to studios and talk to casting directors. If I couldn't get any satisfaction from them, I'd go around to the back of Paramount and jump over the barbed wire, get in, and talk to directors or assistants, producers or production men. The Depression hit us early in the thirties and the Screen Actors Guild became powerful, but I was doing all right financially, even though many smaller people like me couldn't make the same money they did.

I worked for Paramount, RKO, and other studios during this period. Sometimes I made twenty-five dollars, sometimes thirty-five dollars, a day. And sometimes I made one hundred and fifty dollars on a weekly salary, sometimes two hundred dollars. But a day's work could mean fourteen hours. On the "day" check you got overtime; on the "weekly," you didn't. Joan Crawford's *Our Dancing Daughters*, probably her last silent, was just being finished. It made her a big star. But the industry was switching. I can't say that I had much experience with silents. By the beginning of '29, late '28, everything made by a major studio was a talkie, although some small independent companies would still shoot silent and then dub in either the voice or the sound. We did *The Vagabond King* with Dennis King and Jeanette MacDonald. Gary Cooper was at work on *Seven Days Leave*. It was made from an English story called *The Old Lady Shows Her Medals*. Cooper played a Scotch character with kilts. These were all talkies. Toward the end of '29, we did a famous war play called *Journey's End*, in which I played Sergeant Cox. And at RKO, I did something memorable with Rod La Rocque called *The Delightful Rogue*. Also at that time, they were making *All Quiet on the Western Front* at Universal.

The Guild was formed in the middle of 1933, but we didn't get recognition until around May of 1937. Since then, our contracts have been pretty good. In the early days, we frequently worked on a couple of films at the same time. For example, in '32 I worked on *King Kong* at night and *Madison Square Garden* in the daytime. In those days, I had a shock of blond hair. It was hard to double me and harder to duplicate my voice. So I had to go back, after doing retakes on *Madison Square Garden* in the daytime, to shooting *King Kong* at night for four or five days: I collapsed with influenza.

The Depression slowed down production considerably. A lot of actors were out of work, as they usually are today, but today it's a case of making so many runaway productions overseas. Then jobs were just getting scarcer

Stuntman Gil Perkins, as skeleton, with Bert Wheeler and Robert Woolsey in costume house on set of *The Nitwits*, RKO studios. 1935.

All photos: Gil Perkins doubling for Eddie Albert in *The Fuller Brush Girl*, starring Red Skelton and Lucille Ball, Columbia Pictures. 1948.

Gil Perkins as a human torch runs wild in the granary in *The Prodigal*, starring Lana Turner and Edmund Purdom, MGM. 1954.

On lake at MGM studios, lot #3. Chase scene with speed boats and Hyster. Gil Perkins doubled for Red Skelton in *Watch the Birdie*. 1949.

and scarcer. But I had to live. I couldn't afford to go hungry. I watched guys doing stuntwork, and it occurred to me that they were simply good athletes who used their ability in another direction. It so happened that I was an excellent double for Bill Boyd, who later became Hopalong Cassidy. I went out to Pathé where he made his pictures, and they used me right away. Albert Lewin was the executive producer under Irving Thalberg. Frank Lloyd directed. From then on, up to the *Hopalongs*, I did everything for Bill: all those lumber pictures and sea pictures, like *The Suicide Fleet*, a story about mystery ships during the war. When he started the *Hopalongs*, I was at MGM in the original *Mutiny on the Bounty*, with Charles Laughton and Clark Gable. Since I was tied up on that for four or five months, they started to use a cowboy to do Bill. Then I didn't do him regularly anymore, except when there was a really tough gag that none of the others, or his double, would do. Not too long after that, Red Skelton became a big name, and I started to work with him. I did everything he ever did in pictures when it called for action, right up to the time he went into television.

I not only doubled, but I used to lay out all the action and fix up whatever needed mechanical rigging. There was a tremendous amount of mechanical stuff used in *The Fuller Brush Girl*, *The Yellow Cab Man*, *Watch the Birdie*, and *Texas Carnival*. There was plenty of advance work to do. Besides being a double, I worked with the special effects and rigging department. For instance, when we would tear across the prairie in a chuck wagon and the right wheel would come off and then the left wheel and then the body, I would have to jump over a log and land on a seat behind the horses. Of course, all these things have to be rigged.

There were then twenty-five or thirty recognized stuntmen. I aspired to become a top man in the business. Top stuntmen held out for the basic money or more. That was my goal. There were a number of cowboys who were good horsemen, doing their own equestrian stunts and working more or less as extras or as cowboy riders. But all-around men who were good, and were recognized as good, numbered only a few. Then the profession grew and grew. Today in the Stuntmen's Organization, which is a fraternal association within the industry, we have at least one hundred and twenty members, but I wouldn't be prepared to tell you how many of those could be classified as top men. That would be very difficult. Who is going to be the judge and the jury to say which of them to honor as exceptionally good? On the outer fringes you'll find others who don't belong to the Association but work as extras and do a stunt when they can.

What I found interesting about this job is that there was no place to learn, no place to be trained. It was a business, or a bundle of skills, that you learned from experience. In our later years, some of us have taught the younger guys. But we've had no certified training school for stuntmen.

You usually learn by watching someone do a stunt on the set and thinking of a better or easier or a safer way to do it.

Many men would be great whether they had help or not. No doubt if there were training schools, every kid who was a commando in the army or a parachute jumper would try to qualify. When the young hear about how much money can be made, they flock to it. This has already happened to a degree. And it will continue. These days a lot of work is divided into small pieces, and there are guys on the edge of being incompetent taking work away from men who should get it. I say this without sour grapes after a long and good financial career. Pretty soon I'll be of retirement age and I'll get an excellent pension from the Screen Actors Guild Retirement Plan. I really don't have an axe to grind, although at the beginning, it wasn't so easy. For several years some of the top men did their best to stop guys like myself. But eventually they had to and did recognize us.

In a hazardous business, I was young and felt fearless. If you're at all afraid, you should stay out of this activity. One very famous stuntman, Dave Sharp, always said, "If you're not 99 and 44/100 percent sure you can do it successfully without hurting yourself, don't do it." That's a good rule of thumb. The danger in doing stunts varies considerably. I would say that in the great majority of the stunts done today, there's not much danger. But every now and then you get one that you have to cut the mustard on, and it's rough. There is always the danger of killing yourself, or breaking your neck, or breaking your back. In *How the West Was Won*, made in 1962, Bob Morgan doubled for George Peppard. He was through with a stunt, sitting on the edge of a flat car, taking the train back to its starting position. This happened on location in Arizona where he had just been hanging on to logs, swinging back and forth as though they had come loose and were falling down a mountain. He sat there. They started the train. Somebody brought the logs back. He wasn't looking and got knocked down onto the track. Three cars went over him, tore his leg and knee off, tore him apart, damaged one eye. It's a miracle the man didn't die. That's how dangerous this thing can be. And Morgan wasn't even performing a stunt; he had finished with it. Quite a few men do get killed. The overall casualty rate while actually executing a stunt isn't very high. I suppose 1 percent or 2 percent a year at the most. But injuries keep occurring: lumps, bumps, and sprains. A little injury can prevent you from working. It happens less often among real pros, because they check everything pretty carefully; they see what has to be rigged and check it out.

I learned how to fall and tumble at school on the football field. We used to dive out of the willow trees, twenty, thirty, forty feet, and even higher, into the river. I learned how to control my body as a diver. If one's had gymnastic training at school, horizontal-bar training, he knows that his head weighs about twenty-eight pounds, so that whatever he does with it guides his body this way or that way. Appropriate reaction comes naturally to an athlete. It's reflexive.

You also had to know how to rig what you fell into because we used to fall into nets, circus nets or firemen's nets. Today, we hardly use things like that. We use boxes with mattresses placed on top of them. If it's a very high fall, you pile up several layers of boxes and cut the edges off so that the air comes out fast, and when you hit, it's just like going into a soft tissue paper. Or we do it with sawhorses on 1 by 12-inch slats with mattresses underneath and on top. When you hit those mattresses, the 1 by 12 inches bend, even to the point of breaking. They bend three or four feet and then snap off the horses. That cushions you as much as you need. And we use special mattresses, not just bed mattresses. They're thick and made with air in them so that the air expels quickly. We've even gone to what looks like sponge rubber, done up in nets, twice the size of a bed. You can take tremendous falls on one of those, even stop cars. We can do a lot now from the point of view of protection.

In my first stunt, if you can call it that, we marched off the end of a pier at the Isthmus of Catalina, a whole bunch of us, with rifles on our shoulders and bayonets on the rifles. We were supposed to be rinky-dink South American revolutionary troops. Our commander has his attention drawn somewhere else and says nothing—so we just march four abreast into the water with our rifles on our shoulders.

There was no danger attached to that if you knew what you were doing. Instead of keeping to the normal gap between ranks, we doubled it. The four who marched off together made sure they went deep and swam out. The next group went deep and swam out. If they had gone down and come up at the same spot as those before them, their necks would have been broken. When you know those guys are behind you, you're not about to swim straight up. Everyone knew what he was doing in the water and that nobody would have to come off the pier to help.

With a red hairpiece on, I look quite a bit like Red Skelton—in *his* hairpiece. The cameramen used to photograph me from ten to twelve feet away. When we did *Whistling in the Dark*, I got to know Red slightly. The next thing he did was *Ship Ahoy*. They needed a double for him on that. He didn't know my name, but he asked for "that chap who did it on the last picture." Al Schenberg, a nephew of Louie B. Mayer's, was the production man, and he wanted to know what "that chap" looked like.

"Well, he's my height and he's got red hair."

"I can't think of a stuntman like that. I'll ask the casting office." The casting office called me.

"Go down to the set and see Al Schenberg." I went.

"Hi, Gil, what are you doing here?" Al asked.

"I've come to see about doubling Red Skelton."

"I think you'd be great, but he wants the guy who doubled him on the last picture, a big red-headed stuntman. I don't even know one. Do you?"

"Yes, it's me."

"What do you mean, it's you?"

Just then, Red sidled up, "That's the guy."

So Al turned to him. "You big silly jerk. He doesn't even have any hair. What do you mean?"

From then on, we did the *Whistling* pictures: *Whistling in the Dark*, *Whistling in Brooklyn*, and *Whistling in Dixie*. Then came *Merton of the Movies*, *A Southern Yankee*, *The Show-Off*, and *Neptune's Daughter* and *Bathing Beauty* with Esther Williams.

The staples of the stuntman are slapstick and Westerns. Without them, you wouldn't need stuntmen. The essence of slapstick is pie-in-the-face. I was at NBC all last week working on a spectacular called *The Legend of Robin Hood*. In the last part, where we're trying to catch Robin Hood, another fellow and I are supposed to be officers of the army. We're in command, chasing Robin Hood, when pepper and all kinds of stuff are thrown at us as we go through a fair at Nottingham. Then they make a cut to where we've fallen down. As I get up off the ground, boom, a pie in the face. You can't even keep it out of Robin Hood. (Of course, I worked in the original talkie with Errol Flynn. No pies in that one.) When we did *The Good Humor Man* years ago with Jack Carson, we threw 6,000 pies in one week on the stage at Columbia Studios. The L. S. Pie Company trucks came in every day with 1,000 pies. We'd throw them all day long. They were real cream pies. I don't know whether they favored lemon cream or coconut cream. All I know is that I had to do another cream-pie gag once. It was supposed to be in a little school theater. A mule kicks me in the fanny at the entrance of the theater as I am backing out. I go down on my face and keep going all the way down the aisle into the orchestra pit. There was a wire to catch me, but I felt as if I were riding an aquaplane in the ocean. As I slid down, cream pie came spraying up all over the place. When we got through with that picture, it took six or eight months to get the stink of stale cream out of that stage. It had become rancid and unbearable. You can understand why I'm not likely to order pie in a restaurant. Apple pie at MGM is an exception. The same pie chef has been there since the days of L. B. Mayer. He makes the best apple pie I've ever tasted. But outside of that, I wouldn't touch a pie.

I haven't done as much Western work as many of my colleagues. Some of them concentrate on it. But I have done a few. I worked on *Dodge City* and *Virginia City* years ago with Errol Flynn, and, much later,

The Conqueror with John Wayne, which wasn't exactly a Western; rather, it was a Western transferred to Mongolia in the days of Genghis Khan. But you still fell off horses in the same way. I also did *The Alamo* six or seven years ago in Texas with Wayne. For months, we had rearing horses, falling horses, saddle falls, and falls off the fort.

Having learned to ride as a kid was a help. It didn't teach you how to fall off, but that's something you learn awfully fast. Let's say a horse is running, and you want to fall over. You pick a spot where the ground is soft. If it isn't, you get a shovel and a fork and spade and soften it up. Then, when you get ready, you just throw yourself in the direction of that spot. It's best done with your feet lower than your head so that you hit ground on your toes. That way, when you hit you're rolling, which takes the shock out of the fall. That is not, however, the only way to do a fall. Some stuntmen do a dive roll—which is all right if the horse isn't running too fast and if you've got him weighted down so that he is not running wide-open. What happens in the dive roll is that you dive, tuck your head, and hit on your shoulders, which is all right if you're not going too fast to tuck your head so that you won't snap the hell out of it as you roll over. If you're going at a three-quarter gait, you can manage. Some guys, when they are "shot," just kick off backwards. But the trouble with that is that the horse is going one way and you're going the other way. It isn't too safe. If I have a choice, I go off sideways. You hit out and roll, which takes all the shock out of the fall. Of course, we wear arm pads, tail pads, and back pads, if necessary.

Most of our stuff is rigged nowadays by the special-effects department, also known as the prop-shop crew. Quite often, the script helps. But directors tend to have very definite ideas of what they're after in their action. They tell you, "I want this to happen." John Wayne is an example of an actor like that—he thinks he's a stuntman anyway. He was originally a propman at Fox. Wayne started on Western Avenue with Fox when it was Fox Film Corporation. The studio on Sunset and Western Avenue is still there and is used for TV productions. I don't think Wayne worked too long as a propman. In the middle of 1930, John Ford decided he would do *The Big Trail* as a remake of *The Oregon Trail,* a great silent picture. He figured Wayne would be ideal for the lead. But something happened. Ford didn't like the script as they wrote it, or whatever. So Raoul Walsh took over. He still used Wayne. George O'Brien's wife, Margaret Churchill, was the female lead. Before that, Wayne had never done a picture except maybe as an extra. But his beginnings as a stuntman are pure myth.

They went on location with *The Big Trail* first to Yuma, Arizona, then to the Grand Tetons up at Jackson Hole, Wyoming. It took four or five months to make. They came back to finish it. Then he made a picture with Loretta Young, who was borrowed from Warner's for *Three Girls Lost*. I think we made one more, but around 1931, Fox let him go. He didn't do anything for six or eight months. Then an independent producer hired him to make quickie Westerns, turning one out in six or seven days. He used to make, maybe, eight a year. Then early in 1938, Republic, which had gone into and taken over the old Mack Sennett studio, apparently wanted to get rid of Crash Corrigan. They replaced him with Wayne, who made a couple of Westerns there. Later in 1938, John Ford came along with *Stagecoach* and starred John Wayne. From then on he never had to make another quickie.

The war started soon after that. We were short of leading men because a lot of them went into the army. We had Wayne, Cary Grant, Ray Milland, Randolph Scott, Fred Astaire, and a few others, but that's about all. They were working all the time. Wayne now made nothing but big pictures, either at Universal, Paramount, Republic, or MGM—all over the place. After the war, Ford, who had gone in as a commander doing photographic documentaries, started to make pictures like *Fort Apache, She Wore a Yellow Ribbon, Rio Grande*—one after the other—and Wayne got to be an important box-office star.

In the last ten years, I've done more acting than stuntwork. I also set up large action scenes. I rehearsed and laid out the beach landing in a picture which involved 500 Marines and 500 Japanese in Okinawa. We did two big jungle suicide-battles in which everybody was killed. Dawn broke on a battlefield with 1,000 corpses lying around. I rehearsed the performers as if they were really Marines and Japanese soldiers fighting in Okinawa and showed them what I wanted, like how to fall off cliffs with machine guns. On *Hawaii* two years ago, I handled all the action, although much of it was cut in the final editing. But my ambition is to be a second-unit director. I'm sure I could do that very well. Let me explain to you about that.

In many films there are a lot of action scenes to be shot outside the studio while the main company works inside the studio. Let's say you have a chuck-wagon race. We've got to make shots of the wagon losing a wheel or losing a body. The lead, or the comedy lead, like Skelton, gets blown out by an explosion. He is rescued in the desert by Howard Keel and a girl. They pick him up between two horses and put him in back. Esther Williams's horse comes up, she rides alongside the wagon, and he climbs in back. Since you can do all this with a double, a second unit, with a separate director and a separate crew, sets up at a ranch with his camera crew and shoots it with a double. When you come to integrating the film, you may bring the star out for a day to make close shots of him getting on or off the wagon, but mostly you work from the process sheet on which backgrounds are projected. The star sits on a mechanical horse, or on the seat of a wagon in front, while everything goes like mad behind him. He won't be moving, but this is how you keep him safe. A tremendous amount is accomplished that way, and a lot of time can be saved.

The second-unit director doesn't always receive credit. When Yakima Canutt set up and trained almost everybody in the action scenes of *Ben-Hur*, he did a great job, but went unnoticed. Yak, by the way, is one of the best. There isn't anybody better. But there are other men who are very good. Cliff Lyons is excellent. He was trained in the same schools as Yak. When both were stuntmen, they did many pictures together. I've been on quite a few. In *Dodge City* and *Virginia City*, Yak and Cliff and I and a bunch of others were all brought in as stuntmen.

In the forties, Yak got out of doing action. He started directing. Cliff did it in the fifties. Because of their close association with stars like Wayne, they were given special opportunities. Had Skelton stayed in pictures, appearing in two or three a year, all of them jammed with action, I don't doubt that by now I would have been directing. Actually, the director who made most of Skelton's shows, or a hell of a lot of them, had arranged to take me into the production department. He said, "You'll have to remain an assistant director for a year. Then I can let you direct all my second units." At forty-one years of age, three months after that discussion, he died of a heart attack. So it didn't work out despite the fact that I can direct a picture. I need only a script, a set, and a location.

The change would be nice because, after all, at my age, when somebody asks my daughter, "What does your father do?" she has to say, "He falls on his head, of course." Doesn't sound very dignified. Financially, it has been very good, if somewhat chancy. The stuntman gets under contract for one picture that may run eight to twelve or fourteen weeks, if not longer. But when the picture's through, he's through.

There are limits to the stunts I'll do. I've refused to do motorcycle and airplane stunts. With a motorcycle, particularly the big American bike, you have too much power floating between your legs to control. And in airplanes, I think there's too much chance of something happening, as it did two years ago in *The Flight of the Phoenix* when Paul Mantz was killed. A friend of mine, Bob Rose, who goes back to the old silent days, was behind Paul in the plane when it happened. When the plane touched ground, it began to break up in the tail section and started to flip. Bob tells me that it went over once, and then on the second roll, he jerked his safety belt loose and fell out. Bob only broke his shoulder, cracked his skull, and knocked himself out. A Marine helicopter was following the plane. He was picked up and put on a stretcher. The helicopter had him in a hospital in Yuma in twenty minutes. That probably saved his life.

This type of thing is too damn risky. Mantz was killed because the engine shot back and took his head off. Bob recovered. Three months later, he did the same stunt in another plane. If that isn't guts, I don't know what is. But Bob has ice flowing in his veins. He must figure he's had a good long life. Bob is around sixty-seven years old.

There are other ways to get hurt. I came home once last year from a battle scene and could hardly get out of my station wagon because I'd done a stunt on a horse without proper equipment. The horse dragged me something like 150 feet and tore all the ligaments and tendons in my left leg. I was too crippled to work for quite a while. But that was my own fault. I didn't go out on this location to do any stunts so I didn't have the proper equipment. I went out to play a Mongolian, do some fast rides across the valley, and then some cuts of other riders chasing me. I was supposed to step off the horse and go into a sword fight with the leads. The director decided that it was silly for me to *step* off a horse when I wanted to slash these guys to pieces. So he said, "I've got to get you off the horse. So could you slow down as you come between the principals and let one of them drag you off." I was wearing a big heavy Mongolian boot, and I thought I had my foot out on the tip of the stirrup. Instead, it slipped through as I came off the horse. I got hung up in the stirrup, and the horse took off and started kicking the hell out of my legs. I was surprised he didn't kick me in the head. Finally, I managed to jerk my leg out. Now that was my fault. If I had brought the proper equipment with me, it wouldn't have happened. Fortunately, nothing was broken.

Some of the actors do their own stunts. I worked with Tom Mix, and he was particularly good with a horse and even with a car, but he didn't do as much as his publicity would have led you to believe. He had a double there all the time. Similarly, Burt Lancaster is said to do all his own stunts. He has great ability, particularly from heights. He's very well coordinated and does high-wire and trapeze work. But, of course, he does not do all his own stunts. He can ride a horse pretty good now, but at first he was fairly weak at this. Still, it's true that he's done more things himself than most actors have.

On the other hand, in the *Tarzan* movies, Johnny Weissmuller did only some of the small swings. In the original film that Johnny made, toward the end of 1931, the Flying Cadottas, the great circus aerialists, did all the big stunts. That was probably the best *Tarzan* ever made. All those tremendous swings through the jungle, all that aerial business, that was Alfred and Tony Cadotta.

I can't do anything on a trapeze, though I've done a lot of high-wire work. That's when you're strung up in a wire suit fifty or sixty feet above the ground. For example, we had a sequence in *Whistling in Brooklyn* where Red Skelton, another actor, and two girls are trying to escape the heavies by taking an elevator all the way to the top of a building, but it gets jammed against the metal grating at the top of the shaft. To lose the men chasing them, somebody pulls a bolt, the elevator falls, and they are all hanging up there from the overhead grating. Now how do they get down? First, the actor slides down on Red Skelton and hangs onto his ankles. Then one of the girls slides down the two of them and hangs from his ankles. Then the other girl does the same. Now the four of them are swinging fifty feet above the elevator shaft. One of the girls lets go and swings through an open doorway on the fifth floor. Then the second girl swings in. When both girls are safe, they press a button and the cable starts to move. Skelton grabs the cable and both men swing out. Now this doesn't sound like much, but it is three weeks' work because you've got to do it with doubles and with long and medium shots. And then you've got to make close shots of the actors. I did five Skelton pictures like this using wires in every one of them.

Once in a while, stunt accidents are caused by gross negligence, and then you become pretty resentful. I remember a situation when we were on location and a stuntman in an ape suit had to jump about twelve feet to the ground. He was supposed to jump on two men who would break his fall. Now these two men happened to be guys who drink. At lunchtime they had quite a few. In filming this sequence, these two men are supposed to be watching out of the corner of their eyes so that they are perfectly positioned when the jump takes place. It's all precisely timed and marked, and the stuntman has worked it out for them. But when he jumped, these two characters never even came close to the mark. They weren't roaring drunk, but they were intoxicated to the point where their timing was off. So he hit the ground and wrecked his knee. Hurt himself, not seriously, but just enough so that he couldn't work for a while. We all were resentful. He told both men what he thought of them and said that he would never do another job with them again. We all said the same thing. It's stupid and inconsiderate to drink on the job. Most of us drink a little bit. But none of the boys drink when they're working. It's much too dangerous and puts everyone in jeopardy.

Sadly, it was near the end of these two fellows' careers anyway. One of them went into a decline that sometimes happens to great drinkers. You know, "How he could drink two bottles of Scotch and it never bothered him. . . ." And my answer always was, "It will." And it did. As a matter of fact, one of our most beloved and respected stars did everything he could for this man. He was given 104 pints of blood to try to keep him alive. But he died. I won't tell you who the guy was, but I will tell you who the star was. It was Bob Hope. The other man lasted a few more years, but he too drank himself into oblivion.

I've been talking about stunt*men*, but there are other stunt people, such as stuntgirls. The majority of them seem to come out of "cowgirl" backgrounds. Not all of them, but most of them. It seems that these girls learned to trick-ride in rodeos and are excellent on horses. Occasionally, there's a girl aerialist, but most females have come out of the cowgirl ranks. They don't have a great volume of work, although they are needed in certain places. In all the Skelton shows, we had a girl named Helen Thurston stunt for Esther Williams or Arlene Dahl. Helen's still around. She could do high falls, drive a car very well, skid, spin, and power-skid it, could swim wonderfully well, and dive.

But in general, girls aren't used so much because even a skilled girl will never be as good as a skilled man. It's the basic principle of athletics. We've seen many a first-rate female tennis player, but if you put her with a good male tennis player, he'd beat her pants off. So girls are just not called to do the tough work that men do. We frequently disguise a small man for female stunts. Similarly with children. We use midgets for a child's part because the law won't allow a child to be used to do anything dangerous.

In serials, an unusual thing happens. Actors are matched to the stunt-men. A couple of actors got started that way. At Republic, Yakima Canutt, Tom Steele, Dale Van Sickle, and their like stunted most of the serials. I used to work with them on a regular basis. In casting a fifteen-episode serial, actors were picked to match those men. George Burke got going because he matched up with Yakima Canutt. Yak was going to do all the action. It's a strange way to begin a career, but that's how it happened.

Animal work is treacherous and unpredictable. For years Animal Land and Jungle Land supplied most of the beasts. Then Ivan Tors bought Nature's Haven up in the mountains, called it Africa USA, and started to train animals differently. Of a whole flock of trainers, Ralph Helfant and Frank Lansing are the two most important men in Africa USA. They coax the animals, treat them with kindness, avoid whips and chairs, and never beat them. Their training method is very well thought out. Frank Lansing always had a back-up man ready to help in case anything happened. You'd be amazed at how tractable the lions, tigers, and leopards can be when they are fed and taken care of by these people all the time. I have never heard of an untoward incident in that establishmnt.

Before Helfant and Lansing took over, somebody would now and then get bitten on the leg or arm. Not now. One of their jaguars is probably their most powerful animal. They say that he could take a tiger or a lion or any other animal, so they're very careful, using the other jaguars rather than this one which could tear everyone to pieces.

It's difficult to say which of my stunts was the most dangerous. I could pinpoint several, but I'll take one. In 1931, on a Bill Boyd picture, we were up in the High Sierras at a lumber company. Bill's father is on a

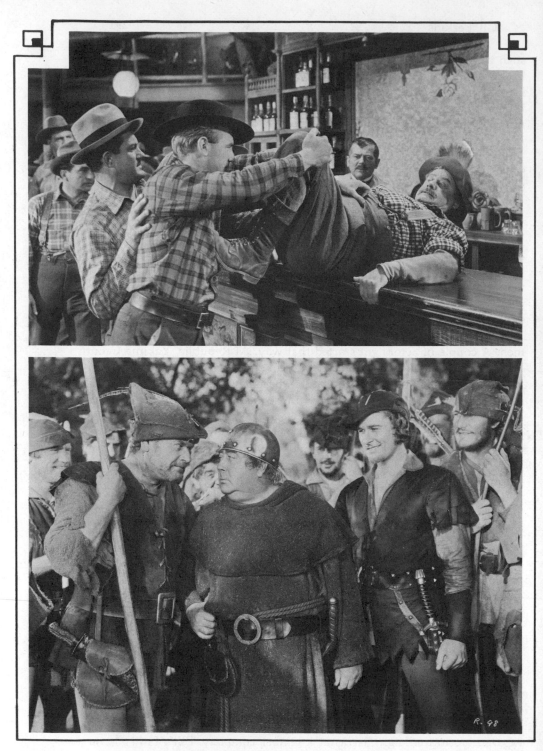

Gil Perkins and Alan Hale in barroom fight in *Valley of the Giants*, Warner Bros. 1938.

Left to right: Gil Perkins, Alan Hale, Eugene Pallette, and Errol Flynn in the Warner Bros. production of *The Adventures of Robin Hood*. 1938.

Gil Perkins as Jacob of Bethlehem in United Artists release, *The Greatest Story Ever Told. 1965.*

lumber train going down the mountains. Bill finds out that the villains are going to sabotage the lumber train, let it run away, and dive off the track. Bill jumps on a log that is on two cables from which the logs are cut. These take him 2,000 feet up to the rail line. Bill runs up, jumps on the thing, and motions for it to be hoisted in the air. Up he goes to about 150 feet, carried through the air at forty or fifty miles an hour, on up through these trees, skimming off the branches. They then drop him on the rail head. This, of course, was me, not Bill.

And that could have killed me. At the director's request, the guy driving the equipment did something I told him not to do. He took me up fast and did the fall at the same time. When the log hit that big steel pulley at the top, it dove all over the place. I only had my hands to hang on with, and my cork shoes were stuck in the log. I wasn't tied on.

Then when he gets to the rail head, he runs across the rail and over to the top of a cliff. The train comes around under it, and he jumps (or rather I jump) twelve feet from the cliff onto the logs. Then he jumps between fifteen cars to the locomotive to rescue his father. The shortest jump is five feet; the longest, ten feet. All the while, the train is snaking down a mountain. I did this several times for different camera set-ups, back, profile, and forward. If I had ever missed and gone down between the cars, I would have been done for. Fortunately, I never missed. I calculated that if I ran fast enough, the momentum would help me keep my balance for the jumps. It did.

Another time, I doubled a cowboy named Tom King who was running away from the heavies. He tries to escape across a gorge. A high cable with a car moves back and forth across the gorge. To release the car, he has to go to the control house. When he gets out of the control house, the car is already on its way, so he can't get hold of it. He looks around and sees a piece of steel which is really a vaulting pole. He takes a run and vaults out over the chasm into the car. There was a net thirty feet below. Thank God, because I missed it three or four times before I got it and landed in the net each time. The only danger attached to that was landing the wrong way and cracking your neck. It's not as easy as getting set, taking off, landing on your back, and turning over.

There have been others like that, but the one on the log car was the wildest, particularly because we had a second-unit director who would do almost anything to get a shot. On one of these runs, before I got to the locomotive, I thought the train had run away. Normally they go at about twenty miles an hour, but this one was really zipping along. I thought it would jump the tracks. I jumped on the end of a flat car, getting ready to bail out before it pitched off the tracks. We came to one of those flat spots where they stop the train and let the brakes cool off before they go down the next section. The engineer stopped the train. That night I talked to a forest ranger who said, "You know something, if you hadn't been shooting a picture today, I would have thought that that train had run away."

"I thought it had too. I was getting ready to bail off it."

Many years afterwards, I was talking to the second-unit director who explained to me what had happened: "The men operating our equipment wouldn't run the train fast enough for me. They claimed the company rule was twenty miles an hour and they were not about to go any faster." And then he reminded me, "I went off on the bush, ostensibly to take care of myself, and when I came back, I started at the end of the train and pulled all the air out of the last fifteen cars. When we started down the grade, our brake pressure wasn't up. That's why the train took off."

Until the locomotive pumped up enough pressure, were were really zooming down that mountain. It was actually a runaway. I might have gotten very badly hurt, but had I picked my spot and bailed off, without having the train come off on top of me, I'd have been all right.

Aside from my torn-up leg, I've never been severely hurt, but I've been shaken up often enough. There have been other close calls. For instance, once when I was making a commercial, a car accidentally turned over. I had an idea that it would, and I told the agency man. He disagreed with me. But it did what I said it would do: the left front tire pulled off, and it did turn over.

Looking back, I would say that there have been a number of big changes in the business. Number one, it has gone from being a fun business to being a very serious production business. We used to have directors like Woody Van Dyke who would play gags and do anything. It was full of laughs. No more. And then, the accent used to be on quality, which is less so today, at least in my end of the business. There was a time when the director would prepare a picture, shoot it, and then sit in on the cutting. Some like Hitchcock and Stevens still do. But half of them never even see the cutting. They may drop in after lunch to see rushes from the day before, but not always. Most of the time, the cutter or the cutter and the producer are on their own.

We also miss saloon fights. We don't do them on the scale we used to. Two of the greatest I ever saw, and I was in both of them, were in *Dodge City* in 1938 and *Seven Sinners*, a year or so later at Universal. On both occasions, we tore the place apart. And we did a pretty good job in *The Great Race* at Warner's with Tony Curtis and Jack Lemmon. We completely destroyed a saloon. Only the roof remained, with a post to hold it up. The structures we destroyed were made of real wood except where you had contact, it was balsa wood. And the glass was plastic. It used to be made of candy, but candy under the lights would just melt.

When you're doing a fight, you always fake it. You learn what looks good from which camera angle and where to throw your punches. Very rarely do we make a mistake and hit the other guy, although I caught one fellow, when we were doing a Skelton picture, high on the chin, with a glancing blow. I never close my fist and hit hard. My fist stays loose so that it doesn't hit with any force. For some strange reason, when you are actually hit, it doesn't look as good as when you're not.

The fake fight looks better than the real! If you watch a picture fight, you'll see that much of the motion is broad. If you're in a real fight and you stop to pull a punch, your opponent will drop you before you get started, or come damn close to it. But if you do a fight with short punches, the way you're supposed to, the camera doesn't see it. To make a brawl look realistic, you have to use long looping punches and then follow through. It's the follow-through that really gives the desired effect.

It's the same with fencing. You've got a foil in your hand, and if you did what fencers actually do, engage, disengage, play with disengagement, lunge, and so on, the viewer would never see anything. Consequently, you make your moves, your ripostes, bigger. With broadsword and saber, you can go into things that look very good.

I learned fencing from a master, Fred Cavens, who did the original stuff for Doug Fairbanks, Sr., the first *Robin Hood, Romeo and Juliet, Captain Blood*, and all his other pictures. He was a fencing master at nineteen in Belgium, and a master of masters at twenty-one. In later years at MGM, he did *The Three Musketeers, Scaramouche*, and *The Prisoner of Zenda*. More recently, John Heremans, another fencing master from Belgium, has worked with the stuntmen.

I was never accomplished in foil or épée; that is, as a genuine fencer. But from the point of view of fencing in pictures, I was. As a matter of fact, just recently, Al Cavens, Fred's son, and a very accomplished swordsman in his own right, and I did some sword play in *Robin Hood* on television.

The great problem of being a stuntman is that it's difficult to get any other kind of work. Those in charge believe that only an idiot takes such chances as we do. Yet, how could you survive to my age and do these things without a little intelligence? I know a number of stuntmen who are excellent actors. They've had the best training available by working with and watching actors all their lives. It's the real way to learn. I can relate all kinds of situations where someone would say, "Why don't you let the stuntman play that part?"

"Not on your life. He's a stuntman. We need an *actor*."

So we have the stigma of being stuntmen. And while they'll let you do small parts occasionally, they'll never give you a part you can really do something with. It's hard to graduate from stuntman to anything else.

The Voice Animator

BILLY BLETCHER

I COME from Lancaster, Pennsylvania, born there, September 20, 1894. My father was in comic opera. He declared, "No son of mine will ever go into show business." I didn't heed his warning. Instead, I started out as a "spotlight" singer in the old silent theaters of Philadelphia. I went only as far as first grade in night school. Show business was in my blood, and there was nothing I could do about it. My brother, though, took father's advice; he's been in the tailoring business all his life and has never left the hometown.

Anyway, a spotlight singer should be explained. On a screen, color slides would be flashed showing, perhaps, a boy and a girl and a beautiful setting. The accompanying song might have been "All That I Ask Is Love," which would be sung by another boy standing in the spotlight. The operator would then change slides, and the "spotlight" singer would do another song.

I met a fellow in Philadelphia, much older than I, by the name of Bobby Heath. He had written a song called "Pony Boy, Pony Boy, Won't You Be My Pony Boy." Do you remember that theme? So, I went into the music-publishing business with Bobby Heath. He then wrote a thing called "Oh Gee Dance the Suwee with Me, Ain't It Nice?" and was that a lousy song! It broke Heath and broke me.

With the few dollars I had left, I decided to go to New York. An agent sent me to Sheepshead Bay, about five miles from the Vitagraph Studios, where I got my first job. I worked there every night and doubled

Saturday and Sunday afternoons as a singing waiter—the piano player was Vincent Lopez.

Some of the boys from Vitagraph would come down to Sheepshead Bay to have their highballs and beer, and we'd sing silly songs. One day John Bunny said to me, "Why don't you come up to the studio and just sort of hang around?" The studio was a great big place like a bull pen, with a swimming pool built for miniature scenes and water scenes, backed up with scenery. I asked Bunny, "Do you think they'll let me in?"

"Well, just come to the gate and tell them I sent you."

I went the very next Monday morning, and a guy there roughly sped me on my way: "Oh, go on in. You're another actor, I suppose." I walked in. I met Ralph Ince, who was from the very famous Ince family, and he hired me just like that for a picture he had about ready to go with Mabel Normand. I was the bellboy and she was the maid. I looked just the right type because I was so short, a fresh punk sort of a kid with a lot of guts. The pay was two dollars and fifty cents a day with lunch. If you got five dollars a day, you were playing one of the leads.

Then along came Larry Semon and a team with the name of Montgomery and Rock. I worked in all their films. They were really slapstick in those days, but not quite as bad as Mack Sennett's Keystone Kops (of whom I was one when we first came to California). I stayed there and worked sporadically in feature pictures they made with people like Betty Blythe, Edith Storey, Maurice Costello, and the Bunnys, Mr. and Mrs. Sidney Drew, and Tony Mareno.

However, I got sick and tired of standing around waiting to work as an actor. I wanted to get into the production end of the game at the studio owned by J. Stuart Blackton and Alfred E. Smith. Blackton had engaged William P. S. Earl, a Fifth Avenue photographer, who talked Mr. Blackton into allowing him to direct a picture. Mr. Earl had an assistant who sort of sat around; I used to sit around and watch *him*. This assistant was let go, and I said, "Why can't I do what he did?" They were working on a story called *Mary Jane's Pa* in which there was a printing office. It so happened that as a kid, before I got into show business, my dad had tried to make a printer out of me, and I knew how to set type. So I became Mr. Earl's assistant.

To cast these films, we would stand at an open window high above the "bull pen." A whole crew of actors standing in the yard would be called over whenever we needed them. One day, I called a very tall, fine-looking, beautiful gal up to the window.

"My name is Bletcher, and what is your name please?"

"My name is Betty Blythe."

"There's a part in this picture, and we'd love to have you for it. Would you care to do it?"

Billy Bletcher, bathing beauties, and Vernon Dent with megaphone. 1922.

Left-to right: Billy Bletcher, Alice Howell, Bert Roach, Charley King in a Universal one-reel comedy.

Al Christie comedy (one-reeler) with Jimmy Adams and Billy Bletcher.

"Oh, yes."

It was the first picture she ever worked in, long before she became a famous star.

The assistant in those days had several responsibilities. He made the people up, he checked the wardrobe, he held the slate for the camera, he did all the manual labor, so to speak. I learned all this from watching.

I had to break down the script, the budget, and everything else, because Mr. Earl, a man brought in from the outside, knew very little about the business. I didn't know a hell of a lot myself, but I felt I knew more than he did. In our second picture, *Who Goes There* by Robert W. Chambers, I needed a Prussian officer who could take command of the situation and who knew something about uniforms and military equipment. I remembered an impressive-looking fellow with a European accent, went over and tapped him on the shoulder, and said, "Pardon me, my name's Bletcher."

"My name is Erich von Stroheim."

"Oh, nice knowing you." I didn't know who the hell he was from Adam. "Mr. von Stroheim, there's a part in this picture. Love to have you for it."

Now the assistant director made all the deals in those days. We'd pay actors off at the end of the day. We carried several little packets. One would say $5, which was for the leading people; another packet said $2.50; and another said $1.50 with lunch. Von Stroheim wanted to know how much we were paying.

"It'll pay you five dollars a day, Mr. von Stroheim."

I thought I was doing him a great favor. He wasn't an established actor, but the five dollars made him angry. He wanted more. I went to Mr. Blackton. "I'd love to have this man, Mr. Blackton, but he won't go for that five dollars a day bit. He wants a salary and he'll agree to help us."

"All right, we'll give him seventy-five dollars a week."

That he grabbed immediately, and as long as von Stroheim was on the lot, we were very friendly. Of course, later on he went to California to direct his own films.

As an assistant, I was making thirty-five dollars a week. In those days, that was a good salary. And then, of course, along came my pretty little bride. She was in the yard doing extra work when we met, and that was it. Then along came a Mr. Burstyn with a job for us making a series of pictures in Jacksonville, Florida. My wife got fifteen dollars a week and I got twenty-five dollars. With forty dollars between us, things weren't too bad.

It was called the Vin Comedy Company. There were several acts. Harry Myers and Rosemary Thebe did the polite comedy, no pie-throwing. There was another team called Pokes and Jabs, who were the rambunctious, pie-slinging, rock-throwing, breakaway type with large mustaches and loud clothing. Those two boys would go downtown to see Roscoe Arbuckle and Buster Keaton in a film, come back the next morning, and do the same damned picture on a smaller scale. So who needed writers?

And there was a road house. Every Saturday night we'd go there and drink beer and eat shrimp. They served pretzels with the shrimp. For entertainment there was big, tall, fat boy with rosy cheeks who'd stand up and sing, in full dress suit, "All That I Ask Is Love" and "Goodbye Rose" and all the old favorites. Mr. Burstyn remarked, "This fellow ought to be in pictures, don't you think so, Bill?"

"Yes, but what have you got in mind?"

"Call him down."

So we summoned Babe (he was always "Babe" Hardy to us), and he came out to the studio the very next day. One of the writers had an idea. He made Babe into "Plump," and a little fellow with a great big mouth became "Runt." I was the utility man, so I had to put whiskers on and play the character parts to these two fellows. Then when the company disbanded, Babe went to California.

My wife and I returned to New York, but William P. S. Earl had promoted some money to make a picture with William Walker in California, taken from a novel entitled *Fran*, the story of a girl in a circus. We went to California, and I was still the assistant director, the business manager, make-up man, and God knows what else. When this was finished, I told my wife, "We're going to stay in California.

"Oh, why? I'm from Brooklyn."

"That's your affair. I'm from Pennsylvania, and it doesn't bother me any."

We decided to stay, so I headed straight for the Mack Sennett Studios. Getting in there was like trying to break into jail, but I had a friend, Bud Ross, who was a fine comedian. He was working at that time with the two Gribbin boys, Harry and Eddie, and Andy Clyde. He got me into the studio. They put a cop's uniform on me, and I took the same abuse for three or four months. I was a Keystone Kop. It was rough, too rough for me. You had to move real fast. They used a slow crank camera, but by the same token, when you saw a car coming at you, you had to get out of there, and believe you me, I wasn't a stuntman. I told myself, "The hell with this. I'll find something easier."

I'd read about Al Christie of The Christie Brothers, who produced the Christie Comedies. The stars were Bobby Vernon and Dorothy Devore. I stayed with them for ten years. They had a marvelous studio at the corner of Sunset and Gower right across from the Columbia Studio. The Christie boys owned that whole block, not only on Sunset Boulevard, but all the way up to Hollywood Boulevard where there's a theater now. And in the end, those poor guys lost every dime they had. Or rather, from what I understand, they spent it.

Bobby Vernon and I looked a lot alike, so they made a bunch of "mistaken identity" stories. It was an easy format for the writer. He could sit down and spin one off in two days. Al Christie's was about the only studio that put stuff on paper. The rest did everything off the cuff. I think they averaged two pictures a week, with maybe three cameras and three companies of players. One of the directors, Bill Beaudine, Sr., is still directing *Lassie*.

I also made a series of comedies for Universal. Irving Thalberg, though under twenty-one, was the general manager, an authentic boy genius. After that, I had a fairly long career in Westerns. There always had to be a little guy among the gang or the posse in those "they went that-away" pictures. The first one I did starred Tom Mix. It was in '22 or '23. The director was George Marshall. I was always the little guy someone else would pick on, and the big guy would warn, "Let him alone or I'll punch you in the nose." In my first Western, I was put on a horse. We were supposed to do a run-across shot in which the horse galloped like hell across the front of the camera. Little did I know that these horses were well trained, even better than some of the actors. We raced across and I'm holding on pretty good when all of a sudden, the horse stops dead. I didn't realize what was going on. I flew head over heels right over the front of the horse for probably the best comic slapstick scene of my career.

I then went back again into production in 1925. I made a deal for a series of pictures to be filmed in the National Parks, called *The Honeymooners*. It wasn't very scenic, but this was before color. I got a piece of the deal, a salary, and expenses. All I took with me was a cameraman, a property man, and a girl. I couldn't pick my wife because she was "out in the front," pregnant, you know.

In 1928, Walt Disney had a little place down on Vermont and Hollywood Boulevard, a little store not much larger than two small rooms. He was planning to do *The Three Little Pigs*. My friend, Pinto Colvig, invited me to come over and see Walt about this thing. There wasn't much to do except voices saying things like, "I'll huff and I'll puff and blow your house in." That's all there was to it. I sort of made a hit with Walt, and stayed with him for, I believe—now I'm not definitely sure about dates—twelve to fifteen years or more, without ever being on steady salary, but always sure of three or four calls per week. In those days, he only did animated cartoons. Walt himself was the voice of Mickey Mouse. I was the Big Bad Wolf and another character, Pegleg Pete. Pegleg Pete was a tough sort of a guy who snarled all the time. It was a lovely engagement.

I was able to do voices and dialects well. Very often you had to pick up a script and they would say, "Now, Billy, here you do Pete," but at the same time, you did the Irish cop over there on the corner, or you did that Dutch fellow with a dialect. At that time, I dare say, there were only four or five pros like myself, including Mel Blanc and Pinto Colvig and Clarence Nash. We didn't make a lot of money, but we had regular work. It came easy to me because when I was a kid I used to sing all the old dialect songs like "I'm Not Homesick for Germany." You picked up a sheet of music that called for a dialect, and you did it that way. In vaudeville, almost everybody except basso profundos used dialect.

I watched the Disney operation grow from the little place on Hollywood and Vermont. Walt soon engaged space across the street from the Paramount Studios. He used to do his recording over there with rented equipment. He didn't have his own. He was still small time. But suddenly, he became a big factory.

For a feature picture like *Snow White*, it would take two months to do five or six minutes of animation, and these were only scratch animations, like doing preliminary sketches. Walt would say, "No, you have to do it over again, boys. There's something wrong here someplace." He'd a great mind for humor, although he was a very serious person.

I said to Walt when he started casting the voices for the seven dwarfs, "Walt, I only work here three or four days a week. Why don't you let me do one of these damned dwarfs?"

"I would be glad to, Billy. The only trouble with that is you're too well recognized in these shorts we've made."

"What the hell difference would that make?"

But that's how he felt about it, so I never got to do a dwarf. Billy Gilbert did one, Sneezy. Remember? In the old days, we got no screen credits. Also, the voice people were never under contract. Graphic artists made the real money. We received seventy dollars for one session, and a session could last all day, although we tried to get out as quickly as possible.

My friend Pinto was not only a good cartoonist, but also a good voice man, so he was on steady salary. Pinto played "trick" flute and "trick" piccolo. He was a very valuable man for Walt. Pinto one day picked up his flute and played what eventually turned out to be "Who's Afraid of the Big Bad Wolf?" In those days, cartoons were jammed full of quick-gag dialogue. I saw *Tom and Jerry* in the theater the other night, and there wasn't a word spoken. Things do change, don't they?

As I said, I gained a fairly substantial reputation for doing odd voices and dialects. I remember being called to dub voices for *The Wizard of Oz* at MGM. They called Pinto and myself to work at night on the sound stage. We had to lip-match some of these little characters, like the one who sang "I'm Mayor of the Munchkin City. . . ." In the original sound

Billy Bletcher and Chic Sale in RKO comedy series.

W. C. Fields and Billy Bletcher in *The Dentist*.

Billy Bletcher.

Left to right: Helen Wood, unidentified, Claude Gillingwater, Billy Bletcher, unidentified, James Burke, Jane Withers, Slim Summerville, Sara Haden in *Can This Be Dixie*.

track, you could hardly understand him. Well, I'd watch his lips, they'd slow-crank, and I'd put that voice in his mouth.

Synching was the main problem. It wasn't too difficult once you learned to start the minute the line in the film began. You just had to be careful of your speed. In that film all the midgets used to sing "Ding dong, the witch is dead, which old witch, the wicked old witch." There was a fellow working at MGM who used to sing, "Ding dong, the bitch is dead, which old bitch, the wicked old bitch." So they fired him. They didn't think it was very funny.

The odd part of that job was that you were paid at the end of each workday. The cashier had to stay on the job until you were finished. We'd work from eight o'clock at night until three or four o'clock in the morning. We might have $150 to $200 in cash when we went home. There had been several robberies right outside the studio. Consequently, when we left, Pinto and I put our money in our socks. It would have made a good film if anyone had watched us trying to get home safely with our money.

Incidentally, before they improved the sound systems, one of the big problems was in re-dubbing the noisy crowd scenes. I recall Cecil B. De Mille spending anywhere from ten days to two weeks on the dubbing stage. When he initially photographed foreground action, the masses in the background were so damned noisy that the dialogue in the foreground was inaudible. Something was always wrong with it. I think I worked on the sound stage with him on every big picture that he made until the time he died. He was a perfect gentleman. A lot of people didn't care for him because he was a bit of a perfectionist—but I always found him quite pleasant.

I've done my share of vocal work in this business, believe you me. I made a very successful album with Capitol Records, a thing called *Rusty in Orchestraville*. In it, I'm the old German professor, who does lines such as, "Now, now. Listen Rusty, you must learn to play the piano because, if you don't play the piano, you'll wind up. . . ."

On that record each instrument was given an animated voice. In other words, one instrument would say, "Good day, Rusty," which a girl did by holding a microphone at her throat, you know. She synched her voice to the music of the instrument. I believe that record was originally done in 1943 with Billy May's Orchestra. At first, it was on funny old wax records, but recently, they put it on an LP.

In recent years, our specialty has become quite competitive. Unfortunately, we never formed an association, so it can be quite tough. It's not like the early days when there were only a few of us. Today the agents call for character voices. And hell, they'll send as many as twenty people out on a single call. It's unfair for them to do that. We call them "cattle calls." It's very demeaning to the actor. What happens is that you are given a script and told to sit in the lobby and look it over. Then they call you into a room, and men from the advertising agency then say, "Don't call us. We'll call you and let you know." If you're lucky, your agent will call and say, "O.K., Billy, be at studio such-and-such at ten o'clock to-morrow morning." If you do commercials, though, it is possible for an hour's work, to earn several thousand dollars in residuals in a year's time. So it's not all that bad.

Once sound films came into being, I went almost completely out of acting and into the voice business. I've done small parts in a few films. The last picture I acted in was *The Chase* with Marlon Brando. I had one good scene in it. That's all.

Still, there's nothing so nice as to get a job in a picture like *The Chase*. You sit around and gab with your fellow performers, and there are usually a lot of laughs. There's no rush, there's no hustle and bustle. However, when you're doing a TV show, you've got to have it on the ball and be on your toes. Seldom are there retakes, and the schedule is very tight. You can't even go to the toilet. If you ask the assistant director, he'll probably say, "O.K. But cut it short. You should have done that before you came on the job." So, naturally, films are more relaxed than TV, and the money in films is better too.

One of my most interesting experiences occurred in 1949, when George W. Trendle, from the King Trendle Broadcasting Company of Detroit, came to California to make a serial: those things the kiddies loved to see in the theaters, particularly on a Saturday afternoon. An audition was held at the old Republic Studios in North Hollywood. Forty to fifty actors came out to audition. I was number 44. I fell asleep. I was in back of the set when all of a sudden I heard a man call, "Hey, Bletcher." The man was Jack English. He tapped me on the shoulder, "Come on. You're next."

"Hell, I'm going home."

"No, wait and do this thing."

So I made a record for the voice of the "Lone Ranger," which was to be a series. Engaging someone to do this was a bit surprising since the films had already been made, but the man who had been photographed didn't sound anything like the voice that so many children and grownups were accustomed to hearing. We had to lip-match everything he said and put the voice into the image of the actor seen on the screen. To my amazement, about two weeks later, my agent called me and said, "Trendle's in town and he wants to see you."

"What's this all about?" I said.

"He wants you for that Lone Ranger job."

I didn't believe him but it was true. Anyhow, I dubbed the first series, twelve episodes of two reels each. About four months later, they made another serial, and I dubbed that one, too. Then, in 1950, Mr. Trendle called me on the phone and said, "Will you come and do the radio show of *The Lone Ranger.* Stay for six months or longer if you like."

"What am I supposed to do, Mr. Trendle?"

"I want you to understudy Beemer, Brace Beemer."

"I'd be very happy to do that. Can we get together on the money?"

"I'll give you three hundred dollars a week and your train fare."

We didn't travel much by plane in those days. So I went to Detroit, Mr. Trendle met me at the train, and took me in his car to the radio station. We walked in, and he announced to the crew fellows, "Here's the new 'Lone Ranger.' " You should have seen those guys when they took a look at me. You know, I'm only 5 feet 2½ inches short. They said, "What! You're the 'Lone Ranger.' Impossible!" Anyway, it was one of the nicest engagements I've ever had. Profitable too.

I stayed on for eight months when along came that awful cold weather. Mr. Beemer was often sick, and whenever that happened, I'd have to walk into the studio, pick up the script, and do a live show without rehearsal. We never knew whether Beemer would show up. If he walked in at the last minute, naturally he'd do his show. But I had to be there, and the days that he did show up, I'd work on *The Green Hornet* and play character parts on *The Lone Ranger.* What's fascinating is that my voice matched Beemer's perfectly. Of course, the radio station people knew there were two of us. But no one else knew about it.

In the past few years, I've done English dubbing on foreign films. It's not too difficult. You listen to the sound track. Then you turn their track off. You do a little silent rehearsing to yourself, and by the time you rehearse it a couple of times, you can hit things pretty well on the nose. You must get the tempo of the foreign language and the character's speaking pattern. And there's a marker on the film which helps you hit your cues in synch. It isn't hard to do at all.

In a way, you might say that the last part of my career has been something of an accident. I never had any voice training. Never in my life. It's just one of those natural things, I suppose.

The Director

WILLIAM HADDOCK

MY FOLKS MOVED to Boston from Portsmouth, New Hampshire, five
years after I was born in 1877. I grew up in Boston and knew
from early childhood that I would go on the stage. I saw my first play,
Marked for Life, when I was seven years old. The star was a man named
Sidney Francis. It must have been written for him. The next play I remember seeing was *Peck's Bad Boy*. From that time on, I got to the
theater whenever I could.

I started out as an accountant and ran a fairly prosperous fire-insur-
ance agency, but my strong desire for the stage never left me. I kept up
with a couple of amateur dramatic clubs early in '99. I tried to get into a
Boston stock company, but that didn't work. Then in August of '99, Agnes
Booth, the sister of Edwin Booth and the wife of John Scofield, who owned
a traveling theater in Boston, put on a benefit for the Sharon Sanitarium.
That summer she needed someone to play a small part. It was just a bit
part, and but for Agnes Booth's presence, no one would have realized I
was there. One of the reviewers wrote that the young man who played
with Mrs. Scofield showed talent. How in the hell I showed talent, I don't
know. Then along about the first of January in 1900, I was in town again,
and on a hunch I went up to the Castle Square Stock Company again. I
saw the director and had an interview with him. He had forgotten me, of
course.

"What have you done, Mr. Haddock?"

"Well, the last thing was a play with Agnes Booth Scofield at the Sharon Sanitarium."

"Oh, you were the young man who played with her, were you?"

"Yes."

"Give me your name and address. I may call upon you."

A couple of weeks later, I got a card inviting me to come in and see him. On February 18, 1900, I opened in a new play, a dramatization of a book by Conan Doyle. I stayed with the company until August, 1901. The old stock companies would put on a new play every week and have a matinee every day. I got marvelous training. Alfred Lunt received his training up there, too. Jimmy Montgomery, who wrote *Irene*, opened the same day I did.

In August, I decided that I had been in stock long enough. That brought me to New York, where I couldn't get to first base. I was almost resigned to another year in Boston stock. However, I met Walter Perkins on the street, and we chatted.

"What are you doing, Bill?"

"Looking for an engagement."

"How would you like to play for me in *Man from Mexico* this season on the road?"

"Fine."

We went on the road. I left him and *Mexico* in Seattle. In March, 1902, I joined Charles Dalton in *The Sign of the Cross*. The following season, I went out with *Alice*, and the next with *Lover's Lane*. The year after that, I did stock in Memphis. After Memphis, I returned to New York. Ed Rose put on a vaudeville act starring a lady friend of his, and I got into that. I was with Ed on and off until I went into pictures. I worked for him when he had something for me, and when he didn't, he placed me elsewhere. The act was called *Chicago Twenty Miles Away*. It was supposed to be a comedy. Outside of New York, it was. We got so many curtain calls in the three towns we played that the curtain man had to call for an assistant to help him. We thought we had a hit. But in New York at Keith's 14th Street Theater, we went on about twenty minutes to three and at a quarter past three, we were out in the alley. We died standing up.

Then Ed Frohman produced a play of his own called *The Square Deal*. I was stage manager and played a part in it. We ran in New York for fourteen or fifteen weeks. Doggone good play, but badly handled by the management. Then Frohman decided to put Sissy Loftis out on the road in an act. So we got ready for her. She had two Englishmen she wanted in the act, and Ed insisted I go along to handle the act and play a part in it. We opened in Cincinnati, and on Wednesday night, one of the actors didn't show up. We tried to locate him at the hotel and couldn't.

Finally the house manager informed me that I'd have to go on. He couldn't wait any longer. The program had already been turned around. I said, "Miss Loftis, we'll go on next."

"But how will I get my cue?"

"Don't worry. You'll get every cue. We'll go on."

I played both parts. I was afraid of one thing. I had to draw a gun which the lead was supposed to knock out of my hand onto the stage, she was to pick it up at the end of the act, and if she didn't, there was no act. But I managed to fumble it as I pulled it out and dropped it. Strange to say, the act never went as well as it did that night. It simply proved that my part was superflous. We ended the act in Chicago.

Once when we were rehearsing *The Square Deal*, I got the third act set with everything marked out on the stage and turned to Ed.

"All ready, Governor."

"The stage is yours," he replied, and walked out of the theater.

So I had to direct it. I complained that night. "Ed, you pulled a dirty trick on me today."

"What's that?"

"Turning over the direction of the play to me cold turkey like that."

"Come, come, you're going to be a director some day. You might as well start now."

We did several more plays on the circuit for a couple of years. In 1908, I was off two or three weeks just before Christmas, helping the secretary of Actors' Equity with his desk work. A chap walked into the office, asking me, "Can I get an actor here? I'm with the Anderson Company, and we're going to Newport to make a picture for the government."

"Oh, we've lots of actors around here," and I turned him over to the secretary. I had planned to go to Boston for Christmas with my folks. He told the secretary, "We'll go up over the weekend till Wednesday, and then I'm going to Boston to spend Christmas with my sister." "It would be right up your alley, wouldn't it, Bill?" the secretary said.

He looked me over.

"No, you're not tall enough."

"I knew there'd be a catch. What part of Boston are you going to?" "What part of Boston are *you* going to?" he turned the tables.

"Dorchester."

"Dorchester! That's where my sister lives. I'll take you along."

"What is the pay?"

"I'll pay your expenses."

"To hell with that," I thought.

"All right, I'll give you five dollars a day."

Afterwards, I found out that five dollars was standard pay for actors in pictures, no matter whether they were walk-ons or leads. And, of course,

Eclair Studio, Fort Lee, New Jersey. 1912.

William Haddock and company on location for a one-reel western in Pawnee, Oklahoma. 1913.

The Eclair Company departing for France. 1912.

there were no stars. When we got to the Newport Naval Training Station, I discovered he was doing stuff that didn't look right from a theatrical point of view. I said to him, "Mr. White, do you mind if I make a suggestion?"

"Of course not," he said.

I recommended such-and-such and such-and-such. He felt that I was right. From then on, after doing a scene, he'd ask, "How did it look to you, Bill?" I had to okay it. If I didn't, he would make changes.

Well, that stint was over, but one day not much later I was at the Actor's Society when Jim White came in again. He proposed that we get some people together and go out to Orange, New Jersey, to make pictures He wanted a couple of girls and three or four fellows. I found friends of mine who weren't working and we went out to Orange.

"Come on Bill. We'll look up some locations."

I didn't know what he was talking about. Look up locations? The only locations I knew were in studios. We started driving around. He'd point somewhere, "Now there's a good spot." So I just yessed him to death. We drove back, and he told me the story I was to do on these locations, no continuity or anything else, just the story, and told me to make-up the cast while he was setting up the camera. Well, I addressed the cast, "Boys and girls, I didn't know it, but I'm your director."

We made two pictures, and we were on the third when it started to snow—which killed us in Orange, New Jersey. My Scotch blood didn't like the idea of all that money wasted. I remembered that Lakewood had a warmer climate than the rest of Jersey. So I went to the Central New Jersey Railroad on 34th Street and asked them if there was snow in Lakewood. At first, they didn't know, but later they found out and notified me on the phone that there wasn't. I called Jim and he drove over in his car so damn fast that the police gave him a ticket for speeding. We raced out to Lakewood the next day and finished the picture. We made one more, and then I went back on the road.

The films were comedies; there were four or five; we had no written continuity for any of them. It was all improvisational, and I was an improvisational director. The actors simply did what they were told by their director. Remember, this was for the Edison Company, and there was no sound on any of it, although I'd had experience with synchronized sound in 1907 working as an actor for Cameraphone. On the early sound films, records were made first to which the actors had to synchronize their actions and mouth the words.

When I became a director, I got deeply interested in trick photography and made several trick pictures. At first I knew absolutely nothing about pictures. As a matter of fact, when I was in vaudeville, I didn't like movies. I made one called *The Boots He Couldn't Lose*, which was quite well known. This was the story line: a young man bought a pair of boots, got home, and put them on with some difficulty because they were so tight. He threw them out of the window, a tramp came along, found the boots, went into the woods, and put them on. He walked around and then went to sleep under a tree. The shoes unleashed themselves, walked down the road and back, and up the side of the house, and into the owner's window. When he got out of bed in the morning, there they stood alongside his bed. No matter what he did to get rid of them, they always came back. Finally, he strung them to the end of a train down at the Orange depot, and they were dragged away. That didn't even come to one reel, but it created quite a lot of talk at the time. It only came to 350 feet of film.

Well, as I say, vaudeville opened up, and I was playing Keith's Providence, going from there to Lowell and from Lowell into Percy William's Colonial. I received a letter from White. The Edison Company was sending a group to Savannah, Georgia, to make pictures, and they wanted me to come along as the director. They were leaving the fourth of March, and I didn't know whether Williams would permit me to leave in mid-week. They finally decided that I was to engage the company later or that it would leave as planned, and that I'd arrive as soon afterwards as possible. But as it turned out, I did leave with them. I'll never forget that day, the day of Taft's inauguration, when an awful blizzard descended on us. We were due in Washington at one o'clock, but at that hour, our train was just pulling into Philadelphia. We got to Washington at one o'clock in the morning.

Ed Porter went with us and made the picture. I learned what little I could from him. We finished on a Tuesday, and he said, "I'm going back to New York tonight, Bill. White will be back tomorrow. Here is $125. Spread it around amongst the boys. When Jim gets here, he'll have the rest." I divided the money. Next morning I was to meet Jim at the train. But no Jim. I went back out to the boys. From those who hadn't spent their money, I took it away. I had no idea what was going to happen, but I had a hunch that cash would be needed. We went on for two or three days, and still no Jim. I didn't dare to wire New York. I suspected that Jim was on a drunk in Havana, and I didn't want the New York office to know. Things deteriorated. Creditors were after us, and I got tired of waiting. I took a car. I found the camera Porter had used. You can't imagine how little I knew about a moving picture camera. Only after I went into Savannah and got access to the darkroom of a photographer would I open that camera. I figured out how it should be threaded and went to work. I was the director, the cameraman, the property man, and what have you. We worked for three or four days, and on the day I finished the picture, Jim White showed up. I was never so glad to see a man in all my life. We finished our time down there with quite a number of pictures. I couldn't say, now, how many. With the end of that stint, I was engaged to go up to Edison's studio in the Bronx. Eventually they sent me down to take charge of their studio on 21st Street.

We had to turn out at least one picture a week. Nobody cared if it was a 350-footer or a 1000-footer. A 1000-footer was one reel. Every director had to produce at least one a week. He had to write his own stories. If he could find one he could buy for ten dollars, all right. Otherwise, he furnished his own. Boy, the *Saturday Evening Post* was our bible. When I couldn't dream up stories, I stole them. For the first three years that I was directing, I did a picture version of every play I had ever worked in. Copyright laws didn't bother us. What were they? You changed the title and moved the narrative around a bit.

Then the Edison talking pictures came along and I was assigned, in 1909, to work with the man who invented them. Unfortunately, I didn't get along with the production manager. We had a couple of run-ins. I laid out the studio which they set up on 43rd Street, way over near 12th Avenue. The architects made their plans. On blueprint there was a cameraman's office, Mr. Haddock's office, and so on. Sure enough, I never got over to make it up. I let them fire me.

At that point, I joined Carl Laemmle's first company. I was the third director to work for him. He had Bill Raynos, then Harry Salder from Biograph with Florence Lawrence, the original "Biograph Girl," and I was the third. The only difficulty we ever had with Laemmle was getting money enough for petty cash to work with when we went out on location. We knew later that the films were making money. Some years later, I was talking to John Cochran, who had been his general manager, and asked him about it. He laughed, "Didn't you know? Laemmle was taking $3,000 out of the business every week. He didn't believe the bonanza would last. While it did, he had to keep his." It was over money matters that I left.

My pictures were gaining recognition. John Chalmers, who was editor of the *Moving Picture World*, seemed to believe that I was the only director alive at that moment. I don't know where he got the idea, probably from a picture of mine that he liked, but whenever anyone asked John for a director, he'd say, "See if Bill Haddock is working."

One part of my reputation was a name that I had been given, "Silent Bill." And then again, I never made a picture that lost money. I had also done a good deal of photography. For example, I made a picture called *The Haunted House*. In it, there was, among other things, a fellow spending a night at a haunted house on a bet. Suddenly a very charming girl appears in front of him. He takes hold of her cheeks to kiss her. As he moves in to kiss her, he comes up with a donkey's head in his hands. Another time when he wants to take a drink, he picks up a bottle and a glass which suddenly turn into a baseball bat and a baseball. Another time, he sits down on the couch between two beautiful girls, and they immediately changed to witches. Trick stuff like that. I figured them out. I don't know where I got the idea.

It's ironic, but many years later, a couple of the *Variety* reviewers said there's stuff in one of the new pictures that every director should see. So I went to see it, and, good God, they were doing things that we had quit doing years before. There they were, advising us to see stuff which we had long since forgotten. Now, of course, they process trick photography. However, we didn't have a processing technique in the early days. We had to do it in the camera. We had seen Méliès's *A Trip to the Moon* and used that film as our model, even though we don't know today how he did some of it.

Getting back to 1909, Chalmers sent me to old man Méliès, Gaston Méliès. He was the twin brother of George, who did his wonderful work in Paris. Gaston was only making Westerns. He engaged me, and we worked awhile in the East, then moved on to San Antonio, staying there until the spring of 1911, and winding up in Sulphur Mountain Springs. It was my happiest period in pictures because I loved horses and I rode one every day. I just lived in riding britches and boots. It was a happy time, all right, but only when I could keep old man Méliès tame—which was some job. But I know I did well for him. In those days, prints were sold on "standing" orders—that is, orders from the exchanges to the manufacturer. They had to order two weeks ahead, figuring that the sale of twenty prints got cost-of-film back. When I started with Méliès, his largest order had been between twenty-five and thirty prints. When I left him, his standing orders were between ninety and one hundred—and he had signed a contract with the Vitagraph Company according to which, after he got through with the negatives in this country, they were able to buy the foreign rights. He was guaranteed one hundred prints of every picture and paid two cents a foot for every foot of film they used. Now you know, that was a nice sweet reward.

Back in New York, Campbell MacCullough was just starting out. George Brennan, who produced *The Clansman* as a play, had arrangements with the Campbell MacCullough Company to film it. I was engaged as the director. Brennan was never overgenerous with money, even on Broadway. On the road, he was even stingier. You can imagine the kind of actors he'd have with a play as old as *The Clansman* going on one-night stands through states like Texas and Arizona. But he agreed to lay them off and make the picture. We tried to locate in several places. Finally, I chose Natchez, Mississippi, where we worked for two or three weeks, which was long enough for him.

"Now, we've got to go on the road again."

"How are you going to finish this picture?" I wondered out loud.

"We'll finish it on the road."

"A company will play one-night stands. It moves every day. Do you expect us to make pictures at a different location every day? It can't be done."

"Oh, yes, it can. Go ahead, do it."

We traveled for a week, and I got disgusted and left for New York. We showed what we had done to several people, among them Frank Woods, a motion picture editor. Later, in 1915, Frank was with Griffith in Hollywood, and Griff said, "Frank, I'd like to do a big picture, something really big." Frank remembered *The Clansman*, which he had seen. "Why don't you do Tom Dixon's story?"

"Can you get it?"

"I think so."

Frank signed a contract with Dixon for *The Clansman* and the sequel to it. That's how Griffith got *The Birth of a Nation*, through Frank Woods, who was interested in what little I had done on it.

We made the first version of *The Clansman* in color and sound. It ran thirty-two frames. Still pictures ran sixteen frames a second. The Campbell MacCullough sound ran thirty-two. One frame was taken through a green filter and the other through a red filter. They were superimposed on the screen so rapidly that they appeared to be one picture. The technical problem was that when you were at right angles to it, you were apt to get fringe. And not only that. It wasn't successful because the camera had to have a special head.

Unfortunately, I was hanging around for some time trying to complete the picture, but I couldn't get financial backing. As a last resort, I took the case to court and secured a judgment for $1155 in salary, but that was all. We had more than a reel of *The Clansman*. It was never completed, and to my knowledge it was never shown. I haven't the slightest idea where it is now.

The Birth of a Nation turned out to be a great picture. In it, Griffith thought he invented the close-up. Not so. Ed Porter had it in *The Great Train Robbery* at the very end. George Barnes, who is the highway robber, shows just his head and shoulders, and he's pointing a gun. And even that wasn't really the first close-up, come to think of it. The first close-up was made by Edison in *The Kiss*, just the head and shoulders of John C. Rice and May Irwin. I do believe that was the first close-up.

In 1912, John Chalmers sent me over to Fort Lee with Eclair. For my first picture, I got Bob Frazer and Barbara Tenant as leads. Eclair kept them both and made stars out of them. Actually Carl Laemmle started the "star" business when he took Florence Lawrence away from Biograph, where she had been known only as "The Biograph Girl." He featured and starred her by her own name in the winter of 1909. The idea was a good thing for films; it created interest. Since then, I do think they've let it get away from them. Management is to blame for that. They've allowed the stars to take over instead of keeping a tight rein on them. Directors used to run the show. Players took direction, or they didn't work, that's all.

In the fall of '12, Eclair sent me to Pawnee, Oklahoma. I went to Pawnee Bill's ranch to make Westerns. Up to that time, I had had two plans for an around-the-world trip. The first was to have been for Edison, who planned on sending a company around the world making pictures and phonograph records in native languages. He even had a portable laboratory set up in San Francisco. I was to go along to handle the picture-making—for some reason, Edison called it off.

The next plan was conceived by Méliès. He intended, in the fall of '11, to start an around-the-world trip making pictures. He was going to start in October or November of that year at the latest. But by that time, he had three different directors, none of whom could get along with him, and he had given up. In January or February, he took an actor I had picked up in Texas and made him the director. They started out and got as far as New Zealand, where the director and the old man had a fight. They called off their expedition—and that's the last I ever heard of old man Méliès.

Eclair was negotiating to build a studio in Tokyo. I was supposed to take a company to Oklahoma and go from there to Japan. Naturally, at the last moment, they canceled this trip. I left Oklahoma and took a vacation. Upon my return, as I was entering the studio, I saw a girl running across the yard. I called the casting director, an old friend of mine from theatrical days. "Sam, who's that girl?" He told me her name, and I insisted on having her in my next picture. In November, I married her.

I left Eclair for All Star to direct Dustin Farnum in *Soldiers of Fortune*. We made that film in Santiago, Cuba. That finished, again I came back to New York, and the night before Thanksgiving of 1913 I was in Jesse Lasky's office in the 46th Street Theater with De Mille and Goldfish, as he was known then, from quarter-past five until quarter-past seven. Lasky, De Mille, and Goldfish wanted me as a director. They offered $300 a week and stock in the company. I had till the following Monday to make up my mind. I took some bad advice and turned it down. I was told that they only had $25,000, that they would make one picture, close it up, and I would be held responsible for their failure. Everybody said, "You've got a good reputation, Bill, don't lose it." A couple of years later when Lasky got together a group of people to form Famous Players, the stock I would have had was worth over a million dollars.

I kept working. I directed *Paid in Full* with Tully Marshall, his first picture, just as *Soldiers of Fortune* had been Dustin's first picture. By then

A scene from a one-reel film about Puritans and witches, Eclair Company. 1912.

Marion Brent toasting Priscilla Dean in an interior shot, Eclair Studios, Fort Lee. 1912.

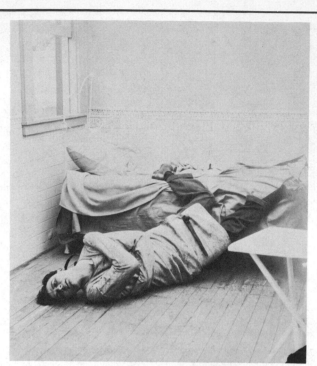

Robert Frazer in scene from *Why Our Jane Never Married*.

On location in Santiago, Cuba. A scene from William Haddock's *Soldiers of Fortune*, starring Richard Harding Davis and Dustin Farnum. Haddock used an entire company of Cuban soldiers as extras in this film. 1913.

Robert Frazer and Barbara Tenant in scenes from *Why Our Jane Never Married*, Eclair Company. 1912.

we used scripts. Gustav Thomas said that he couldn't make a scenario out of the play *Paid in Full*. They got an outside man to write the scenario. Thomas read it: "No, that will never make a picture." It was handed to me without my knowing what Thomas had said. I said, "Yes, I can make a picture out of it." And with Gus pretty unhappy, I made a hell of a good picture out of it.

Then I made *The Education of Mr. Pipp* from the musical comedy that Digby Bell had starred in for years. It was originally a series of pictures drawn by Charles Dana Gibson which Thomas had made into a musical comedy. We created a straight silent film. I had a little argument with Thomas over a scene involving a French count who had three lines to speak, supposedly in French, to the two girls playing Pipp's daughters. I was going through the rehearsal of that scene when Thomas appeared.

"Oh no, Bill. Wait, wait. He should speak those lines in French with the proper French dialect."

"What the hell difference does it make if he's speaking in French or in Choctaw? The audience can't hear it. They won't know."

"Ah hah, but what about the lip readers?"

"The lip readers are going to have quite a job catching his accent."

But he spent an hour and a half, teaching this guy to read two lines of French with what he called a proper French accent.

One day Chalmers sent me to see Bob Wright. Wright was general manager for the Kalem Film Company. Chalmers said, "Wright wants someone to make pictures for him here in the city." So I signed a contract with Wright. I don't think there was ever another contract like this in the picture business. He agreed to buy everything I made, and the price he was to pay for it was decided before I started the picture. Even if he didn't like the picture, he couldn't refuse it, and he had to pay. Pathé gave out similar contracts. They offered me one, but theirs was subject to screen examination. I wouldn't sign. But Bob Wright did much better by me.

However, I was short of cash at the time. For the first picture I calculated my costs and signed my contract with the agreed-upon price. Then I discovered I was short $400 of what I originally thought the picture would cost me. It was only one reel, and I decided to take the risk, determined I wouldn't pay a bill I didn't have to pay until I delivered this picture. Our bookkeeper approached me one day.

"Mr. Haddock, I understand you're going to make some pictures for us."

"Yes."

"When will you start?"

"Tomorrow."

"You'll want some money, won't you?"

"Yes."

"How much?"

If I could have thought quicker, I would have said more, but all I could think of was the $400.

"Do you want it in fives and tens?"

"Certainly."

If he had said in twos and threes, I would have said, certainly. Then he left for lunch, due back about two o'clock. I was there at a quarter of two. He came in. He had the money. I got it and got out. I was afraid he'd see Wright and find out I was supposed to finance myself. Kalem financed me though they didn't know it. I made enough on the entire deal to put me on easy street, a lot of money.

Chalmers told me that Wright said to him one day, "I don't know how Haddock does it. He's giving us better pictures than we're getting from the Coast, and they're not costing us as much." He couldn't get it through his head that when I stopped working, my overhead stopped. I only had studio expenses when I was working in the studio. That's how I could do it. However, if I had known he felt that way, it would have cost him a lot more money. The association continued until I heard about a new company called the Gotham. They had already made one good picture and sought me out to direct the next one.

I was strolling along one day on Broadway when I met a chap named Opperman, who had been general manager at Eclair. He wanted to know whether I could see a Mr. Bradford at the Knickerbocker. He'd been talking to Mr. Bradford, who was sorely in need of a director. I made my way to the hotel; as I got out of the elevator, I ran into another friend, a lithographic paper salesman. What does he say but, "My God, Bill, come here. I was just talking about you." He took me in and introduced me to Bradford, "Bradford, this is the director I was telling you about." How could I lose? I found myself at Gaumont, a French outfit headed by Paul Gaumont, originally the Gaumont Brothers, who had a studio in England. That winter, they packed up and went to Florida to do their shooting, and we left in the spring when Gaumont stopped producing in America. This was in '15, and I came back in '16. Gaumont quit this country because he refused to pay any more than ten dollars for a story. Bradford told me he had informed Gaumont that no one could get stories for that price. Gaumont's response was, "In that case we will leave this country," and they did.

That put me out in the cold again, but I wasn't worried. I had money. And then George Cahn, who was Laemmle's private secretary, sent for me, and I was engaged to go to Key West, Florida, and do some experimental work on underwater photography. Unfortunately, the job needed an engineer, or someone who knew more about it than I did, because I found out, the first time I went out to shoot, that there were some faults with the diving bell. I returned to shore and redesigned it, but every time I went out, I'd find something new. An engineer would have discovered every flaw at the start, but I had to experiment. We got a few not very good results, and we could have done better with a little more time. But then in 1917, war was declared, and everybody with a camera either had to give it up or get out of town in twenty-four hours. And we, of course, got out of town.

I had an offer from a company that was forming in San Francisco, and for a while, I was baffled about why that didn't materialize. But some time later, I met the San Francisco man, and he pointed out that my agent wanted him to pay the commission. I was nonplused because my agent had asked *me* to pay the commission too. That guy was too damned avaricious.

After that, I don't remember what I was doing, I guess not much of anything. A friend of mine had a yacht which I was using for the summer. I did a picture here and there, usually a small job. I went to work with Burton King on a serial featuring Harry Houdini. When we finished that, the war was over.

And on the first of January, I went with Harry Grossman to handle the production of a serial called *The Carter Case,* written by Arthur Reeves, the Sherlock Holmes of America. I handled the production on that, and when it was through, I quit. I laid off. I bought myself a yacht. Meanwhile my wife and I separated. I didn't care too much about anything. I lived on the yacht and had a good time generally. But after that, I lost damn near all I had. It didn't take too long before I lost the rest of it.

Then through the secretary of the chamber of commerce out in Morristown, New Jersey, some fellow had arranged to do film commercials about the town. He'd shoot pictures of industries in the town and tell a little story about how Morristown was settled. The industries would pay for their footage. He got me to organize a company for that purpose. We did very well at it. This fellow's name was Cooper. That is, we knew him as Cooper. Well, I got frightened. I was scared to death that a sheriff would put his hands on my shoulder one day for something Cooper had done. He was that kind of a guy. You couldn't trust him across the street. But we made good money with that, and I quit. I was lucky, I guess, because I heard a couple of years later that Cooper beat the sheriff across the bridge at El Paso to Mexico by about a foot and a half. Then I went with the Foundation for Children. I managed the theater. Anyway, 1919 was the end of my film-making career, and I went back to my first love, the theater. I've been acting ever since and appeared in my last role at the Lincoln Center Repertory Theater in 1966 at the age of eighty-nine.

FRITZ LANG

My FATHER WAS an architect; my mother, a housewife. We lived in Vienna, where I was born eighty years ago. I ran away from home. Every human being should do that. Unlike most people of my generation, I really like contemporary American youth. I was asked in New York this year to make a picture about young people. If I had, the theme would have been: It's not you people, but your parents, who need an education. That gives you a little idea of my point of view.

I went to the Realschule and to the equivalent of an American university, the technical high school. I found it terribly boring. I wanted to become an artist. I went to Belgium. I longed to learn as much as possible of the world, so first I stopped in Nuremberg and Munich, and then went on to Frankfurt. In these days, around 1908, such towns had a lot of what was called good art in their museums. I was always interested in people, too. Finally, I landed in Brussels, where I ran out of money. So I started to sketch postcards and sold them. There I fell in love with a woman. Her mother was from Indochina; her father was an officer in the French army. Later on, when I recuperated from that affair, I went to Paris and on through the Orient. After a year of traveling, I returned to Paris, where I started to paint.

Once, while I was painting in the street, a man offered me paints, brushes, and canvases if I would paint for him. I was very happy to do that. He gave me old paintings for canvases. I didn't know that I was forging the canvases that I painted over. It turned out that he sent them to

New York. And at the same time, he would write a letter to the New York Customs' officials to this effect: "Watch for some fake paintings. Remove the surface paint and you will find. . . ," I don't know, a Renoir or something. Under my painting, there really was a forgery of a Renoir or of some other famous painter. The customs' officials certified it as an original, for which full duty had to be paid. Then the conspirators could sell it at a high price to an affluent art collector. I discovered all this by accident.

I remained in Paris until 1914, living in Montmartre and working in Montparnasse. When the war broke out, all my friends left in time—but I stayed on. I finally took the last train out of Paris; we were stopped at the Belgian border and arrested. Some of us broke out of jail. We passed over the German frontier. In Germany, I didn't have a penny, but I could travel by train wherever I pleased. And so, I came back to Vienna just before the first hostilities.

I served one year "voluntarily" in the army. In Austria, no one with such an education as I had was forced to serve three full years. You entered the military for one year, and at the end of that time you became an officer. I was twenty-three years old, and I had passed all the examinations three times. But I was unable to serve because of a hernia, which I later corrected, so I was free. Instead of enjoying myself, I suddenly suffered a rash of patriotism and felt it my duty to go. Four years later, after I had been wounded three times, I had had it up to here. First I was in Russia, then Rumania, and finally Italy.

I was the leader of a very well-known scout patrol. I belonged to an artillery battery. The Austrian army first went forwards in Russia and Galicia and then moved backwards. It was in Rumania when we should have gone on the offensive, under German supervision. Their intelligence service was faultless—only no one told them that the Russians had just removed and shipped all this artillery to the North. Now they used the artillery against us, and the whole offensive in Rumania was killed. We were sent to Italy. I was wounded and returned to Vienna.

I was working there with the cadre, a lieutenant by then. I had a sweetheart and no money. Including sickness and hospital compensation, I got exactly 120 kronen, which would equal maybe $30 a month. One day, I was sitting in a café in Vienna worrying about where to lay my hands on a little money when a man approached me. I wore a monocle and a few fancy decorations.

"Please forgive me, Mr. Lieutenant, but would you be willing to appear in a Red Cross play?" said the man.

"Who are you?" I said haughtily.

"My name is Peter Ostermeyer."

"That can't be helped," I told him, haughty as haughty could be.

"I'm the director," he added.

And I, who had never been on the stage, but had already become interested in motion pictures in Paris, inquired, "What are you paying?"

"Seven hundred and fifty kronen."

Now, I had about 120 kronen, so my heart fell. But sometimes I have a bright moment, and I had one this time when I said, "That's not very much."

"We couldn't pay more than one thousand," he replied.

"O.K."

I was supposed to play a *Prussian* officer, but I couldn't. With the best will and the best coach they were able to give me, nobody with my Viennese accent could portray a *Prussian* officer. Then something which only happens in fairy tales took place: since I had a contract, he had to give me not the subsidiary role I couldn't play but the main part, that of a wounded Viennese lieutenant who is captured by the French.

In Paris, I had become interested in motion pictures for a particular reason. I wanted to be a painter, and it thrilled me to see *pictures in motion!* I spent many long hours viewing motion pictures. While performing in these plays, I was introduced to a man who eventually became very important in my life. He was Erich Pommer, who died only a short while ago. Erich Pommer was responsible for the golden years of the German film—1919 to 1933—the Weimar period which lasted until Hitler's time. Pommer, at first, didn't want to know anything about me. He had seen me with the monocle and thought I was an arrogant son-of-a-bitch. Finally when we talked (he wrote this somewhere), he got interested in me and offered me a job as a *dramaturg* (in his company in Berlin)—which is a man who checks manuscripts that writers offer to a motion picture company. I was something like a script editor. For this job, you must have the ability to judge, to suggest to the front office that such-and-such a script should be done.

In the meantime, I was still officially in the Austrian army. I went to a friend of mine at the cadre who had the authority to ask for a furlough for me because Pommer had told me, "Look, we will go to the German High Command to have them free you from your duties as an officer." That seemed to be a good idea. I left Austria two months before the revolution in Germany which ended the war. Erich Pommer was working not in Berlin but in Rumania. After five or six weeks in Berlin, I got a letter from my friend in Vienna telling me, "You must come back. Your furlough is over!" I asked, "What about the German High Command?" It turned out that the Berlin film company hadn't approached the high command and I was practically a deserter. But being technically employed, I didn't have to go back. I was writing scripts which everyone liked very much, but I wanted to be a director.

After four or five months, they gave me a chance to direct my first

film, which I had to shoot in four days! From 1919 on, I was a director.
The first was a feature-length picture. It took Monday, Tuesday, Wednesday, Thursday, Friday. Hold on, five days.

Many years—ten or eleven—later, I had contract problems with Ufa,
the biggest German film company. I was disgusted and decided to make
no more motion pictures. At that stage, and most perversely, I wanted
to become a chemist. I don't know why. It was one of those stupid ideas.
(When quite young, I had seriously, foolishly, wanted to become a detective.) Anyhow, someone else asked me to make a picture for him. I refused because I didn't want to work with him. On the one hand, I had
a law suit with Ufa. On the other hand, this man came and came and
came every weekend until finally I succumbed: "All right, but under one
condition. I can make whatever I please, and you have nothing to say." I
was married at the time. I asked my wife, "What is the most despicable
crime that you can imagine?" We started to talk about the idea, and suddenly I thought, "A murderer who kills a child because of sexual deviation."

The picture that resulted was *M*. Now, I'll show you the difference
between this picture, *M*, and my first American film, *Fury*. *Fury* was an
anti-lynching picture. The victim, accused of having raped and killed a
child, was an innocent white man. He really hadn't done it. But at least
I could say something about lynching. If you want to make a real lynching
picture, though, it should be about a *colored* man who rapes a white
woman, which *proves* that lynching is wrong, but in America, I was
forced to use a *white* man who really was *not* a rapist. In *M*, the lead part
was a child-killer, and I said in the end: "Whatever you do to him is unimportant because it doesn't bring dead children back to life. What is
important is we have to watch the little ones much better." That is the
difference.

I stayed in Germany till the rise of Hitler. In my final German picture, called *The Last Will of Dr. Mabuse*, I put Nazi slogans into the mouth
of an insane arch-criminal. He says, "I have to shake the confidence of
the bourgeoise in just those authorities he himself has appointed. When
the average citizen finds out that the authorities don't work, they will revolt and topple the whole structure into this chaos we will create. . . ."
Where Hitler referred to "our realm of a thousand years," Dr. Mabuse
promised to create a "realm of crime." I finished this picture, and presently
two men in uniform materialized. I told them, "When you think you can
confiscate the picture of Mr. Lang, do so." They did.

One day, I got an order to visit Mr. Goebbels. I didn't feel very
happy. I wore the official uniform for visiting a minister, cutaway striped
trousers, stiff collar. I walked into the Ministry of Propaganda. There was
a desk on the left with two men in uniform. One of them asked, "What
do you want?"

Fritz Lang. 1927.

Fritz Lang directing Joan Bennett in *The Woman in the Window*. 1944.

Fritz Lang in the cutting room.

Fritz Lang with model of set for *Hangmen Also Die*. 1942.

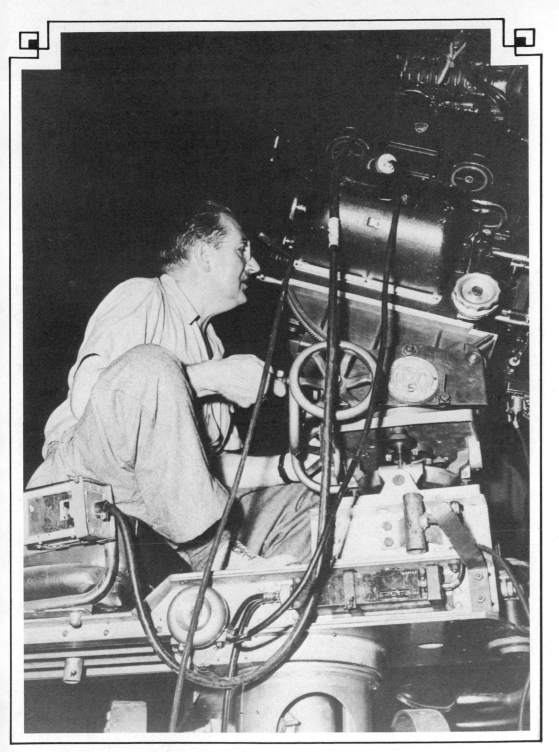

Fritz Lang shooting *The Secret Behind the Door.* 1947.

"I want to see Mr. Goebbels."

"You mean the Minister of Propaganda?"

I showed him the order.

"Go down that corridor and on the next crossing you go right and you will find his office."

The corridors were very wide, with big stone floors. You walk and you hear every step. It was not very agreeable, believe me. I came to two guards in uniform, with pistols, on the right and left. "What are you doing here?" they asked. I told them, and after an eternity, I wound up in a round room and there was a door. I got to the door. Just as I was about to knock, it opened, and a man asked, "What do you want?"

"My name is Lang."

"Oh yes," very polite, "certainly. Please will you wait, the Minister is. . . ."

I waited ten or fifteen minutes; then the man came out.

"Mr. Lang, please."

It was a long, long room and on one end, very far down, was a desk. Goebbels approached; he limped, as you know. He was a charming man when he wanted to be. He said nothing about the picture, never mentioned it until the end. He said that the *Führer* had seen two pictures of mine, *Metropolis* and *Die Nibelungen*, and afterwards declared of me, "This man will make us *the* Nazi picture." I was wet all over my body.

"I'm tickled pink, Herr Minister," I said.

What else could I say? To myself I said, "Get out of here as fast as you can." It must have been half-past twelve, and I knew the banks closed at two o'clock. Outside was a post with a big clock on top of it. When you looked out the window onto a little square, you could see the time. Goebbels continued, "We would like you to head up the German film industry. We know your pictures."

"Wonderful, wonderful."

I kept looking at that damn clock and finally it was two o'clock and I knew I couldn't get my money out of the bank. At the end, he came to *Dr. Mabuse:* "I'm terribly sorry, but we have to change the last reel."

"What would you propose?"

I was now expecting him to say that the slogans would have to go. Oh no!

"In the end, Dr. Mabuse goes insane. That is wrong. He has to be killed by the people, by the fury of the people."

"That is wonderful."

At last, I could go. I was sweating, simply soaking all over my body. I went straight home, and the same evening, I left Germany, with almost no money, with nothing. Fortunately, I had a passport with visas for London and Paris where I had business connections. I had big collections of Chinese and South Seas art objects. I always had 5,000 marks, which is a little more than $1,000, in the house. That was all I could take with me.

I made a picture in Paris called *Liliom*. Erich Pommer, who was Jewish, left sooner than I, advising me to stay and see what could be done. One was very stupid in those days. He worked for the French Fox for whom I made *Liliom*. I did not know the author, Ferenc Molnar. The only correct copy of this film is at the Cinématheque in Montreal.

In those days, it was fashionable in Hollywood, when a producer or an agent came over to Europe on a spree, to bring a famous person back to Hollywood. Mr. David Selznick and his brother, Myron, who was an agent, chose me as a trophy for MGM. I had no idea of what to expect— or I might not have come at all. My colleagues and I knew only that American pictures had developed terrific technique. I had never heard of *producers* in Germany. For instance, with Erich Pommer, I made *Die Nibelungen*, a German epic. In one scene, over a hill came 400 Asiatic Huns. Pommer calls me (we were very good friends), and he says, "This scene costs a lot of money. We have to shoot it next week. Think about whether it's necessary." I thought it over, and went back to him, "Erich, I want to tell you something. I don't think that we should compete with American mass scenes. I believe we can drop it."

"Fritz, I thought it over too. I believe we *should* do it."

I was not warmly received when I arrived in Hollywood. My reputation did not really precede me. In Germany, credits went like this: *M*, a film by Fritz Lang, followed by the other credits which were listed alphabetically: writers, architects, also the crew. It was really a collective enterprise. Here a producer is responsible to the top. I do not like producers. In the beginning, I spoke very little English and what I did speak was lousy. Later on, well, I am one of the very few people who liked Harry Cohn, the head of Columbia. With him you could talk. He used very dirty language, but you could talk to him. I didn't want a long-term contract. I preferred an arrangement either working on a picture of mine or collaborating on an idea with a writer. I'd make one picture at a time. That way I supposed there would be less trouble.

I have always been a loner. I have had too much to do just thinking about the art of motion pictures. You have a vision if you are creative. You have an idea which is very vague. If you try to grasp it, it goes away. You can, *maybe*, when you are with a very good friend, talk about this vision over coffee, over a martini, and then in a long conversation that goes on for weeks. How can you convince a producer in one short meeting? And not just one producer, you have to convince five or six people. It's very hard.

For one year, while under contract to MGM, I wasn't assigned to any pictures. After a year, they wanted to kick me out, very politely! "Mr. Lang, we will let you go." I went to a man who is dead now. Mannix was his name, the right hand of L. B. Mayer.

"Eddie, I am the most famous director in Europe. I came here and I never had a chance to do anything."

Mannix was once a bouncer, and maybe as a man who came up the hard way, he was responsive to my plight.

"All right. What do you want to do?"

I had found a four-page story by Norman Krasna—I wanted to do that. Then I located a writer, Bartlett Cormack, who is also now dead. We wrote the story together, even though I knew very little English.

My best ideas come from newspaper clippings. This happened with *Fury*. I missed only one thing in that lynching picture. You know what it was? A real lynching had happened in San Jose, and in San Francisco, a conductor stood in front of three buses and yelled, "If you want to see a lynching in San Jose, come with us." They waited in San Jose until buses arrived to lynch the guy. Unfortunately, I didn't have this vignette in my picture. Since Stephen Foster was something new for me, I made one scene of a colored girl hanging laundry on a line. She is singing, "I want to go to a happy home where all the darkies are free," and a colored man answers her with another song while he is washing a car. I made a scene in which the district attorney speaks to the jury! "There have been so-and-so many lynchings a year." Then I showed a dilapidated car in the South. Inside was an old white-haired Negro; outside, a very buxom colored girl and a boy and two children. From the car radio came the accusing voice of the district attorney. The only reaction of the listeners is that the old man nods knowingly. That scene was taken out of the picture after my first cut because L. B. Mayer was against showing colored people in films. *Fury* was a great success, and for years publicity called me "Fritz (Fury) Lang."

After that, I did no more work at MGM. Only twenty years later, when everything was forgotten and L. B. Mayer wasn't there anymore, I made another picture for them. I took it only so that I could say I was back. The next film in America I made for Walter Wanger, *You Only Live Once*. Then I got a job as producer at Paramount, where I made one lousy picture—*You and Me*.

I'll tell you a typical story about a producer. I was once in New York at Keen's English Chop House, just sitting there. A woman and a man came along and sat at another table. He showed her some photographs (slides). They laughed, and I thought they were looking at dirty pictures. But in reality, these were photographs of their food, the meat they were about to eat. That incident gave me an idea for a scene I used in a picture called *While the City Sleeps*, with Dana Andrews and Ida Lupino. I had a scene in which the lover of Ida Lupino, played by George Sanders, who was working for a kind of Hearst paper, says to Ida Lupino, "You have to help me to get him [Dana Andrews] on my side. You can do whatever you want." He adds, "Whatever you do, I know you will do for me." She understands that she should sleep with him if necessary. She tries to find Dana at a reporters' hangout. She finds him alone, sitting at the bar, half drunk. He greets her, and she says, "Hello, how are you?"

"Can I offer you a drink?"

She orders a fancy concoction with two drops of Pernod. They start to talk. Finally, she opens her handbag and takes a slide out. She looks at it and smiles, and he's dying to know what's there. She played the scene so well that you positively knew it was a picture of Ida Lupino naked. He keeps exclaiming, "Let me see it, let me see it." She refuses and there is a little bantering. He grabs, and it falls behind the bar. The barkeeper, a character I showed as a learned man with glasses, absolutely different from the usual type, jumps over to the picture and looks at it. We see for the first time that it is a naked baby on a rug. I thought that was very funny.

Mr. Producer didn't like it. My contract specified that I had the right to show it at the preview in my way. The producer violently objected, "No, that is not funny. Cut the scene out." I had to fight five days for something that was written in my contract. I won my fight. It comes to the preview and my scene is in the picture. I tell you very honestly, I was sweating blood and water because now everything depends on the audience. When the scene is finished and they see the little baby on the rug, the audience applauds and roars. Gene Fowler, Jr., was my friend and cutter on this picture. He stands outside; the producer comes along: he is furious. Gene says, "Lang was right." The producer yields nothing. "Yes, he was right now. But I will preview this picture until I find an audience that doesn't applaud, and then I will cut it out." It never was cut, but that's unmitigated vanity. They cut themselves in their own flesh.

Let me tell you another case. I made a picture originally called *Chuck-a-Luck*. It was all based on that word, "chuck-a-luck." Howard Hughes, who was then owner of RKO, without asking me (because he is God personally), changed it to *Rancho Notorious*. It's a Western. Somebody tries to find a murderer who has killed his fiancée. All that's known about the culprit is that one word "chuck-a-luck." There was a song in the picture about chuck-a-luck. Now the name of the picture has to be *Rancho Notorious*. What is chuck-a-luck? I asked a man from the Howard Hughes' Tool Company, who was running RKO. "Why did he do it?"

"He thought in Europe they wouldn't understand what 'chuck-a-luck' means."

I couldn't suppress an ironic comment. "It is a good thing they know what 'rancho notorious' means."

As a young man, I roamed around the world. I really had an education in life, as a director should have. I wrote too, but I am not a writer. I dabbled in many things, in religion and in everything else that interested me. Nothing is more important for a creative artist than that he be curious. In this respect, the artist is like a creative scientist, only he should take care not to become specialized.

I'll tell you another story, this one about Jerry Wald. He wanted to make a picture about the unemployed, based on Odets's *Clash by Night*. Wald wished to place it in Monterey among fishing people. He asked me if I knew anything about fishing? What could I say? "Jerry, a director doesn't have to know. If I do the film, I *will* know." That is the crux of the matter. Superficial knowledge isn't enough.

I made an American Western after living very long with the Navajos. On a busman's holiday, I was the first to photograph Navajo sand paintings. I made many friends among the traders, too. Later I made a Western called *Western Union*, which was a perfect example of several things. Zanuck bought a Zane Grey story, but our picture had nothing in common with the book. To Zanuck, "Western Union" signified the colors yellow and blue. He wanted something yellow for the telegraph company and blue for God knows what. So the covered wagons were yellow and blue! Zane Grey's hero was married and had seven children, but naturally, he had to be a bachelor for the picture. The only adventure which actually took place during the building of the line from Sioux City to San Francisco involved buffalo rubbing off ticks against telegraph posts, which thereupon collapsed. That was all. Naturally, we had *everything* that could possibly happen in the picture!

But Zanuck was a very good producer in those days. When the picture was released, I got a letter from Flagstaff that ran like this:

"Dear Mr. Lang: We have seen *Western Union*. It is the first picture to depict the West that really was. What authenticity!" How is that? From a European director? In fact, my picture was not at all like the old West. But the whole spirit of it was true: what we captured were the old-timers' dreams about their past. And that, too, is a species of reality.

I've said motion pictures are the *art* of our century. Certainly finance is a headache, but I have never found that honest pictures lose money. Practically all of my pictures showed a profit. I had only one flop, and it happened when I tried to copy Brecht in *You and Me*. It was the only really lousy picture I ever made precisely because I wasn't being myself, and it didn't work. However, I made certain pictures which I detested, and made them just because I needed the money. There was a time, during the McCarthy affair in Hollywood, when I couldn't find work. Everybody believed I was a Communist. After a year and a half, Harry Cohn gave me a job and the whole thing blew over.

I like audiences. Producers don't. They used to say that audiences had the mentality of a ten-year-old child. Ridiculous! On the lowest level, my picture M is a cops-and-robbers story. On a higher level, it's a police procedure. On a still higher level, it is a documentary of the times. And on a very high level, it is an indictment of capital punishment. Here you have all the possibilities in one picture. You have to satisfy yourself, and you should not underestimate yourself. You make the picture for yourself. You are interested in life, in what's going on. The producer is just interested in making money. I did an anti-Nazi picture called *Hangmen Also Die*. And the publicity department was upset. They panicked because it had no love interest. What could they publicize? By being interested only in money, they wind up by never being able to make it.

Hollywood is peculiar in so many ways. I had a very good friend, Ruth Chatterton, who was really a star. We saw each other every day. I had a rented house in Santa Monica, and she had a wonderful house just south of Sunset Strip, with a British butler and so on. She was a literate woman. When she didn't want to make films anymore, she wrote one or two best-sellers. Out of the blue, she says, "Fritz, I'm leaving."

"Ruthie, where are you going?"

"Oh, I have to go."

She gave up her house, her library, her dogs, and disappeared. I didn't hear from her for six years. For a long time we had seen each other every day. Then, poof! No more Ruthie. I was crossing Madison Avenue at two or three o'clock one afternoon when I heard somebody yell, "Fritz." And there's Ruth Chatterton. She had married and now acted as if nothing had happened. She came back to California and wrote a novel, but not one person invited her out for Christmas. They use you as they would cardboard in the studio. In Germany or in Europe, when you are under contract, you have the *right to work*. They can't just pay you and say that's that. You can break any contract if you don't get work. I didn't want to be used like a piece of cardboard. You are filed somewhere. When they need you, they take you. When they don't need you, you get your money.

In a certain way, this complex extends to the social community as well. It's only interested in you as long as you are in the limelight. Income alone makes you acceptable as a poker player. If you earn $500 a week, you cannot play poker with someone who makes $5,000 a week because he will bluff you out of everything.

Only people in the same income bracket can be found together. In Europe, I could name you many, many actors and actresses who get old and are still beloved. Here? Nothing. I am told that Mary Pickford in her

Fritz Lang and Edward G. Robinson on set for *Scarlet Street*. 1945.

Fritz Lang. 1967.

heyday was once manhandled at a station where her train stopped. They treated her without any respect or love, pawing around and tearing her blouse. It is the same thing with actresses in New York! They can play two years in a successful play, and then have no job for the next two years. Take any newspaper and look at the advertisements. You will find producers mentioned. Naturally, they're most important. Directors, too, but you will seldom find the writer's name. Hollywood created the star system. First you had one star, and then one wasn't attractive enough so you had two, then four, and so on. Stars, stars, stars, stars.

From the standpoint of the industry, the star system was not a mistake. From the standpoint of motion pictures, it was and is. This system didn't exist in Europe when I began. In Europe one asked: What is the play about? What is the picture about? Above all: *What do you have to say?* It was the story that sold *M*.

The writer was very important in Europe, but here he is transformed into a mechanic. In any major studio, there are ten writers working on a single script. You never know which was the first. This has not changed. How can you expect anything to come of it? How can an idea be developed by ten different people who are competitors, who don't know each other? When I was under contract at MGM in 1934, one man got a script which I found was extremely good. We had the following exchange:

"I have to rewrite almost every line of it."

"But why? The script is fine."

"Yes, the script is fine, but how can I prove to them that I earned my money? I have to rewrite, even though it will not be as good as the original. They gave it back to me, and I have to do something."

It is a vicious circle.

I always fought very hard in Hollywood, and as a result, some things I made there are as good as what I did in Germany. Now and then I won a battle and beat the system. That could come to pass because I was a free agent. Nobody under contract really fights. An executive of a big company once put it to me: "Mr. Lang, we are not interested in making good pictures. We are interested in making successful pictures with as little risk as possible." Theoretically, a producer could be of great help to the director. He could move big stones from the director's way. What he should never do is write a scene or otherwise interfere with the director. Every picture has a certain rhythm which only one man can give it. That man is the director. He has to be like the captain of a ship.

I'll tell something about Thalberg that relates to me. One day he said to his writers, "Now, you bastards, I will show you a *picture*." He showed them *M*, the story of a child-murderer with *no love interest*. When it was finished, he asked them, "Well, what did you think of it?" They all said that it was a wonderful picture. He recommended that they study it and learn. But one of the writers got bold and ventured a question, "Mr. Thalberg, what would you have said if I had brought you the script of this picture?" Thalberg answered, "I probably would have said, 'Go to hell.' " There you have it.

One producer I know gave his directors exactly twenty to twenty-one days to make a picture. On the first picture *he* directed he took eighty-seven days. I knew producers who, when they started to make the schedule for a picture, ordered so many shots per day. If a unit manager claims the schedule's impossible, he's told to shut up: "Give the director so many shots. Otherwise he will get too uppity. This way, he'll try to work fast, fast, fast." There is no respect, no *esprit de corps* or comradely feeling. I read a defense of producers, written or spoken by a producer, according to which he alone should choose the material. Most men of this ilk use best-sellers, period.

I recently saw Jack Palance on TV in *Dr. Jekyll and Mr. Hyde.* I had once seen the film version with Freddie March and Miriam Hopkins, Rouben Mamoulian's piece. Also I know it with Spencer Tracy and Ingrid Bergman. Now I saw Palance. I became interested. It had been so long since I'd read the book that I reread it. I still have my copy. Not one picture version had anything to do with Robert Louis Stevenson's novel. Stevenson's Mr. Hyde is younger than Dr. Jekyll. Everybody who sees him has an indescribable feeling of repulsion because he is *evil.* That's all. But nowhere does it say that he looks like a monster. And all those stories with girls—you'll find none of them in the book. The producers never read Stevenson. They only saw one picture which feeds on itself.

I took myself out of the Hollywood film-making process ten years ago. Next year I may do something in Paris, but I don't ever want to do anything in Hollywood again.

The Cameraman

HAL MOHR

I AM SEVENTY-SIX YEARS OLD, a man of mixed immigrant background, born and raised in San Francisco. My mother's maiden name was Remarque, as in Erich Remarque—no relative of ours. There's a little story about that. I was doing a picture with Marlene Dietrich at a time when Erich was pursuing Marlene pretty earnestly. He used to sit on the set with her, and once I tried to be friendly. "Your name is Remarque. We could be related. My mother was a Remarque." And he got on his high horse, sputtering, "This is not possible." He was a pretty snobby man, but at any rate, there's no connection.

I was the sixth and last of my parents' children. Father ran a wholesale woolens firm in San Francisco. I was raised and educated in San Francisco; I was there at the time of the earthquake and fire, pardon me—only fire, you shouldn't call it an earthquake—and our home was destroyed at that time. We moved up to my grandparents' place, which was in Petaluma, the chicken and egg center of California.

My schooling was spotty. I started in a Catholic convent across the street from our home. My father was Jewish, but my mother was a Catholic. I was excused from religious services at the parochial school and was excused from school during the Jewish holidays. My education was pretty badly neglected, I must say. I only completed two years of high school.

I had never seen a motion picture until after the earthquake, or the fire. Little variety and vaudeville houses started up all around the city. Sid Grauman's father was a theatrical man who had the Empress Theater,

part of the Sullivan–Considine circuit in San Francisco. He was in what
we called the junk-exchange business. The "junk" dealers would get
clips of film and sell them to vaudeville houses. At that time this was
bigger and more profitable than production. It was before *The Great Train
Robbery*. At one of the little vaudeville houses, I saw my first motion
picture, just a train going by the camera. I got so fascinated, I wanted to
find out what it was. I couldn't understand how they did it—which must
sound stupid now but the process was brand new. It's true that I had
"magic lanterns" and that I was always experimenting, investigating. I
had an inquisitive nature.

At Polytechnic, my high school, they didn't know what a motion picture was. We did have a manual arts section, though, with woodworking
and a machine shop. I liked dabbling in those things. There was also a
nickelodeon near my home. I ingratiated myself with the operator. He
used the old machine they cranked by hand in those days and didn't
mind letting me crank the machine for him while he did other things.
In that way, I learned what film was and what made the pictures move.
I managed to pick up a toy projection machine called an opto, a tiny
machine through which a spool of film was cranked. It had a shutter like
a barrel and cut the picture on and off. This little machine, which pre-
ceded the motiagraph, was a very fine projector for that period.

I took this toy to school and built myself a camera, a light, tight
little box with a little projection machine set in it. You had to load and
thread the film in a dark room, close it, bring it out, take your photograph,
and then unload again in the dark room. I managed to pick up little
scraps of film from a firm in San Francisco owned by the Miles' Brothers,
for whom I subsequently went to work. They had a cameraman working
for them, an Italian chap named Jim Saroni, who had a very fast horse
and buggy into which he'd load his camera and tripod and dash all over
the city photographing things. They had their own little laboratory, but
it was a secret thing because at this time, there was a patent company,
a trust, that controlled the motion picture industry through its patents on
the loop used in threading projection machines. They did take my camera
away from me. The patents people put detectives on my trail, when they
found out I had a camera.

During this time, I was photographing little news events around San
Francisco and running them in Sid Grauman's father's place at intermission time. When something extraordinary happened—for instance, when
President William Howard Taft came out to San Francisco to break ground
for the Pacific International Exposition in 1912 or 1913—I photographed
it. Since I had just a projection lens, I fixed up a little laboratory for
developing my negative, using the camera as a printer. Then I'd send it
over to the Orpheum and the Empress for their runnings.

I violated the patents; my camera had a loop. Everybody taking pictures was a patent violator. The loop was essential, allowing the film to stand still for an instant, then pick up, and move again. The loop was a slight piece of film between the sprocket and the movement of pulling the film off the roll—giving pictures their intermittence. Beyond that intermittent movement was another sprocket and loop between it and the sprocket which fed film to a take-up spool or magazine.

Before the trust was broken, two detectives, Kelly and Smith, were working for the company. They actually had to see our film in the form of a loop before claiming infringement. I had a friend, a big husky Swedish boy who worked as a stevedore. He would go around with me, keeping people away from the camera. If they got curious, he'd just stand in the way, and if they got too curious, he'd give them the elbow. But Kelly and Smith reached me, and I was—hell, I was sixteen years old. These two got me on the pretext that they were a couple of oilmen who wanted to make a film of their oil fields. Being the stupid kid that I was, I showed them my equipment. They took a good look at the camera, and that was my undoing. In a few days, I was served an injunction to seize the equipment. They confiscated my camera. I subsequently got it back, but only after the company had been broken. The thing that finally broke the patents monopoly was the fact that the shuttle in a sewing machine is really a "loop," too, although this is a matter of hearsay with me.

After that, I got a job at Sol Lesser's Film Exchange. I cut school for six months before my family knew about it. I'd leave the house every morning for the cable car to connect with the electric car to get to Polytechnic High School. It was during the last few months in school that I built my camera. Mother and father were against my doing anything but getting an education. So I was a juvenile delinquent. I got along pretty well until they finally caught up with me. That was the end of my schooling. There I was in 1913, on my own, with the folks, who were well-fixed, still convinced that I should be a doctor.

That year the Panama–Pacific International Exposition was to be built a few blocks from my home. The Exposition people had given a charter, a commission or a license, to Doom and Harder, film-makers in San Francisco, to photograph it. But I kidnapped films against the license that had been issued to Doom and Harder, photographing stuff that was not to be photographed. Nothing could be done about it once I had my films. I got outside the Exposition grounds while the fair was on and photographed one of the flyers. There was exhibition flying every day. That was one of the big features. I photographed—what's his name?— who used to do the "falling leap and uncontrolled spin." He'd recover from the fall just before reaching the ground. Only this day, he didn't recover, and I happened to photograph him going straight down into the

Mary Pickford in *Little Annie Rooney*. Cameraman—Hal Mohr. United Artists. 1925.

Bay alongside a transport. That was a sensational shot. It was for news-reels at that time.

I made stuff for newsreels, getting one dollar a foot for film they used, which was pretty good since it cost me eighty cents a foot. I first worked for Sol as a film inspector. When the film would come back from the theater, I'd run it between my fingers, feel a broken sprocket, patch it up, and get it ready for the next showing. But that took place before I really got into photography. I worked in the film exchange while play-ing hooky, just to make enough money to buy film to do the things I wanted to do.

Then the camera couldn't tilt, but I devised a way. I knew that in a still camera, you could raise and lower the lens to avoid distortion, so I built such a device on my second camera, mounting the lens on a little board that worked between two tracks out in front. I had a lever going so I could raise and lower the lens. I also hooked a finder to the same thing, on which I could slide the lens up and down. Now I could see what I was doing. I still had to crank the camera by hand since there was no such thing as a motor in those days. And I could only tilt within a limited area, up or down, using the finder to show what I was doing.

I earned seven or eight dollars a week in the film exchange. Sol was always generous and kind. He wanted to start a newsreel to be called *The Golden Gate Weekly,* and he gave me the job because he knew that I would be interested. He formed the Progressive Film Company. We converted a little store on Ellis Street into a laboratory, with developing tanks, a drying drum, the printing machine, and so on. Sol financed the enterprise, and I turned out *The Golden Gate Weekly* for him. We made five or six prints every week, which were released throughout California and the West Coast states. I photographed, developed the negative, and made the titles. I was also salesman for the firm. It was a one-man opera-tion.

We got close to Exposition time in San Francisco. Until then the Barbary Coast was a notorious place. San Francisco had kept its vice re-stricted to ten square blocks or so near Chinatown. That was the "Tender-loin," a cheap district that appealed to sailors and soldiers who came from everywhere. On one little street especially, Pacific Street, you found ladies of easy virtue, who were forerunners of our "B" girls and café entertainers. In the dance halls they would grab fellows and inveigle them into buying beer or champagne.

The city fathers decided to clean up this section before the 1915 Exposition. They decreed that the Barbary Coast was to be closed, that its final night was in the offing. The dance halls were going to be boarded up, 10,000 prostitutes, along with their "call houses," or "crib houses,"

had to be eliminated. Sol thought it would be splendid to make a film of
this last night of the Barbary Coast.

I set about making this film. I went over before the night of the closing, carrying my camera, stalking into alleyways lined with "fast houses"
on either side of the street. San Francisco's lots were all very narrow as
you know. They were twenty to twenty-five-foot lots with four- and
five-story buildings built right on top of each other. The "parlor houses"
and "crib houses" were situated in the center of the block back away
from the street itself. You'd have to go through one of these passageways
to reach them. I ventured down there on a Sunday morning to get exterior
shots. I couldn't photograph them at night because the film was very slow.
And, oh, I got into terrific rows. I mean, I'd have the camera set in the
middle of an alley, getting a long shot of fast houses, and I would be de-
luged by chamber pots being thrown from open windows.

I had managed to get hold of a couple arc lights which I strung
around telephone poles. Each one had a feeding apparatus and a bowl on
the bottom. I built a pair of bracketed stands and linked them up. To this
day, I don't know how the hell I did it. A kid with the limited knowledge
I had. With a theater electrician, I mounted two more arc lights, and we
took them out on the street, which was packed with people. It looked like
New Year's Eve on Times Square. With these, I photographed the mobs
on Pacific. I photographed the inside of a disreputable café called The
Failure in which many murders had been committed. Frequently, a sailor
would come in from a long trip with his pockets full of money, enter this
kind of place, and that was the end of him. The gals would get sailors
drugged or rolled and dump them into the alleys or kill them, or whatever
the hell had to be done. It was pretty rough. I also photographed The
Hippodrome and The Midway, which were dance halls. I made one shot
of a Salvation Army gal coming along with a tambourine. People were
always very generous to the Salvation Army.

So I actually photographed a one-reel, full-length picture of Pacific
Street on its last wide-open night. Of course, features eventually became
two-reelers, three-reelers, and even five-reelers—but the average then was
one reel. I used everything I shot. We didn't waste film in those days. I
shot a thousand feet, or maybe twelve hundred with leaders and what not.

I developed the negative, assembled it, and made titles. I had one
printing machine, and it was very slow, four frames a second at top speed.
That's all I had. There was no automatic printer of any kind. Through a
ruby glass, you could see the negative, with the positive film. It had strings
that pulled the light back and forth to regulate densities. I speeded this
mechanism up and made something like—I don't think this is a exaggera-
tion—200 prints of this *Last Night of the Barbary Coast* off one negative.
Sol sold them on a "state's rights" basis. That meant that a film exchange,

which served theaters in, say, the state of California, would buy so many prints. You were guaranteed that nobody else in the state could buy them. It gave you exclusivity in the whole area.

My association with Sol lasted a couple of years. You might say they were the years of my apprenticeship. Actually, I was an apprentice to myself. After Sol dissolved his company, I served a second apprenticeship. I realized my shortcomings photographically and took a job with the leading portraitist in San Francisco. God almighty, the prices they paid him! He made "ivory prints," six by eleven inches, through a carbon transfer process put on white celluloid. There were no enlargements as yet. They were contact prints. He photographed on plates up to sixteen by twenty inches and then printed directly from them. He was an exquisite photographer. So I went to work for him. I'd clean out his studio, carpet-sweep it, dust all over every morning at the crack of dawn, working through his whole loft.

I was rather an ingratiating kid. I mean, I *made* people like me. I was a bit of a smoothy, I guess, because he took a fancy to me and taught me. I helped him in the darkroom developing his plates. He did it all by hand, by the "brush development" process. He started with a very slow solution. When the image appeared, he would use different strengths of solution to bring some out here and move some out there. It saved quite a bit of retouching, although we did that too. His sister-in-law and I were the entire staff. I got six dollars a week for God's sake! During the Christmas rush, we just slept and worked. The second year, he raised me to eight dollars, but by this time, I was doing his printing and developing his negatives. His sister-in-law did the finishing work. By the end of the Christmas rush of the second year, I had learned about all there was to learn for my purposes. I asked him for more money. He wouldn't give it to me, and I quit.

I worked in Berkeley for Arthur Rice, another very fine still-photographer who was interested in motion pictures. He had a first-rate studio. In his motion picture enterprise, he had a partner, Alfred Einstein, the son of a banking family in Fresno. The last I heard, Alfred was president of the Fresno National Bank or the First National Bank of Fresno. Well, I began to learn, really learn, from Arthur about motion picture photography over and above what I had already taught myself.

I worked for Arthur until he left for Los Angeles in 1915. The Exposition was over, and Arthur went to work for Universal as a director. That was the year Universal moved to what is now Universal City. They had a little studio at the corner of Gower and Sunset Boulevard, the old Christie Studios. There was a location ranch, and just to give you an idea of how early this was, they had men on horseback patrolling the area to keep the patents company out. Tom Ince had a studio in the Santa Inez

Canyons, a big studio in which he made "bronco" films, where I worked very briefly. In the meantime, I promoted a studio in Berkeley. An Italian fellow had started a school of acting and had built a studio in Berkeley on Telegraph Avenue which had a little outdoor stage and a kind of office building. He used to charge a fee to teach people in the Italian colony how to act, and pretend that he was making pictures of them. Then the police caught up with him. I moved into this studio and started promoting. My dad gave me $500 to use as initial capital. He had seen that it was impossible to stop me by this time and advanced the money. The war had just broken out in Europe. We were not yet involved. Now our best pictures were coming from Europe, chiefly from Italy and France. A tremendous feature, *Cabiria*, came out of Italy. In that picture, for the first time I saw a camera moving. Do you recall those shots through the palaces before the volcanic eruptions and the earthquakes? A suspended camera went traveling through columns and over bacchanalian festivals.

It was the first time, to my knowledge, that a moving camera had ever been used. I went to the people who had been students of the guy in jail, men who had been house painters and decorators and vintners. Their association began to buy stock. One man, Johnnie De Maria, known as the "King of the Barbary Coast," owned a lot of real estate which he rented to houses of ill-repute. He also operated a flat-iron building at the corner of Pacific Street and New Montgomery. Johnnie put up a large part of the cash. He helped finance me. I was the producer. I would make the pictures and have disposal rights over them. I was going to do all these things, and if I succeeded in selling the pictures, I was to get something like thirty-five dollars a week and a 5 percent interest in the company, or some ridiculous arrangement like that. I had a year's contract at twenty-five dollars a week.

I had read a wonderful book and misappropriated its theme. The book was *Pam's Mountain*, if I recall correctly. I renamed it *Daughter of the Guards*. That title had to go, too, because someone else had just used it. But I made my picture. I took all my talent from the Italian colony in San Francisco. The leading lady was my sweetheart, a nice little Italian girl sent to me by a theatrical agent. I paid the cast three or four dollars a day. They desperately wanted to be in pictures. Extras for mob scenes I paid one dollar a day. I got them from an agency in Oakland and I had almost finished this picture when I ran out of money. Johnnie wouldn't give me any more, so I cut what I had of the unfinished picture and took it to New York to William A. Brady, who *was* the World Film Exchange, a big man in the motion picture industry. I showed the film to his people. Oh, I got pushed around something terrible. I had a hell of a time. Meanwhile, back in Berkeley, Johnnie saw a chance to get out from under. While I was stuck in New York with the film, he put our company through bankruptcy out on the Coast. The picture was never released, and I was broke again. Dad had lost $500, which wasn't such a terrible tragedy for him, but it was the end so far as I was concerned.

At that point, Arthur Rice found a job for me as film-cutter at Universal. I went to work the first year they were at Universal City in 1915 and edited films. They had fifty-six directors on the lot, of whom Arthur was one. Nine of us cut film for fifty-six directors. After two years at Universal, I went to the Rolins Studios, run by Hal Roach and Ralph Whiting. They were making *Lonesome Luke* pictures with Harold Lloyd and *Toto the Clown* pictures. They had Bebe Daniels and many other people. I went to work as a director. By this time we were at war.

I directed Harold Lloyd in a couple of pictures at Rolins Fairfield Studio. He had been "Lonesome Luke" but had become the boy with the glasses, the young college chap. No more mustache. Daniels was the leading lady. The studio owned something like a little school bus on which we would load the company and, without a script, would just go out and shoot.

I was a lousy director, but no one cared with the war on. They clung to me. I'd been deferred. Mother was dependent upon me. So I was—what? Class F? Whiting, Hal Roach's partner, thought, "Oh, well, we're going to lose all our people. We'd better grab this guy." So they grabbed me as a director, and Alf Goulding as the alternate director. For a while, Roach himself directed the series. Alf would be making a picture one week while I prepared a script, and then I'd direct the following week while Alf prepared another story. I made only two pictures before they called me into the army. But the second one opened the Criterion, a spanking new theater in downtown Los Angeles. It was *the* chic theater. They featured a good film, and the accompanying comedy was my comedy, *The Big Idea*. I made it with Lloyd and a chap who used to be Lloyd's chauffeur, Gil Pratt. You may recall that name. He became a comedy director. Harold asked if I would let this Gil work with me to learn how to become a director, so I took him on as an associate, and he got to be a director after I was drafted early in 1917.

Once in the army, I immediately applied for a transfer into aviation as a photographic observer. The only photographers were aerial observers for aviation, and aviation was just nothing. Nevertheless I put in for a transfer. Instead they made me company clerk. I rather liked that job because I figured it would get me out of duties like KP, latrine police, and such nonsense. I became a corporal. My transfer didn't come through, and when we went overseas, I was still in the infantry. A month or two before the Armistice, the transfer finally arrived. I got packed in a hurry and headed for a train to Paris. By then, the photographic section had been divorced from aviation. It was now in the 66th Service Company

Signal Corps. I remained in Paris for a whole year, dying to get home. But Paris was fun. George Siegmann, the great heavy for D. W. Griffith who chased virgins all over the place—in pictures I mean—was my commanding officer in the photographic unit. We were in Tours when the Armistice was signed. He and I got gloriously, roaringly cock-eyed! I talked George into transferring us back to Paris, and we were there on Armistice night. Oh, my God, that was exciting.

Al Kaufman, head of Paramount Studios for quite a while, was our adjutant, the captain under Major Hardy, and Major Hardy liked it in Paris because he was doing all right. He got a major's salary and lived high-on-the-hog surrounded by beautiful women. He concocted the idea of making up photographic albums for the commanding generals of different divisions, of which there were thirty or forty. We'd make up documentary films for each division. It was an excuse to keep us there for over a year.

After this military experience, I worked a bit for Miles Brothers in San Francisco, just to get re-established in civilian life, making industrial films. Then I got a job in Portland to finish photographing the first picture Jean Hersholt made as a star. I worked there for a year and returned to Hollywood. I had to fight "poverty road" for a while, and I finally wound up with Ince, photographing a picture for his brother Ralph. It was a one-man operation, and after his death, there was no "general" anymore, only "buck privates." He died on William Randolph Hearst's yacht. Ince's death has always been a mystery. There've been theories: everything from the most gruesome type of murder to an accident to a lot of other things, but these are all pure rumor.

Before going to Ince, I'd made one-reeler Westerns. Outdoor action presented no particular problem except for light. Without it you were lost. During this period, new photographic techniques and new cameras, like the Bell and Howell, had come in. We learned all about changing camera speed in slapstick comedy. For a fast chase, we'd crank the camera a little slower. When a cowboy would dive off a cliff, we'd speed up the camera to beat hell. We contrived ways of chasing along in an automobile. Naturally, we knew nothing of hand-held cameras. Credit for shooting from a moving automobile, as you know, really belongs to Billy Bitzer. He and Griffith were a team. It was Billy who created the first "soft focus," diffusing by putting gauze in front of the lens. Later we developed diffusion disks. I knew Billy in the final days of his life. I met him in New York. He taught me a few little things, but the poor guy was broke by that time, on the ash heap—like Griffith. Billy was a technical genius who, after the glory days in Hollywood, did all right in New York until he came to be considered passé.

After the Ince studio closed, I went to work for Mary Pickford. I spent a year working with one of our greatest cinematographers, Charles Rosher. He was an Englishman, an exquisite photographer, a marvelous cameraman, and I learned a lot from him. He was noted for his exquisite portraitures of Mary Pickford. I did a couple of pictures, one with Charlie Rosher called *Little Annie Rooney* and then *Sparrows*.

Cameramen were no longer processing their own film. We had laboratories. At the old Ince Studios there was a laboratory behind one of the sets. We were still using racks to develop film, no machinery. Men worked there, but some of us particularly wanted to develop our own negatives. Then came the first Consolidated Laboratories in Hollywood with a drum-system development. I encountered it when I was with Rosher. Terrific overexposure followed by very light development produced a soft negative with lovely tonal quality and gradation. In time, you no longer developed your own negatives. Soon there were commercial laboratories, one or two run by master craftsmen. Gradually the cameraman got away from photography. The modern cameraman is not a photographer.

Being of the older generation, I'm very jealous of our experience. It was only through men like Rosher, Arthur Miller, Arthur Edeson, myself, and a few others, who went through a hard school, that a craft and a profession I'm damn proud of came into shape.

What changed it all was not so much division of labor as the regimentation of industry. The "automobile assemblyman" began to get into our industry. The efficiency experts wanted even more money than they were making. God knows, they were making enough. But to get still bigger profits, they began regimenting different jobs and pigeonholing certain types of work. The cameraman of today is like a man in the assembly line of an automobile factory who puts in upholstery or marks the engine or performs some limited task of that nature. We were in the handicraft stage, and suddenly it was industrialized. I don't mean to say, though, that remarkable photographic effects aren't being achieved right now.

I'm on the Board of Governors at the Academy of Motion Picture Arts and Sciences as chairman of the Cinematographic Committee. I look at a lot of foreign-language pictures with a view to nominating five of them to be voted on for an award by the members of the Academy, so I'm in a good position to contrast them with the Hollywood product. Something's happened to Hollywood since the advent of television. You'll find a new breed of directors in the industry. Some of them are very talented. They've brought wonderful things to film. But the majority are as phony as a three-dollar bill, bluffers, tight-pants Madison Avenue types.

On the other hand, I looked at a picture the other day made by a French director, Lelouch. He got the Academy Award for *A Man and a Woman*. Lelouch made that picture with practically no money, but he showed a spark of genius, and I think the award was well deserved. This year he did *Live for Life*. Now, there's a picture that is of the real new school. It's what these tight-pants phonies, who were ushers in television yesterday and the darlings of the motion picture industry today, think they're doing. They can't hold a candle to someone like Lelouch.

He takes a distasteful subject like fornication and does it so beautifully that it's not offensive. Lelouch inserted directorial touches everywhere; he *used* his cameras. Nowadays directors, not cameramen, use cameras. There are just a few of the fine cameramen left who do their own photography. But Lelouch! On *A Man and a Woman*, I understand he photographed as well as directed, wrote the story, and produced it himself. Although he doesn't take credit for photographing this one, you can recognize his touch. Maybe I'm off-base in eulogizing the guy so much, but I believe that that picture is an outstanding example of what the phonies do so badly.

I would give my soul to do a picture with Lelouch. I see an opportunity of developing things for that man and helping him with his own creative ideas. I can contribute as much to him as I contributed to the directors of my early days. I'm an old man now. What the hell, let's face it. I can't hang on the front of locomotives as I used to, but my professional abilities have not slackened in any way. I've kept up with the parade, and I've kept ahead of it. After this hysteria we're going through now finally filters out, there'll be a major breakthrough. There'll be some really brilliant people, a renaissance of creative minds, not one, but a group, making great pictures. Not as we did them in the old days, but as pictures in the old days were made by creative minds. A new school, a whole new school.

In our time, there'd be a director, a production manager, an assistant director, a cameraman, and maybe a writer. That was the unit, and they made the picture. All their thoughts worked together. Everybody was equal in thinking capacity. They worked things out together. The pictures they made then weren't as good as the best pictures we are making now, but they were a hell of a lot better than the bad pictures we're making now. I think the old type of production will have to be restored for creativity to flourish again. In the early days, we were really attached to the director and to the stars as well. I had earned a reputation as a photographer of women. I could make them look beautiful. I would travel with stars, such as Dolores Costello. They accepted me.

I was under contract until a few years ago. Now there are no more contracts for cameramen. I was the highest salaried cameraman in the industry for quite a while, probably the first cameraman with a salary up to four figures. It was quite an accomplishment. I stipulated that any publicity had to indicate that I was the director of photography. All that's a thing of the past now.

I'd done most of the important pictures at Warner Brothers for some time. And I was there when the Crash took place. They were in pretty bad financial condition. Their backs were to the wall. Most of the time we didn't know whether we were going to get our salaries. Sam Warner, a charming guy, introduced the Vitaphone, which was the first vaudeville or variety type of talking picture. Edison had first tried with a hooked-up phonograph and succeeded technically, but not commercially. Well, Sam's Vitaphone showed promise just for making shorts. They figured it might be a way out of their difficulties.

All this led to *The Jazz Singer*. Jessel was supposed to be the lead. I don't know what happened. Georgie might have been afraid that he wouldn't get his money. Jolson had made one silent picture with D. W. Griffith. It was awful, and Jolie didn't want to have anything more to do with motion pictures. Jack Warner thought of trying to get him to do *The Jazz Singer*. The idea was to have somebody sing and talk on the screen. That might be the thing. They proved that it was. Alan Crosland was assigned to the picture, and I went along with Alan. Jolson agreed to make a test. They wanted to see how he looked on film. Jack talked to Alan and me. We realized the importance of this test, made it with Jolie, and he liked it. Thus, *The Jazz Singer*.

Sound was a sensation. But it produced new headaches, new challenges. The camera was noisy, arc lights sputtered, our film was not sensitive to the red incandescent light. We had the old autochromatic film that was sensitive to the blue light. And we couldn't use arc lights with a microphone on the set. On location doing exteriors we'd hang down a branch of a tree so that it would cut into someone's head to hide the microphone. The soundman was God. Whatever he said went. In an interior set, the microphone had to be within eighteen inches of my mouth. To conceal that, I put a little piece of glass in front of the camera, and on that, I painted a picture that had to be on the wall. Or we'd hide it in a big vase of flowers on the table.

The camera became stationary again for a while. On *The Jazz Singer*, we rehearsed a scene and ran it. Jolie sang a song running approximately three minutes. It was photographed *in toto* like "live" television with three or four cameras on the set. It would have been impossible to record. So we built "iceboxes" and put the cameras in them. We locked the assistant and the operator inside, and the poor bastards would suffocate for the duration of those scenes. We had to hide microphones for all these cameras. If you have ever looked at some of the early talking pictures and seen incongruous things all over the set—for God's sake!—those are "microphone hiders." We used all sorts of devious tricks both in the background and in the foreground.

One day we read our "declaration of independence": "Now look, here's how we're going to photograph, and you get the best sound that you can." We have difficulty to this day with soundmen over their microphone shadows, but not as much as we did at the beginning. In order to get a moving camera shot, we had to move the whole icebox in closer. We didn't have the zoom lens, you know. Heavens, what a job that was—but it didn't last too long. We had to assert ourselves and restrict the soundmen.

We finally compromised, and of course their equipment began to improve. They developed directional microphones which gave them perspective and distance. For some time they stayed with the disk and, my, it was cumbersome. They could never cut without dubbing. A reel of film suited the length of a record. Some of the reels were so short that the operator would just have time enough to turn on his other machine. With two separate mechanical units, there would be slippage. The operator had to resynch and speed up the record or slow down the film to get them together. You can see why the projectionist had to be highly skilled. It was up to him to synch the record on the picture. Sound meant the beginning of recognition for projectionists. That was what gave them the chance to do something worthwhile.

Nathan Levison, a musician at Warner Brothers, figured out the way to dub sound, so that we could take many different records that were still on wax, have them all running and cutting and put on a master. He deserves a chapter in film history. He became the sound engineer at Warners'. The man's a forgotten hero.

I stayed with Warners' until I got into trouble over *Noah's Ark*, a big biblical epic. Zanuck and I didn't see eye to eye on a few things. *Noah's Ark* needed an enormous flood with plenty of sets all collapsing at once. On Sunday we were rehearsing a scene that had to be photographed the following day. A gigantic temple with huge columns was going to collapse. They had water spillways on top of the columns, each one with several tons of water in it, which were going to be dumped on people down below. We had stuntmen who knew what they were doing, but we also had several hundred other people who didn't know what it was all about. The trick specialist, the producers, the director, and I were all there. They started talking about how to do it, and I objected, not as a cameraman, but as a human being, for Christ sake, because it seemed to me. and I could have been mistaken, although at the time I didn't think so, that they were going to kill a few people with these tons of water and huge sets falling on them. I knew the stuntmen could guard themselves to some degree. But what about the others? So I walked off

Dolores Costello and George O'Brien in *Noah's Ark*. Cameraman—Hal Mohr. Warner Bros. 1929.

The flood scene from *Noah's Ark*. Cameraman—Hal Mohr.

Scenes during filming of *A Midsummer Night's Dream* which won an Academy Award for Cameraman Hal Mohr. Warner Bros. 1935.

the picture. I wouldn't have any part of it. They were trifling with lives—and did modify their plan somewhat. But some stuntmen were seriously hurt. I don't know whether they left just the stuntmen and took the others out or not.

I forget where I went from there. But what the hell. I could walk out of this studio today and into that one tomorrow. I was so independent. I had a good reputation.

I won a couple of Academy Awards, but that takes us back to Warner Brothers again to a point after the horrible strike in 1933. I was out with an army of other people. We were having deep trouble. And I had just gotten married. I had been working with Will Rogers. Warner Brothers started making *A Midsummer Night's Dream*. It was kind of mixed-up. They had the German producer Max Reinhardt and another German, William Dieterle, directing the picture. The cameraman was good, but he apparently didn't insist on what he wanted. They had built a set—the art director was a very ambitious guy—a magnificent forest set on two enormous stages, which were simply impossible to photograph. And they had been ten weeks or so on the picture when they finally realized they couldn't make it. They were in terrible trouble.

Now, I hadn't been back to Warner Brothers since the *Noah's Ark* incident, and I'd also had some difficulties with the production chief. A top man (I'll keep him anonymous) called me over to *A Midsummer Night's Dream*. "Don't be ridiculous," I said, "Jack Warner wouldn't want me around the place. Furthermore, I don't believe in taking another man's job. You've got a damn good cameraman on that picture. What's the matter?"

"But he can't photograph it."

"Well, if he can't photograph it, I can't."

"Look, will you come on out? I'll pave the way. Just come on out and talk to me."

I went. A very dear friend was asking me. The film looked pretty bad. They couldn't get exposure. There was no fantasy to it at all, no imagination injected from a photographic point of view. I asked, "May I work with the chap who was photographing it for a few days and see if I can help him? I'd be glad to do that with no charge to you or to anybody else. He may still be able to handle it."

"No, that's out of the question."

In that case, I made some stipulations. I'd have to be given complete authority over the art director and anybody else who might stop me. They talked and talked. It was a delicate thing between them. At last we agreed. I said, "Well, all right, tonight I want a good-sized gang of painters on the set, and we'll be ready to shoot tomorrow morning. You're going to see a radical change in that set. It will still be there, but it will be entirely different."

They quit shooting that afternoon. I went up with the boss painter and the electricians. We lit all the lights on one side of the stage to get the visual effect of light coming through the trees and across the grass. (The two stages of that tremendous set were as big as a square city block.) I told the painters, "Make up an aluminum paint and get your spray guns, bring your gang of painters, and move in on that side with the lights. Wherever you see light, spray it with aluminum." I pointed out places where no light was hitting: "Spray aluminum on that same side and on the other side where no light is hitting. Take orange shellac and spray all the trees, all the shrubs, all the foliage, spray everything with orange shellac."

They thought I was crazy. I stayed with them for two or three hours and saw it was working. About midnight, I went home. I walked in again at six o'clock the next morning. The painters had finished. You could see nothing but aluminum paint and orange shellac. I began to concoct things with cobwebs and with sparkles on cobwebs and created a lot of crap. By the time Warner and the rest of them walked in, they also thought that I had gone insane. Everyone thought so—until they saw the first rushes and then they were jubilant. I got an Academy Award for that.

I took over one other picture, this time for Herman Shumlin, a wonderful stage director and stage producer who had recently scored with *Watch on the Rhine*. It was the same kind of a situation, only with very different photographic treatment. Once again, we were faced with the arrogant attitude of one department toward another department. And once again, the cameraman didn't have strength enough to insist, "This is how I must do it." It took a lot of gumption and integrity to defy the studio and say, "I'm going to take a fifty thousand dollar set and ruin it on you!" Christ, this is beginning to sound as if I'm selling myself. I'm not trying to do that. I'm trying to sell the profession. Well, they had started Shumlin's picture version of *Watch on the Rhine*, with Bette Davis and Paul Lukas, a hell of a cast and after eight weeks, they were ready to call it off.

They had a dialogue director working with them who was a little schnook, and their cameraman was weak. The director of photography has to be a general. He has to command and coordinate when necessary. Shumlin had never made a picture and he was lost, working at it like a stage play. Nobody had enough imagination to help him, and the director was in conflict with the cameraman. Things were fouled up to the point where they were going to give up. Under the circumstances, I wanted to help this cameraman. I did nothing to the set. I simply took hold of the damn picture and made it. We did rather well, if you recall, with *Watch on the Rhine*. For me, it was just a case of engineering. The first thing I said to Shumlin was, "Please rehearse the scene exactly as you did it on the stage. Let me watch." The sets were more or less like the stage sets. He would rehearse; I'd take a script clerk and break it all down. As he did a scene I would say, "There is the camera, and we'll move it across to here," without changing his action at all. In this way, I wrote my own shooting script. Shumlin would rehearse and leave the set. I'd mark the camera positions, mark the stand-in positions, call Shumlin back, show him exactly what I intended to do, and he'd give me the go-ahead.

I didn't win another Academy Award for that, but I did for color on a remake of *The Phantom of the Opera* with Claude Rains. I could tell you so much more, but let's talk for a moment about the American Society of Cinematographers. It's not a labor union, but rather it is a professional organization, or a guild. In 1927 or 1928, we organized the International Photographers. We started with a few hundred members including still-photographers and directors of photography. At present, the membership is somewhere around two thousand. Television did a lot to increase the number of jobs. The rank order is approximately as follows: director of photography, operator, cameraman, special effects photographer, first assistant cameraman, second assistant cameraman, film loader, newsreel cameraman, optical cameraman, electronic cameraman.

Nowadays, personality counts for more than ability—and there's the same old acquiescence by cameramen to whatever the director says. In many cases, the camera treatment is so ridiculous, you can't follow the story. Some directors of the new school, although this can't be a blanket condemnation, are complete incompetents. Too many of today's cameramen do only what they're told to do. A director issues an order. "Put the camera here and photograph into that light." He doesn't explain why. A good director will say, "Look, I'd like to get an effect here. I think that maybe if we could get some kind of a flaring light coming across the man, it would partly obliterate him. Now you go ahead and figure out how to do that." You'd do that and show him, trying to make it photographically and artistically proper. And he'd respond with, "That's great," or "No, that's not what I want." The intelligent director works creatively with his cameraman, never treating him as a mere photographer. I'm still eager to associate with that kind of man.

The Sound Director

DOUGLAS SHEARER

I WAS BORN in 1899 in the little town of Westmont, which is inside of Montreal, something like Beverly Hills inside of Los Angeles. I had Scotch, Irish, and English grandparents. My Scotch grandfather came to Montreal in 1838 by sail ship, with about a pound in his pocket, from way up in Cape Ness County, North Scotland. One more step and you are in the Arctic Ocean. He got started in the lumber business, then in contracting and building. He built up the James Shearer Company. My father married late in life, his father did too, so in a way I belong to Queen Victoria's era.

My other grandfather became a clergyman after graduating from Cambridge, Trinity College. He and his wife had their first-born prior to leaving for the New World. A famous doctor sailed over with them to establish a medical practice in Ontario, Canada. He told my grandmother that they'd better bring along a milking goat with them so that if she became seasick, the baby would have something to drink. She did that. They eventually set up a couple of church centers in Canada. The first was just a log cabin in the woods, and Indians were a part of the parish. Finally, they set up a permanent church where my grandfather spent the rest of his life as minister of that congregation. My grandmother had twelve children. You can imagine the spread of time that took.

My grandfather on the other side of the family built himself a house at the end of a road which they named Shearer Lane, now Shearer Street, where he had the lumber yard. He sold that to the Northern Electric Company. It's at the corner of Shearer and St. Patrick streets yet.

I grew up in Montreal and stayed there until I was twenty-five, although I worked in other places. I quit high school before receiving my final grades and went to work for the Northern Electric Company, which, in Canada, is the equivalent to the Western Electric. I also learned something about technical equipment because I had studied signaling with the McGill Officer's Training Corps and I intended to join the Royal Air Force. But it so happened that I was a victim of that first epidemic of flu in 1918. You know there were millions who died of it. Actually, had I not gotten ill, I would have gone into the Royal Air Force and I wouldn't be here at all because most fighter pilots lasted only a month. Anyway, when the war wound up, I couldn't afford to go back to school because my father had met some financial adversities, so when I was about nineteen, I had to go to work.

I spent about two and a half or three years in a machine shop and became a bit of a machinist. Then the firm I was working for took on, as a sideline, industrial power plant equipment, so I learned a good deal about various principles and aspects of mechanics. After a period of time in the machine shop, the company sent me out on the road as their representative. I came in contact with the top mechanical engineers and mechanical supervisors of the big industries all over Canada. In this way, I'd meet what turned out for me to be great teachers. I'd sit and talk with a chief engineer of an enormous paper mill and spend a night or two like that. Next time, I'd see some guy running a tire factory up in Ontario and so on. I appreciated this experience as a substitute for the education I would have had under normal circumstances. I went to all kinds of places. Glue factories, soap factories, everything you could think of. I was fortunate. Later I'd be hiring guys with college educations. The paper mills were one of the things that interested me most. They were in the backwoods. In those days almost the whole country was a strip of settlements around the St. Lawrence River.

Then strangely and abruptly, in 1920, I got into the motorcar business. I had a dealership of Model-T Fords with a partner. He was the sales manager, and I ran the shop.

A year or so before that my sister Norma started her career in New York. A lot of people think it began in Hollywood. My youngest uncle was in show business and had married a wonderful actress, a young, very clever, redhead. They managed shows on one-night stands all over the country and Mexico, too. One year he visited us and got to talking about Norma, who was barely out of her childhood then, a young teen-ager, but she was quite able and played the piano. So, since his wife was an actress and he was a manager, he suggested that Norma should go into the picture business. He knew certain people in New York who were in film production, and he gave her a letter of introduction to one of them. She went to New York with our mother and played a little part in an early movie *The Flapper* in which the young starlet Olive Thomas also played.

Then during the Depression in 1920, she went to work posing for photographers. She and Mother had to earn a living. She began to study herself from the hundreds of stills that were taken and was able to move around without any awkwardness. She was noticed in one of her little films and received an offer to come out to Universal with the possibility of a contract. Well, Mother wasn't any fool, I'm telling you. Somehow, she'd heard of Universal and didn't quite like the outfit, although they were fairly important in the early days of pictures. No reflection particularly, but Carl Laemmle was somewhat rigid. So she turned Universal down. Later, she got an offer for an interview with MGM. They went out to Hollywood. This is what she tells me. There has been nothing written about it. She went into an office in the corner of the MGM lot, and there was a young man of twenty-seven sitting behind the desk. It was Irving Thalberg, the same one who had made her the offer at Universal and who had instigated the merger of Metro-Goldwyn-Mayer.

Thalberg had become the top organizational manager. Although Mayer was the official head of the studio, Thalberg had the primary voice in many things. There was a lot of squabbling, of course, but it was to be expected. Mayer was not so hard to get along with if you just didn't give in to him. He was initially a hard man, but he had a very alert sense of values for certain things. He was partial to certain films like the Mickey Rooney series, or that repetitive kind of stuff. He was very good at that. But Thalberg had an eye for big picture quality. He picked up Al Lewin, Harry Rapf, talent of that sort, and formed a nice group of production heads who turned to Thalberg for the last word.

Anyway, I hadn't seen my mother and sister in quite awhile, so I came to visit them in California. I had a return ticket, too. It was during that visit that I became involved in some publicity promotions. At that time, Norma was in a picture called *Slave of Fashion*, which, as a part of the star, featured particularly nice clothes. As the film was being run, a radio broadcast was picked up by a receiver at a theater in San Francisco. The film and the radio broadcast ran at the same time. I was invited to see the show, and I suggested a way they might be able to tie the picture and the dialogue parts more closely together. I went to see the head publicity man, Pete Smith, who was quite a guy. I pursued this idea and it worked out pretty well. There was quite a report on that in June of 1925.

I had recorded on a phonograph record the talk that my sister Norma and Lew Cody had used in San Francisco over KPO radio. From that, I was able to get the timing between the words by putting them on a paper sheet and punching holes in it. It worked much like a pianola. The words were spaced according to their different tempos of expression. In short, I timed the talk they had recorded. The basic problem was that different people have different word timings, but by spacing and typing the words up on a large sheet and running it through an ordinary washing-machine wringer, with an attached crank and metronome, you could proceed at an even rate.

In one section of MGM there were two monitor rooms with a glass window between them. I took a couple of cameramen with me to show them what I had done and then connected the camera to a movieola screen. However they didn't take me too seriously. They talked as if I had invited them to come down and chat about their picture, *Slave of Fashion*. So when they came in, we exchanged a few cordial greetings. Meanwhile, the camera and the movieola were going. The movieola now had a film version of the paper tape. On that film was a recording of the words going by, synching their voices with their words. I had invented a tie-up between the film of the actors delivering the talk and the paper tape with words on it in natural cadence. You might say they were a little surprised. Once I had that, I was able to generate many copies. By using some of the illustrations of the costumes Norma wore in between the dialogue sections, we created an eight- or ten-minute film out of it. I made fifteen copies and they went to theaters all the way to Long Beach and Pasadena. We supplied them with metronomes that I had calibrated to click together, took the motor drives off the projectors, and added a crank. So by 1925 we had a sound movie projector in fifteen theaters, including Loew's State in downtown Los Angeles.

I was now working for MGM, employed for this particular publicity stunt, which was what they called it. For that they paid me very well, seventy-five bucks. And I decided it was time I sold my return ticket for Montreal and stay on. I had become fascinated by the country as well as the industry. I had had enough background in industrial plants and mechanics so that I thought the competition wouldn't be too tough. I visualized the possibilities of a place for myself. And the weather was fine compared to that of Montreal.

I had been interested in photography as an avocation since the time Eastman enabled you to process your own pictures. Well, I applied for a job in the camera department as assistant cameraman. Thirty dollar-a-week jobs were just as hard to get as those for thirty thousand dollars a week. Plenty of people were available. I had met Jack Warner at my mother's and sister's house at dinnertime once or twice. I went to see him. I said, "I'd like to stay around here. Have you got anything for me to do?"

"We can put you in the prop room, building and moving furniture," he said.

They were making Rin-Tin-Tin pictures in those days. So for thirty dollars a week—all the jobs paid the same amount, thirty dollars a week— I said, "Fine." After that I began working with directors as a propman.

The propman is the one who sees that the chairs and all such accessories you needed on the set are there. The propman was also assistant animal guy on the set. If they needed pigeons for a rooftop shot, I would get them, clip down their wings so they couldn't fly, and put them up early in the morning before the company came to shoot. I was also responsible for three cows, fifty chickens, and some pigs. I had to buy the food for them, feed them in the morning, and put the pigeons out. I remember at that time, we were making a picture starring Syd Chaplin, Charlie's brother, in it. I used to eat the pigeon eggs because at thirty bucks a week, if you had a few eggs, it helped. Syd used to steal the eggs from me—he liked them, too.

While I was working at Warners', I got a call from MGM for an assistant cameraman job. I stayed there for a while and did some photographic accessory work, or "trick shots." I kept at that pretty much until the advent of sound. Sound came in at Warners' and Vitaphone on disk records synchronized to the picture.

I'll tell you briefly about the history of sound. The Bell Telephone Laboratories developed the equipment, design, and what not. Then Western Electric mass-produced it. Amplifiers were first designed by Bell Laboratories, built by Western, and became the basis for long-lines telephony. The Signal Corps used them too. These amplifiers were the first of the type that could run properly reproduced phonograph records and long-distance telephone lines. The Electrical Research Products Company was formed as a sales group of the Telephone system in order to market by-product quantities of the same amplifier. They went to Warner Brothers and suggested that disk records with amplifiers connected to movie projectors in theaters would make sound pictures. I believe this was in '27, but don't take my word for it. A lot of facts have a little rubber in them. At any rate, Warners' started using the Victor Phonograph Association for phonographs and Western Electric amplifiers and formed the company called Vitaphone, under which name it was advertised to show these sound pictures. In their first sound movie, a small part of *The Jazz Singer* was reproduced that way and tagged on to the end of a silent picture.

MGM didn't want to be left behind. Eddie Mannix, the general manager, quite a wonderful chap, was in New York as comptroller for Loew. The New York bankers were sending money to Hollywood and wanted to be assured that the money was being spent properly. By the way, Eddie Mannix had previously been the bouncer for Palisades Park across the Hudson River in New Jersey. Later on, he had supervised the building of Loew's theaters. He had been working for Nick Schenck, seeing that the

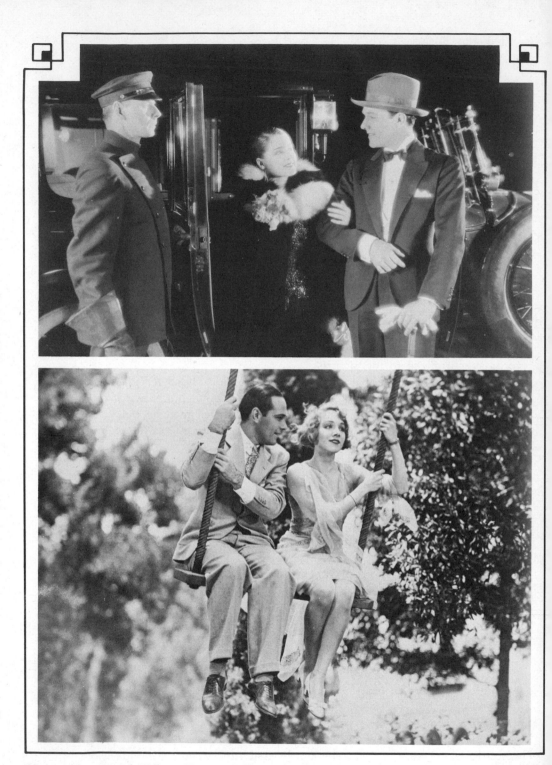

Norma Shearer and William Haines in *Slave of Fashion*. Sound experiment by Douglas Shearer. Metro Goldwyn. 1925.

William Haines and Leila Hyams on set of *Alias Jimmy Valentine*. Sound by Douglas Shearer, MGM. 1928.

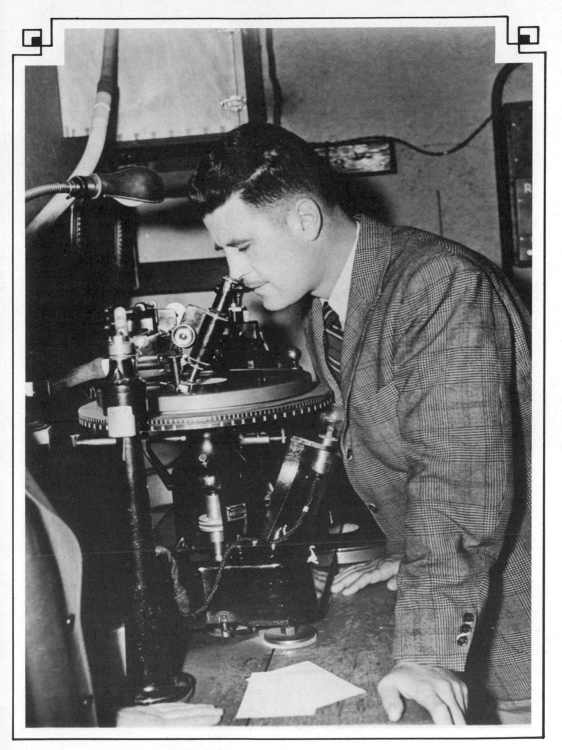

Douglas Shearer at work. Circa 1933.

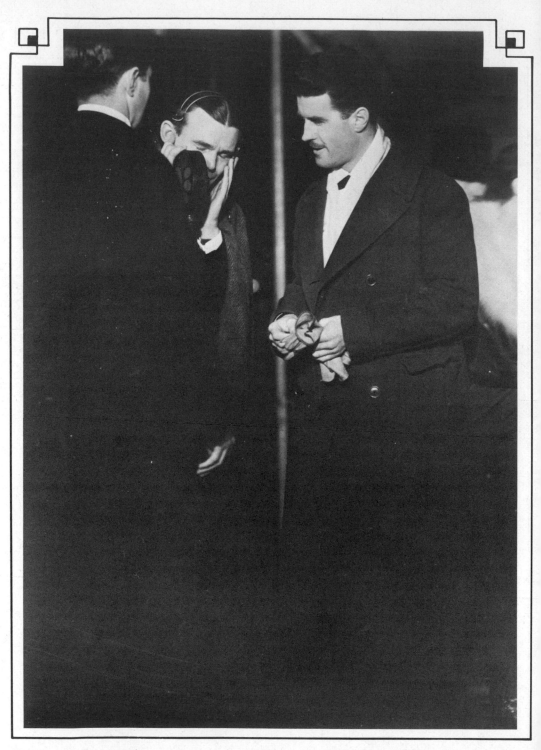

Douglas Shearer, recording engineer, at the world premiere of *The Broadway Melody* at Grauman's Chinese Theatre in Hollywood. 1929.

Loew's theaters were built properly, the equipment was delivered when needed, and that the people were there to work every day. Schenck, who was later president when Loew died, made Mannix comptroller. He became so valuable to MGM that they eventually made him vice president and general manager. I got along well with him. He never made an enemy either, his rough character notwithstanding.

When sound came in, Mannix said, "We've got a fellow down here in the special-effects department who does camerawork and trick stuff. Why not throw the sound problem in his lap?" Overnight I was the one-man sound department. They ordered me to do the job; they didn't just give it to me. Incidentally, there was no connection with Norma in all this. Around '27 or '28, she married Thalberg, or he married her. Anyway, their marriage worked. Oh, a great pair! Gosh, they were like that! Wonderful.

At any rate, I had to learn a whole lot about electronics. I had some knowledge of it from my prior work. I had handled electrical equipment and knew, to a certain extent, what made it operate. But when this happened, I said, "I've got to get out of here for three weeks or a month and go to Bell Labs to see what's happening there and learn a bit about the system." No longer were disks going to be used. Instead it was to be done on film with a couple of ribbons that oscillated and a beam that regulated the amount of light reaching the film which, in turn, produced the sound change. So off I went to Bell Labs and learned about sound. I also had to pick up a sound crew, which I stole from every which where. I had one guy from Bell Labs, another one from somewhere else, a few from the colleges. I built up a bit of a crew and started the sound department. That's the highly personalized part of this. It sounds like a guy blowing his own horn. The facts are fairly supportive.

The first sound job I did was two reels at the end of a picture called *Alias Jimmy Valentine*. I'm surprised I remember since I've worked intimately on about 1400 pictures and sometimes their titles slip by. Anyway, it was an interesting sound problem, because it centered on a guy whose fingers were sensitive to the clicks on the dial of a safe. We had originally made that as a silent picture. We were charging into sound production because the competition was so great at that time. For example, Paramount had already beaten us by a little bit to the equipment at Electrical Research Products, Bell Lab, and Western. They called it ERPI, a terrible name, but everything is letters, even today. So we went over to the lab and made the last two reels of the picture over again.

This wasn't exactly the first sound we did because we made musical scores for pictures first. I didn't do the scoring. I did the technical part of it. We had some very good musicians. I'm musical only insofar as I'm sensitive to variations in sound. I know sounds that are good and those that aren't, and that includes music. The first picture we scored was done in a church auditorium of the Victor Phonograph Company in Camden. We didn't have our own equipment yet, but the group I had organized was growing into an excellent crew. Oddly enough, Bell Labs and Western Electric didn't know what making a movie was. They thought you just made a movie by sticking films end to end and that made a picture.

Consider the problem of photographing a person talking to someone else. The important part of what he's saying might be the listener's re-action, so you have to make a reverse angle of this actor listening to the fellow talking. If you made sound and picture together on one film, you must make a sound transfer, back to the time when you inserted the picture of the guy listening. There were several approaches to the same problem. Fox used a method which made the sound right in the camera. There was another where the sound was recorded on one film and the picture on a different one. In this case, sound track and picture can be edited independently of each other and the cutbacks are introduced more readily.

But we had no equipment to do those kinds of transfers and cutbacks or for combining music under the dialogue. We had to develop all that equipment at MGM. Once we had separate sound tracks for film and picture, we were able to edit much better. But, of course, we still had to be able to re-record a track onto a negative with the music inserted. It wasn't long before I went to work on *The Broadway Melody,* the first big musical of that stature we put out. It was sort of the culmination of all our efforts in the sound department.

Over the years, many people associate my name with Cedric Gib-bons because we were almost always listed together in the screen credits. My association with him began with our first full-length feature. He had terrific taste for the appearance of things. His was basically an architectural background. He was kind of an architectural Thalberg. He was a very close friend, too, and not only because we had to work on the same prob-lems. We got along quite well together, although I didn't know him much off the lot. Gibbons was essentially what is called an art director, although I prefer the term motion picture engineer. For instance, there was no use building an ordinary living room for a set. How are you going to light it? You have to have slots in the walls, and you have to photograph it so they don't show. Gibbons could solve that kind of problem and placement of the sound equipment with ease and taste.

For the sound apparatus, we originally had electrical parts come in on cables to a central plant downstairs. Only microphones were used on the set. They had to be hidden or made to function directly above the camera line. On the first stage over here, I had a couple of gantries built, which would run up and down on both sides of the set and contained a bridge from which you could let down the microphone. They were also constructed so that they could be suspended to any part of the stage from above. At one of our early tests, Eddie Mannix came in and looked at this monkey business. He said, "Hey, what's the matter with an old wall sweep?" Do you remember the wall sweep with the bucket and rope on the end of it? He said, "Why don't you have one of those instead of all that junk up on the roof?" That's Mannix for you. So, in about half an hour or forty-five minutes, we had one constructed in our carpenter shop. Out of that simple off-the-cuff idea came the microphone boom. It's served pretty well ever since, except later we made them lighter so you could hold them. It was so simple, but I hadn't thought of it. Credit that invention to Mannix.

In time MGM set up an original research department. In our research we were confronted with many questions. For example, we might have had to copy an actual palace existing in Europe for a set. We couldn't be wrong about it. So our research department would bring the materials to the art department, and their men would develop the most practical way of building a set which looked like the original.

And then we had costume designers. The head of the costume department at that time had great ability. He showed up on a picture we made, *The Student Prince*. We used a research man from Europe to help him who knew the costumes exactly, and we made the picture his way. It was the drabbest thing you ever saw. Just terrible. Our own man was able to retain the true character of costumes in Marie Antoinette's day and yet build them into an appearance that was as modern as all get out. You saw the thing, it was beautiful, and still nobody could question its authenticity.

Thalberg always wanted to know what was going on with the sound, costumes, and photography. He would be quite critical. For example, he saw the set of *Mutiny on the Bounty* and instantly commented, "Those sails on the *Bounty* are too gray for a bright sunny day." He'd spot such faults. And then we'd do retakes, a Thalberg specialty. Some of the retakes were replaced with material already photographed, but most of it was additional footage. We truly put together a superb team in all departments.

It was hard work, but we were having fun. I lived in Santa Monica Canyon and many nights I couldn't drive all the way home without pulling off on the sand strip, up by a golf club on the hill, and taking a nap for fifteen minutes. I had to work long hours, especially at the beginning because we didn't have enough sound stages. We'd use one in the daytime and use it again at night for another picture.

In the early days, we engaged in block-booking by the year. We had 170 theaters in the Loew's circuit, half of which we owned and with a half interest in the others. For the product we were making, that was literally only a few theaters. However, in addition we had 13,000 independent exhibitors who bought our product by the year, just as one would subscribe to a national magazine. In subscribing to a magazine, one doesn't expect that every issue will be a knock-out; nevertheless, one feels that it is a good magazine to receive each week. The block-booking principle was the same. The studio was assured of a big yearly sale. In addition, we didn't want some theater to use another studio's picture subscription instead of ours. All this time, the competition was strong. And the world market was important, too. For that, we had Loew's International, which operated more or less according to the same principles. And so we worked quite hard at trying to produce quality pictures.

Of all the work I engaged in over the years, redesigning the theater horn system gave me the most satisfaction. The problem was basically this: In a large theater, the speakers, which were composed of "horns," produced a sound distortion, so that in certain parts of the theater it was difficult to hear with clarity. The original amplifier projected sound, but not without distortion. So I developed the "Shearer horn," which distributed the sound properly throughout the theater area. One of my Oscars is for that. It was introduced at the opening of *Romeo and Juliet*. We tried one new horn in the Loew's theater in New York and one in Montreal, just a few days before Thalberg died, in 1936. But Western Electric and Bell Lab had already developed a new system which had a mid-horn and a bass horn. The bass horn was a good one, but it was enormous and therefore quite cumbersome. I went to see our president in New York and told him I didn't like our new horns. He said, "What are we going to do? We have to stay with the times." I said, "Well, it will take about a year." So he gave me the go-ahead. I went to work and designed a horn composed of only two elements that's now in standard use.

Initially, it was a one-man research and development department. After a few years, I had several associates who made enormous contributions to the technical aspects of film. Occasionally I branched out of the sound department and worked in the camera department. I evolved the big screen, the 70-mm stuff that is known as "Panavision." I got rid of the deep curved screen which was characteristic of Cinerama.

I like to consider myself an applied physicist now, looking for challenging problems that need to be solved so that the quality of films can be improved. I tinker a bit in many areas and in recent years have worked on improvements in color-processing.

I don't see retirement in the offing for myself. I wouldn't like to go out to weed the front lawn. I've seen too many people get sick doing that. Although I'm beyond retirement age, I'm not required to meet any union stipulations on that score. There are a lot of men who look forward to retirement, but I'm not one of them.

The Music Director

❦⟡❦⟡❦⟡❦⟡❦⟡❦

MAX STEINER

I CAN TELL YOU when and where I was born, but not why. It all happened in Vienna in 1888. I was an only child. My father was one of the greatest impresarios and producers in the theatrical business. Our family owned many theaters in Vienna. The family business was begun by my grandfather, Maximillian Steiner, after whom I am named. He discovered Strauss and brought Offenbach to Vienna. He originally produced *Tales of Hoffman*, *Orpheus in the Underworld*, and Papa produced *Die Fledermaus* and *Night in Venice*.

There is a wonderful story about my father. Johann Strauss, on whose lap I sat when I was a kid, playing the piano with one finger and accompanying him, had written a new operetta, *Night in Venice*. My grandfather and father were sitting in the audience at the opening performance, and Grandfather said to Father. "You better go down and tell the maestro he stole this note for note from *Light Cavalry Overture* by von Suppe." He answered, "I can't do that." Johann Strauss was conducting the orchestra. Then my father said, "Why don't you go?" And my grandfather replied, "He doesn't love me. He loves you. You'd better go." Strauss truly loved my father. So Father went over and said, "Maestro, you can't do this. It's note for note from the *Light Cavalry*." Strauss looked at him and said, "What the hell, he's dead and he doesn't need it anymore."

As I said, my father was the very biggest theater operator in the city. We owned the Crown Theater, the Theater on the Wein, the Orpheum

Theater, the Apollo Theater, and an exhibition park. In that park there is a big Ferris wheel which is frequently shown on picture postcards and is known the world over. Papa built that. When I was a kid, I was the one to pull the switch the first time it ever turned.

I was well educated. I went to the Gymnasium. Then to the Academy of Music. In those days, it was a four-year course of study. I made the four years at the Acadamy in one year and received the Gold Medal of the Emperor. Within four years I had a symphonic suite played by the Vienna Philharmonic. Mahler predicted that I was going to be one of the greatest composers that ever lived. Little did he know that I would end up with Warner Brothers. He thought that I was going to be a symphonic composer, which I could be if I wanted to, but I'm too lazy and it's too uninteresting for me. And now it's too late. I studied harmony with Hermann Graedener, counterpoint with Hermann Fuchs, organ and choir work with Brenner, and composition with Mahler. You'd never believe it because I'm in this industry. I'm almost ashamed. I can read and write, which I can't say for all the producers. But I would never tell anyone about my education. I wouldn't dare. They wouldn't let me stay in Hollywood anymore.

When I was seventeen years old, I went to England to conduct the *Merry Widow* in His Majesty's Theatre. I stayed there until 1914. During my stay, I became associated with the London Opera House as conductor and orchestrator. It was a fantastic place. We had a vaudeville show with a one-hundred-and-ten-man orchestra. There were two hundred stagehands and eighty bathing beauties. This experience was very important to me when I finally came to the United States. After World War I broke out, I was an enemy alien in England, and I had to leave the country. They were going to intern me. The Duke of Westminster was my friend; he obtained a passport for me, and over I came to the United States with thirty-three dollars in my pocket. I landed in New York and was rather green, for as soon as I came off the boat a drunk "borrowed" five dollars from me. For a while, I starved. Then I started to play piano for vaudeville artists and copy music.

I went to work for William Fox, who was one of the finest men the world has ever known. He was a truly wonderful person. I was the conductor at the Riverside Theater where we were showing a picture called *The Bondman*. I had an idea. Until about 1915 there was no special music written for motion pictures. We just used to take the albums publishers put out and would play "Hurry number one, hurry number three, love scene number six." I said to myself, "This is a lot of baloney. I'd like to do something new." I talked to Mr. Fox and told him I wanted to write music for the picture.

"You're nuts," he said.

"I'm not."

"Go ahead and do whatever you want."

"Can I have my orchestra?"

"How many men do you want?"

"A hundred."

"O.K., you've got it."

And I went down and wrote the music for William Farnum's *The Bondman*. We put together another one-hundred-and-ten-man orchestra. After that, Mr. Fox always called me professor. The orchestra came from different theaters we owned, from Mr. Fox's circuit, Jack Loeb's, and others. We had a big opening at the 14th Street Playhouse, opposite the City Theater, which we owned too. I was the boss and now I had one hundred and ten men, but what one hundred and ten did I have. They were put together from all the theaters we owned. But these theaters used to have ten men in a band, one trombone, two trumpets, a piano, a fiddle, a banjo. Now you put a hundred of them together and what do you get? Something that sounds like a hundred banjos. I wanted to make it a symphonic orchestra. There was only one cello in the ten theaters. Not much choice. Yet we were a success. The thing sounded like Sousa's Brass Band. When we accompanied a love scene, you never heard so many trumpets in your life.

Mr. Fox was the sweetest man. We used to have theaters in Jamaica, Long Island, and up in the Bronx. I would have to drive from one theater to the other in order to check up on what these different orchestra leaders were doing. I was the head of eighty theaters, and I had to see what was going on. So on Christmas, 1917, I was at home in #43 on 43d Street. The doorbell rang, I opened the door, and there was a man standing outside with a cap on like a policeman.

"Mr. Steiner?"

"Yes."

"Here's a letter from Mr. William Fox, and I wish you would sign the receipt and come on down with me."

"What's the matter?"

"I've got a car for you downstairs."

"You've got what?"

"Come on down," he said.

There was no elevator. I lived up five flights. We walked down and there he had a little car. It turned out that Fox had bought me a car so I could get around to the different theaters in the winter.

In 1929 I did a show called *Sons O' Guns* with Jack Donahue and Willie Damaker. William Le Baron, who was then the head of RKO, saw me in Boston with the show. He thought it was the greatest orchestra performance he'd ever heard. So he invited me to come to Hollywood. He gave me a fairly decent contract. Now it's not even worth talking about, but in those days it sounded pretty good, and I quit the show. I was smart because the week after I left, Donahue died and so did the show. I came to Hollywood, to RKO, as an orchestrator.

It is very difficult for any person who is not a musician to understand the difference between orchestrator and arranger. An orchestrator is a man who takes a composition and puts it into orchestra parts. An arranger is a man who takes a melody, puts different harmonies to it and fixes it up, and usually ruins it. However, he is called an arranger. They should all be shot. The orchestrator just takes what he is given to do and if he has any ideas of his own, he had better not show them.

So I came out as an orchestrator for Harry Tierney, who was also my great friend. He had written the song "Rio Rito" and "Alice Blue Gown." I came out to do the movie *Rio Rita*, which was then supposed to be done as a musical at RKO. That was the first really successful musical extravaganza. I was paid $450 a week, which wasn't bad, but wasn't that good because of the great expense of living in Hollywood. I really came out because I figured this was for me. I thought this was it. I had a hunch that I knew more about the picture business than some of these people out here, and I was right. That's how I came to Hollywood.

Soon after *Rio Rita*, there was a picture going to be made called *Cimarron* with Richard Dix and Irene Dunne. William Le Baron and I had done a show together called *Apple Blossoms*, with Wesley Rodgers directing. When it was finished, Le Baron called me and said, "Who are we going to get to write the music for *Cimarron*? We need a big composer."

"Let's get Stokowski."

And I called Stokowski. And he agreed.

"When can he come?" Le Baron asked.

"Tomorrow."

"How much does he want?"

"*Three hundred thousand dollars.*"

"What about Gershwin?"

I went back, called Gershwin, and said, "Do you want to write the music for *Cimarron*?"

"I'd love it. I love the story," he said.

"How much do you want?"

"Two hundred and fifty thousand dollars."

"How long will it take you to do it?"

"About a year."

When I told Le Baron, he screamed, "My God, we're opening in four weeks." Now we were down to the bottom of the barrel. We called Percy Grainger. Grainger said, "If every note that I write is going to be published

Clark Gable and Vivien Leigh in a scene from *Gone With the Wind*. Music by Max Steiner. 1939.

and put on records, everything, I'll do it for three hundred and fifty thousand dollars. But I want a year."

Le Baron again screamed, "Four weeks. Four weeks. What'll we do?"

"I have no idea," I said.

So William Le Baron said, "Max, put a temporary score on there, do you mind?"

"No, I don't mind."

"Write just a few lousy things."

The picture opened. The next morning, the papers came out and reported that the picture was excellent. And what about the music—it said it was the greatest music that ever was written. Their faces dropped, and I got a raise of fifty dollars.

The way I approached writing music for films was to fit the music to what I thought the dramatic story should be and score according to the way a character impressed me, whoever he might be. He may be a bastard, she may be a wonderful woman, he may be a child. I write what I see. This is very difficult for anybody to understand. Especially for anybody with such bad eyesight as I have. But I see a character on the screen and that is what makes me write the way I do. That is also the reason that people enjoy what they hear because it happens to fit.

I never write from a script. I run a mile everytime I see one. If I started to write when I first saw the script, I would have been in Forest Lawn long ago because what they can do to a script is unheard of. I had one very bad experience like that. There was a picture called *Pursued*. It starred Robert Mitchum. So I read the script and thought it was the finest I had ever seen. I sat down and started writing themes for the picture. And I did the entire score. Then I saw the picture. It was terrible. What I had seen in the script was completely changed when the movie was released. I've never been so disappointed in a picture in my life. Since that day, I've never looked at a script, because all the characters appear different to me in the script than in the picture.

As musical directors, we take the scores, orchestrate, conduct, and add material. We make bridges between scenes. One of the first I did was *The Gay Divorcée* with Edward Everett Horton. I did *Top Hat, Follow the Fleet, Roberta,* and *Melody Cruise,* which was the first picture with Phil Harris. It's the first time he sang "Lazy River." That's many years ago. These were all at RKO.

Strangely, in a musical, the musical director doesn't do anything. You're told what to do. They say, "There's a number; orchestrate it." That's all there is to it. Otherwise, there's a very technical aspect to this. That is, when you score or orchestrate for a sequence, you have to get it in proper timing with the film. There's a whole elaborate mathematics involved. You start with cue sheets. Everything is measured to a split second.

I write a cue that may last for one minute and two-thirds seconds. It might be only a chord or some kind of musical trick. But I wait to do this until the picture is finished, unless, of course, they need some music for a song or a dance sequence while it is being shot. Otherwise, I never do until it's entirely completed. Then I look at it once, maybe twice, but very rarely more than that. I have a photographic memory. I look at a picture once, and then the second time I run it with my cutter and my editor and tell them where to put the music. Then I get my timing, my cue sheets on which everything is written down. For example, there might be the line, "Darling, I love you." It says five seconds. Then after ten seconds he sits down, at fourteen seconds he gets up, at twenty-one seconds he punches her in the nose, at twenty-five seconds, and so forth. And then you write against that. I said in a book I once wrote years ago that to me the toughest thing for a film composer to know is where to start, where to end; that is, how to place your music. You can ruin a scene with music in the wrong place, and on the other hand, you can help it. Silence may be the most difficult problem of all.

For me, there's no doubt about the way the character or a scene hits me. I can help a scene that may be too slow, or I can help a scene that's too fast. You might change the tempo of your music, and, if it's an uninteresting scene, the music can make it so exciting that you think they really said something, even though they didn't say a damn thing.

Yet, it's a great fallacy to think that a bad picture can be saved by good music. It may be helped a little bit, but that's all. Similarly, a good picture can't be ruined by the worst possible music. But sometimes I wonder. The straight scoring that you hear these days is enough to drive me out of the theater. It's just a theme. I hear music that doesn't belong to the picture, and it's very disturbing to me. There is the use of instruments which interferes with the dialogue, taking a person right out of the mood. I can't stand it, nor do I understand it, so I'm glad I'm not doing anything anymore.

It's very hard to explain. There are things that clearly belong in certain places, that are absolutely appropriate. You wouldn't want an elephant to be put in a bar, even if he looks beautiful. He doesn't fit in a bar. If you want an elephant, put him in a living room. It's the same with music. In my mind, much of the recent scoring doesn't belong.

Certain pictures which I did, like *King Kong*, were really modernistic and, therefore, unusual for their time. Really screwy. Everyone in Hollywood was bothered because I had this "screwy" music. I got some good notices from Moscow in those days. In Russia, they thought it was just great. They even invited me to come over, but I declined. I've written *The Beast with Five Fingers* and other pictures with modernistic scores. But that doesn't mean that everything should be done that way. I have

A scene from *The Informer*. Left to right: Una O'Connor, Heather Angel, and Victor McLaglen. Music by Max Steiner brought him the first of three Academy Awards in 1935.

Max Steiner.

Ingrid Bergman and Leslie Howard in a scene from *Intermezzo*. Music by Max Steiner. 1939.

A scene from *The Lost Patrol*, starring Victor McLaglen and Boris Karloff. Music direction by Max Steiner, RKO. 1934.

phobias. I don't like a single instrument even with orchestral background, because they interfere with the dialogue. It cuts right through, whereas an orchestra, a full orchestra, doesn't do that. But one lousy clarinet can kill a scene and even the entire movie. And this is taught and learned only by experience.

I always worked independently. If a director or producer interfered, I would take my coat and walk out and he would never see me again. Once the film was completed and I composed the score, that was it. If they didn't like the result, they could always get another composer. Fortunately, this never happened to me. Take *The Treasure of the Sierra Madre*, for which I won the Venice Film Festival award. I never saw Huston. He was in Europe. Most composers are in the same position. Yet, some of them are so afraid they're not going to get paid next week, they don't act independently. Some guys are shaking in their boots. They're hungry, and the director, who thinks he's a genius, a musical genius, which he is not, may say, "You know what I think this should be?" and the guy says, "Yes, okay, Mr. Monster Director, anything you say." If this was ever said to me, I would say, "Oh, no." I wouldn't be very insulting because that isn't done. I would just say, "Okay," and then I'd do exactly what I wanted.

Getting back to my career, I worked for RKO, where I made 111 films until 1936, and then I went to work for David O. Selznick. In 1937, I moved over to Warner Brothers and first did the score for *The Charge of the Light Brigade*. I was loaned out, thank God, in 1939, to do *Gone With the Wind*. The picture had a strange history for me. Only thirty minutes of the entire 222 minutes are without music. In Europe and Asia, it was considered the best score ever written. But the Academy voted the Oscar to *Stagecoach*, which was a picture using old cowboy songs. Anyway, I did it in three months, and I wrote a picture called *Intermezzo* at the same time. I would start to work at nine o'clock in the morning, lie down about midnight for a few hours, I'd be awakened by my butler at five A.M., and then I'd go back to work. The doctor would give me an injection to keep me awake, and I'd keep going.

Before that I had done *The Informer*, which, without the music, would never have been what it was. Music did just the little bit needed to put it over, because in that movie, Victor McLaglen was great. But the music with the pennies, the money that fell down, was a good touch. I put the music in the harp when McLaglen sold this guy down the river. And in the very end, I had him sing when his mother forgave him in church. It brought a few tears.

There are many pictures I liked but which did not win Academy Awards. *Sierra Madre* is one. Although I won with *Since You Went Away* and *Now, Voyager*, I thought I should have fared better with *Johnny*

Belinda. That year it was won by *Red Shoes*, which did not have original music. The workings of the Academy are very mysterious. Surely, I have had many disappointments, but that is a part of this business. And then again, I feel bad about Jack Warner, who did not even say goodbye after all those years with him.

But over the years, I had a few marvelous, close friends. George and Ira Gershwin, Oscar Levant and I were the four indestructables. We were always together. My friendship with George Gershwin goes back to the old days in New York when I conducted Broadway shows and orchestrated. He had done a show called *Dear Mabel* which I was to help him conduct. In it, we had a song about a dog, the music to which was called "This Is My Lousy Dog." After that, I told Max Dreyfus, who was then a music publisher, to keep an eye on George.

George was an accomplished musician, having studied with Madame Boulanger in Paris, Libling (of the 12-tone scale) in New York, and at the Juilliard school. He was a wonderful pianist. The only thing he didn't do at first was orchestrate by himself. "Rhapsody in Blue" is written in four lines. I was with him from first to last while he composed it, and we together worked all night until we finished. Then we still weren't satisfied with the orchestration. Jules Ganser, who was the president of Cartier jewelry, sponsored the whole thing, and he originally made Georgie write it. He had Paul Whiteman play it.

I was instrumental in bringing Whiteman to New York. I had seen him with a little combination of eight men in a San Francisco restaurant, and I was so impressed with what he did with just eight men that I went home and told Flo Ziegfeld to sign him to a contract. Flo Ziegfeld sent Frank Slocum, who was the manager of the show I was with, which shouldn't happen to anyone because it was a terrible thing, to San Francisco. Frank agreed, and that's how Whiteman came to New York.

We used to have our little circle. Sometimes we would get together and play music, discuss what I wrote, what the other guy wrote, have a few drinks, get plastered, and go to bed. Those were the good old days. Later, when we were in Hollywood, Gershwin and I didn't see so much of each other. As a matter of fact, I don't often participate in the social events of Hollywood.

Oscar Levant was also part of our small circle. He is a great humorist. I remember once, after a première of *Blue Moon* by Sigmund Romberg, Oscar, Max Dreyfus, and I were walking down the street, and Max said to Oscar, "What do you think of the music?" Oscar said, "It's the kind of music you whistle before you hear it." Unfortunately, over the last few years, we haven't gotten together too often.

We music people have had our problems in Hollywood. For a long while we weren't getting paid for our background music, so in 1942 I organized the Screen Composers' Association. I'm very proud of that. It took a lot of money and effort during the first year of organizing, but now we are an accredited association. If the producers want to start anything, they have to fight the entire organization, which means about 300 or 400 composers here in Hollywood. There are many of them whom I admire a great deal. Elmer Bernstein is excellent, and another, Franz Waxman, who recently passed away, was a real craftsman. Of course, in the last few years so many new faces have come up that I don't know most of them. I don't get to the movies too often, and I've only seen three pictures in the last year. That's partly because a couple of eye operations make it difficult for me to see, particularly in color. For the past three years, I haven't done a picture. It would have to be a very good one for me to write again. After all, I did over 250 scores, so the next picture has to be the very best. I suppose that makes me retired.

The Writer

ANITA LOOS

I WAS BORN in the northern part of California. In 1900, I was six, which, of course, makes me seventy-six now. My grandfather on my mother's side was a pioneer. He had gone to California in '49 as soon as he heard of the gold strike, settled in the northern part of the state, and discovered a very rich mine. When the mine went dry, he developed his enormous acreage into a wheat ranch. I was born on that ranch.

My father initially came from Ohio to publish a newspaper. He had established himself quite near to my mother's family in Yreka City, a small town in the mountains. We lived there until I was about six years old and then moved to San Francisco, staying there until I was about eight.

Loos is a French name. It isn't pronounced Loos, but everybody calls me Loos. It was a Huguenot family, and in 1618, when the Huguenots were scattered all over Europe, our name was dispersed all over Europe and Australia. So that's why there are Dutch and Scandinavian Looses as well as a number of them in Paris.

I grew up between San Francisco and San Diego, and then Los Angeles and San Diego. I had one brother and a sister who died when she was about eight. We were a close family. My brother became a very important man in the medical profession because he invented the thing that is now called Blue Cross in New York. He invented it in California. He and one of the Lodges in Boston worked out the entire medical plan.

When he died, he had twelve buildings in southern California, all given over to medicine. It was the same program as group medicine. My brother was a stable, conventional citizen, and the one credit to our family.

My mother was tremendously unsophisticated, if not to say naïve, and a typical, very feminine, housewife. My father was a newspaper man. He was a wit and, you might say, a very smalltime Aly Kahn. He led a very gay life. I adored him. We were great pals.

I was self-taught to a great degree because I learned French very, very early and I read my way through the Carnegie Library in San Diego. I graduated from high school when I was twelve years old. I didn't have aspirations; I was just a writer. My father owned a printing-press plant and a newspaper. Oh, I couldn't have been more than ten years old when I wrote for his newspaper. So I never even thought about whether I wanted to write or not, I just wrote. I guess it was needed in the family. In addition, during my high school days, I became a "stage" child and continued for a time as an actress. I played Little Lord Fauntleroy in a stock company in San Diego with Harold Lloyd.

My whole life was led as a professional. I never knew anything but professional life, so I can't say that I had any ambition to be anything else. (The time finally came when I was earning more money as a writer than as an actress, and I said, "This is where I quit acting.") My father owned a magazine in San Francisco called *Music and Drama* that was roughly comparable to *The New Yorker*, but slanted more toward the theatrical affairs in San Francisco, and through him it was easy for me to become an actress. In those days stock companies would go out from New York and hire children in the various cities they played. They didn't bother to bring a child actress from New York. So I just naturally fell into the place of being the child in San Francisco. I played with all the stars of that day because the stars would go to San Francisco. I played in the first production of *A Doll's House,* as one of Nora's children, and in the first production of *Quo Vadis.* As I say, my career unfolded so normally and gradually that I didn't even know it was there.

Mother didn't exactly object to the stage, but she was horrified by the movies. By then theater actresses had already gotten a little standing, but movie actresses were the end. Mother considerd them "trash," whereas father gave me his complete support. However, I actually got into the movies as a writer, which my mother also thought was disgraceful. You see, I had been writing for D. W. Griffith for two years without ever having met him. I would mail the scripts to his studios in Los Angeles and New York where he divided his time making films. When finally settled in Los Angeles, he sent for me since he had been buying my scripts at a rate of—I don't know how many hundred a year. This was when I was fourteen. I still have my old ledger with a list of them.

In those days movies were either half a reel or one reel. They were very short. There was no dialogue. One simply did synopses of three or four typewritten pages. I'd turn them out by the hundreds, literally. When I finally met Griffith and he discovered I was a "stage" child, he wanted to put me right into the movies. That was when my mother balked and dragged me out of the studio. I didn't see him again for about a year. But I went right on writing for him. It took awhile for mother finally to decide that writing was respectable enough, so I joined Griffith at the studio and began work in Hollywood.

I recall that first story I had produced—it was called *The New York Hat*. They now show it at the Museum of Modern Art. It was seen here prior to my arrival in Hollywood, and I believe I received twenty-five dollars for it. I wrote hundreds of slapstick comedies, and for these I'd get fifteen dollars. When they began to make movies longer, my productivity declined somewhat. One time, at the very beginning of my association with Griffith, I became quite angry with him and left the organization. I thought he didn't appreciate me, so I joined Mack Sennett. I didn't stay with Sennett very long because Griffith jerked me back, saying, "What do you mean by leaving home?" Anyway, at the old Griffith lot, we had a slapstick comedy company similar to the Keystone Kops. It had two stars, a man named Eddie Dillon and a comedienne named Faye Tincher. I turned out hundreds of scripts for them. But when movies got longer, I began to move away from slapstick. One of the first dramas I wrote was for Mae Marsh. That ran into two reels, and I began to get fifty dollars a reel for them. Then the price went up and up and up. When Douglas Fairbanks joined the studio and made his first picture there, they paid me five hundred dollars for the script. I was rich.

When I first met Griffith, he was between thirty and forty years of age. We were in awe of him because he had a powerful presence. Whenever he came into the studio, everyone immediately snapped to attention. It was not that he required an audience, for he was anything but conceited, but he was just magnificent, and he frightened us because we were kids. He was a very serious man. It was the man and his fundamental character that we respected. He was very handsome and bore an Olympian personality. None of us, except Lillian Gish, ever got close to him. Complete formality pervaded the lot, and nobody ever was called by his first name. He was always Mr. Griffith. Maybe some of the older people around the studio called him D. W., but we never dared call him that. I was always "Miss Loos" and Lillian was always "Miss Gish." It was a rarefied atmosphere. But at the same time, Mac Marsh, Norma and Constance Talmadge, and I behaved like school kids. Naturally, we were young and there was so much fun to be had around the lot. The lot was very big, and he couldn't be everywhere at once. Of all the girls, only Lillian realized that we were doing anything at all of importance or even interest. To me, it was like being paid for doing nothing.

I kept in contact with him and many years later wrote his last picture in New York. By then, he was finished professionally. He was in the throes of alcoholism, really down and out. He sent for me and begged me to write a script for him. I wrote one that wasn't at all my cup of tea, a very soggy soap opera. It was called *The Struggle,* a sound film. It is now shown at the Museum of Modern Art in New York City, if anyone wants to see it. It was a terrible flop and deserved to be. They called me from the museum when they got a copy of it and asked if I didn't want to see it. I said, "No. It certainly isn't good, is it?" They said, "You'd be surprised. It is really an excellent film." So I told Lillian Gish about it and she went over and saw it. She came back and said, "Don't go near it. It's awful."

In retrospect, it seems to me that Griffith could not keep up with the times. He was terribly shy. He was a man with a faulty education, but great ambition to be a playwright and poet. He never wanted to be in movies. And actually he was a poet because I think of his silent films, perhaps all of his films, as works of poetry. But with his limited education, it seemed that he was afraid of being with people more sophisticated than he. He found it very difficult to meet people and that accounted for a large part of his decline. If he had kept up with the kind of people from whom he could have learned, it would have been of great help to him, for it was necessary to keep pace with changing modern life and the film industry. Unfortunately his attitude was pretty corny. And as his perspectives on everything got cornier and cornier, his pictures began to reflect those views. There are those who thought he was too extravagant. That was only to the extent that every penny he earned was put back into his own movies. After he made *Intolerance,* he repaid over a million dollars because the bankers who financed the picture accused him of incompetence. So he took the money out of his own pocket just to compensate them. He was deeply hurt because he knew that he had made a great picture. And he died in poverty just because he spent money on his own pictures.

At the studio there were two people with whom Griffith had a very close relationship. One of them was Frank Woods, an old editor, who wrote *The Birth of a Nation.* He was a wonderful man and Griffith's one confidant on the lot. As long as Woods lived, he kept Griffith up to date and in pace with the times. When Woods died, Griffith felt quite alone. He also needed Billy Bitzer, the cameraman who strangely, like Griffith, was an uneducated but extremely talented man. Griffith always worked closely with Bitzer. He would put problems to Billy and frequently Billy would insist that the things Griffith wanted couldn't be done. Griffith would go away, brood, get drunk, and then decide he'd do it Billy's way. So many cinematic innovations came to fruition in just that way.

The Birth of a Nation was both a success and a great tragedy for Griffith. It was regarded as an extraordinary film contribution, but at the same time Griffith was accused of racism, which was the very last thing in his mind. He had a wonderful old colored cook who, when she saw the picture, broke down and cried because of the accusation against him. The criticisms nearly killed him. He looked at The Birth of a Nation as a great dramatic story. He would have been the last to think there was any racism in it, which certainly there was. And then he made Intolerance, which was, in a way, an act of repentence by him.

Up through The Birth of a Nation, I did only very minor films. The Mutual Studio was quite large, and besides the pictures that he personally made, which were the essential reasons for the studio's existence, he had six or seven directors who made movies under his aegis. Those were the films that I wrote. Many of his directors were very good, men like Vic Fleming, who later directed Gone With the Wind. The man I later married, John Emerson, also a very important director, came out of that group. The middle-aged directors weren't too good, but younger ones became important.

When I first joined the studio, the subtitles for the pictures were "That Morning," "The Next Day," and "After a Year." I invented the more complete subtitles which came about through doing scripts for Douglas Fairbanks. Griffith had hired a few people from the New York stage, Douglas Fairbanks among them. Griffith had made screen tests of Fairbanks, found that he couldn't act, and didn't know what to do with him. Among his New York imports was John Emerson, one of Frohman's stage directors. Emerson and Fairbanks were great friends. They were both members of the Lambs, and they used to sit around on the lot and be homesick for New York. Emerson was looking for material when he ran across several of my scripts that Griffith had bought and placed in the files. He began reading them and went out of his mind with joy, "Good heavens, this is material for Fairbanks." So he went to Griffith, "Will you let me make a comedy with Fairbanks?"

"Don't waste your time, Emerson, because that man can't act."

"But I've found some comedy material here that is perfect for Doug."

"Those can't be shot because the comedy is all in the lines."

"Well, why not put the lines on as subtitles?"

"Because people don't go to the movies to read. They go to see pictures."

"Well, would you let me make one of them before his option runs out?"

"All right, go ahead if you want to waste your time, but it can't be done."

Then Emerson asked Griffith, "Why do you buy these things if they can't be shot?"

"Because I like to read them myself."

So anyway, he made the picture. I think about an eighth of it was made up of subtitles. They got Griffith into the projection room to look when it was finished. He looked and said, "You'd better put this one on the shelf because it isn't a motion picture at all. It's a book."

Ultimately, that film got on a shelf in New York. When the Strand Theatre ran out of films one day and their new film hadn't arrived, they rushed this thing over to fill in the gap. Before they put it on, Mr. Rothafel, who ran the theater, came out and announced to the audience that the film was on its way and they would show a substitute until it arrived. They would then take the substitute off and put on the regular program. By the time half a reel was over, the house was rocking with laughter. Rothafel told me afterwards, "If we would have pulled that film off, they would have mobbed the theater." *The New York Times* critic reviewed it and said, "Yesterday, films came out of their infancy." So then Griffith, who was the first to recognize a mistake when he made one, put me on every film the studio made. At that time, *Intolerance* was ready to be put together. It was being edited and he told me to write the subtitles. That's how subtitles were born.

It was lots of fun writing subtitles. In a sense, it amounted to kidding the picture. And when I look back over the years, none of the work I ever did at a studio was anything but fun. I'm the one writer in the world who had nothing but wonderful experiences in Hollywood. I worked for people who were so great that it was an inspiration to be with them. First Griffith, then Irving Thalberg. When Thalberg died, I looked around and saw that the ship was going to sink and got out.

Thalberg was just the most revealing and inspirational character of all. In his way, he was a greater man than Griffith because he was talented in so many areas. He was an excellent businessman. He ran the studio superbly. And then he was a fine artist. We did fifty-two pictures a year, and every single one of them was a smash hit. All the time I worked for Thalberg, there wasn't one picture that wasn't an absolutely staggering sensation. You see, I now look on movies much as they are looked at by intellectuals who reflect on them and say they were works of art. I didn't know they were of such stature at the time. But I now think that they are.

Thalberg had the capacity to judge with perfect taste and an ability to innovate. As soon as there was a hit in Hollywood, everybody else would copy it. If Thalberg had a hit, he would say, "Now that was just fine. So let's do exactly the opposite." And it's the way things went.

Anita Loos. 1918.

Anita Loos and her husband, Director John Emerson, in front of their Long Island home. 1918.

Anita Loos and husband, John Emerson, working at home. 1918.

Anita Loos and Jesse L. Lasky. 1923.

I wrote *Gentlemen Prefer Blondes* when I left the Griffith studio. I had decided to retire at that time. However, it was only temporary. I wrote that book in 1925 just to amuse myself. I actually left before '25. We had become so very rich. In those days, we had no income tax, and the movies were paying exhorbitant prices for writers. We just retired, my husband and I, and quit working. He was a very good director and made an early Shakespearean film, *Macbeth,* with Herbert Tree and Constance Collier. I wish to heaven they could find a copy of it because I'm sure it was a very fine film.

My recollection is that in the beginning, Hollywood was a gypsy camp and everything was fun. The villains were all the bankers in New York. We didn't have to face them, so that was easy. But then the producers began to move in; they became the real villains. They soured the atmosphere considerably. There would be terrible frictions between writers, directors, and producers. But, as I say, I had a lucky time because I worked only with great people. It was sheer luck; I could just as easily have been handed over to L. B. Mayer. Actually I did work for Mayer, but I never saw him. I worked for MGM for years, but my boss in those days was Thalberg. Then when Thalberg died and I saw that I was going to be thrown to the lions, I got out. I left very quickly when wholesale vulgarity took over. There was never any vulgarity in the Thalberg outfit. I came out of retirement and joined them just after the Crash when I had lost all my money. By that time, Thalberg and Mayer were together at MGM. I stayed eight years on the MGM lot. When Thalberg died, I had just finished a script called *San Francisco* for Clark Gable. Thalberg was to have produced it, but he died in the meantime.

When I returned to the picture business, I was faced with doing a different kind of script than I had ever attempted before. My only experience up to then was with silent films and the subtitles. Talkies represented an entirely new conception for me, and I was a bit frightened. But then the first script I did for Thalberg, which was called *The Red-Headed Woman,* turned out to be the best thing I ever wrote. So I was left very secure after that.

In Thalberg's time, it was the producer's day. He was the important person in making a film. Goldwyn was another great producer. So was De Mille at that time. They were great vulgarians. Before that Griffith was both director and producer. And the writer only worked for the boss. But no matter whom I worked for, I never had any trouble at all with scripts being chopped up. I am almost unique. I think it was because I was working with talented men.

Even censorship was a great benefit in my case. For example, in *San Francisco,* I had a scene where Gable fought with Spencer Tracy, who played the part of a Catholic priest. The censorship board sent for me and said, "Here, you can't have Spencer Tracy sock Clark Gable."

"Well, let me think it over. I'll see if I can find a way out."

I went home and thought about it. I returned and said, "Now look, suppose I write a scene in which we show that Spencer Tracy could knock the block off Clark Gable. So that when Clark Gable strikes Tracy, we know Tracy could kill him, but he won't do it." So I wrote a scene which opens with the picture of two men boxing in a gymnasium, and Tracy floors Gable. All it needed was that scene to make our point. It didn't matter how much Gable socked the Catholic priest. That change actually made the picture.

I only had one bit of trouble with censorship. I wrote a play for Helen Hayes called *Happy Birthday*. Kate Hepburn was dying to do the film version, but it was turned down by the censorship board. We never got it past them, but never, because the girl in it solved all her problems by getting tight, and they said that that was very wicked, that every girl in the audience would go out and get tight. As far as sex was concerned, it was the cleanest picture in the world. But the girls got tight and had a good time and that was too evil.

Certainly, Hollywood has influenced the world. I used to find, on going to Europe, that Hollywood had infiltrated every culture in every nation. I remember when stars had to put on black glasses because of the Hollywood sun and suddenly black glasses became the rage all over the world. And they're still worn by people who don't need them; that is, they don't need them for protection from the sun.

The Critic

ARTHUR KNIGHT

M Y INITIAL INTEREST in films goes way back to 1922. The first picture I can remember seeing at age five was a Harold Lloyd comedy called *Dr. Jack*. I can still recall some of the scenes in it like Harold Lloyd climbing down a well after a baby which actually turns out to be only a baby doll. That was supposed to be terribly funny back in those days. But what I remember best is that after the film was over, my mother tried to drag me out of the theater and I refused to go. I just clung there as long as possible, seeing as much as I could, before being hauled away. All that transpired in Germantown in Philadelphia at the Orpheum Theater.

I would go to the movies every Saturday morning and every Saturday afternoon. Sometimes I'd manage to get over to my aunt's on Friday night because then she also would take me to the movies. Summertime was the best of all: I could go almost every day. My aunt had a top floor which she rented out to a family. The son in the family was projectionist of the local movie house. He became my hero. What a privilege to climb up into the projection box! Then, when I was in junior high school, still in Germantown, I began writing a movie column.

I preferred seeing the comedians. That includes not only Buster Keaton, who I thought was even better than Chaplin, and I'm still not sure that I wasn't right, and Harold Lloyd—not quite so good. I thought that there were some run-of-the-mill comedians at the time like Douglas MacClean and Johnny Hines, who, I think, deserve to be looked at again to see if they weren't really better than we thought. I was reminded of them when I saw the latest compilation of Laurel and Hardy. And Charlie Chase was marvelous. You know, there were many more.

I think the most important single influence on my life was the film critic on *The Philadelphia Ledger*, a man named Eric Knight (no relation). He wrote the *Flying Yorkshireman* stories and *Lassie, Come Home*. However, it was at the time that he was writing on *The Philadelphia Ledger* that he probably made me decide that that was what I wanted to do. It was because of Eric Knight's reviews that I started my column in the junior high school paper. Then I wrote film reviews in the high school paper and then at City College in New York. When I was sent overseas during the war, I started a film review column for the base paper. I never wanted to be a film-maker or an actor. I had the rare good fortune of knowing pretty much what I wanted to do from the start. At City College in 1935, I switched from day session to evening session and began working at the Museum of Modern Art, just before the building on 53rd Street opened in 1939. I started off in charge of the book part of the film library —the film books. And ended up there. I stayed for ten years and became assistant curator.

I got the job because I used to hang around so much that finally, when they needed a librarian, they said, "How would you like to come around here and get paid for it?" Actually my first job in the museum was to set up the book collection. Up until that time, the books had been on shelves arranged alphabetically by author. With something like 2500 titles, they realized that it wasn't the best way to shelve their collection. And so with Bernard Karpel, who's now librarian of the museum, I worked out a classification system for books—for film books—which had never existed before. When I was back in New York recently, Bernard told me that they still use that system and they've only had to make one alteration in it over the past thirty years—and that was only because new material came into the field.

In 1949, I thought it was time to look around. Ten years is a long time, and I began thinking of my job as the "fur-lined rut." Also I was married. The museum didn't pay very well. And, anyway, I decided that the time had come to make a change, so I began teaching and also started the *Saturday Review* column at that time. I began free-lancing. I taught at the New School for Social Research for a year and then went up to City College. It was a little bit scary at first, but I found I enjoyed it more.

During my stay at the museum, I was constantly writing. I sold my first article in or around 1939 to *Theatre Arts*. And from that time on, I kept writing. Some of what I wrote, I gave away; some, I sold. You begin to find that you're a professional writer when finally you're giving away less than you're selling.

I always wrote about film. I did many reviews for what was then called *New Movies:* it's now *Films in Review,* the National Board of Review magazine. I was on a committee of that group from the time I got back after the war. Primarily it meant critical writing. In addition, I did historical and encyclopedia pieces, accounts of the motion pictures. Very often, the encyclopedias bring out a *Book of the Year,* and I've done a number of entries under that heading.

The field of film criticism has grown considerably in recent years because more and more people have come to take films seriously. That's due in part to the Museum of Modern Art, which made it possible to look at old films. The museum began circulating film programs in 1937. From that year on, instead of just seeing funny old movies like *The Flicker Flashbacks,* it became possible to study films. And soon a great proliferation of film courses developed around the country. Out of them have come more people who want to make and talk about films. They constitute an increasingly sophisticated and intelligent audience for films.

Today you can hardly turn around without finding a new film magazine and many, many more film books are published than ever before. In the *Los Angeles Times* there was an interview with Milton Lubovitsky, who has the Larry Edmond's bookstore in Hollywood. He said that there have been more film books published in the last two years than in all of the preceding time—especially with the stuff that's pouring in from Europe.

In 1924, Gilbert Seldes wrote *The Seven Lively Arts.* From that time on there has always been an intellectual coterie willing to concede that film might be an art form. Seldes was able to convince a goodly number of people. And the Museum of Modern Art gave it a sort of prestige. You could no longer just dismiss the whole thing as an aberration of little magazines.

At first, we didn't have much of an audience. There were few serious film critics at that time, although among those we had some good ones. Agee was writing then; Manny Farber was swell; Otis Ferguson of *The New Republic,* I'd consider one of the best film critics we've ever had in this country. I believe that Agee derived a great deal from Ferguson. Manny Farber would be the first to admit that he did. These people were able to respond to the film directly. They articulated their reactions extremely well without having any tremendous backlog of filmology to worry about. I'm not at all sure about the competence of these film critics who come into the field now. Particularly, I'm thinking of the new approach to film which requires you to be well rounded in dialectics and everything else before you start criticizing. That doesn't strike me as the best way to go about film criticism.

That's why I like Pauline Kael so much. She gives you a direct response. The best thing Pauline does is to hide the fact that she knows a great deal more about the film medium than most people who teach it. She has absorbed everything but is still able to give an immediate, personal response to the films she writes about. The good critics are on to this, that there is a special immediate experience in viewing films. A painting on a wall can be looked at for ten minutes or a half hour or the next ten days, but a picture that's flashed on the screen is there for less than $\frac{1}{24}$ of a second. And you will never go back to that one frame again unless you sit through the next two hours, and even then the nature of that first reaction will have changed in those two hours. Ordinarily when I review a film, I see it only once. But there are films that require going back to, and then, if possible, I do it.

Drama critics, who are very serious and concerned about a play, will manage to get hold of the text, and, not infrequently, they quote from it. We film critics don't have much opportunity to see scripts, believe it or not. That's because the studios feel if they let a script off the premises, somebody will swipe their property and make another film of it. In most instances, it's a puzzle why they made the film in the first place, but they are still nervous about theft!

My own experience in film-reviewing is that there's nothing more disastrous than trying to outguess an audience. At one point, I was doing film reviews for *Scholastic Magazine*, which goes to high schools, junior high schools, and elementary schools. One of my most devastating experiences was reviewing a Doris Day picture, *On Moonlight Bay*. It was a really dishonest review because I didn't like Doris Day pictures, but I knew that she was big with the school kids at that time. I thought, "Well, I'd better just go along with them on this one." And so I praised this picture, which was, to my mind, no worse than anything else she'd ever done. I received more letters on that than on anything else I've written. And they were all to this effect: "Why don't you get a good critic like Louella Parsons?" or "What's the matter with your critic, does he have rocks in his head?" I had no comeback because the mistake was mine. I never made it again. They chose me for *Scholastic Magazine* thinking I could write reviews that would interest their readers, but no one told me I had to review in a certain way or how many checks I had to assign to this picture or that picture. It was foolish on my part to try to measure up to some imagined editorial policy.

I consider myself a critic rather than a reviewer. The critic's work is to go into the film much more than one can simply at the plot level, which is the only level you find in trade papers. The critical function is to examine a picture and indicate what works, what does not, how problems were solved, and if they weren't, why not. I don't think you'll too often find in my writing the statement that this is a great film or that this is a terrible film or this one is all right. Rather, I write an exposition of what the film-maker has tried, what interesting things have been achieved, what didn't come off, and why it didn't.

The fact that I was at the Museum of Modern Art for so many years and sat in the galleries almost as much as in the auditorium has influenced the kinds of reviews I write. And my music collection is also important. It gives me an extra dimension. Also I think it's unfortunate that professional critics don't have much contact with a real audience. More often than not, we see films in a small screening room. The film is really built and timed for audience reaction. I can't think of anything more deadly than seeing a comedy or even a Hitchcock thriller in an empty room.

I had a good experience seeing *The Apartment* just before I left New York—up at Loew's 72nd Street—a fond memory. The audience was primed for another Billy Wilder comedy similar to *Some Like It Hot*. And United Artists was selling it as a Billy Wilder comedy. The audience laughed its head off at Jack Lemmon. Shirley MacLaine tried to commit suicide, which was funny because she failed at it. Lemmon made spaghetti for her and strained it in a tennis racket, and that was hilarious, and so on. But I found the film absolutely heartless and couldn't respond well to it no matter how hard everyone laughed. When I started my classes at USC, I was able to borrow the film and showed it one evening before a small class, whose reaction was completely different. Without the predisposition to laugh and the sustaining qualities a whole audience laughing at one time has, the film played as a sort of bittersweet, almost tragic affair. It was not the big, wild comedy that it looked like at Loew's 72nd Street.

I've been aware of this discrepancy any number of times. I remember one day having to do a film review in a hurry. I called Universal to let me see a film that I knew was just about to open, called *Come September*. They obliged. I saw the picture on a Monday morning all by myself in a screening room over there and came out of the theater knowing that I couldn't review it. I had no frame of reference. It was a comedy that didn't work, and I really couldn't say whether it was the film or me or the hour or what. Instead, I wrote a piece about comedy.

Sometimes the same film seen a second time, after some years, appears quite different to you. Here's a very good illustration. I don't know if you've seen *The Grapes of Wrath* in recent years, but *The Grapes of Wrath* in 1939 was criticized very severely for not having been as slashing as it might have been, for pulling punches, and that sort of thing. Looked at today, and I've seen it again within the past year, *The Grapes of Wrath* seems almost as radical as *Potemkin*. In part, it's the changing times which make you see things differently. That creates rather a serious situation if you see pictures over again. You begin to ask yourself, "How could I have thought what I thought?" and you're probably being unfair to yourself. Yet you hope to recognize that difference in yourself and in the times.

If I were writing reviews for the New York *Daily News,* they would have to be much different from those for the *Saturday Review* or for *Scholastic.* Perhaps I can carry it a step further and say that if I were to write for the *Daily News* as I do for the *Saturday Review,* I wouldn't be on the *Daily News* very long. Other magazines, such as *The Partisan Review* or *Commentary,* have a very specific readership for which I've not written. There's something to the idea of water seeking its own level, and I believe the film critic finds his own level too.

We film critics are quite unlike one another. Some, like Andrew Sarris, operate on principles I just don't understand. I can't see how anybody could put *The Countess From Hong Kong* on his "ten best" list. And, I daresay, Andy looks at my list and wonders how some of my selections got there. It can't be helped. We're working from different, or even mutually unintelligible, principles.

When I do a "ten best" list, it's really on the basis of what Hollis Alpert and I can agree on as the ten best films of the year. Several times, when *we* couldn't agree on the ten best, we extended it to the twelve best, accommodating both parties. We pay no attention to anyone else's list.

Sometimes, daily reviewers feel pressure about affecting the box office. I haven't had that kind of experience. In the *Saturday Review,* one of the first columns I did was a review of *I Was a Communist for the FBI,* which was a terrible picture. But it came out during the McCarthy investigation, producing a very hot potato. I thought it might be wise to see if the magazine had any policy about this sort of thing. The answer was "No, you write your review and we'll run it." I wrote it and they ran it, and I've never made that kind of call again.

The other type of pressure, the "bought" review, has not come up either. In this instance, it was *Viva Zapata!,* the film of Elia Kazan's which was personally produced by Darryl Zanuck as his prize baby for the year. They were very anxious to have the *Saturday Review* cover; they flew a print in specifically for Hollis and me to look at with the idea that which ever one of us liked the film better would do the review. They also sent a lot of beautiful pictures of Marlon Brando in big Mexican hats. We saw the film. The lights went on, we looked at each other, and decided that this wasn't a film for the *Saturday Review* cover. Since we only have four cover pictures a year, we consider those our private "Oscars." So it did not go on the cover. If I'm not mistaken, they put on a Daphne DuMaurier novel instead, which I'm sure was no better than *Viva Zapata!* But at least, our integrity was secure. Now it wasn't until months later, and then not from the people at *Saturday Review* but from the people at Twentieth Century-Fox, that I learned that there was a full-page ad hanging on that cover. If the magazine had put *Viva Zapata!* on the cover, they would have had a full-page ad inside. The magazine was not fat in those days, but there was no mention at any time of the ad, no request that we change our opinion. Surely all this depends on the editor and the publisher.

The studios rarely use critics to preview films before distribution to get an estimate of the success of the film. I think they're so nervous about the picture themselves that they don't want to chance it. We have considerable freedom of action. So, for example, sometimes there may be an attempt at corrupting a critic they want to win over. They do this with "Won't you come out and have a drink?" or they invite you to a cocktail party or to a dinner. But I really have found there's not much of that.

Specifically, before the showing of *Hurry Sundown*, Otto Preminger had a small dinner party at one of the swankier places in Beverly Hills, brought the party to the studio, and showed the picture. We went back to his office afterwards to have a drink, which was a little embarrassing for me because I thought the picture was awful. I'm sure that was a warm-up process. I wrote a review which was called "Uncle Otto's Cabin," and that was the last I heard from Mr. Preminger for quite a while. But then a short while ago, he returned to town and was about to start another picture and called and said, "Hello, this is your Uncle Otto." But this just means that he's got another picture and that he hopes this one will do better or that I will like it better, but you know, that's hardly bribery. And either a critic has too much to drink at the dinner that evening, or too much to eat and falls asleep, or he responds to the film as he would to any other.

Over the past twenty years, the main thing that's happened with me is that I've come out to Hollywood. It's been seven years (now) and I feel that I know a bit more about the back-behind-the-scenes part of production than I ever did before. That exposure has given me more sympathy for people who make films. It's made me more admiring of a picture that comes out well. So many things can go wrong in the making of a film, there are so many areas where compromise has to take place, and so many conflicts of will, that if a picture comes out as well as, let us say, *In Cold Blood*, you know what a struggle Brooks had first merely to get to the point of making it. Just imagine, here's a picture on a substantial budget—I think it's three and a half million—made in black and white at a time when the studios insist that everything has to be in color because of color television and outdoor theaters. They know that in many countries, color automatically brings higher rental than a black-and-white picture. Again, a three-and-a-half-million-dollar picture with no stars and very few actors you ever heard of. And a picture that has all sorts of opportunities to exploit violence that Brooks pulled back from. It takes a lot of courage in a commercial enterprise that film-making in Hollywood really is.

There have been films I thought were difficult and films that tried to do something different and succeeded, and I was able to call the turn on them. This gave me great personal satisfaction. I guess the best example is *Marty* because the people who made it have told me that it was our cover in the *Saturday Review* that made United Artists pay attention to it. That, for me, is the greatest satisfaction a critic can have: to influence public opinion in support of a film that might otherwise get lost in the shuffle.

The other source of gratification is teaching at USC, which I enjoy tremendously. In Los Angeles it's so much better than it could possibly be in New York. Week after week I have people coming down to my classes who are only the best writers, the best producers, the best composers, right across the line. We get full cooperation from individuals in the industry. They're concerned about their craft. They like to have their work seen and discussed by knowledgeable students. It's been an extraordinary experience. We get films in advance of their release, so students are able to talk about them without the preparation of having read somebody else's review.

The Liveliest Art came about in a curious way. I had been asked to take over a book of essays on the film by Iris Barry for New American Library. The contract was still in force and the book hadn't appeared. They showed me the outline she had prepared and I agreed to do it, but felt in addition to the listed topics there should be at least one chapter, possibly two, on film history. Out of those introductory chapters came *The Liveliest Art*. After I had written them there was no room for anything else. Writing film history also has its special problems. What I was trying to do in *The Liveliest Art* was not to say such-and-such was done first by so-and-so, but rather to show the development of the aesthetics of the film. To show that development means that you have to begin someplace and explain more or less consecutively that somebody did something else and then somebody did something else. However, that preoccupation can be irritating. For one gentleman I know, that was his whole bag. He spent all his time checking out everything ever so carefully. I can't tell you how many phone calls I had from him, asking, well where did you get this fact or how do you *know* that. He had discovered something else that contradicted it. In another book, you have an author who devoted years to tracking down just what section of line it was on the Delaware and Lackawanna that they used in *The Great Train Robbery*. I couldn't care less. What does interest me in the development of film art would be to say that with *The Great Train Robbery* something happened. *The Great Train Robbery* was where it happened and it greatly affected the next decade of film-making.

I can't think of any other field apart from film where a magazine or a newspaper or a learned journal would publish something on an art form by somebody who's had no experience whatsoever in that art. It would be scandalous to have a music critic who didn't know how to read music. You can't imagine an art critic who hasn't been to an art gallery— he needn't paint himself, but he has to have been exposed to visual art over a number of years. In film, alone, all too often the critic is yanked off the sports desk, or he happens to be in the office when a preview is taking place and he gets sent out to write a review. This kind of thing is changing and it will change more in the next few years.

An accompanying misconception is that anyone can make a film. That's really my whole hangup on the underground film world. The man who makes such a film knows that if he wrote a short story and sent it out for publication, he'd get it back very quickly—if he enclosed a six-cent stamp. But if he makes a film, he can take it down to Jonas Mekas, who'll put it on at the Cinematheque at the drop of a hat. What you have in the Underground is a denigration of all of the art of the film that has been built up over the years. These people have the same approach to film that George Eastman had to the Kodak camera: you press the button, we do the rest. They're so egocentric they feel that just because their eye is in back of a camera, that makes it art.

I had a good instance of this about a year ago, when a young and fairly well-known actor in this town went back East and, falling under the influence of Andy Warhol, decided that he, too, was a film-maker. Until then, he was just an actor. He bought himself a camera, went down on the Strip, and photographed the statue that revolves and says "Welcome to the Riviera," you know, the cowgirl. He photographed it in slow motion and he photographed it in fast motion, and he used a zoomar lens, of course, and he zoomed in and he zoomed out. I was present at the unveiling of this masterpiece. On that occasion, he bitterly complained about the laboratory not understanding why, when the thing went faster, the film got darker, and when it went slower it got lighter. He had consulted with the laboratory, it turned out, and was told that for X number of dollars, they could correct that, but he'd have to splice on forty more feet of film so they could make proper light markings. He thought that was outrageous. It never occurred to this budding film-maker that there are things like turning the lens to accommodate for different speeds and the amount of light that enters into the camera. Well, this kind of no-knowledge—of yahooism in film—I find insufferable. It is the kind of eagerness for self-expression that no artist in any other field can possibly condone. If you see enough of these films, and I think I've seen enough of them, you are able to say, "This man is a film-maker and this one is a phony." That again is something a critic has to do.

You wouldn't mistake an Ed Emshwiller film for a picture by somebody else even if both seem to be made up of random shots. But it's impossible to pass that information or that perception along by the printed word. What you can do, if you're acting as a responsible critic, is to say, look for the work of Ed Emshwiller and contrast it with superficially similar work by somebody else. I think Emshwiller's wonderful. He has a beautiful sensuous feeling about the world. But you know he's also a great cameraman, and what's most impressive about *Hallelujah the Hills* is the camerawork he did on it.

Before you can make a picture that has any validity as art, you have to know a lot more about the camera than the fellow who made the "revolving girl" picture. You have to know about the camera, about film, about editing. You have to know what can be added with sound. And you have to know a great many techniques. You go to a school like UCLA or USC or NYU or Northwestern, or any of the half dozen that teach film, and you at least get those fundamentals. Then you can start on your own creation. I'm not saying that you *have* to go to a school and learn the classical ways. You can kick all rules out of the window as soon as you've mastered them. But at least you have to know what has been accumulated over these past sixty years. Only after you've learned the rudiments is it time to make a film; then make it your way.

Rightfully, the key person in producing a film is the director. And the director should, in every sense, be creator of the film. No director's earned that stature until he's put his own idea on film. In other words, much as I admire *In Cold Blood*, it's still no more than a skillful adaptation of somebody else's work. When you turn to Jean Luc Godard's films, they're nobody else's. They're Godard. If you look at the films of Bergman —it's nobody else's work. It's Bergman, the creative-film-maker.

In Hollywood, everybody is more or less a journeyman. The writer is not a creative writer. He is the writer who's making over somebody's play or somebody else's novel or short story and turning it into practical script form. The director takes that script and tries to cinematize it. You seldom get the sense of total creation that's necessary to art.

People like von Stroheim fell by the wayside. He was working at a time when the studio factory was the thing, and he was not willing or able to conform. Today, I think the nonconformists are in a slightly better position. Conformity works more for television than for films. TV is doing the equivalent of "B" and "C" films. With the kind of grind they have, doing a half-hour film in three days or a full hour in six, maybe seven days, TV has no time for experimentation. In the past, time wasn't so expensive. Buster Keaton could spend a week or more working out a gag, perfecting it.

Remarkable films were made when you didn't depend on the script. Today, before a film goes into production, everything has to be written down, and marvelous visual gags just don't happen. You have one-liners or clever dialogue. You may have chase scenes sketched out, but not the kind of thing that Keaton or Chaplin would do. The elaborate mechanisms they worked out for developing one situation can't be reduced to paper— which is no substitute for talk and repeated experimentation.

Words are no substitute for visual actions. They have their place, and I'd feel much better about film as art if producers who buy scripts could really visualize what's down on paper. I'm not at all sure that they can.

Montgomery and Rock in scene from *Lovers Not*.

INDEX

PHOTO CREDITS

Photos on pp. ii–iii, 18–19, 24, 25, 26, 36, 37, 38, 42, 43, 57, 74, 75 (top), 81, 88, 89, 104, 105, 116, 117, 182, 183, 201 (bottom), 207, 214, 215, 224 (bottom left), 225, 248, 249, 250, 259, 354, 365, 366, 367, 378, 380, 391, 394, 395 (top right and bottom), 407, 408, 409 from The Museum of Modern Art/Film Stills Archive.

Photos on pp. 46, 52, 53, 66 (bottom), 425 from Joe Rock private collection. Photo p. 66 (top) by Planet News, Ltd., London, from Joe Rock private collection.

Photo p. 75 (bottom) from Adolph Zukor private collection.

Photos pp. 136, 137, 146, 147 (bottom), 148 from Dore Shary private collection. Photo p. 147 (top) is Bob Brooks Photo, Maritime Star Weekly Rep., Yarmouth, Nova Scotia, from Dore Shary private collection.

Photos pp. 166 (top), 167 from Arthur Mayer private collection. Photo p. 166 (bottom) by Reni Photos from Arthur Mayer private collection.

Photos pp. 192, 199, 200, 201 (top) from Blanche Sweet private collection.

Photos p. 224 (top and bottom right) from Edward Everett Horton private collection.

Photos p. 258 from Dagmar Godowsky private collection.

Photos pp. 268 (bottom), 269, 270 from Wini Shaw private collection. Photo p. 268 (top) by Bert Longworth from Wini Shaw private collection.

Photos pp. 279, 280, 281, 292, 293 from Gil Perkins private collection.

Photos pp. 301, 302–303, 308, 309 from Billy Bletcher private collection.

Photos pp. 318–319, 320, 321, 328, 329 from William Haddock private collection.

Photos pp. 337, 338, 339, 346 from Fritz Lang private collection.

Photo p. 395 (top left) from Max Steiner private collection.